This Is a *Thriller*

This Is a *Thriller*

AN EPISODE GUIDE, HISTORY AND ANALYSIS OF THE CLASSIC 1960S TELEVISION SERIES

by Alan Warren

with a Foreword by Donald S. Sanford

McFarland & Company, Inc., Publishers
Jefferson, North Carolina, and London

Frontispiece: "Thriller" host Boris Karloff (courtesy of Ronald V. Borst/Hollywood Movie Posters)

The present work is a reprint of the library bound edition of This Is a Thriller: An Episode Guide, History and Analysis of the Classic 1960s Television Series, *first published in 1996 by McFarland.*

LIBRARY OF CONGRESS CATALOGUING-IN-PUBLICATION DATA

Warren, Alan, 1952–
    This is a Thriller : an episode guide, history and analysis of the
classic 1960s television series / by Alan Warren; with a foreword by
Donald S. Sanford.
        p.   cm.
    Includes bibliographical references and index.

    ISBN 978-0-7864-1969-2
    softcover : 50# alk. paper ∞

    1. Thriller (Television program)   I. Title.
PN1992.77.T564W37   2004
791.45'72 — dc20   96-32736

British Library cataloguing data are available

Cover photograph ©2004 Comstock

Manufactured in the United States of America

McFarland & Company, Inc., Publishers
  Box 611, Jefferson, North Carolina 28640
  www.mcfarlandpub.com

Dedicated to

DOUG BENTON
ROBERT BLOCH
WILLIAM FRYE
DONALD S. SANFORD

the men who put the thrill into *Thriller*

ACKNOWLEDGMENTS

The author wishes to thank the following individuals whose recollections, advice and insights helped to make this book possible: Forrest J Ackerman, Doug Benton, Robert Bloch, Ronald V. Borst of Hollywood Movie Posters (with special thanks for supplying the photographs), the late Macdonald Carey, William Frye, Russell Johnson, Ken Kaffke (president of the Thriller Fan Club), Mike Matthews, John Radice (who coined the term "crisscrossing genres," which I have made free use of throughout), Don Sanford, Mike Warner, and Phil White.

TABLE OF CONTENTS

Acknowledgments   vi
Foreword by Donald S. Sanford   1
Preface   5

Part I. Introduction

Putting the Thrill into *Thriller*   8

Part II. Episode Guide

FIRST SEASON, 1960–1961

The Twisted Image (September 13)   28
Child's Play (September 20)   30
Worse Than Murder (September 27)   31
The Mark of the Hand (October 4)   33
Rose's Last Summer (October 11)   34
The Guilty Men (October 18)   36
The Purple Room (October 25)   37
The Watcher (November 1)   41
Girl with a Secret (November 15)   43
The Prediction (November 22)   45
The Fatal Impulse (November 29)   48
The Big Blackout (December 6)   50
Knock Three-One-Two (December 13)   52
Man in the Middle (December 20)   53
The Cheaters (December 27)   56
The Hungry Glass (January 3)   59
The Poisoner (January 10)   62
Man in a Cage (January 17)   65
Choose a Victim (January 24)   67

Hay-Fork and Bill-Hook (February 7)   68
The Merriweather File (February 14)   71
The Fingers of Fear (February 21)   73
Well of Doom (February 28)   74
The Ordeal of Dr. Cordell (March 7)   78
Trio for Terror (March 14)   80
Papa Benjamin (March 21)   84
Late Date (April 4)   87
Yours Truly, Jack the Ripper (April 11)   88
The Devil's Ticket (April 18)   91
Parasite Mansion (April 25)   94
A Good Imagination (May 2)   97
Mr. George (May 9)   98
The Terror in Teakwood (May 16)   99
The Prisoner in the Mirror (May 23)   103
Dark Legacy (May 30)   106
Pigeons from Hell (June 6)   109
The Grim Reaper (June 13)   116

SECOND SEASON, 1961–1962

What Beckoning Ghost? (September 18) 120

Guillotine (September 25) 122

The Premature Burial (October 2) 124

The Weird Tailor (October 16) 126

God Grante That She Lye Stille (October 23) 129

Masquerade (October 30) 131

The Last of the Sommervilles (November 6) 133

Letter to a Lover (November 13) 135

A Third for Pinochle (November 20) 137

The Closed Cabinet (November 27) 138

Dialogues with Death (December 4) 140

The Return of Andrew Bentley (December 11) 142

The Remarkable Mrs. Hawk (December 18) 145

Portrait Without a Face (December 25) 148

An Attractive Family (January 1) 151

Waxworks (January 8) 153

La Strega (January 15) 156

The Storm (January 22) 158

A Wig for Miss Devore (January 29) 160

The Hollow Watcher (February 12) 163

Cousin Tundifer (February 19) 165

The Incredible Doktor Markesan (February 26) 167

Flowers of Evil (March 5) 169

'Til Death Do Us Part (March 12) 171

The Bride Who Died Twice (March 19) 173

Kill My Love (March 26) 174

Man of Mystery (April 2) 176

The Innocent Bystanders (April 9) 179

The Lethal Ladies (April 16) 181

The Specialists (April 30) 183

Part III. Appendices

A. Ancestors of *Thriller*   186

B. Descendants of *Thriller*   188

C. The Top 25 *Thriller* Episodes   190

Bibliography   191

Index   193

FOREWORD

by Donald S. Sanford

Alan Warren's admirable scholarship stirs a field of dusty but very agreeable memories for this former member of the *Thriller* team: that superb actress Ida Lupino skillfully directing her cast without ever giving an acting lesson; Jerry Goldsmith's luminous scores, especially the signature theme for the little girl heroine in the "Mr. George" episode. And Boris Karloff, consummate professional and gracious gentleman, whose likes are rare, if not nonexistent, in these cacophonous times. There were many others whose creative talents gave *Thriller* its unique style and quality — very especially producer Bill Frye, whose meticulously skillful hand guided us all. *Thriller* was Bill's show.

And I was a helluva lot faster at my typewriter — and on the tennis court — when *Thriller* debuted in September 1960. Over three and a half decades ago! Probably the biggest break in a rags-to-riches-to-rags, etc., writing career (spanning more of those hectic decades than I care to acknowledge) was the day producer Bill called me into Universal Studios to offer a polish job on a script titled "Mark of the Hand." The fee was $500. The polish was supposed to be minimal. For minimal read top-to-bottom rewrite, which is what happens when the rewriter thinks it's necessary to take a sharp plot turn in the original storyline. There followed another rewrite assignment. Same bucks and another plot fix that I couldn't resist. Having an extravagant sense of plot logic can be a costly and greedy time consumer, since a writer's only product is what is in his head and the time it takes to commit it to paper.

At any rate, I had no other employment at the time, having fired my agent several years before when it became apparent that the guy was relying on me to do all the job hustling while he toiled to take his 10 percent commission. So I was relying on past contacts and word of mouth to keep working. (Definitely *not* recommended in today's market.) Bottom line is, I felt that *Thriller* had the potential of making it through the first season, which meant the possibility of more assignments. Thankfully, there followed a full rewrite of "Worse Than Murder" for the munificent sum of $1,750. This deal, however, was packaged with an assignment to adapt Dorothy Hitchens' "The Watcher" provided that my work on "Murder" resulted in that script being shot. It was. So was "The Watcher."

1

Thus started a two season association which was one of the most enjoyable and productive in all of my decades of professional work. *Thriller* was a complete change of pace in a career which had concentrated almost entirely on the private eye, metro police station and cowboy-western genre, totaling some 150-plus episodes on more than three dozen series.

Why am I recounting all this personal stuff? Because at a dinner party not long ago, the guy sitting to my left, a lawyer who was a wannabe scriptwriter, asked how I came to write the screenplay for the Universal Picture *Midway*. He knew that the film had grossed several hundred million and said he never missed seeing it whenever it reappeared on television. (The kind of dinner companion a writer loves to be seated with!) Little did he know that all writers are starved for praise and tend to prolong those rare moments of gratification. So instead of answering his question directly I gave him the full history, as follows:

I finished the '60 season writing three more *Thriller* episodes, an original titled "The Prediction," Robert Bloch's fascinating tale of "The Cheaters," and "Well of Doom," a John Clemons story. Then, just before hiatus time, Allen Miller, production manager for Universal Studios, called me into his bungalow. (Yes, the lot was then graced with lovely bungalows which housed production teams and the various stars of the moment.) With Bill Frye's approval, Allen offered me a nonexclusive contract to write 12 *Thrillers* for the '61 season. Bill and his associate producers, Doug Benton and Jo Swerling, Jr., would supply me with 12 stories which I would adapt into teleplays. This one-man script assembly line was designed to speed up the creative process, avoid writer's block, and meet *Thriller*'s rigid production schedule. (There's nothing so daunting as staring at a blank page that wants you to tell it a story.)

It worked marvelously. Bill and company gleaned ten intriguing black comedy and blacker horror stories from old pulp magazines and God knows where. Off the assembly line came ten episodes, among them "The Remarkable Mrs. Hawk," which was one of three scripts nominated for the 1961–62 Writers Guild of America Anthology Drama Award.

Some sage once said, "Never trouble till it troubles you." None of us did, but trouble came anyway. The assembly line silently halted when Bill and staff were unable to find stories number 11 and 12 required by my contract. We all searched. We all failed to uncover suitable material. Meanwhile, the gap was filled by writers with original stories and teleplays. I extended my contract for six weeks, gratis. It didn't help. Then *Thriller* was abruptly killed by NBC. Bill and Doug and Joe went on to other projects.

After a decent interval of mourning for a series that should have had an extended run, I contacted Universal's business manager in charge of television contracts. Since my 12 script contract had a pay-or-play clause, I requested payment in full for the two episodes I was unable to write because of no fault of mine. The biz manager, who will go nameless, went ballistic. No way was Universal going to pay me for work I hadn't done. "To hell with the contract," he spat. Yep.

His exact words, knowing that he was putting me in the position of filing a griev-ance with the Writers Guild. The Guild lawyers could most certainly get the monies due me. But at what cost? Being barred from working on any Universal produced series, no doubt. Mind you, no formal blackball notice would be given to the studio's producers. Just a quiet word passed along by this zealous guardian of Universal's purse. Faced with the very probable loss of access to a major employer, I screwed up my courage and caved in. I suggested that he find me two assignments on any of the other series that the studio was producing. He grunted something unintelligible and hung up.

The next day, the business manager's secretary telephoned. "You have an appointment with Mr. Champion at 10:30 tomorrow," she said. Not "Can you be available at...?" or "Would you be interesting in meeting with...?" She didn't even say who the hell Mr. Champion was. Of course, I was in Mr. Champion's outer office the next day promptly at 10:30. The best part of an hour went by before I was shown in to meet my new employer. His first name was John. He was the producer of a successful western series, *Laramie*, and he was doing a poor job of concealing how pissed he was. He observed how happy he was with the writers he was employing and that he resented being "instructed" to hire me in order to satisfy a contract on a series he didn't give a damn about and that was already history. A good start to a productive relationship, right? Right. I couldn't help but sympathize with the lousy position the studio had put him in, and I sorta liked the guy. Sometime after that initial encounter, in fact, we became close friends. Besides, he was a damn good tennis player. Eventually, I wrote four episodes for him; they turned out rather well. Then *Laramie* was canceled.

"And that," I said to the scriptwriter-wannabe lawyer, "is how I came to write *Midway*."

He gave me a blank stare. I continued:

"Five years later, John called me from Goldwyn Studio where he was pro-ducing a feature picture for the Mirisch Company. It was in script trouble. I rewrote it."

"*Midway*."

"No. *The Thousand Plane Raid*. *Midway* was the fifth feature I wrote. But not for John. For Walter Mirisch. He'd fired John by that time."

"Oh," he muttered. He left the table and I think he abandoned the idea of becoming a scriptwriter. For his sake, or that of anyone who wants a sane and secure career, I hope so. Very few writers ever find a creative and financial haven in a *Thriller*.

Donald S. Sanford
Studio City, California
April 1994

PREFACE

In recent years television has become the graveyard of horror. Most of the series purporting to be horror anthologies either make the mistake of telegraphing their punches or, conversely, ladle out gore and special effects at the expense of story, mood and characterization. Such recent efforts as *Tales from the Crypt*, *Nightmare Cafe*, and even the resuscitated *Twilight Zone* and *Alfred Hitchcock Presents* indicate that television, as a medium for the horror story, is a lost cause.

Such was not always the case. In the late fifties and early sixties, with the glitches and technical shortcomings of early television a thing of the past, there was a brief period in which televised horror was not a contradiction in terms. Anthology series such as *Way Out* and *Great Ghost Tales*, and certain episodes of *Twilight Zone* and *The Alfred Hitchcock Hour* constitute a high watermark in terror. And perhaps the crest of that wave was Boris Karloff's *Thriller*.

Each of these series had its own distinct identity: an episode of *Thriller* was quite different from, say, *Twilight Zone*, which frequently presented morality plays employing science fictional trappings. *Thriller* rarely descended to moralizing; its vision of life was darker, its snap endings appropriately bleaker and more uncompromising. It also employed a more self-consciously Gothic approach to the genre, adapting stories by acknowledged horror specialists such as Robert E. Howard, August Derleth and Robert Bloch. Its chief failing was its near-schizophrenic attitude toward subject matter: although approximately half of its 67 episodes could be categorized as horror, an equal number were unmistakably crime oriented, leading to an inevitable quandary among viewers confused by the program's apparently random alternation between two distinctly different genres.

My purpose in writing this book was twofold. First, I wanted to analyze *Thriller*, to indicate certain themes and motifs employed during its two-year run, and to appreciate its literacy and individuality. Second, I was interested in a somewhat nostalgic look at an unjustly neglected period in television history in which drama took precedence over action and special effects. Each episode is listed in the order in which it was initially broadcast over NBC from 1960 to 1962, and the dates indicate the original telecasts.

Alan Warren   *July 1996*

5

Part I
Introduction

PUTTING THE THRILL
INTO *THRILLER*

Thriller, the NBC television series that Stephen King has called "Probably the best horror series ever put on TV," had a remarkably short gestation period. The brainchild of NBC programming head Hubbell Robinson, it was originally intended as a Hubbell Robinson production for Revue Studios at Universal, for which he would serve as executive producer. An early television pioneer, Robinson had worked on *Startime* in 1950 for the now long-defunct Dumont network. Throughout the fifties he produced *Climax!, Studio One*, and the prestigious and Emmy-winning *Playhouse 90*, often acclaimed as the finest television series of all time. By 1960 he was a top-echelon network executive. According to writer Donald S. Sanford (who later became an important contributor to *Thriller's* success):

> The rumor at the time was that Hubbell, when he was terminated as head of programming for NBC, was given two one-hour slots of prime time on the network to fill in as he pleased. The slots were his for two seasons only. Apparently this was in lieu of big severance pay.
> Hubbell came to Universal/Revue where *Thriller* and a show called *Precinct 54* [actually, *87th Precinct*] were dreamed up.

One of Robinson's most important decisions (and one which would later determine the eventual direction of the series) was the choice of host. Since an anthology series presents a different cast of characters each week, the host is the only continuing "character" as such, and thus provides a strong thread of continuity. Robert Montgomery, host of the long-running *Robert Montgomery Presents*, and Alfred Hitchcock, host of his own NBC series, thus acted as touchstones for their series, not only introducing each episode in a distinctive and individual manner, but in a sense embodying the essential concept of the series itself.

In this respect, Robinson made a superb choice. He selected Boris Karloff.

Karloff was born William Henry Pratt in England in 1887. He had struggled for years as an actor, appearing onstage in Canada and America, and landing mostly bit parts in silent films. Finding the name Pratt unsuitable for an actor, he changed it to Karloff (after a relative on his mother's side); he adopted the name Boris simply because it sounded appropriate. His film debut came in either 1916 or 1919 (accounts differ). He was working at Universal in 1931 on a film called *Graft* when he was approached by the studio's ace director, James Whale, and asked if he would mind testing for a certain role. When he asked Whale what for, the director replied, "For a damned awful monster!"

The resultant film was, of course, *Frankenstein* (1931), and Karloff was singled out by critics for his milestone performance. It took Karloff's special insight to realize that, as he put it, "That monster is one of the most sympathetic characters ever created in the world of English letters."

Throughout the thirties, Karloff reigned as Hollywood's king of terror — a position he cheerfully accepted despite his reputation as one of the gentlest and best-liked members of Hollywood's English colony of actors. He consolidated his position with appearances in *The Old Dark House* (1932), *The Mask of Fu Manchu* (1932), *The Mummy* (1932) and *The Black Cat* (1934), among others. He reprised the role of the Monster in Whale's *The Bride of Frankenstein* (1935), the apotheosis of the Hollywood horror film. After appearing as the Monster one last time in *Son of Frankenstein* (1939), he settled in for a long career in roles requiring less makeup. Some of his finest acting was done for producer Val Lewton in *The Body Snatcher* (1945), *Isle of the Dead* (1945), and *Bedlam* (1946). He also scored a personal triumph on Broadway in *Arsenic and Old Lace* (1941–44).

In the late fifties Karloff temporarily abandoned film work. For five years (1959–63) he was absent from the screen, the longest such hiatus in his career. He had made his television debut in 1949 on *Chevrolet on Broadway* for NBC, and had since appeared as a guest star on such programs as *Suspense, The Best of Broadway, $64,000 Question, The Dinah Shore Show*, and even *The Shirley Temple Storybook*. He had also hosted the short-lived series *Starring Boris Karloff* in 1949.

By selecting Karloff as host of *Thriller*, Hubbell Robinson immediately provided the series with a warmly remembered screen icon whose very name was synonymous with horror. Karloff's introductions established the proper mood of mystery and intrigue from the outset, and his tag line "As sure as my name is Boris Karloff, *this* is a '*Thriller*'!" became a memorable catch-phrase. (Although in retrospect it seems he introduced every episode with this memorable spiel, in fact he only did so on two occasions: in "The Cheaters" and "The Premature Burial.")

Thus equipped with the perfect host, *Thriller* seemed assured of success. Certainly, Robinson's prefatory statement promised greatness from the start: according to him, *Thriller* would be "The *Studio One* of mystery, a quality anthology drawing on the whole rich field of suspense literature...." Moreover, Robinson promised that the series would be his personal project. Consequently, *Thriller* was sold without a pilot — a rare event in 1960 as well as today. Production of the first episode began in late February.

Problems set in almost immediately. As Gary Gerani and Paul H. Schulman recount in their book *Fantastic Television*:

This was the first of several big mistakes. Robinson's description of *Thriller*, though high-sounding, was actually vague. Consequently there developed between Robinson, producer Fletcher Markle and associate producer-story editor James P. Cavanagh a running ideological battle over the nature of the series. Where, for example, does a thriller end and a horror tale begin? What about black comedy? Is graphic violence necessary to a crime story? There were many differences in taste and concept, and, as the production deadline drew nearer, tensions escalated.

These tensions manifested themselves in an ongoing conflict between Robinson and his producer. Fletcher Markle, the husband of actress Mercedes McCambridge, had come to television

Boris Karloff, the most gentlemanly of horror stars, in a characteristically genial pose (courtesy of William Frye).

through films; his credits include *Night into Morning* (1951) and *Man with a Cloak* (1951), an offbeat mystery with Joseph Cotten as a mysterious crime solving stranger revealed as Edgar Allan Poe. Markle's *Thrillers* rank among the poorest of the lot; they indicate he saw little difference between the new series and the long-running *Alfred Hitchcock Presents*. Douglas Benton, associate producer of the later *Thriller* episodes, recalls that "Fletcher Markle was a bright guy, but he made a tremendous gaffe; he tried to do film noir, but it just wasn't film noir."

The time slot chosen for the new series was Tuesday night between 9 and 10 p.m. Its competition included a western, *Stagecoach West*, on ABC, and two comedy series, *The Tom Ewell Show* and the very popular *Red Skelton Show*, on CBS. In the midst of such furious infighting, the first episode was broadcast on September 13, 1960. "The Twisted Image" was produced by Markle and based on a novel by William O'Farrell. The plot dealt with a psychopathic office boy with delusions of grandeur. Critical comment was unanimously negative: "A preposterous mystery," said one, "silly in its narrative construction, unpleasant in its production." The second episode, "Child's Play," was worse, and the third entry,

"Worse Than Murder," indicated that *Thriller* was foundering. Ratings were low, and critics were sneering at the series that had been launched with such high hopes. According to Jay Allen Sanford, author of "Karloff Through the Looking-Glass": "Most of the first stories, and even a few of the subsequent episodes, show little style or attempt to deviate from the blandest ingredients of the most lackluster *Alfred Hitchcock Presents*. The hour-long episodes seemed to last forever, moving along like Southern California traffic ... lightning fast one moment and a dead standstill the next."

Drastic steps were taken. The word "Thriller" was redefined as having two specific meanings: the crime story and the horror tale. Robinson announced: "Our new formula immediately eliminated whole vast areas of material ... we now had a narrower interpretation of the word 'thriller'."

These changes necessitated the removal of Fletcher Markle. To take his place, Robinson brought in two veteran producers, each with a specific task. Maxwell Shane was hired to produce the crime episodes. He had already written one *Thriller*, "Rose's Last Summer," and had been a screenwriter at RKO and Universal, where he had produced and directed such films as *City Across the River* (1949) and *Nightmare* (1956). He had also co-written *The Mummy's Hand* (1940), depicting the Mummy as a slow-moving, unstoppable engine of destruction, which became the blueprint for all further movies in that series. In general, his screen work was competent but unexceptional. The quality of his *Thrillers* is highly variable: his gritty, hard-edged crime episodes could be outstanding, or simply mediocre. Thus, "The Fatal Impulse," one of the most suspenseful of *Thriller*'s crime entries, was followed by "The Big Blackout," one of the weakest. Shane's finest *Thriller* is probably "The Ordeal of Dr. Cordell," a compelling crime drama with science fictional overtones.

The other producer, hired specifically to handle the horror episodes, was to have a far more significant influence on the series — he would, in fact, take over *Thriller* and remake it to fit his own image. His name was William Frye.

Bill Frye recalls:

> I fell into *Thriller* on a weekend. I only met Hubbell Robinson once, and never saw him again. Fletcher Markle, who started it, was asked to leave on a Friday, and by Monday his name on his parking space had been painted over. That's the way they do things on TV.
>
> I looked at two or three [*Thrillers*], and I didn't like them. They asked to see me again on Monday, and when I came in they asked me to produce the series. The five or seven [episodes] that had already been done, I had to intersperse them with the others. And so Robert Bloch and Donald Sanford and I did the series. It was a nice little group of people to be working with.
>
> Fletcher Markle and I never had one word. I was brought in on Saturday, and started on a Monday. The only resentment I ever had was that Hubbell Robinson had a credit, and I never even got a telephone call from him.

The man who was to make such radical — and necessary — changes in order to save *Thriller* started out as a talent agent before producing such shows as *Johnny Dollar* and *Tales of the Texas Rangers* on radio. He moved to television in the early fifties, and did the pilot for *Four Star Playhouse* with Charles Boyer and Andrea King. ("We really only had three stars," Frye recalls with a laugh. "We were supposed to have Rosalind Russell and Joel McCrea, but they never did it. Roz was horrified at the thought of doing television. Eventually, we got David Niven and Ida Lupino.")

A close friend of Ronald and Benita Hume Colman, Frye went on to produce *The Halls of Ivy*, an early sitcom with Colman as a college professor and Hume as his wife, but the series came to an abrupt end in 1955. "It was too erudite for the times," Frye recalls. "The market just wasn't ready for an Ivy League professor."

William Frye, the man who gave *Thriller* a new lease on life after an inauspicious beginning (courtesy of William Frye).

Following *Ivy*, Frye went on to produce *General Electric Theater*, featuring then-actor Ronald Reagan as pitchman and occasional star, for six years. Following that, Frye, a close friend of Ray Milland, worked on his late fifties detective series *Markham*, alternating between that and the crime drama *Johnny Staccato*, featuring a young John Cassavetes. Thus, by the time he took on *Thriller*, Frye was a television veteran.

The first episode produced by Frye was "The Purple Room," broadcast on October 25, 1960. A ghost story set in a supposedly haunted mansion, it was *Thriller*'s first horror entry, moodily directed by Douglas Heyes, and today remains one of the best *Thrillers* ever. Frye followed this up with an equally strong crime drama, "The Watcher," featuring a young Richard Chamberlain. "He really was totally unknown when we used him," Frye observed, "and that show opened up the door for him: He went on to do all those other things afterwards, including *Dr. Kildare*."

Despite Frye's innovations, certain elements present in the earliest episodes remained intact. One of these was the show's graphics designed by Jerome Gould. These consisted of straight white vertical and horizontal lines that crisscrossed the screen, forming a suitably bizarre background for *Thriller*'s logo. This design was probably inspired by Saul Bass's similar design for the titles of Alfred Hitchcock's *North by Northwest* (1959). Laid on top of this was Pete Rugolo's blaring *Thriller* theme. "We try to use this theme as often as possible, usually when the villains are on camera," the Sicilian-born composer explained. Indeed, in the early episodes he virtually drove the theme into the ground through overuse. Following Frye's advent, Rugolo's strident soundtracks would give way to the subtler orchestrations of Jerry Goldsmith and Morton Stevens, though his jangling main theme for brass and bongos would continue to be heard over the main title.

Another standard device carried over, and improved upon, was Karloff's introductions. Through his theatrical training and polished delivery, he could always be counted upon to impart great moment to these often bombastic lead-ins. Donald S. Sanford recalls: "As to Boris' introductions: They were written by the writers of the individual scripts. He was marvelously able to read complex sentences which were necessary in order to squeeze a great deal of introduction into a very limited amount of time." These introductions were usually filmed out of sequence, four or five at a time (as were Hitchcock's), usually in Hollywood but occasionally in New York (depending on Karloff's whereabouts), and were usually great fun. They were often imaginative and sometimes playful. In "Hay-Fork and Bill-Hook," an episode dealing with suspected witchcraft, the actors' faces were superimposed over a fiery cauldron. For "Man of Mystery," concerned with tycoons and high finance, the actors were shown as images on a $10,000 bill. In "The Premature Burial," the cast was introduced, one by one, lying in their respective coffins. And in "Guillotine," the actors' heads were seemingly removed from a basket. Karloff would deliver his spiels with tongue in cheek, occasionally hammy or properly somber, as the occasion demanded.

Following the initial success of "The Purple Room" and "The Watcher," the show's ratings began to climb. These episodes, unfortunately, were followed by several that were mediocre: "Girl with a Secret," "The Prediction," "The Big Blackout" and "Man in the Middle." Then came two of the strongest horror entries: "The Cheaters" and "The Hungry Glass," both based on stories by Robert Bloch. To this day, "The Cheaters" is considered by some to be the high-point of television horror; "The Hungry Glass"—which Jay Allen Sanford considered the "turnaround" episode, establishing the show's district image—featured a strong performance by a young William Shatner.

Even here, however, a perplexing problem was apparent. Following these two milestone horror offerings, *Thriller* returned to crime episodes. Although some of these were outstanding (such as "The Merriweather File" and "The Fingers of Fear") the juxtaposition of a Gothic horror piece one week with a standard crime entry the next reflected a bipartite approach that threw the viewer off balance.

As Jay Allen Sanford points out, "It was hard to guess just which type of *Thriller* would be aired each week, a dilemma that could have led to eventual viewer disenchantment. While a handful of the crime-drama episodes did manage to successfully integrate supernatural themes into the mix ... for the most part *Thriller* seemed like two separate programs." Sadly, this fundamental error plagued *Thriller* to the very end; even today, television critics remark on its "schizophrenic" image. To add to the confusion, many horror episodes actually took on crime elements as they went along, creating an entertaining mix best described as "crisscrossing genres." But in terms of viewer response, the mix of crime and horror was a mistake.

Under William Frye's aegis, *Thriller* took on a different look and feel. The horror episodes took place in a Gothic, nineteenth-century atmosphere replete with cobwebs and a predominant, almost palpable atmosphere of decay and death; even when the stories were set in the present day, the physical surroundings imposed a timelessness that lent credence to supernatural (or *apparently* supernatural) events.

Frye's influence was everywhere. As Donald S. Sanford recalls:

> Bill Frye ran the show with a very firm hand. He was excellent at casting, knew the art of storytelling, was meticulous about how the sets were decorated (much to the annoyance of the studio's set designers and decorators and the prop people). He was also a better costumer than any of the professionals at the studio. And he had an absolute rule with his directors and casts: no one was allowed to change a line or a word in a script without his approval. This last was a boon to his writers, as all of us, all too frequently, have had our material butchered by some thick-headed, egotistical director or actor."

Frye hired Doug Benton as associate producer. This proved to be another inspired choice. Benton recalls his first days on the series:

> When Bill Frye was put on the show after the original producer had made a mess of it, I came over to work for him as I had on *General Electric Theater*. The first thing I did was call Richard Matheson, and he said the man who knew this particular genre was Charles Beaumont; they were both satellites of Ray Bradbury's.
>
> As it turned out, it wasn't the right sort of thing for Matheson. And Chuck Beaumont said he didn't want to do television; he said, "Look, I just got a feature picture [to write]." He said, "Call Forry Ackerman, and get his complete file of *Weird Tales*. He just bought it from me." I called Ackerman, and, sure enough, he had trunks and trunks of *Weird Tales*. I said, "Do you want to sell them?" He said no, he'd had enough trouble finding someone to buy them from. So he rented them to me with the proviso that they would all go back to him. I started taking ten of them home at night with me, and I'd read them, and every time I thought one was a possibility I'd mark it. I'd take the ones that were feasible [story properties] and give them to Frye, and he would either agree, or he would say, "I don't know what you see in this." Eighty percent of the shows that we did were *Weird Tales*. We had a whole legal staff tracking the authors down, and we paid them two or three times as much as they were paid for the stories in the first place. Then, usually, the story became the last two acts [of the *Thriller* adaptation]. Don Sanford had a knack for building up to the final two acts. And people were surprised at how good, how macabre and hair-

raising and terrifying our stories were, but it was because these guys were so good in the first place.

For *Thriller*, Benton selected lesser-known works by Robert Bloch, Cornell Woolrich, Harold Lawlor, Margaret St. Clair, and others. No less than eighteen *Thriller* scripts originated from stories published in *Weird Tales*, though other pulp sources were used as well. As Stephen King has written:

> One of the most significant things about the *Thriller* series from the standpoint of the horror fan was that it began to depend more and more upon the work of writers who had published in those "shudder pulps" ... the writers who, in the period of the twenties, thirties, and forties, had begun to guide horror out of the Victorian-Edwardian ghost-story channel it had been in for so long, and toward our modern perception of what the horror story is and what it should do.

Thriller had at last acquired an identity of its own, quite distinct from that of *Twilight Zone* or *Alfred Hitchcock Presents*. Frye credits much of the show's success to the creative personnel assembled: "I had the same editor [Danny Landres], the same makeup man [Jack Barron], the same set decorators [Jack McCarthy and Julia Heron], and we tended to use the same directors — Ida Lupino, John Brahm, Herschel Daugherty. It was a very nice little group."

Perhaps most importantly, Frye selected writers uniquely suited to *Thriller's* needs — Donald S. Sanford, John Kneubuhl, and Alan Caillou, among others. After the presentation of "Yours Truly, Jack the Ripper," based on the classic short story by Robert Bloch, they decided to go to one of the prime sources for material: they called in Robert Bloch. This proved to be an inspired move, for in many ways Bloch was the quintessential *Thriller* writer.

Chicago-born Robert Bloch (1917–1994) was attracted to the macabre at a very early age. "The first film that shocked me out of my wits was *The Phantom of the Opera*," he recalled. "Lon Chaney had a traumatic effect on me." He also encountered the work of H.P. Lovecraft in *Weird Tales*, and began a correspondence with him. Lovecraft encouraged Bloch to write, and his story "The Feast in the Abbey" was published in the January 1935 issue of *Weird Tales* when Bloch was 17. He began making steady sales to that magazine. These early stories show the heavy influence of Lovecraft, particularly in their avoidance of dialogue. "I didn't really begin to write properly for nearly a decade following that first sale," Bloch wrote many years later. "Not that I was necessarily any great shakes at it even then, but at least I'd begun to diversify my style and divest it of some annoying mannerisms." Many of these stories, including "Waxworks" (1938), "The Weird Tailor" (1950), and "The Cheaters" (1947) later become grist for *Thriller's* mill.

Following Lovecraft's death in 1937, Bloch began to evolve a style quite different from that of his formative years. Partly influenced by Raymond Chandler, dialogue began to play an increasingly more important role, and by the time he wrote "Yours Truly, Jack the Ripper" in 1943, he had stepped out from behind

Lovecraft's shadow. Dramatized on radio and frequently anthologized, it enhanced Bloch's reputation, and led to his writing a short-lived radio series of his own, *Stay Tuned for Terror*.

During the forties and fifties, Bloch turned to writing novels. *The Scarf* (1947) was the first-person account of a serial killer, and later novels such as *Spiderweb* (1954), *The Will to Kill* (1954), *The Kidnapper* (1954) and *Shooting Star* (1958) continued this trend. Another novel, an Inner Sanctum mystery entitled *Psycho* (1959), was "bought blind" for the movies by MCA, representing the actual purchaser, who of course was Alfred Hitchcock. As Bloch recalled: "I was not told who wanted it. All I received was a flat offer ... Hitchcock ... asked if I was available to do the screenplay. The person he talked to was an MCA agent. And it took that agent three seconds to say 'No, Bloch is not available.' Because at that time MCA was in the talent business and wanted to sell one of their own clients."

For the rights to *Psycho*, Bloch was paid the princely sum of $9,000. Joseph Stefano got the job of writing the screenplay. Hitchcock's film, of course, became a classic, as well as the highest grossing black and white film up to that time, with rentals of more than $9 million. Consequently, Bloch began getting more scriptwriting offers than he could handle; these included *The Cabinet of Caligari* (1962), *The Couch* (1962), *Strait-Jacket* (1964), *The Night Walker* (1965), *The Deadly Bees* (1967) and *The House That Dripped Blood* (1971), none of which he particularly admires. "There are too many producers and directors and cameramen who do horror films who invalidate what they are trying to achieve," Bloch pointed out. "That's why for every good film of this sort there are innumerable bad ones."

Bloch also began writing for television, both original teleplays and adaptations, for such series as *Lock-Up, Star Trek, Journey to the Unknown*, and, of course, both *Thriller* and *Alfred Hitchcock Presents*. "Films or TV have seldom given me an opportunity to exercise my craft as best I can," Bloch opined; "a few Hitchcock shows, some of the *Thriller* shows, a 12-minute segment of *Strait-Jacket* just about comprises the output which satisfies me in the visual media." On another occasion, in discussing television, he said, "In general, TV never quite comes off—there are too many fingers in that particular pie—but *Thriller* was in a different category entirely. Almost invariably my first draft teleplay was shot exactly as I wrote it. The director didn't try to change the story."

The first of Bloch's teleplays to be aired was his adaptation of his story "The Devil's Ticket," followed by "A Good Imagination," an expansion of the story of that title. In all, ten episodes featured Bloch stories. When asked which of these he preferred, Bloch responded, "I think 'The Grim Reaper' is my favorite adaptation of another writer's story, and 'The Weird Tailor' might qualify as a favorite adaptation of my own story. Though perhaps it's just that I compare it to the altered version of the script I did as a film episode some years later [*Asylum*]."

By now, *Thriller* was operating at full throttle. Most episodes were genuinely horrific, with the occasional crime entry thrown in as a change of pace. One out-standing episode, "The Ordeal of Dr. Cordell," featured a young Robert Vaughn as the protagonist, and an even younger Marlo Thomas as one of his victims. This casting highlighted a *Thriller* characteristic: its ability to showcase up and com-ing stars in both major and minor roles. Besides Richard Chamberlain in "The Watcher" and William Shatner in two episodes ("The Hungry Glass" and "The Grim Reaper"), many others would turn up in the future: Ron Ely, later to play Tarzan on the small screen, appeared in "Waxworks"; Ursula Andress starred in "La Strega"; Bruce Dern was seen in "The Remarkable Mrs. Hawk"; Elizabeth Montgomery turned up in "Masquerade"; and Mary Tyler Moore was featured in both "The Fatal Impulse" and "Man of Mystery."

One measure of the show's increasing popularity was the number of com-mercial tie-ins exploiting both the series and its star. Time Records released an LP titled *Original Music of Thriller* featuring Pete Rugolo's jazz-oriented main theme and musical cues. The album featured liner notes purportedly written by Karloff, in which he stated:

> A good thriller is exciting, spine-chilling fun … after a bit over a quarter-century of film roles devoted primarily to thriller-type themes, I've become something of a purist on the subject. I don't consider … horror or violence a basis for such drama because such ingredients are apt to revolt one rather than provide an interesting bit of entertainment. There can be little suspense or excitement in the chatter of gunfire or brutal pistol-whippings; such elements are far too crude for the true enthusiast.…

Another, longer-lasting tie-in was a comic book, *Boris Karloff's Thriller*, published by Gold Key. Like the similar *Twilight Zone* comic, it did not adapt stories done on the show, but rather featured *Thriller*-like horror and suspense stories considerably less macabre than those presented by its namesake. The pub-lication would continue long after *Thriller* left the airwaves, under the modified title *Boris Karloff Tales of Mystery*. A more logical tie-in was also planned: a paper-back anthology of the most successful stories that appeared on *Thriller's* first sea-son, but unfortunately this collection never saw print.

As *Thriller* evolved, music began to play an increasingly more important role in the series' overall impact. As Randall Larson remarks in *Musique Fantastique*, his excellent study of sci-fi and horror film music:

> Much of the style of *Thriller*, both aurally and visually, seemed to have been influenced by Hitchcock's *Psycho*, a good example being the music for the episode "Pigeons from Hell," which used a predominantly string orchestra. The episode also featured a striking use of female voice heard at the end when the apparition appears.

Pete Rugolo's jazz scores continued to dominate the crime episodes and even the occasional horror entry, but as the focus began to shift to the macabre, the producers came to rely on two noted composers: Morton Stevens and the leg-endary Jerry Goldsmith. Between them, Stevens and Goldsmith scored 42 of *Thriller's* 67 episodes.

Stevens was born in New Jersey in 1929 and educated at Juilliard. During the sixties he worked as an arranger for popular vocalists and did the music for such TV series as *Tales of Wells Fargo* and *Checkmate* (with Rugolo). His most notable *Thriller* scores include "The Ordeal of Dr. Cordell," "The Prisoner in the Mirror" and the aforementioned "Pigeons from Hell." His other television credits include *Apple's Way*, *87th Precinct*, *Hawaii Five-O* (with Rugolo), *Kodiak*, and *The Wild, Wild West*, and such TV-movies as *Poor Devil* and *The Horror at 37,000 Feet* (both 1973).

Goldsmith was born Jerrald Goldsmith in Los Angeles in 1929. After studying piano with Jakob Gimpel and theory and composition with Castelnuovo-Tedesco, he studied music at Los Angeles City College. He sat in on Miklos Rosza's sessions on film music at the University of Southern California, and wrote music for CBS radio and television programs. His TV scores include *The Man from U.N.C.L.E.*, *The Girl from U.N.C.L.E.*, *Archer*, *Cain's Hundred*, *Dr. Kildare* (with Rugolo), *The Line-Up*, *Police Story*, *Police Woman*, *The Waltons*, and *The Twilight Zone*. His motion picture credits are too numerous to list, but among the most notable are *Freud* (1963), *Seven Days in May* (1964), *Seconds* (1966), *Planet of the Apes* (1968), *Patton* (1970), *Chinatown* (1974), *The Omen* (1976, for which he won an Academy Award), *Star Trek: The Motion Picture* (1979), *Poltergeist* (1982), and *Psycho II* (1983). His work for *Thriller* was outstanding, as Randall Larson notes:

> "Mr. George" utilized effective, somewhat discordant violin figures under a pleasant woodwind tune, in a clever chamber variation of a lullaby theme ... "Yours Truly, Jack the Ripper" was given a dirgelike motif for strings in addition to a mellow saxophone theme for Jack; faint use of accordion was also in evidence from time to time.

Donald S. Sanford remembers Goldsmith with special fondness:

> I'm a classical music fan, and sometimes I used to go down and sit in on the scoring sessions with Jerry. You know, they had some of the best musicians in the world, the guys who played in those scoring sessions. Really great stuff. That helped the show — I would say maybe 25 percent of the value of the show was in the score sometimes.

By mid-1961 *Thriller* was at its peak.* After 35 episodes the show had acquired its own distinct image, and the ratings were consistently high. In addition, the compromises and occasional ineptitudes of the earlier shows were gone.

And so was Maxwell Shane. With the telecast of "Papa Benjamin," the 26th episode, the crime specialist bowed out. In some ways this was unfortunate, since Shane had produced a number of fine episodes — notably "The Ordeal of Dr.

It was also a good period for anthology series, or at least for those in a horrific vein: for one brief period in mid-1961, Thriller, Twilight Zone, Way Out, One Step Beyond, Great Ghost Tales, and the semi-horrific Alfred Hitchcock Presents were all on the air at the same time.

Cordell," "The Merriweather File," and "The Fatal Impulse"—but it can hardly be denied that William Frye had turned the show around and steered it from almost certain early cancellation to its present critical and popular success. From now on (with but two exceptions: "The Innocent Bystanders" and "The Specialists") all *Thrillers* would be produced by Frye. (By now, Hubbell Robinson had little or nothing to do with the show, hence Frye's continuing displeasure that he was still receiving on the air credit: the logo "A Presentation of Hubbell Robinson Productions" appeared on every episode.)

On June 6, 1961, *Thriller* presented its best-remembered episode, an adaptation of Robert E. Howard's "Pigeons from Hell." Directed by John Newland, the host of *One Step Beyond*, and starring former child actor Brandon DeWilde, this episode—set in an abandoned Southern mansion—went further than anything previously seen on *Thriller* in its bloodletting and visceral horror, doing full justice to Howard's sanguinary tale, and remains the firm favorite of many *Thriller* fans. Even today, more than 30 years since its initial telecast, it is still remembered by many as the most frightening single episode of any series.

The makers could not have known it at the time, but *Thriller* had peaked. There were still many excellent episodes yet to come — indeed, Robert Bloch's outstanding adaptation of "The Grim Reaper" followed one week later — but, in a sense, "Pigeons from Hell" marked a high point that the series would find increasingly difficult to attain. There was nowhere to go but down.

Thriller began its second, and last, season on September 18, 1961, with an adaptation of Harold Lawlor's "What Beckoning Ghost?"

"There was a lot of talk about going to color for the second season," Donald Sanford recalls. At this time (the 1961-62 season) most programs were still done in black and white. Sanford today feels that if *Thriller* had switched to color the series would have done better in syndication, though it's hard to imagine the chiaroscuro photography—by now part of the *Thriller* style—replaced by color. Fortunately for purists, *Thriller* would remain in black and white for the duration of its run.

By now, *Thriller's* method of adaptation had evolved into a formula. With the writer providing the first two acts, the original story (usually from *Weird Tales*) then kicked in, and the result was a strong one hour drama free of the obtrusive padding that had been noticeable in the earliest episodes. The average *Thriller* took five days to shoot ("Believe it or not," Doug Benton adds), and cost between $125,000 and $150,000.

One disappointment was the lack of bigger stars. NBC had issued this announcement at the beginning of the second season: "While not designed primarily as a star vehicle, *Thriller* for 1961-1962 will have a larger cast budget which will permit more frequent use of 'name' performers in its suspense dramas." Whether this was their actual intention or simply hyperbole, few "names" signed on. Whereas the first season had featured Mort Sahl, Mary Astor, Macdonald Carey, John Ireland and Brandon DeWilde, among others, the best the second season could offer was Jane Greer, Robert Webber, Jo Van Fleet, Richard Carlson (and, of course, Karloff). The salaries offered were certainly no inducement: "Most name actors wouldn't work for our $2500 top," Doug Benton says. "We could (and did) get great character people, however." These included George Macready, Oscar Homolka, Walter Burke, and the uniquely skull-faced Reggie Nalder, seen in two episodes.

Donald S. Sanford, who was responsible for more *Thriller* scripts than any other writer (courtesy of Donald S. Sanford).

There had never been any real danger of cancellation — the ratings had improved dramatically, and the show was receiving critical cachets; moreover, *Thriller* was enjoying new-found respect in the industry that must have been doubly pleasing after its initial desperate struggle for survival. Unfortunately an even greater danger was hovering just over the rise, but in the fall of 1961 this specter was not yet in view.

One major change was *Thriller*'s new time slot. It was now broadcast on Monday evenings, from 10 to 11 p.m. It faced stiff competition from *Ben Casey*— soon to become one of the most popular shows on television — on ABC, *Hennessey*, a popular novel comedy starring Jackie Cooper, and *I've Got a Secret* on CBS.

"What Beckoning Ghost?" was followed by "Guillotine," Ida Lupino's third *Thriller* and the best of their Cornell Woolrich adaptations. That was in turn followed by "The Premature Burial," a loose adaptation of the Poe story, and the first episode since "The Prediction" to feature Karloff as an actor — rather a surprise, since he was obviously one of *Thriller*'s prime assets. Moreover, Karloff did not merely walk through these assignments (as he did with some of his films): he approached them with his usual dedication and enthusiasm. As Donald Sanford recalls:

One of my contract understandings was that I agreed to write all of the episodes in which Boris Karloff starred. They were all original stories and teleplays. It was a great compliment and a pleasure because I was very impressed with Boris. He was a fine actor and a classical gentleman.

Producer Bill Frye, contrary to most producers, encouraged his writers to attend first cast readings and to adjust any lines or words that a particular actor might have difficulty with. At the readings it was all too often apparent that very few of the actors had even bothered to learn their lines or had any handle on the interpretation of their roles. Boris, however, was always letter perfect in both areas. He came to rehearsals having done his homework!

One other remembrance: Mrs. Karloff (whose first name I don't recall) was most always in attendance at rehearsals and shooting. Never intrusive, but always quietly taking care of Boris. She was a very attractive woman. In every way.

Sanford also discussed the writers' financial arrangements:

A monetary note: the "top of the show" as far as dollars were concerned was $3000 for a one-hour teleplay and $3500 for an original story and teleplay during the first year of the series. The second year I was able to squeeze $4000 out of Universal for story and teleplay. Today writers are getting eight to ten times that amount for a one-hour episode on the most modest of series.

The Writers Guild contract with the networks and the studios at the time provided for rerun payments from one through six nationwide showings. No payments were due after the sixth run.

Inevitably, due to the show's crushing production schedule, some intended episodes never got made. These include "The Black-Eyed Stranger," "A Secret Understanding," "The Loving Enemy," "An Air That Kills," "Passage of Guilt," "Tomorrow Is Here," and "King's Ransom." None of these ever made it past the scripting stage, but there was a tantalizing rumor of an entire "lost" episode scripted by Bob and Wanda Duncan from a story, "Tamara, the Georgian Queen" by Harold Lawlor (which appeared in the July 1943 *Weird Tales*) and directed by *Thriller* veteran Herschel Daugherty. The plot concerned a married couple who consult a fortune teller, Madame Yalta Salkov. She tells the wife of her previous incarnation as Tamara, the Georgian Queen, who reigned between A.D. 1184 and 1212, and had her lover of the previous evening thrown to his death from her castle the following morning. The couple, after hearing this, find young men dead on the sidewalk below their apartment.

This enticing rumor was, alas, just that — a rumor. Although this episode was scripted, it was in fact never shot. "We bought the story and script," Doug Benton recalls, "and Herschel Daugherty *was* picked to direct, but it never got made. Hubbell Robinson wanted to do the pilot instead ["The Specialists," the last episode]." As Benton puts it, "Universal was a little like a packing house: they didn't buy anything they didn't use."

Ironically, the most famous unmade *Thriller* became a very famous movie, *What Ever Happened to Baby Jane?* Bill Frye recounts:

I was going to do it as a *Thriller*, but then I took a second look at it, and said to myself, this is too good for a *Thriller*. I gave it to Bette Davis, Olivia de Havilland

and Ida Lupino, and I hoped my agent Lew Wasserman would buy the book, but he hated it and he hated Bette Davis too! So while I was in Monaco preparing a program for Princess Grace, I learned that Robert Aldrich was doing it, with Bette Davis.

In addition to unmade episodes, there were unused introductions. *Good Stuff*, the magazine of the *Thriller* club, recounts one of these, recalled by Assistant Director Willard Shelton:

> In one of the *Thriller* series there was a doctor, and a big lab; and they would cut off the arms and legs of people, and throw then into vats of brine to preserve them (he was going to try and put them on other bodies). There were some shots of these huge vats, and Boris Karloff would come along and look into one vat, and he'd take a stick and stir it, and you'd go to an insert, and the vat was full of legs — all made out of foam rubber, of course. Another vat would be full of arms in this boiling stuff. We finished all that and we were going to end up the day with a big, beautiful set of an ancestral castle, with a long flight of stairs. Boris was going to appear at the top of the stairway, coming down the stairs, looking very satisfied at what he had just done in the laboratory.

Despite the lack of "name" stars, the show strove to showcase character actors. Doug Benton remembers:

> Bill Frye was more interested in who was going to star in it. Bill was more interested in above the line people. All the character people were generally hired by the director and me. We used Henry Daniell several times: he was perfect for that sort of thing. You used the appropriate people; if Rondo Hatton had been available, we would have used him. I remember we tried to get Basil Rathbone — I don't think he wanted to be subservient to Karloff. We tried to get him a couple of times. He was a nice man, but he had a healthy ego. He *did* do a *Dr. Kildare* later: he didn't object to that. We tried to get Victor Jory, but he didn't like TV. And Peter Lorre didn't want to do television, either, although he wound up doing some — not by choice. And the awful truth about Lon Chaney, Jr., is that he wasn't very reliable. He and Brod Crawford used to drink an awful lot.

By now, *Thriller* was well enough established to attempt some experimental or offbeat episodes. "Masquerade," aired on Halloween of 1961, was a tongue-in-cheek vampire yarn (perhaps one should say fang-in-cheek) based on a story by Henry Kuttner. It featured a young, pre-*Bewitched* Elizabeth Montgomery, Tom Poston, and horror veteran John Carradine, later featured in "The Remarkable Mrs. Hawk." But, once again, straight crime dramas were interspersed among the horror offerings. Thus, "Masquerade" was followed by "The Last of the Sommervilles," a murder yarn featuring Karloff, and this was in turn followed by "Letter to a Lover" (actually the first episode shot for the second season) and "A Third for Pinochle," two crime stories which, whatever their respective merits, must have confused fans expecting *Thriller*'s usual horror fare.

One episode, "The Return of Andrew Bentley," ironically represents Richard Matheson's only contribution to the series. Although he had been one of the first writers approached when Frye became producer, his teleplay (based on a story by

August Derleth and Mark Schorer) was rewritten without his knowledge or approval, and Matheson, displeased with the result, never did another. This was unfortunate but probably inevitable, since Matheson's brand of fantasy, with its strong ties to the prosaic realities of everyday life, was simply antithetical to *Thriller*'s moody, Gothic *mise-en-scène*.

This was followed by "The Remarkable Mrs. Hawk" (nominated as one of the four best written anthology dramas for the 1961–62 season by the Writers Guild of America) and "Portrait Without a Face," one of the best crisscrossing episodes, intermixing supernatural horror with straight suspense.

It was around this time that the specter that had hovered nervously in the background finally appeared, with disastrous results. His name was Alfred Hitchcock.

For some time *Thriller* had been drawing consistently higher ratings than *Alfred Hitchcock Presents*, the show it had originally attempted to emulate, and this fact was not lost on the Master of Suspense. "Don't think that Hitchcock and Joan Harrison [the producer of *Alfred Hitchcock Presents*] weren't watching *Thriller*," says Bill Frye.

Hitchcock, irked by *Thriller*'s consistent high quality, issued an ultimatum: he wouldn't go on unless *Thriller* was withdrawn for one year. This was tantamount to cancellation; the network hesitated, but as Frye ruefully recalls, "Hitchcock's clout at NBC was greater than Karloff's."

The decision was made to axe the series.

After such excellent episodes as "Waxworks," "A Wig for Miss Devore" and "The Incredible Doktor Markesan" (the last to feature Karloff), the series declined, and the final eight episodes were considerably below *Thriller*'s usual level. Of these eight, the only one with any real punch was "Man of Mystery," written by the always dependable Robert Bloch. The final episode, "The Specialists," was not produced by William Frye; as unlikely a *Thriller* as can be imagined, it seemed a throwback to the show's earliest days. (It was, in fact, a pilot for an unproduced NBC series.)

And so, after 67 episodes, *Thriller* came to an end. It had been a heady two years. William Frye recalls being "very disappointed" when the decision was announced. Doug Benton was unfazed. "I wasn't surprised when *Thriller* was cancelled," he said later. "The ratings were marginal and Universal had to split the take with Robinson. They saved their clout for their own shows." In retrospect, he adds, "I do think it was the *only* good horror series."

As for Hubbell Robinson, the man who started it all was still receiving credit as executive producer despite having nothing to do with the series. He announced, "The show simply did not have enough time to find its identity," thus neatly ignoring the fact that after the first batch of turgid episodes, *Thriller* had forged an identity of its own and had successfully sustained it throughout its lifespan.

On April 30, 1962, with the telecast of "The Specialists," *Thriller* ended its run. Reruns followed, and in July the series left the air.

As expected, *Alfred Hitchcock Presents* benefited from *Thriller*'s demise. Now retitled *The Alfred Hitchcock Hour*, the series began presenting unabashed horror episodes, something Hitchcock had previously steered away from. William Frye observed this metamorphosis with undisguised annoyance. "Not only did they begin using similar stories," he points out, "but they started using the same directors — John Newland, John Brahm, and so on."

Meanwhile, the creative personnel behind *Thriller* went their separate ways. Frye left television altogether to produce movies, including the very successful 1966 comedy *The Trouble with Angels* (directed by Ida Lupino) and its follow-up, *Where Angels Go ... Trouble Follows* (1968). He also produced two high-grossing *Airport* sequels, *Airport 1975* and *Airport 1977* (which presented horror veteran Christopher Lee in a straight role), and the less successful *Raise the Titanic!* (1980). Doug Benton went on to a successful career as a television producer, overseeing such series as *Dr. Kildare*, *Columbo* and *The Girl from U.N.C.L.E.*, among others.

Robert Bloch stayed active on television, writing for the Hitchcock series and various others, including *Journey to the Unknown*, *Night Gallery*, *Darkroom*, and *Star Trek*. He also wrote screenplays for such films as *The Night Walker*, *Strait-Jacket*, and the atrocious remake of *Cabinet of Caligari* (which was completely rewritten without Bloch's knowledge or approval by its director, Roger Kay). Don Sanford also went on writing for television, as well as scripting such films as *The Thousand Plane Raid* (1969) and *Midway* (1976).

John Newland continued directing for television (including an episode of *Star Trek*, "Errand of Mercy"), and hosted an updated version of *One Step Beyond*, retitled *Next Step Beyond*. This follow-up was not nearly as successful as the original.

Ida Lupino and Herschel Daugherty also remained active in television, as did John Brahm, who crafted some memorable episodes of *Twilight Zone* and *The Alfred Hitchcock Hour*.

And Boris Karloff...

Karloff entered the final stage of his career. He remained active on television (reprising his role as the Frankenstein Monster on *Route 66*, donning the headpiece and heavy makeup at the age of 74!). He also returned to movies in 1963 in Roger Corman's tongue-in-cheek version of *The Raven*. Following this, he went to Italy to appear in Mario Bava's *Black Sabbath*, a *Thriller*-like compendium of horror tales; did a horror sendup, *The Comedy of Terrors*, with Price, Rathbone and Lorre; and starred in *Die, Monster, Die!*, which insulted its marvelous source, H.P. Lovecraft's "The Colour Out of Space." He also made numerous guest appearances on television series, including *The Wild, Wild West*, *I Spy*, *Shindig*, and *The Girl from U.N.C.L.E.* One of the few bright spots in his later career was his performance in Peter Bogdanovich's *Targets* (1968), in which the 80-year-old Karloff, playing an aging horror star, virtually summarized his entire screen career. Following that, he made a few more movies and television appearances; then this most gentle of monsters died on February 2, 1969, in England. A commemorative plaque at St. Paul's Covent Garden bears this quotation from Andrew Marvell:

> He Nothing Common Did or Mean
> Upon That Memorable Scene

As for *Thriller* itself, it went into syndication soon after its cancellation, and played in many parts of the country. It became a great favorite in Europe (particularly in England), Australia and elsewhere. William Frye recalls his surprise when he went abroad: "When I did *Airport 1977*, Jimmy Stewart and his wife and I went on a tour to promote the film, to Hong Kong and Bangkok, and, much to my amazement, in Sydney and Melbourne and Tokyo and places like that, they were more interested in hearing about *Thriller*! *Thriller* had just finished playing in Australia in 1977."

Despite its success in the overseas market, *Thriller* has not enjoyed the syndication popularity of such series as *Twilight Zone* and *The Outer Limits* (both of which will probably be rerun well into the twenty-first century). Apart from occasional revivals on local stations, it had little air play in recent years. All that changed in 1994 when MCA released six episodes (three with Karloff) on videotape and laser disc. The collection includes "The Grim Reaper," "The Incredible Doktor Markesan," "The Terror in Teakwood," "The Prediction," "Masquerade," and "The Premature Burial."

Even before this recent development, fans made a concerted effort to make *Thriller* available once again. In 1989 the *Thriller* Fan Club was formed in San Francisco; the club, headquartered at 537 Jones Street, No. 1850, San Francisco, CA 94102, provides tapes of all *Thriller* episodes and publishes *Good Stuff*, the official catalog and magazine of the *Thriller* club. The club's president, Ken Kaffke, reports that they have around 300 members across the nation (as well as such faraway locations as England, France and Germany). Equally devoted to such memorable but largely ignored television series as *Way Out, Great Ghost Tales, One Step Beyond* and *Suspicion*, the club feels that *Thriller*'s revival is long overdue.

Today, more than three decades since its demise, *Thriller* stands alone as the very model of a successful horror series. In many ways it was a fluke: uncompromised by network censorship or interference, blessed with a producer of taste and intelligence, well served by a team of craftsmen who knew and respected the genre, and hosted by a beloved screen icon, it has stood the test of time remarkably well. Perhaps in coming years, as it is seen by new generations unimpressed by the vapidity of what passes for contemporary horror fare, it will once again be taken up by aficionados of the macabre, who will quiver in the delicious anticipation of fear as its venerable host intones his memorable salutation:

"As sure as my name is Boris Karloff, *this* is a *Thriller*!"

Part II
Episode Guide

FIRST SEASON, 1960-1961

"The Twisted Image" (airdate: September 13, 1960). Produced by Fletcher Markle. Directed by Arthur Hiller. Teleplay by James P. Cavanagh, from a novel by William O'Farrell. Director of Photography: Lionel Lindon, A.S.C. Associate Producer: James P. Cavanagh. Music: Pete Rugolo. Edited by Danny Landres. Assistant Director: Carter DeHaven III. Art Director: Arthur Lonergan.

Cast: Leslie Nielsen (Alan Patterson), Natalie Trundy (Lily Hanson), George Grizzard (Merle Jenkins), Dianne Foster (Judy Patterson), Constance Ford (Louise), Virginia Christine (Marge), Carol Kelly, Ray Montgomery, Victor Sen Yung.

"The Twisted Image," *Thriller's* premiere episode, hardly constitutes a proper introduction to the series. The first of *Thriller's* crime episodes, it's a study in psychosis with little to recommend it aside from some fine acting by the four principals.

Lily Hanson (Natalie Trundy) stares at advertising executive Alan Patterson (Leslie Nielsen) at the newsstand and at lunch. She finally sits down at his table and talks with him, then shows up the following day at his office, ready to be taken to lunch. She explains that she has a plan; unbeknownst to Alan, that plan includes marrying him despite the fact that he is already married and has a small daughter.

Merle Jenkins (George Grizzard), another employee in the same building where they both work, has been stealing items from around the office. Like Lily, he is living a fantasy: he has been writing letters to his family implying that he will soon be vice president, which is Alan's position; he actually works in the mailroom. He has a nasty confrontation with his sister Louise (Constance Ford), who bullied him during his childhood.

Meanwhile, Lily is calling Alan constantly, disrupting his home life and convincing his wife, Judy (Dianne Foster), that the two of them are having an affair. Merle approaches Lily, telling her he's a friend of Alan's, and the two have a discussion over drinks. They exchange fantasies: Lily tells Merle that Alan will leave his wife for her; Merle boasts that he will soon have Alan's job. But when Merle tells her he looks like Alan, she laughs at him. They quarrel, and Merle strangles her. Just then, Alan arrives at Lily's apartment, determined to have it out with her. Merle knocks him unconscious, then clears out. Alan awakens to find Lily's body. Leaving the apartment in haste, he is seen by one of the other tenants. Instead of going to the police, he takes out after Merle himself.

Merle, meanwhile, steals Alan's car, then shows up at his apartment, frightening Judy. When Alan arrives home, Merle snatches up his small daughter and runs out. Alan pursues him, and the chase leads to a room filled with bric-a-brac. Merle sees Alan and strikes at him with a poker, but it is only a mirror image and shatters, giving back Merle's twisted image.

Although "The Twisted Image" is not one of *Thriller*'s finer hours, it's superior to many of the straight crime episodes to come. The concept of Merle being the "twisted image" of Alan Patterson gives the story a thematic unity that is emphasized throughout: Alan's secretary describes Merle as a "kind of smudged-up carbon copy" of Alan, and Merle is constantly seen patting the scar on his cheek just as Alan does. Merle's identification with the more successful, handsomer man increases with each new theft: he steals Alan's wristwatch, his car, and finally his own daughter.

"The Twisted Image" features better than average acting. Leslie Nielsen, now firmly typed as a comedian, is fine as the lead. Previously a stiff, colorless performer, Nielsen revealed his comic range in *Airplane!* (1980) and has gone on to great success as the blinkered cop in the *Naked Gun* series. He's best known to genre fans as the stalwart captain in *Forbidden Planet* (1956), though he made an engagingly offbeat hero in the *Thriller*-esque *Dark Intruder* (1965).

Geoge Grizzard makes Merle Jenkins a distressingly believable antagonist. Grizzard usually appears as a sneaky character in films and on television. He had a memorable role in *Advise and Consent* (1962) and was featured in *From the Terrace* (1960) and *Warning Shot* (1967). On television he appeared in *The Twilight Zone* and in the memorable final episode of *Bus Stop*, an adaptation of Robert Bloch's "I Kiss Your Shadow," which Stephen King said "has never been beaten on TV — and rarely anywhere else — for eerie, mounting horror."

Natalie Trundy was a strikingly beautiful young actress, and her piercing gaze sets the tone of "The Twisted Image" from the first shot. She married Arthur P. Jacobs, producer of the highly successful *Planet of the Apes* films, and appears in the second (as a mutant), the third (as a human scientist), and the fourth (as an ape). She's suitably demented as Lily Hanson.

The other performers, including Dianne Foster as Alan's wife, are all adequate. If you look fast, you'll spot Victor Sen Yung, Charlie Chan's number two son, in a bit as a bartender.

One other performer deserves special mention, not for what he does, but for his near-total absence from the episode. In recent years everyone (or so it appears) seems to think Karloff is in "The Twisted Image." In his otherwise excellent article "Karloff Through the Looking Glass: Horror on *Thriller*," Jay Allen Sanford writes, "Even Karloff's venerable presence, acting in ... 'The Twisted Image' ... couldn't salvage its muddy look and trite storyline," and adds, "He had a much meatier role in the tenth episode, 'The Prediction.'" What's even more strange is that there's no conceivable role he *could* have played — certainly not Alan Patterson or Merle Jenkins! (Another missing performer, originally announced for the episode, is John Cassavetes; it's equally questionable which role he would have played.)

Although "The Twisted Image" has come in for its share of hard knocks, it's really not that bad. There's a pervasive feeling of sympathy for its characters, particularly the unfortunate Merle Jenkins, and it's far more watchable than some of the *Thrillers* that would shortly follow. It simply had the misfortune to be the first episode telecast, and, as such, didn't live up to the publicity that had preceded it.

"Child's Play" (airdate: September 20, 1960). Produced by Fletcher Markle. Directed by Arthur Hiller. Written by Robert Dozier. Music by Pete Rugolo. Associate Producer: James P. Cavanagh. Director of Photography: Bud Thackery, A.S.C. Film Editor: Danny Landres. Art Director: George Patrick. Assistant Director: James H. Brown. Editorial Supervisor: David J. O'Connell. Set Decorators: John McCarthy and Julia Heron.

Cast: Frank Overton (Bart Hattering), Bethel Leslie (Gail Hattering), Tommy Nolan (Hank Hattering), Parley Baer (The Fisherman), George Werier (Other Fisherman).

Despite its intriguing premise, "Child's Play" bogs down into a verbose domestic drama with only a smattering of thrills.

The Hattering family moves into a mountain cabin for a summer vacation. Eleven-year-old Hank (Tommy Nolan), a boy with an overactive imagination, has fantasies about a notorious highwayman called Black Bart, much to the chagrin of his parents, Gail (Bethel Leslie) and Bart (Frank Overton). "He can be vivid at times," Bart says. Gail wants him to take Hank hunting, but Bart, a writer, is too busy preparing an article to pay much attention to either his wife or his son.

Still enmeshed in his fantasy involving Black Bart, Hank takes one of his father's rifles off the shelf, loads it, and goes off in pursuit of his imaginary enemy. While he is gone Gail reveals to Bart that Hank was expelled from summer camp for shooting an apple off another boy's head with a gun. An argument ensues; Gail accuses Bart of taking little interest in their marriage, and suggests that they consider separating. Meanwhile, Hank has captured a fisherman (Parley Baer), thinking he is Black Bart, and is holding him at gunpoint. He tells him he will keep him captive until he decides what to do with him.

Gail and Bart continue to argue. Bart finally decides to take Hank hunting with him, but then finds his rifle and shells missing. Gail realizes that "Black Bart" is actually Bart himself. "He's taking out his resentment toward you on this Black Bart person — in his mind, it's you," she tells Bart. They go looking for Hank. The boy, meanwhile, has decided to offer the fisherman a chance to escape by putting an apple on his head so that Hank can shoot it off. The fisherman reluctantly complies, but before Hank can fire, Bart arrives; he puts the apple on his own head. "I'm Black Bart, isn't that right, Hank?" he says. Hanks shoots the apple off his father's head, then collapses in tears. "I didn't want to hurt him," the boy sobs. "I just had to scare him a little, didn't I?"

Despite its potentially exciting storyline, "Child's Play" devolves into an endlessly talky (and overwritten) drama of marital discord; Bart and Gail discuss Bart's shortcomings as both father and husband in exhaustive detail, and the promised thrills never arrive. There's some inventive direction by Arthur Hiller, cutting back and forth between Gail and Bart haranguing each other and Hank firing his rifle and holding the fisherman hostage, but overall the episode suffers from contrivances. The ending is telegraphed well in advance, and the symbolism of "Black Bart" being a stand-in for Hank's father seems obvious and even hackneyed. In some ways the episode is a precursor of the *Alfred Hitchcock Presents* segment, "Bang! You're Dead," which also dealt with a loaded gun in the hands of a small boy, with almost equally unmemorable results.

The performers are all fine. Bethel

Leslie (seen in a later *Thriller*, "The Merriweather File") is very good as Gail Hattering, though the role itself is unflattering: she seems content with so little in her marriage that one wonders why she ever wed Bart in the first place.

Frank Overton (seen as Gig Young's father in the memorable *Twilight Zone* episode "Walking Distance") is every bit as unappealing and unpleasant as the role demands. It's a little unbelievable (to say the least) to see Bart risk his life at the end out of sheer love for his family. It's too tidy a resolution, but since the whole thing seems so achingly contrived, it's hardly a surprise. Overton was a regular on the sixties series *Twelve O'Clock High*.

Tommy Nolan, a child actor busy in the fifties and early sixties, is adequate as Hank. (He also appears in a later *Thriller*, "Parasite Mansion.") He was the lead in a short-lived western series, *Buckskin*, aired in 1958.

"Child's Play" seems to confirm the worst doubts critics were having about the fledgling series. Although Hubbell Robinson himself blamed the quality of the early scripts on a TV writers' strike raging within the industry, it was becoming increasingly obvious that more serious problems were plaguing the series.

"Worse Than Murder" (airdate: September 27, 1960). Produced by Fletcher Markle. Directed by Mitchell Leisen. Teleplay by Mel Goldberg, from a story by Evelyn Beckman. Music: Pete Rugolo. Director of Photography: John F. Warren, A.S.C. Associate Producer: James P. Cavanagh. Assistant Director: Jack Doran. Art Director: Howard E. Johnson. Edited by Danny Landres.

Cast: Constance Ford (Connie Walworth), John Baragrey (Dr. Ralph Mitchell), Christine White (Anne), Harriet McGibbon (Myra Walworth), Dan Tobin, Jocelyn Brando.

A man lying in a hospital bed dreams of someone smothering a woman. He cries out "Myra! You mustn't!" and then dies.

The man's niece, Connie Walworth (Constance Ford), learns that her uncle Archer has died intestate, just as her husband has done. The money will go to Archer's sister. There is one small consolation: a diary Archer kept. Connie takes it home to read; when her wealthy mother-in-law, Myra (Harriet McGibbon), learns of it she tries to buy Connie off, without success. When Connie reads the diary she finds descriptions of Archer's dreams, specifically a nightmare describing a murder. Looking up old newspaper files, Connie finds a reference to the death of an 84-year-old woman, Mrs. Gedney. She also locates Mrs. Gedney's nurse, and forces her to admit that the old woman was given an overdose of insulin. Myra has been paying her off ever since. When Connie tells Myra she knows that Myra and Archer killed the old woman (who was Myra's stepmother), they are overheard by Myra's daughter, Anne (Christine White). Connie tells Myra she wants $100,000 to hold her tongue, and within 24 hours.

Anne breaks into Connie's apartment looking for the diary, and finds it just as Connie arrives. The two women struggle, but Anne gets away with the diary. Connie goes after her. Meanwhile, Dr. Ralph Mitchell (John Baragrey), who has been attending Myra, hears the whole story from her just before she dies.

Anne makes it back to her home and throws the diary into the fireplace. Connie arrives and, not seeing the money Myra has left for her on a nearby table, pulls the burning book out of the fire. The flames spread to the drapes, and the house is soon ablaze. Anne barely escapes with her life. The $100,000 is burned along with the house.

Although directed by Hollywood veteran Mitchell Leisen, "Worse Than Murder" is an unremarkable effort. It has become fashionable to take potshots at the early *Thrillers*, and, in *Fantastic Television*, Gary Gerani and Paul Schulman sneer, "The next show was called 'Worse Than Murder,' and it was." Actually, the episode isn't *that* bad, but it did seem to indicate that *Thriller* was marking time in search of an identity of its own.

The performances are adequate. Constance Ford, a brassy blonde, is perfectly cast as Connie. Very busy in the sixties, Ford appeared on *Way Out, The Twilight Zone, The Untouchables, Perry Mason*, and many other series. Her film credits include Robert Bloch's version of *The Cabinet of Caligari* (1962). She was memorable in "I Heard You Calling Me," perhaps the most frightening episode of the long-unseen series *Way Out*. Like many other actresses, she found steady employment on soap operas. She died in 1993.

John Baragrey, seen in the much later episode "A Wig for Miss Devore," is adequate as Ralph Mitchell. He's not a particularly memorable actor, and his role here is likewise forgettable.

Christine White is very good as Anne. A tomboyish actress popular in the early sixties, White appeared in a small role in William Castle's *Macabre* (1958), and starred in a short-lived television series, *Ichabod and Me*.

Actually, the most notable debut on "Worse Than Murder" is that of writer Donald S. Sanford. Though uncredited, Sanford did a rewrite of Mel Goldberg's teleplay. Over the next two years Sanford would become one of the most important principals involved with *Thriller*.

Born on March 17, 1918, Donald S. Sanford began his career as a page and tour guide for CBS Radio in Hollywood. World War II interrupted his budding writing career, and he served in the Navy for four years. Afterward, he worked for the United Nations as the supervisor of their disc recording division, then joined the Dumont television network. There he worked as a cameraman, technical director, stage manager and audio engineer. He also begin writing for *The Plainclothesman*, an early police series that developed into one of Dumont's most successful programs. Later he wrote, edited, and co-produced the series. He resigned from Dumont in 1950 to become head writer for the successful *Martin Kane, Private Eye* at NBC. He also began writing for the popular anthology series *Telephone Time* (one episode which he wrote — "The Golden Junkaman," featuring Lon Chaney, Jr.— won the first Writers Guild of America Award for best half hour anthology drama) as well as *Ellery Queen, Passport to Danger, Perry Mason, M Squad*, and *The Loretta Young Show*.

He was actually summoned to work on *Thriller* before the series' debut. "My first assignment was in July '60," Sanford remembers, "a polish of 'Mark of the Hand,' written by Steven Gethers. That was followed by another polish of 'The Black-Eyed Stranger' by Howard Rodman, and a rewrite of Mel Goldberg's 'Worse Than Murder.'" Owing to the vagaries of the production schedule, the last of these was televised first. "The Black-Eyed Stranger" was never made.

In all, Sanford did 15 *Thrillers* — more than any other writer. Following this, he wrote for such series as *Laramie, The Virginian, Dr. Kildare, The Outer Limits* (the memorable episode "The Guests"), *Twelve O'Clock High, Gunsmoke*, and others. His motion picture work includes *Casino Royale* (1967, uncredited), *Submarine X-1* (1968), *Mosquito Squadron* and *The Thousand Plane Raid* (both 1969), and *Midway* (1976), a very successful World War II drama featuring Charlton Heston, Robert Mitchum, Henry Fonda and others. Sanford's novelization of his screenplay was published by Bantam Books.

All of Sanford's scripts for *Thriller*, along with various drafts, research notes and the like, are in the Donald S. Sanford collection at the University of Wisconsin. The collection also includes the entire files of the more than 200 prime-time network scripts he wrote since the early fifties. Sanford adds:

> No, I did not attend Wisconsin. They sought me out as one of the industry's dinosaurs. A kind of poor man's pioneer of TV drama. Anyway, my files were pushing me out of my office, so I was happy to get the use of their space. It was a helluva lot cheaper than building an extension onto my office.

Now retired, Sanford looks back on his scripts for *Thriller* with special fondness: "Of all the things that I've done in television — westerns, *Perry Mason*s and so forth — I had more fun doing *Thriller* than anything I've ever done, except maybe feature pictures. It was a ball — I loved it."

"The Mark of the Hand" (airdate: October 4, 1960). Produced by Fletcher Markle. Directed by Paul Henreid. Teleplay by Eric Peters, based on the novel by Charlotte Armstrong. Music: Pete Rugolo. Director of Photography: John L. Russell, A.S.C. Associate Producer: James P. Cavanagh. Edited by Danny Landres. Art Director: Howard E. Johnson. Assistant Director: James Hogan. Set Decorator: Julia Heron.

Cast: Mona Freeman (Sylvia Walsh), Shepperd Strudwick (Doug Kilburn), Jessie Royce Landis (Mrs. Kilburn), Judson Pratt (Lieutenant Bill Gordon), Berry Kroeger (Paul Mowry), Terry Burnham (Tessa), Rachel Ames (Betty Follett), Jon Lormer, John Alvin.

The fourth *Thriller*, "The Mark of the Hand," is a slight improvement over "Worse Than Murder," but it shows the series was still foundering. Clearly a change in direction was needed, but it wouldn't come until the seventh episode, "The Purple Room."

In a large home, a shot rings out. The family comes running in, only to find an eight-year-old girl with a gun in her hand and a dead man lying on the floor.

The police investigate, questioning Doug Kilburn (Shepperd Strudwick), the girl's father. The girl, Tessa (Terry Burnham), is under sedation. Sylvia Walsh (Mona Freeman) and Paul Mowry (Berry Kroeger) are questioned by Lieutenant Gordon (Judson Pratt). They tell him that Tessa was playing with the gun when it went off, firing a bullet into a chandelier and another into houseguest Charles Mowry, Paul's brother. "Do you think she's normal?" Gordon asks regarding Tessa. When he questions her she says she's never going to speak again, "no matter what."

Gordon then queries wheelchair-ridden Mrs. Kilburn (Jessie Royce Landis), the child's grandmother. She insists that Tessa did not fire the gun. When Gordon tells her the mark of her hand was on the pistol he adds that, unless he is told the whole truth, he will have Tessa placed in a state institution for observation. Meanwhile, Paul Mowry is being watched by Tessa, and Gordon finds out that the little girl has been under the care of a psychiatrist in the past.

Some time later, Gordon gets a call from Paul Mowry, who seems on the verge of spilling some new information. Gordon goes to see him, but just then there is a scream from the Kilburn house. Rushing over, they find Sylvia shouting that Tessa tried to kill her. Gordon finds the little girl with a knife in her hand. Sylvia subsequently admits that Tessa killed Charles Mowry deliberately. "The child is insane," she tells Doug Kilburn. "I didn't want to tell the truth, for Tessa's sake." Paul Mowry backs up Sylvia's story. Gordon goes upstairs to question the little girl. "Tessa! Was it an accident?" he demands. Having had enough, Doug punches the policeman. "I didn't think your daughter meant that much to you, Mr. Kilburn," Gordon says. He then tells Kilburn he will have the child institutionalized. Doug tells Tessa he doesn't believe she shot anyone, nor that she tried to kill Sylvia. Later, he tells Sylvia he's confident Tessa will speak by next morning.

Paul Mowry, apparently summoned by Sylvia, drops by. He tells Sylvia he won't burn for her: a quick marriage to Doug, followed by a quick divorce and a settlement to divide among the three of them (including his brother Charles), was the original plan; he didn't count on murder. "You put the gun in the child's hand, *I* didn't," he points out. Charles was about to divulge the scheme to Doug when Sylvia killed him. When Sylvia realizes that it was Mrs. Kilburn who summoned Paul, impersonating Sylvia's voice, she dismisses him. She prepares to kill Mrs. Kilburn, then leave the gun in Tessa's hands. "I'm here, Sylvia — waiting," Mrs. Kilburn says. But Doug and Lieutenant Gordon are also waiting, just outside the door, and disarm Sylvia.

An unconvincing crime yarn, "The Mark of the Hand" suffers from predictability. Since a little girl is accused of murder, we know she's innocent, making it easy to spot the real killer: the person telling the lie. It also includes two flashback sequences showing the killing, first as an accident, then as a deliberate murder; these are imaginatively filmed with tilted camera angles, lending an air of unreality. But since both are lies, the flashbacks are a cheat, something Alfred Hitchcock realized when he included similar flashbacks in *Stage Fright* (1950), later dismissing them as a mistake. In addition, since reptilian Berry Kroeger confirms Sylvia's story, we know she must be lying!

The actors are a mixed bag. Judson Pratt is particularly good as Lieutenant Gordon, but Mona Freeman (a former juvenile actress) tends to overact, with wild facial gyrations and overdone reactions, as Sylvia. As for Berry Kroeger, he's his usual loathsome self. (Bill Warren called him "one of the great slimy creeps of movie villainy ... [h]e's the kind of performer you half expect to see leaving a slimy trail behind him.")

Paul Henreid's direction is competent, but no more. He later rose to the occasion on the far superior episode "The Terror in Teakwood."

"Rose's Last Summer" (airdate: October 11, 1960). Produced by Fletcher Markle. Written and directed by Maxwell Shane. Director of Photography: John L. Russell, A.S.C. Music: Pete Rugolo. Associate Producer: James P. Cavanagh. Edited by Danny Landres. Art Director: Howard E. Johnson. Assistant Director: Edward K. Dodds. Set Decorator: Julia Heron.

Cast: Mary Astor (Rose French/ Mrs. Goodfield), Lin McCarthy (Frank Clyde), Jack Livesey (Haley Dalloway), Dorothy Green (Ethel Goodfield),

Hardie Albright (Willet Goodfield), Lois E. Gridge (Mrs. Cushman), George N. Neise, Percy Helton.

One of the least thrilling of all *Thrillers*, "Rose's Last Summer" involves impersonation, an inheritance and attempted murder, but the resulting stew is unconvincing and distinctly uninvolving.

Rose French (Mary Astor), once a beautiful film star, now a drunken has-been, is struck by a truck. Among the onlookers is a man named Willet Goodfield (Hardy Albright). When Frank Clyde (Lin McCarthy), operator of a rehabilitation center for alcoholics, goes to visit Rose in jail, he finds that someone else has already bailed her out. When he sees her at her apartment, she tells him she has a job. Eight days later the newspapers announce that she has died of a heart attack.

Her ex-husband, Haley Dalloway (Jack Livesey), goes to see Frank. Together, they go to the garden where Rose died. Frank notices they are being watched from the house. Dalloway questions Mrs. Goodfield (Dorothy Green), the elderly owner of the house where Rose had gone to work. He asks if she can tell him anything about Rose's death. "Tell me — do you know the Sweet Marie doll?" Mrs. Goodfield asks. Downstairs, Frank finds a map similar to a partially burned one that Rose had. "I think these people killed Rose," Frank tells Dalloway.

Frank travels to San Francisco and learns that Horace Goodfield invented the Sweet Marie doll, which made him a fortune. After he talks with the executor of Goodfield's estate, the man reports back to Willet Goodfield and his sister, Ethel.

Back at the Goodfield house, Mother Goodfield turns out to be Rose in makeup and wig; the job she applied for involved impersonating the old lady. Training under her, she adopted her looks, voice and walk. The Goodfields had been looking for someone to carry out the impersonation, in the event Mother Goodfield should die before she reached 65, in which case the money would go to a health food foundation rather than to the family.

In the meantime Frank and Dalloway figure out the scheme and realize that, since Mother Goodfield is dead — she was made to look gradually younger, and was buried as Rose French — and her sixty-fifth birthday has passed, there is no reason for them to keep Rose alive. They contact the police; in the meantime Willet and Ethel are preparing Rose for a fatal "accident." Rose manages to escape from them, but they pursue her and are trying to run her down when the police arrive. "Rose, let's go home," Haley Dalloway says.

There's not much mystery in "Rose's Last Summer." Almost from the beginning, it's apparent that Rose isn't dead, and as soon as Mrs. Goodfield (supposedly played by "Helen Quintal," but actually enacted by Mary Astor) turns up, it's apparent that Astor is performing in a wig and glasses. Thus robbed of any possible suspense, the story plods along to its unexciting climax.

The only enjoyment to be had is in some of the performances. Mary Astor, star of silent films as well as such memorable talkies as *The Maltese Falcon* (1941) and *The Great Lie* (1941) — for which she won an Academy Award — has a fine time as Rose French and Mrs. Goodfield. She's photographed in an unflattering light and made to seem older (she was 54), but she still has star quality and is enjoyable to watch, as is veteran actor Jack Livesey as her ex-husband. Lin McCarthy (featured in the very last *Thriller*, "The Specialists"), on the other hand, is robotic and Robert Stack–like as Frank Clyde.

All in all, "Rose's Last Summer" is one of the least interesting *Thrillers*, a sure indication that the series was in a rut. Renewal was one episode away.

"The Guilty Men" (airdate: October 18, 1960). Produced by Fletcher Markle. Directed by Jules Bricken. Written by John Vlahos. Music: Pete Rugolo. Associate Producer: James P. Cavanagh. Director of Photography: John L. Russell, A.S.C. Film Editor: George Nicholson. Art Director: Howard E. Johnson. Assistant Director: James Hogan. Editorial Supervisor: David J. O'Connell. Musical Supervision: Stanley Wilson. Set Decorator: Julia Heron.

Cast: Everett Sloane (Lou Adams), Frank Silvera (Charlie Roman), Jay C. Flippen (Harry Gans), John Marley (Dr. Tony Romano), Dorothy Greene (Ethel), Anne Barton (Martha Adams), Argentina Brunetti, Tony Caruso, Ralph Neff.

"The Guilty Men" is an adequate crime episode bolstered by strong performances.

During the twenties, a boy running from the police meets with his friends atop the roof of a tenement. He has stolen $200 to pay for his father's funeral, but his brother, Tony Romano, refuses to take it, telling him a man who lives by violence will die the same way. Outraged, the boy, Cesare Romano, tells Tony, "He who takes, gets." He vows that, someday, he will be Mr. Big.

Years pass. By 1960 Cesare, now known as Charlie Roman (Frank Silvera), tries to get his crime syndicate to allocate money to spend on a project to help neighborhood children. His lawyer, Lou Adams (Everett Sloane), advises other syndicate members to go along with Charlie, but they are opposed by Harry Gans (Jay C. Flippen) who wants no part of it. During an argument with Gans, Charlie has a near-fatal heart attack. He is attended by his brother, Dr. Tony Romano (John Marley), despite his distaste for Charlie's line of work. "You're scum, Charlie, and you know it," Tony tells him. "What good is tearing down the slums if you keep bringing in narcotics?" Lou advises Charlie to drop the narcotics and says he will bring the matter up at the next syndicate meeting.

Gans goes to see Lou. He tells him Charlie should step down as head of the syndicate; Gans intends to take over, and warns Lou not to oppose him. Despite his heart condition, Charlie attends the next meeting. When he suggests staying out of the narcotics racket, the others object. Gans stalks out. He is persuaded to return; Charlie makes an impassioned plea to turn legitimate, but Gans refuses. The two men quarrel, and Charlie has another attack. Gans holds Lou immobile so he cannot help Charlie, and the stricken man dies while reaching for his pills.

At the funeral Tony reads Charlie's last testament leaving his money to the children of the other mobsters. One of them, Johnny Longo, breaks down and is about to reveal Gans as Charlie's killer. As the mobsters file out Tony observes, "Soon they will eat each other alive."

Lou pleads with them once again to end the narcotics traffic. When they vote in favor of continuing the practice, Lou and the others walk out. When Lou goes to see Johnny Longo, he finds his body hanging from the ceiling; the killing has been made to look like suicide. Lou admits to his wife, Martha (Anne Barton), that he is involved with the syndicate. He telephones the head of an investigating committee, telling him he will testify against the syndicate, unaware that his phone is being tapped. As he is leaving his house, he is gunned down by Gans and his men. The police give chase, and as Lou lies dead on the sidewalk, there is the sound of a car crash.

"The Guilty Men" is an adequate, if conventional, crime episode featuring a fine performance by Everett Sloane. Charlie Roman's fervent desire to keep the syndicate out of drug trafficking prefigures Don Vito Corleone's similar concern in *The Godfather*, and the presence of John Marley in the cast heightens the comparison. Apart from this, the episode is quite similar to the overheated theatrics of the popular ABC series *The Untouchables*. The strongest scene occurs midway, when Harry Gans holds Lou Adams immobile while Charlie reaches for his heart pills; it's melodramatic, but undeniably gripping.

The cast is a major asset. Everett Sloane is, as always, affecting and believable as the beleaguered Lou Adams. Like Elisha Cook, Sloane was one of the most distinctive character actors of all time. He was originally brought to Hollywood by Orson Welles, and began his film career as the obsequious Bernstein in *Citizen Kane* (1941). His other films include *The Lady from Shanghai* (1947), *The Men* (1950) and *The Big Knife* (1955). He was memorable in the classic *Twilight Zone* episode "The Fever." He shot himself in 1965. One of his last appearances was host and narrator of *Hercules and the Princess of Troy*, an ABC special broadcast that year.

Frank Silvera is equally impressive as the altruistic Charlie Roman, though his dialect and mannerisms are far from subtle. His film career was routine, apart from appearing in the early Stanley Kubrick film *Killer's Kiss* (1955). He was especially effective in the *Alfred Hitchcock Hour* adaptation of Ray Bradbury's

"The Life Work of Juan Diaz." He died in 1970.

Jay C. Flippen is broad but effective as Harry Gans. A burly type who normally played cops and sheriffs, his film career dated back to the thirties. He was memorable in Kubrick's *The Killing* (1956). He died in 1971.

John Marley is quite good as the noble Tony Romano, but then the role is made to order for him. An effective character actor throughout the sixties and seventies, he played Ali McGraw's father in *Love Story* (1970), but is probably best remembered as the producer who found the horse's head in his bed in *The Godfather* (1972). He died in 1984.

"The Guilty Men" hardly stands out among the early *Thrillers*. It reflects the hit-or-miss approach that was then imperiling the show's future. Fortunately the very next episode would finally put the foundering series on the right track.

"The Purple Room" (airdate: October 25, 1960). Produced by William Frye. Directed and written by Douglas Heyes. Director of Photography: Bud Thackery, A.S.C. Music: Pete Rugolo. Assistant Director: John Bowman. Editing: Danny Landres. Art Director: Howard E. Johnson. Set Decorators: John McCarthy and Julia Heron.

Cast: Rip Torn (Duncan Corey), Patricia Barry (Rachel Judson), Richard Anderson (Oliver Judson), Alan Napier (Ridgewater), Joanna Heyes (Caroline Vale), Ray Teal (Wiley).

After six disappointing episodes, *Thriller* struck pay dirt with the seventh, and the result is a memorably creepy ghost story — the first *Thriller* classic.

In the purple room of Black Oak mansion, a frightened young girl lies in bed calling for Jeremy and fires her gun at something she sees approaching.

One hundred years later, in modern day San Francisco, Duncan Corey (Rip Torn) sits listening to lawyer Ridgewater (Alan Napier) reading his late brother's will. Corey is to inherit Black Oak mansion, provided he lives there for one year. If he chooses not to, the house will pass on to Rachel and Oliver Judson. After one year Corey will be free to sell the house, which suits him fine, since the property is in an area ripe for development. There is just one snag: Ridgewater tells Corey that after remaining in the house for one night, he may not be willing to stay. Scoffing at his fears, Corey leaves for Baton Rouge.

Corey arrives at the house with Rachel (Patricia Barry) and Oliver (Richard Anderson). The electricity is off and the only bed made up is in the purple room, which is purportedly haunted. "A nice place to visit ..." Corey remarks. "But you wouldn't want to die here," Rachel replies. Oliver warns Corey that his brash smugness will antagonize whatever is present in the house. Corey shows off a gun and tells them that, if any ghost appears, he will put a hole through it.

Oliver explains that the bed in the purple room was occupied by Jeremy Ransom's young bride, Caroline. In the middle of the night Caroline awoke, hearing footsteps. Jeremy went downstairs to investigate, leaving Caroline with a pistol. Caroline waited in the darkness, hearing footsteps that were not Jeremy's, fumbling, shuffling, coming closer, finally reaching the door. Caroline fired point-blank at a shape. When she lit a candle, she began to scream. When the servants found her, Caroline was raving mad and Jeremy lay dead with a knife in his chest. He had been stabbed by the prowler, but had forced himself up the stairs.

Corey laughs off the ghost story.

"This place is all yours — and everything it contains," Oliver warns. He and Rachel leave. Corey locks the door.

Sometime later Corey hears a door close, followed by strange noises. "Ah, the old creaking stairs — that's truly a creative touch," Corey calls out. Drinking, he keeps up a running conversation with whatever is making the sounds. Realizing too late that the liquor has been drugged, he collapses.

When he awakens, the door is open. Going downstairs, he hears footsteps. "That's enough," he calls out. A dagger lands at his feet. "All right," he announces. "That does it. From now on I take no responsibility for what happens." He sees something coming toward him from the shadows — a ghostly figure with a knife in its chest. When the figure keeps approaching, he fires at it, over and over again, to no effect, and then collapses. The figure bends down over him, listening for a heartbeat, then removes its mask to disclose the face of Oliver Judson. He calls for Rachel and tells her Corey has died of a heart attack — something they hadn't counted on.

Oliver and Rachel carry the body out, put him in their car, and drive to a nearby swamp. They leave the body in the car so it will appear Corey suffered a heart attack and ran off the road. They prepare to return to the house, but Rachel has misgivings. "Next thing you know, you'll be believing it's haunted, too," Oliver says. "It is — now," Rachel answers.

Back at the mansion, Rachel tells Oliver that she has a premonition; she was frightened while waiting downstairs, sure there was some other presence in the house. Oliver tells Rachel he was not afraid of Corey, since he exchanged the bullets in his gun for blanks.

Later that night in the purple room, Rachel awakens Oliver. There are noises downstairs. Rachel tells him it's

Jeremy. Oliver gets up to investigate. "Please don't leave me alone here," Rachel pleads. Oliver gives her the gun, this time loaded with real bullets, and goes downstairs despite her pleading. He sees something in the shadows and runs. Rachel, meanwhile, waiting in bed, hears footsteps on the stairs, coming closer. At last the figure shows itself: it is Duncan Corey. Rachel pumps all six bullets into him. She runs from the room and finds Oliver on the stairs. "He didn't even touch me," he says. Just then a sheriff (Ray Teal) arrives, having heard the shots; he also ran into Corey, who said his name was Jeremy Ransom. Despite Rachel's protests, the sheriff insists on going upstairs.

"The Purple Room" was the first *Thriller* produced by William Frye, and it is an auspicious beginning. Gone are the murderous diaries, guilty men and twisted images of early episodes: in their place is a haunted house story heavily laden with the Gothic atmosphere that would dominate *Thriller's* horror episodes. Even though the story's resolution rationalizes the ghostly proceedings, it does not dispel the heavy supernatural atmosphere. It is the first example of "crisscrossing," or intersecting, genres, which "thriller" would exploit in forthcoming episodes. Appropriately, it was first telecast just before Halloween 1960.

Douglas Heyes, of course, deserves much of the credit for the look and feel of "The Purple Room." His first job was as a cartoonist at Walt Disney studios, where he learned about motion picture techniques, particularly the process of storyboarding. "I started thinking of drama in terms of what you could see, and I still try to think of how many scenes will play visually," he said later. He wrote his first novel, *The Kiss-Off*, and broke into television by writing teleplays for *General Electric Theater* in the early fifties before graduating to director. He did a number of episodes of *Maverick* and became known for solving logistical problems such as those faced by *Twilight Zone* producer Buck Houghton. "I think that 'Eye of the Beholder' is probably the most difficult director's job that ever came down the pike," Houghton recalled. "I was scared to death of that, the problems of making that picture in such a way that the tag wasn't foreseen long before you got there." Heyes solved the problem (not showing the actors' faces until the climax) through complicated camera movement and discreetly angled shadows. It worked, and Heyes directed a number of other memorable *Twilight Zone* episodes, including "The Howling Man," "The After Hours" and "The Invaders."

In retrospect, Heyes was a logical choice for *Thriller*, even though he seems to have taken undue credit for its change of format. He told *Twilight Zone* magazine interviewer Ben Herndon:

> *Thriller* was not a scary show when it first began. The first five of six episodes were gangster stories, crime stories, adventure stories — and the series was not doing well. I was called over to Revue, Universal's television department, and I was called into a conference with Alan Miller, who ran the department, and Hubbell Robinson ... They asked me what was wrong with *Thriller*? Why wasn't it getting the good ratings? To me, it seemed like a terribly obvious answer. When you say, "Boris Karloff presents 'Thriller'," then people believe you're going to show them something scary, something spooky. Something indigenous to Karloff's work on the silver screen. They asked me to write and direct one which had those elements in it, to see if that was really what the public wanted. So I

Their schemes undone, Patricia Barry and Richard Anderson are haunted by what happened in "The Purple Room" (Ronald V. Borst/Hollywood Movie Posters).

wrote and directed ... "The Purple Room," and I threw in everything. I threw in ghosts and people rising from the dead and secret passages and portraits that moved. I threw in *everything*! Clanking chains, candles that blew out — everything in the genre. The ratings began to rise after that.

(Associate Producer Doug Benton disputes Heyes' claim, saying "Doug Heyes had nothing to do with *Thriller* changing its format. That all originated with Bill Frye. Isn't it wonderful how some people rewrite history?")

Heyes' teleplay is an unofficial adaptation of the classic ghost story

"The Gentleman from America" by Michael Arlen. This powerful but flawed tale, a staple of anthologists, tells a similar story, though there are differences: in the story, the girl's sister goes downstairs to investigate the strange noises, and the gentleman from America, who spends the night in the room on a bet, goes insane, avenging himself on the perpetrators of the hoax some years later. (A more faithful adaptation was done on *Alfred Hitchcock Presents*.) The story is undeniably effective, but impaired by the grotesque parody of American speech that the author, an Englishman, forces into his titular hero's mouth: "Aw, have a heart!" he growls at one point. "You get a guy so low with your talk that I feel I could put on a tall hat and crawl under a snake."

Thriller's version evokes supernatural dread from the very first scene, depicting a frightened Joanna Heyes (the writer-director's wife, also seen in his later episode "The Hungry Glass") and moving on to Richard Anderson's telling of the story of Jeremy Ransom. In place of flashbacks the tale is related in a voice-over while the camera tracks through the house, emphasizing the locations in which the action took place. It's an effective cinematic device.

All this, of course, sets the stage for Duncan Corey's ordeal in the purple room. For that, Heyes trots out all the basic tenets of the haunted house story, and then skirts the edges of parody by boldly calling attention to every cliché, from the moving portrait to the rapping sounds, causing us to suspend disbelief while he sets up an arsenal of hoary devices, exhausting them of their theatrical effectiveness, and then disposes of them to relate a non-supernatural, yet undeniably effective tale. Admittedly, it's a disappointment when the fearsome-looking ghost turns out to be Richard

Anderson in a costume, but the suspense that has been generated by then makes it easy to forgive.

Of course, none of this would work if the performances by the three principal actors were weak or unconvincing, but, in this respect, "The Purple Room" succeeds admirably. Rip Torn, a much undervalued actor, delivers a tour de force performance as Duncan Corey: cynical, smug, self-reliant and, finally, terrified. It's one of the strongest performances in any *Thriller*. Torn has rarely been used to advantage in his 30-year screen career, which included such films as *Sweet Bird of Youth* (1962), *The Cincinnati Kid* (1965), *Tropic of Cancer* (1970, as Henry Miller) and *Payday* (1973). His performance in "The Purple Room" is one of his best.

Patricia Barry would be seen in two later *Thrillers*. For more information on her, see the entry for "A Wig for Miss Devore."

Richard Anderson became an inescapable face on TV and in movies during the sixties and seventies. He was the murderous, centuries-old medico in *The Night Strangler* (1973), and he turned in an impressive performance in Kubrick's *Paths of Glory* (1957), but most of the time remained a bland presence in many forgettable TV shows. He was a regular on *The Six Million Dollar Man* and *The Bionic Woman*.

"The Purple Room" marked a definite change in direction for *Thriller*. Although there would be several missteps ahead, Frye was moving the show in a different direction. *Thriller* was at last acquiring an identity of its own.

"The Watcher" (airdate: November 1, 1960). Produced by William Frye. Directed by John Brahm. Teleplay by Donald S. Sanford, from the novel by Dolores Hitchens. Director of Photography: Neal Beckner. Music: Pete Rugolo. Art Director: Howard E. Johnson. Assistant Director: William Dorfman. Set Decorators: John McCarthy and Julia Heron.

Cast: Martin Gabel (Frietag), Richard Chamberlain (Larry Carter), Olive Sturgess (Beth Pettit), Stu Erwin (Uncle Florian), Irene Hervey (Mrs. Pettit), Alan Baxter (Sheriff Archer), James Westerfield (Matthews), Nelson Olmsted, Gloria Clark.

Producer William Frye followed "The Purple Room" with "The Watcher," one of the strongest early episodes, a warning against sexual repression and religious fanaticism that thankfully stops short of overt sermonizing.

Frietag (Martin Gabel) drowns a young girl and makes it look like an accident. Sometime later he spies on young lovers Beth Pettit (Olive Sturgess) and Larry Carter (Richard Chamberlain), then types up a message for the police: IS THERE ANOTHER CORRUPTER ABROAD? I MUST BE SURE BEFORE I KILL AGAIN. Frietag visits Larry, who is working at a boat house, and accuses him of often seeing the murdered girl. "I suppose a good-looking young man like you doesn't have any trouble finding feminine companionship," Frietag observes. "Must be a problem for you — I mean, avoiding unwelcome attentions." Frietag reveals himself as a religious fanatic determined to help Larry avoid what he calls the "dark paths" of life. Larry shrugs off the warning.

Beth and her uncle Florian (Stu Erwin) keep Beth's romance with Larry a secret from Beth's mother. That night, during a rainstorm, Beth sees Frietag on the dock, watching her. She tells Larry, but he sees no one. Larry and Beth make plans to marry, unaware that Frietag is watching them outside in the rain.

In the meantime, Frietag mails his warning to the police who haven't had an unsolved murder in recent years. Sheriff Archer (Alan Baxter) has never believed the young girl's death was an accident, but the town is a summer resort and a murder would scare off tourists. "Only a psycho could write a letter like this," Archer declares. "Someone who reads his own corruption into everything he sees." Archer decides to investigate on his own.

Frietag, meanwhile, continues to spy upon Larry and Beth. He mails another letter to the police reading: I AM NOW CERTAIN I MUST KILL AGAIN. He follows the two lovers out to the lake. When they return to their car they find one tire has been slashed. Larry hitchhikes over to a garage while Beth stays in the car. Frietag approaches from behind some shrubbery and tries to get to Beth, but suspicious locals frighten him off before he can harm her. Frustrated, Frietag drives to the gas station, where he knocks Larry unconscious, then lowers a car on him. Larry is saved from certain death by a tire iron which prevents the car rack from crushing him.

Larry is recuperating at home before being admitted to a hospital. Beth goes to see him. Frietag goes up to Larry's room, intending to kill them both. Beth and Frietag struggle; she hits him with a water pitcher and Frietag falls through the window to his death.

"The Watcher" remains a powerful warning against the dangers that may lie behind a facade. Frietag, though a murderous fanatic, is able to gain people's trust through his circumspect appearance. Likewise, Beth's mother is excessively concerned with appearances.

There are no major surprises or plot twists in Donald S. Sanford's script. It's a straightforward account of the downfall (literally) of a fanatic (though his climactic tumble from the window seems contrived). According to Jay Allen Sanford, "The Watcher" went from a first draft script on February 8, 1960, well before *Thriller*'s debut, to a final script on September 23.

John Brahm's direction is, as always, atmospheric. Frietag's voyeuristic compulsions are emphasized visually: we see him through window curtains, and he watches the young lovers through fish nets. The most frightening image is Beth's sudden view of Frietag standing in the rain during a thunderstorm. Although "The Watcher" is not a horror episode, per se, the image is as frightening and disturbing as any in Brahm's more macabre assignments.

The acting is above average. A very young Richard Chamberlain, just a year away from playing Dr. Kildare, is (as always) very good. Savaged by critics early in his career, Chamberlain bounced back, winning plaudits for his performance in *Petulia* (1968), and from then on became king of the television miniseries, appearing in *Shogun* (1980), *The Thorn Birds* (1983), *Casanova* (1987) and *The Bourne Identity* (1988), among others.

Martin Gabel is slightly theatrical — his performance isn't particularly subtle or shaded — but effective as Frietag. He's convincingly fanatical, yet canny enough to create the right impression around others. Gabel was primarily a stage actor (he played Professor Moriarty in *Baker Street*), but made occasional films, including *Fourteen Hours* (1951), *The Thief* (1952), *Lord Love a Duck* (1966) and *The First Deadly Sin* (1980). He was particularly memorable as the victimized banker in Hitchcock's *Marnie* (1964), though he may actually be best remembered as Arlene Francis' husband. He died in 1986.

Olive Sturgess was a pretty, young starlet whose career didn't go much further than Roger Corman's version of *The Raven* (1963), in which she played Vincent Price's daughter. (Her suitor was a very young, very wooden Jack Nicholson.) She's adequate as Beth Pettit. She also appeared in a later *Thriller*, "The Closed Cabinet."

Stu Erwin's Uncle Florian seems intended to show that not *all* adults are fools or fanatics. His level-headedness is in complete contrast to his fifties TV role in *The Trouble with Father* (a.k.a. *The Stu Erwin Show*), in which he's the quintessential father as boob. Erwin's screen career went back to the twenties but included mostly forgettable films. He died in 1967.

Irene Hervey, as Mrs. Pettit, is appropriately severe. Hervey, a leading lady of the thirties and forties, was the lead in two of Universal's most enjoyable horror mellers, *The House of Fear* (1939) and *Night Monster* (1942).

After more than 30 years, "The Watcher" remains a compelling episode, one that pulls no punches. Despite many similar cautionary tales presented over the years, its dramatic power remains undiminished.

"Girl with a Secret" (airdate: November 15, 1960). Produced by Fletcher Markle. Directed by Mitchell Leisen. Teleplay by Charles Beaumont, from the novel by Charlotte Armstrong. Director of Photography: Lionel Lindon. Music by Pete Rugolo. Associate Producer: James P. Cavanagh. Art Director: Jack Doran. Set Decorators: John McCarthy and Julia Heron.

Cast: Fay Bainter (Geraldine Redfern), Paul Hartman (George Stafford), Myrna Fahey (Alice Page), Rhodes Reason (Tony Page), Cloris Leachman (Beatrice Stafford), Harry Ellerbe (Walter Devon), Ellen Corby (Mrs. Peele), Victor Buono (Carolik), James Seay

(Herb Innes), Esther Dale (Ellen), Anne Seymour, Rex Holman.

Charles Beaumont's first *Thriller* teleplay, "Girl with a Secret," is unfortunately an uneven entry, a predictable espionage tale that works up little excitement.

Tony Page (Rhodes Reason) and his wife, Alice (Myrna Fahey), are at an airport when his attaché case is stolen by a man who was watching them on the plane. Tony seems strangely unconcerned about the theft, but shortly afterward they are nearly run off the road by a strange-looking man (Rex Holman). When they drive on to visit his family in Pasadena, Tony asks Alice not to mention what has happened, saying there's no sense in upsetting them.

Alice meets Mrs. Redfern (Fay Bainter) and George Stafford (Paul Hartman), as well as Beatrice Stafford (Cloris Leachman) and a mysterious man named Walter Devon (Harry Ellerbe). But when Tony leaves her with his family, he goes off to meet with the man who stole his attaché case. When the man asks Tony if he's studied the information in the other case, Tony tells him someone's on to him, and describes the man who tried to run him off the road. Unbeknownst to them, the man in the car is working for a criminal named Carolik (Victor Buono), who is furious that he didn't kill Tony.

Shortly afterward, Tony receives word that he must travel. He tells Alice he is leaving for Minneapolis alone; he explains that she can stay with his family. In the meantime, Walter Devon reports to Carolik that Tony is about to leave. Carolik seems unconvinced that Minneapolis is his real destination. Alice finds plane tickets to Mexico in Tony's coat and asks her husband why he lied. Tony finally explains: he is an undercover agent, and has been feeding unim-

portant information to enemy agents. He thinks the head of the gang is in Pasadena. Tony tells Alice she will have to keep his secret, since his life will depend on it. But the maid, Mrs. Peele (Ellen Corby), knows Tony's real destination and blackmails Alice into giving her a pair of earrings, a treasured family heirloom. But when she wears them around the house, she is fired. Beatrice Stafford remarks that Alice is keeping a secret, and suspects that she paid off Mrs. Peele. Devon, meanwhile, is reporting all this to Carolik.

Alice is forced to pay off Mrs. Peele, giving her $300 to keep her secret. But Carolik's hit man arrives to question Mrs. Peele, and winds up killing her.

The family is shocked by Alice's involvement in Mrs. Peele's death. Devon suggests sedating Alice, after which he will take her to a friend of his (actually Carolik) and get the truth out of her. But Mrs. Redfern has Alice spirited away to a drugstore in Los Angeles. When Tony returns from Mexico, Devon has him followed to the drugstore. Devon and Carolik's hit man prepare to murder both Alice and Tony, but the druggist shoots the killer first. "I've had this gun in the drawer for twenty years ... never used it before," he says.

It's too bad that "Girl with a Secret" is a routine entry, since the adaptation of Charlotte Armstrong's novel is by Charles Beaumont, one of America's premiere *fantasists*. Born Charles Nutt in Chicago in 1929, he was one of the three principal writers for *The Twilight Zone* (the other two being Rod Serling and Richard Matheson), and his memorable teleplays for that classic series include "The Howling Man," "Perchance to Dream," "Shadow Play" and "Printer's Devil." His screenplays include *Queen of Outer Space* (1958), *The Wonderful World of the Brothers Grimm* (1962), *The*

Haunted Palace (1963) and *Mister Moses* (1965). He died in 1967 at the youthful age of 38, the victim of a bizarre medical disorder that made him appear a man of 90.

For such an unremarkable episode, "Girl with a Secret" boasts a surprisingly strong cast. Fay Bainter, who plays Mrs. Redfern, was a noted character actress who started in films in 1934. Her screen appearances include *Jezebel* (1938), for which she won an Academy Award, *Our Town* (1940), *The Human Comedy* (1943), and *The Children's Hour* (1962). She died in 1968.

Lovely Myrna Fahey, who plays Alice, had a brief film and television career. She appeared as the doomed Madeline Usher in Roger Corman's Poe adaptation, *House of Usher* (1960), and starred in a short-lived sitcom, *Father of the Bride* (1961).

Rhodes Reason plays *the* hero, a role without shadings — the same role he played throughout his career. He's virtually indistinguishable from his twin brother, Rex Reason, and appeared mostly in second features. He was the lead in a TV series, *White Hunter* (1958), and was a regular on the short-lived *Bus Stop* (1961-62).

Ellen Corby, who plays Mrs. Peele, was a reliable character actress who played mostly spinsterish roles; she's amusing as the blackmailing maid, a role written to order for her nosey persona. She appeared in Val Lewton's *Bedlam* (1946) and William Castle's *Macabre* (1958), and played Victor Buono's mother in *The Strangler*, but she's best known as Grandma Walton on the long-running *The Waltons* (1972-81), for which she won three Emmy awards.

Cloris Leachman became a notable TV star on *Phyllis*. Her films include *Kiss Me Deadly* (1955), *The Rack* (1962), *The Chapman Report* (1962), *The Last Picture*

Show (1971), for which she won an Academy Award, and *Young Frankenstein* (1974). Unfortunately, she has little to do as Beatrice Stafford.

Victor Buono, making the first of his two *Thriller* appearances, shines as the villain, Carolik. Though his part is small (he isn't even allowed a death scene), Buono makes the most of his limited screen time. The massive, powerful Buono etched a gallery of memorable screen portraits: *What Ever Happened to Baby Jane?* (1962), for which he was nominated for an Academy Award, *The Strangler* (1964), *Hush ... Hush, Sweet Charlotte* (1965), *Who's Minding the Mint?* (1967), and many others. Hollywood made poor use of his talents, casting him mostly as villains or in comedic parts; given the proper roles he could have been another Laird Cregar. Instead, he's probably best remembered as King Tut on *Batman*. He died in 1982.

There isn't much to be said about "Girl with a Secret." After the double punch of "The Purple Room" and "The Watcher," it seemed to indicate that *Thriller* was content to tread well worn paths.

"The Prediction" (airdate: November 22, 1960). Produced by William Frye. Directed by John Brahm. Written by Donald S. Sanford. Director of Photography: John L. Russell, A.S.C. Editing: Danny Landres. Art Director: Howard E. Johnson. Music: Pete Rugolo. Assistant Director: Edward K. Dodds.

Cast: Boris Karloff (Clayton Mace), Audrey Dalton (Norine Burton), Alan Caillou (Roscoe Burton), Alex Davion (Grant Dudley), Abraham Sofaer (Gus Kostopopulos), Richard Peel, Seymour Green, Keith McConnell, Murvyn Vye.

Unfortunately for *Thriller* fans, William Frye's third episode (and the first to feature Karloff) is a disappointment. "The Prediction" is itself predictable, hampered by a too familiar plot line and weak acting.

The episode begins with Clayton Mace (Boris Karloff), an English headliner billed as "Mace the Mentalist," doing his stage act. "I challenge you," he announces to the audience, "to refute the predictions of Nostradamus, or to deny that down through the ages every major event has been foretold by someone — a pagan priest, an oracle, an astrologer, or just some simple man whose mind was responsive to the vibrations of the cosmos ... I propose tonight, ladies and gentlemen, to reveal to you some of the remarkable occult powers that lie on the very threshold of man's knowledge." After this impressive spiel, it's disappointing to learn that Mace's act consists of simply answering questions from the audience, but in answer to one man's query regarding an upcoming prizefight, he prophesies death: "someone will die in that fight." Following this, he collapses.

When he revives, he demands to be taken to the boxing arena to stop the fight. Instead, Roscoe Burton (Alan Caillou), father of Mace's accompanist (Audrey Dalton), offers to go to see the manager of the fighter Mace has singled out for death.

That night, Gus Kostopopulos (Abraham Sofaer) sponsors a party in Mace's honor. Norine, Mace's accompanist, meets her boyfriend, Grant Dudley (Alex Davion); he wants to marry her, but has to dodge her father, who disapproves of him. Burton returns, drunk, and has a row with his daughter. The fighter's manager also arrives, blaming Mace for the young man's death; what's more, Burton has cashed in on his foreknowledge by betting against the boxer. Mace accosts Burton, but he shrugs it

off. "I didn't kill the boy," he says. "If anyone's to blame, it's you." Mace has another of his predictive flashes; "Burton, don't leave, don't go," he pleads. "Something is going to happen." Something does: a few moments later, Burton is killed by a robber. Mace blames himself. "Maybe I was responsible for Burton's death," he says. "Did I foresee Burton's death, or did I will it to happen?"

An innocent man is arrested for the killing; Mace's friend, Gus, calls the police with an anonymous tip, since Mace knows the identity of the real murderer. Mace asks Gus if he knows a man named Harcourt. Gus says no. "Don't cross the stage to meet him," Mace warns. A moment later, Gus is told a man named Harcourt is waiting in his office for him. Mace prevents Gus from crossing the stage just as a counterweight comes crashing down, barely missing him.

Gus meets Harcourt, who is from the C.I.D. He tells him that they have found the real killer. Meanwhile, Mace is doing his act and makes another prediction, this time aimed at Grant Dudley: "He must not make that trip," he says. "It will end in death!" Dudley meets with Norine; he thinks Mace's prediction was an act designed to keep Norine from leaving the act. He is driving to Dover that night to take a ferry to Calais.

Dudley goes backstage to see Mace. To his surprise, Mace consents to his plan to marry Norine, but the mentalist warns him to turn back from his trip if he sees a sign with the legend EDINBURGH 50 MILES. Dudley agrees.

That night, after the performance, Dudley and Norine drive off. Having second thoughts, Mace has Gus drive him to an unknown destination. On the road, Dudley has a near-collision with a workman restoring the very sign Mace warned him about. Not seeing it, Dudley drives on. Mace, meanwhile, tells Gus to stop on the main highway, then gets out. Dudley, speeding up to catch the ferry, does not see Mace on the road and hits him. A moment later, the boat station blows up. "That's probably what he saw," Norine says. "He saw the future, and he was resigned to it," Gus says. "I'm sure he was glad that his death was the means of saving your life."

"The Prediction" seems more like an extended episode of *One Step Beyond* or Karloff's little-seen series *The Veil*. The characters are cliché through and through, and the resolution can be foreseen well in advance.

The acting is uneven. Karloff, in the first of his five *Thriller* appearances, is sympathetic and even touching at times, but Clayton Mace is such a boringly good character that there's little he can do to enliven him (Karloff also seems a little old to still be doing a stage mentalist act). It might have been more interesting, and certainly more believable, for Mace to be tempted to profit from his precognitive powers; it might have made Mace a character and not a paragon. Instead, he's a living cliché right up to the very end, when he lays down his life for the young lovers. He's too much like the characters Karloff played in the thirties and forties: the basically decent scientific man who runs afoul of society and winds up as a menace, only to be redeemed by his death. But here there's not even the fun of seeing him go on a rampage; he's staid and boring, and rather begs the question: who wants to see Karloff play a sympathetic old codger anyway? It seems a waste of his talents (not to mention his ability to be both menacing *and* sympathetic). Fortunately, his later *Thriller* roles allowed him greater leeway.

Audrey Dalton, in the first of her three *Thriller* appearances, is inadequate in the role of Norine. An actress of limited ability, her frozen face and flat delivery further weaken the episode. It would be nice to report that her acting improved later on, but unfortunately her subsequent *Thriller* performances (in "Hay-Fork and Bill-Hook" and "The Hollow Watcher") are just as wooden.

Abraham Sofaer (later to be seen in "The Weird Tailor") provides fine support as Gus Kostopopulos, but Alan Caillou is unconvincing as Norine's drunken father: the lowlife nature of the character seems to defeat him; he's much better as the aristocratic Sir Wilfred in "Hay-Fork and Bill-Hook." Doug Benton recalls that Alan Caillou "was quite a character. He was chief of military police in Cairo, and started a British theatre there. He was always writing novels and short stories; he got on John Brahm's nerves a little bit." Caillou went on to write the teleplays for such subsequent *Thrillers* as "Hay-Fork and Bill-Hook," "The Terror in Teakwood" and "La Strega."

Alex Davion, as the hero, Grant Dudley, is as bland and forgettable as the role demands. It's another strike against the episode that the lovers are such cloyingly saccharine types — we never become involved in their predicament.

Doug Benton recalls one incident during filming that illustrates Karloff's extreme professionalism:

"I remember that John Brahm, one of the best Gothic directors we ever had — oh, Tod Browning may have been a shade better — was directing, and the stuntman fell across a little creek. It was really just a stream. And he had to get Boris to lie there in the stream, and take the stuntman's place. It was freezing cold, and the stream was running straight up Boris's leg and up his arm. And John said, "Boris, you don't have to do this..." And Boris said, "Oh no, John — you don't know how *grateful* I am to be able to do this."

Despite Karloff's devotion to his profession, "The Prediction" ranks as one of Frye's weakest *Thrillers*. Fortunately, his later episodes would bear little resemblance to this one.

"The Fatal Impulse" (airdate: November 29, 1960). Produced by Maxwell Shane. Directed by Gerald Meyer. Teleplay by Philip MacDonald, based on the short story by John D. MacDonald. Music: Pete Rugolo. Director of Photography: Benjamin Kline. Edited by Richard Belding. Art Director: Howard E. Johnson. Assistant Director: Edward K. Dodds.

Cast: Robert Lansing (Lieutenant Brian Rome), Whitney Blake (Jane Kimball), Conrad Nagel (Walker Wylie), Elisha Cook (Elser), Steve Brodie (Sergeant George Dumont), Elaine Edwards (Marjorie Dallquis), Harry Bartell (Mr. Dallquis), Lance Fuller (Larrimore), Mary Tyler Moore (Miss Snyder), Ed Nelson, Antony Carbone, Alice Backes, Cynthia Pepper.

A fairly tense police drama about a race against time to prevent a concealed bomb from exploding, "The Fatal Impulse" is a reasonably suspenseful crime entry, based on a can't miss premise.

A figure with a limp (Elisha Cook) telephones Mayor-elect Walker Wylie (Conrad Nagel) with a death threat; he then calls a newspaper with the same message.

Lieutenant Brian Rome (Robert Lansing) goes to see Wylie, who thinks the caller was a crank — "Killers don't advertise in advance." "That's theory, Mr. Wylie. Sometimes they do," Rome says. Wylie can't think of anyone who

might have made the threat. In the meantime, Elser, the man with the limp, is preparing a bomb. While Wylie's office is being readied for a television broadcast, Elser slips in disguised as a workman and attempts to plant the bomb in Wylie's desk. But when a secretary enters unexpectedly, Elser makes a break, taking the bomb with him and pushing a heavy light onto Rome's sergeant. Elser hides in a closet, then melts into the crowd leaving the building. He gets on an elevator, the bomb still in his pocket. Rome and Sergeant Dumont (Steve Brodie) go after him. Elser attempts to make it across the street, but is hit by a car. Dying, he gasps that he slipped the bomb into a girl's bag on the elevator; it's set for 11:00 that night. He dies before he can say anything more.

A warning goes out over radio and television, but there is no word from the girl. The police discover that Elser worked for the water and power company until he lost his job; Walker Wylie was the water and power commissioner — hence Elser's grudge against the mayor. When Dumont checks Elser's garage, the place, which has been booby trapped, blows up and Dumont is killed.

The police narrow down the list of women in the building to a few names. One, Jane Kimball (Whitney Blake), is at a restaurant with her boyfriend, Larrimore (Lance Fuller). Rome tracks her down and goes through her purse, but the bomb is not there. Jane, a commercial artist, offers to draw the faces of everyone on the elevator. Rome takes the sketch. He inadvertently creates marital discord by pinpointing one of the women as being in the building that afternoon; she was having an assignation with her lover, and now her husband knows.

By now all the names on the list have been crossed out. "So what do we do? Sit around and wait for a girl to get blown up, I guess," one cop grouses. Meanwhile, Jane Kimball remembers another girl on the elevator: a girl with glasses. She sketches her for Rome, and he tracks her down — Miss Snyder (Mary Tyler Moore). But she tells him she doesn't have the bomb; she checked both her bags — her purse and attaché case.

Meanwhile, unbeknownst to Jane Kimball, the bomb is at her house, having fallen out of her portfolio. Rome calls the restaurant, but Jane is gone. He rushes over to her house. The bomb is under a pillow on the couch. Rome checks her portfolio; it is now 11:00. Rome leaves, but then comes running in, finds the bomb and throws it out the window. It explodes harmlessly in the street. Jane, deserted by her boyfriend, asks Rome if he'll stay. "Suddenly I feel a great need for a cup of coffee," he says.

"The Fatal Impulse" (Karloff mistakenly identifies the title as "The Impulse" in the prologue) contains few surprises, but the basic premise sustains it. What hurts is its conventionality. There isn't a character who isn't a cliché: there's the tough, laconic cop, his married sidekick, the beautiful girl with the weak boyfriend, and so on. When Steve Brodie, as the sidekick, starts talking about his wife and their new baby, even the most casual viewer knows that he's not long for this world. One of the few surprises is the way the story casually discards the character of Walker Wylie, the mayor: it seems he will be a central figure, but once the plot is set in motion, he's instantly forgotten. Nor is the pathology of the bomber examined at any length: like Wylie, he's strictly functional; his motive for planting the bomb is suggested and confirmed in a perfunctory exchange of dialogue.

Robert Lansing, as the tough cop

Brian Rome, gives a credible performance. Lansing, a fine but underrated performer, played the *4D Man* in the 1959 film, and gave the character surprising depth and conviction. An intense, driven actor, Lansing has worked mostly on television: he was a regular on *87th Precinct* (in which he played a character much like Brian Rome), *Twelve O'Clock High*, and *The Man Who Never Was*. Bill Warren said of him: "The trouble with Lansing is definitely not a lack of ability, but that he does not have a clearly definable screen personality, or rather that which he has isn't distinct enough to make him sought by producers. He's essentially interchangeable with many other actors, many of whom are not as talented as he is." Lansing died in 1994.

Whitney Blake is competent as Jane Kimball. A regular on TV in the late fifties and early sixties, she's probably best remembered as Dorothy Baxter, employer of supermaid Hazel Burke, on the long-running comedy *Hazel*.

Conrad Nagel's part as Walker Wylie is surprisingly small, considering his notable screen career. A leading man of the twenties who made the transition to talkies with ease due to his excellent speaking voice, Nagel was the hero in the long-lost Lon Chaney film *London After Midnight* (1927). He also intoned the credits for *The Terror* (1928), the screen's first sound horror film. His other credits are mostly routine; late in his career he ran an acting school. In the early fifties he hosted and occasionally starred in his own series, *The Conrad Nagel Theatre*. He died in 1970.

One of the best aspects of "The Fatal Impulse" is watching Elisha Cook play the bomber. It's his only *Thriller* appearance, and, as usual, he's outstanding. Cook made his film debut in 1930; his credits include such genre films as *Voodoo Island* (1957, with Karloff), *House on Haunted Hill* (1958), *The Haunted Palace* and *Black Zoo* (both 1963), and *Rosemary's Baby* (1968). He was memorable in *The Big Sleep* (1946), *Shane* (1953) and *The Killing* (1956), but for most film fans he will forever be remembered as Wilmer the gunsel in *The Maltese Falcon* (1941). He's one of the great character actors of all time.

The rest of the cast is made up of such capable performers as Steve Brodie, Antony Carbone, Ed Nelson (in the first of his three *Thriller* appearances), and of course Mary Tyler Moore in her *Thriller* debut. She would have a much larger role in a later episode, "Man of Mystery."

Despite its conventionality, "The Fatal Impulse" holds the viewer's attention from beginning to end. The same can hardly be said of the following episode, "The Big Blackout."

"The Big Blackout" (airdate: December 6, 1960). Produced by Maxwell Shane. Directed by Maury Geraghty. Teleplay by Oscar Millard, from the novel by Don Tracy. Music by Pete Rugolo. Director of Photography: Benjamin Kline, A.S.C. Assistant Director: James Hogan. Edited by Danny Landres. Art Director: Howard E. Johnson. Set Decorators: John McCarthy and George Milo.

Cast: Jack Carson (Burt Lewis), Nan Leslie (Midge Lewis), Jeannie Cooper (Ethel), George Mitchell (Doc Mulloy), Charles McGraw (Sheriff Cliff Wright), Paul Newlan (Paul Hawkins), Jean Engstrom, Don Wilbanks, Chubby Johnson, Robert Carricart, Ron Harper, Jimmy Cavanaugh, Gil Perkins, Raoul DeLeon, Saul Gorss.

There's little to be said for "The Big Blackout," *Thriller*'s 12th episode. A pointless essay in alcoholism and murder, it's distinctly inferior to producer Shane's previous episode, "The Fatal Impulse."

Ex-boozer Burt Lewis (Jack Carson), a member of Alcoholics Anonymous, is summoned by Ethel (Jeannie Cooper) when a man is found unconscious in a motel room. The man has a large amount of money on him, as well as a note instructing him to assassinate a man known as either Bill Logan or Burt Lewis. Burt spent two years in a recurrent alcoholic blackout, when for long periods of time he couldn't remember his actions, and, after reading the note, he fears he may have killed someone during that time.

Burt is partners in a charter boat business with Ethel, who is in love with him despite his marriage to Midge (Nan Leslie). She tells Burt that when the man, named Adams, awakened, he was asking about Burt.

A man named Paul Hawkins (Paul Newlan) wants to charter Burt's boat. He mentions the name Bill Logan. Burt goes to see Adams, but the nurse says he is under sedation. Burt sneaks in through a side entrance, but Adams is dead — murdered. Burt is questioned by Sheriff Cliff Wright (Charles McGraw), who has a grudge against him because of an injury sustained during Burt's alcoholic period. Shortly afterward Burt is visited by an ex-convict whom Burt knew in prison, along with his sadistic partner. They think Burt killed Adams, and ask about Bill Logan. They rough Burt up and threaten Midge's life, but are scared off by the arrival of Sheriff Wright. The police have found Burt's gun — the one used to kill Adams. Burt tries to question a patient in the clinic where Adams was killed, thinking he may have seen what happened to him, but the man is dead, the victim of a hit and run driver.

Burt telephones an old friend,

another ex-con, for information about Adams. He tells Burt the people who sent Adams are involved with narcotics. Logan smuggled the narcotics into the country and double-crossed the people he was working for. Burt is sorely tempted to begin drinking again, but manages to avoid the temptation. He goes out on the boat with Paul Hawkins. When he asks Hawkins about his interest in Logan, Hawkins tells him Logan killed his son. He had investigators looking for him, and found that he was running a charter boat. He also has a photograph of Logan; the man looks nothing like Burt.

Shortly afterward, Burt's wife and child are kidnapped. Burt drives to a prearranged site and meets with the kidnappers. His wife and child are safe. Burt tells the kidnappers that Logan, who was Ethel's husband, has been dead for three years. When Adams arrived to kill Logan, Ethel got him drunk and put the note in his pocket. Later, she killed Adams with Burt's gun to fix the blame on Burt, whom she still loved.

Burt breaks free from the kidnappers who, shortly afterward, are killed by the police. Burt goes to see the dying Ethel, and asks her whether he was mixed up with the narcotics racket during his blackout. Ethel tells him he wasn't.

Maxwell Shane's "The Fatal Impulse" was a tense, if predictable, crime drama; "The Big Blackout" is a forgettable, overcomplicated farrago of alcoholism, jealousy, narcotics and murder. It's difficult to keep track of the names and events and, after a while, hardly seems worth the effort. We know in advance that Burt is innocent, and there's no real drama in his struggle with the bottle either, since we know he'll triumph over his alcoholism.

Bluff, hearty Jack Carson was a comedy actor born in Canada. His best-known film appearances were in the thirties and forties, and included *Strawberry Blonde* (1941), *Mildred Pierce* (1945) and *The Good Humor Man* (1950). He may be best remembered as the playwright-cop in *Arsenic and Old Lace* (1944). He's competent as Burt Lewis, but little else. He died in 1963.

Gravel-voiced Charles McGraw plays the sheriff. He's a little too ferocious to be believed, and his animosity toward Burt is equally implausible. McGraw was a familiar character player, on both sides of the law; one of his best-remembered roles was in the original version of *The Narrow Margin* (1952). He died in 1980.

The other actors leave little impression, with the possible exception of Paul Newlan as the revenge seeking father. This was Newlan's first appearance on *Thriller*; he would appear in three more episodes in the years ahead.

There's little else to be said about "The Big Blackout." A true failure — but not an honorable one — it could as well be an episode of any mediocre crime series of the period. It certainly ranks as one of the poorest *Thriller*s ever. Its title is singularly appropriate, for even among *Thriller* fans, their memories of the episode are one big blackout.

"Knock Three-One-Two" (air-date: December 13, 1960). Produced by Maxwell Shane. Directed by Herman Hoffman. Teleplay by John Kneubuhl, from the novel by Fredric Brown. Music: Pete Rugolo. Director of Photography: Benjamin Kline, A.S.C. Edited by Richard Belding. Art Director: Howard E. Johnson. Assistant Director: Frank Losee. Set Decorators: John McCarthy and George Milo.

Cast: Joe Maross (Ray Kenton), Beverly Garland (Ruth Kenton), Charles

Aidman (George Milkos), Warren Oates (Benny), Murray Alper (Bartender), Norman Leavitt (Charlie), David Alpert (Hoodlum), Meade Martin (Young man), Clancy Cooper, Lida Piazza, Will J. White, Bunny Bishop, Lillian O'Malley.

Although a compelling crime drama for most of its length, "Knock Three-One-Two" is let down by a contrived ending.

Ray Kenton (Joe Maross) owes money to cover his gambling debts — he has until the following night to pay up, or he will be killed. On the street he bumps into a young man (Meade Martin). In the hotel building the young man has just left, a girl's body is found — the victim of a compulsive strangler of young women.

The next morning Ray's wife, Ruth (Beverly Garland), is reading about the killer, whom the papers have dubbed the Silk Stocking Strangler. There is a coded knock at the door — three-one-two. It is Ray, who is desperate for money. Ruth has a savings account of $4,000, but she refuses to give it to him. Ray tells her they will kill him if he doesn't pay off, but Ruth has heard it all before. "There's just got to be an end to it somewhere," she says.

Later Ruth meets up with Benny (Warren Oates), a feeble-minded man who has a compulsion to confess to the slayings. Ruth tries to explain that, whenever the murders occurred, Benny was at his newsstand, but he is unconvinced. "Believe me, you couldn't hurt anyone," Ruth says, "you just don't have it in you."

Ray goes to see Ruth at the restaurant where she works, and they have a reconciliation. He asks her to borrow the money from her employer, George Milkos (Charles Aidman). She refuses. They quarrel, and George comes in.

"Ray just came to say goodbye — for good," Ruth announces. Ray leaves the restaurant, only to be set upon by the men he owes the money to. They rough him up, then tell him he has until the following night to produce $3,000 — twice his original debt.

Benny finds Ray lying in an alley and takes him to his apartment. When Ray asks him why he has newspapers recounting the Strangler's exploits hanging on his walls, Benny says, "I like to read about myself." When Ray tries to convince him he isn't the killer, Benny refuses to believe it. "The only trouble is I don't remember it when I'm doing it," Benny says. "It's only afterwards when I read it in the papers that I know I've done it again." When Ray reads about the latest murder, he remembers the young man he bumped into.

Later that night Ray runs into the young man again at a bar. He is about to call the police, but then has a better idea. He buys the young man a drink, then drops hints that his wife will be home alone. He shows the young man Ruth's picture and tells him about their "knock three-one-two" code. Suitably impressed, the young man leaves. Intent on having an alibi for the evening, Ray calls Benny and arranges to meet him at the police station, telling him he will convince the police that he's the killer.

George takes Ruth home, unaware the Strangler is watching from across the street. Ray goes over to the police station. Just as Benny is confessing to the crimes, the Strangler is knocking on Ruth's door. Thinking it's Ray, she opens it, only to scream at the sight of the Strangler. At that same moment George suddenly turns his car around and drives back to see Ruth.

Meanwhile, the police do not believe Benny. They call a psychiatrist. Benny is angry because Ray promised he'd make the police believe him. "You lied to me," Benny says. George, meanwhile, hears Ruth scream and breaks into her apartment; he fights with the Strangler and knocks him unconscious. As this is happening, Benny turns on Ray and strangles him. When the police enter the room they find Benny sitting beside the body with a smile on his lips. "Now I bet you believe me," Benny says.

Although it has an intriguing premise — a man using a compulsive killer as a murder instrument — and a gritty, film noir-ish feel, "Knock Three-One-Two" falls down at the end simply because too many coincidences pile up. George suddenly drives back to Ruth's apartment for absolutely no reason, just in time to confront the Strangler (whom he bests rather unconvincingly in a one-sided fight). Likewise, Benny, whom the other characters have described as a gentle soul, suddenly turns on Ray for no good reason. It might have been believable if he'd strangled Ruth, to prove he had killed the other girls, but here it's simply contrived. What's worse, we're not only asked to accept two jaw-dropping coincidences, but to believe that they dovetail together neatly so as to allow Ruth a happy ending (she's rid of Ray and free to marry George).

Beverly Garland, as Ruth, is her usual strong-willed self. It's entirely plausible that she would turn down Ray when he comes looking for money. She always played an aggressive, no-nonsense type; as Bill Warren notes, "she's simply too tough and too intelligent to portray a fainthearted, negligee-clad heroine." Her genre films include *Curucu, Beast of the Amazon* (1956), *It Conquered the World* (1956), *Not of This Earth* (1957) and *The Alligator People* (1959).

Joe Maross is quite believable as small-time gambler Ray Kenton. His lived-in face suggests the character quite

adequately, and he seems as desperate as the role calls for. Maross guested on numerous anthology series (including *The Twilight Zone*) and was briefly a regular on *Peyton Place*.

Charles Aidman seems an odd choice for the hero (a role he also plays in "The Terror in Teakwood"). He seems more like the hero's best friend. He's an adequate if unexciting actor, though *The Twilight Zone Companion* author Marc Scott Zicree gives him special praise for the *Twilight Zone* episode "Little Girl Lost." He filled in for an ailing Ross Martin on the much lamented *Wild, Wild West*, and more recently supplied the narration for the revived *The Twilight Zone*. He died in 1993.

Warren Oates was one of Hollywood's most distinctive character actors; he invariably brought conviction to even the most stereotypical roles. The part of Benny doesn't do much for him, but he infuses it with his usual believability. He started out in supporting roles, made an impression in *In the Heat of the Night* (1967) and *The Wild Bunch* (1969), and became a star, briefly, in the seventies; his best known role was as *Dillinger* (1973). His stardom didn't last, and he drifted back to supporting roles. He died in 1982. He can also be seen in the much later *Thriller* episode "The Hollow Watcher."

"Knock Three-One-Two" is a distinctly disappointing episode, promising more than it delivers. With a stronger ending, it might have been one of the more compelling crime episodes.

"Man in the Middle" (airdate: December 20, 1960). Produced and directed by Fletcher Markle. Teleplay by Howard Rodman, from the novel by Charlotte Armstrong. Music: Pete Rugolo. Associate Producer: James P. Cavanagh. Director of Photography: John L.

Russell, A.S.C. Edited by Danny Landres. Art Director: Howard E. Johnson. Assistant Director: Charles S. Gould. Set Decorators: John McCarthy and Julia Heron.

Cast: Mort Sahl (Sam Lynch), Sue Randall (Kay Salisbury), Werner Klemperer (Clark), Frank Albertson (Charles Salisbury), Grace Albertson (Mrs. Salisbury), Frederick Beir (Alan), Ashley Cowan, Fred Sherman, Anthony Jochim, Bert Remsen, Pitt Herbert.

Another of *Thriller*'s undistinguished crime dramas, "Man in the Middle" is a middling account that illustrates the dangers of not getting involved.

Two men sit in a restaurant discussing the kidnapping and possible murder of a young socialite named Kay Salisbury, unaware that they are being overheard by TV writer Sam Lynch (Mort Sahl) seated in the next booth. One of them, Clark (Werner Klemperer), sees Sam, but does nothing. When they run into Sam again, Clark indicates he will not act on this knowledge. Clark and his companion, Hoffman, then follow Sam to his job at a local TV station and to his home. They are not convinced he will keep his mouth shut and, to ensure this, Hoffman works him over. They threaten to kill him if he talks.

Sam goes to see Charles Salisbury (Frank Albertson), the girl's father; with him is Kay's fiancé, Alan (Frederick Beir). Sam tells them of the kidnapping plot, but Salisbury declines to take any action. Sam meets Kay (Sue Randall), but she is likewise reluctant to believe his story. He takes her captive and drives her to a remote cabin, where he explains the position he is in. He also tells her that Hoffman is the boyfriend of her maid. Kay wants to contact her fiancé, but Sam tells her, "Get in the world, will you? At least, enough to be scared."

Clark and Hoffman meanwhile contact Charles Salisbury, demanding $100,000 for Kay's return. Salisbury offers $80,000 and receives instructions for the drop off of the ransom money. But when he does as instructed, Hoffman takes the money and knocks him unconscious. Salisbury waits for a call from the kidnappers, but receives word from Sam instead, telling him Kay is safe. Sam drives back to the city and arranges with a friend to give a message to Clark and Hoffman, but they brutally murder the friend.

Sam buys a gun, then drives back to the cabin and gives Kay the keys to his car, telling her to drive home. He has left word with the killers to come to his cabin. But on the road, Kay passes the killers. When they force her car to the side, Kay takes flight through the woods. Hoffman goes after her, and Clark drives on alone to Sam's cabin. There he explains his plan to Sam, the plan that has now gone awry. "You're a man who makes plans," Sam says. "I'm a man who does the first thing that comes into his mind, and everything I've done up until now has been wrong. The more I tried to get out of this, the more I got in, deeper and deeper." Just as Hoffman arrives with Kay, Sam pulls his gun and kills both Clark and Hoffman, but is wounded in the exchange of bullets. "You see what this is about?" Sam asks Kay. "I'm sorry, I'm truly sorry, I didn't understand you," she says. "You're not the only one," Sam says.

"Man in the Middle" is unconvincing due to the unbelievability of its central character. Sam Lynch describes himself as a pacifist confronted by the age-old question, "What would you do if you saw a maniac attacking someone with a knife?" We know his answer early on; it's suggested by his repeated advice to Kay Salisbury: "Get in the world."

Unfortunately Sam is a sketchy character; his job as a TV writer is perfunctorily and unconvincingly depicted, and he seems more like an illustration of the dichotomy between thought and action than a flesh and blood character. In some ways he's a slightly more cerebral version of the archetypal Bogart character in *Casablanca* and *To Have and Have Not*: the loner who chooses not to get involved until he is forced to. Like Bogart, Sam is apolitical and uninvolved, truly a "man in the middle," and it is not until his friend is killed that he takes decisive action.

Unfortunately, little of this is suggested by Mort Sahl's performance. Sahl, at this stage in his career, wasn't much of an actor, and his stumbling, lethargic performance does little for the episode's believability. Fortunately there's far more to Morton Lyon Sahl than "Man in the Middle" suggests. Canadian-born, he began appearing in nightclubs like San Francisco's Hungry i in the fifties. Described as "a nice fresh breath of carbon monoxide," his sardonic commentary on Eisenhower, the bomb, McCarthyism and other pungent topics helped pioneer the "hip wits" school of comedy that came to include Lenny Bruce, Shelley Berman, Nichols and May, and others. But when John F. Kennedy took office, liberals didn't take kindly to Sahl's satiric jibes, and his bookings fell off. His impassioned involvement with New Orleans D.A. Jim Garrison's controversial probe into the Kennedy assassination also hurt his career, although he still appears in clubs and on TV. His political stance has become more conservative in recent years, but his barbs are still memorable: "Johnson wounded the presidency, Nixon killed it, Carter buried it, and now Reagan is trying to bring the dead back to life." He was sometimes effective, and even memorable, in small parts (for instance, as a soldier answering a field telephone in *In Love and War*: "Good morning, World War Two."), but as the lead in "Man in the Middle," he's inadequate.

As Kay Salisbury, lovely Sue Randall has little to do. She appeared on *77 Sunset Strip*, *The Twilight Zone* and *Have Gun, Will Travel*, but is probably best known as Beaver's teacher, Miss Landers, on the long-running *Leave It to Beaver*. Her career came to an abrupt end in the mid-sixties when she was seriously injured in an auto accident. She died in 1984.

As for the kidnappers, Clark and Hoffman, they are not much more believable than Sam Lynch. They seem to have stepped straight out of a B movie. It's typical of their ineptitude that they're plotting the kidnapping openly in a restaurant where they can be overheard. And Werner Klemperer plays Clark as a straight, down the line heavy with little nuance or shading. But as with Sahl, Klemperer's other accomplishments overshadow his performance here. The son of distinguished orchestra conductor Otto Klemperer, Werner's screen appearances include *Operation Eichmann* (1961, in the title role), *Judgment at Nuremberg* (1961), *Ship of Fools* (1965) and the *Thriller*-esque *Dark Intruder* (1965), as the demon. But he's best known as Colonel Klink on TV's "Hogan's Heroes," for which he received two Emmy awards.

Frank Albertson is adequate as Charles Salisbury. A natural at playing wealthy businessmen, Albertson was a light leading man in his younger days, appearing in such films as *Just Imagine* (1930) and *Room Service* (1938). He's probably best remembered as the wealthy oilman who tempts Marion Crane in *Psycho* (1960). He died in 1964.

"Man in the Middle" is one of

Thriller's least effective crime dramas, a sure indication that Fletcher Markle's concept of the show was conventional and even trite. Fortunately, the very next episode would prove a resounding success, leaving "Man in the Middle" far behind.

"The Cheaters" (airdate: December 27, 1960). Produced by William Frye. Directed by John Brahm. Screenplay by Donald S. Sanford, based on the short story by Robert Bloch. Photography by John Russell. Edited by Danny Landres. Art Director: Howard E. Johnson. Music: Jerry Goldsmith. Assistant Director: Edward K. Dodds.

Cast: Paul Newlan (Joe Henshaw), Linda Watkins (Maggie Henshaw), Ed Nelson (Charlie), Mildred Dunnock (Miriam Olcott), Jack Weston (Edward Dean), Barbara Eller (Olive Dean), Dayton Lummis (Clarence Kramer), Alan Carney (Burgin), Molly Glessing (Mrs. Ames), Audrey Swanson (Salesgirl), Harry Townes (Sebastian Grimm), Grandon Rhodes (Judge Pfluger), Ralph Clanton (Thorgenson), Joan Tompkins (Ellen Grimm), Henry Daniell (Dirk Van Prinn), John Mitchum (Policeman).

Based on the story by Robert Bloch, "The Cheaters" is one of *Thriller*'s most notable early successes. From its opening scenes, it establishes a mood of foreboding that never falters, yet the most remarkable thing about the episode is its unity. Despite telling five separate stories and introducing a multitude of characters (many of whom are subsequently murdered), the central motif of "the cheaters" remains consistent throughout.

Karloff's ominous introduction sets the tone: "When a man shuts himself off from his neighbors, when he conducts experiments behind locked doors, there is bound to be talk. There were those who whispered that Dirk Van Prinn was

a sorcerer — and worse. He might never have been remembered at all had not his research led him to the discovery of a most unusual formula for making glass." Van Prinn (Henry Daniell) has already perfected his formula, and the result is a pair of spectacles, or "cheaters." Putting them on and then looking into a mirror, he sees something so horrifying he begins to scream — and goes on screaming. Before dawn, he hangs himself.

Years pass. Joe Henshaw (Paul Newlan), a salvage operator, is arguing with his wife, Maggie (Linda Watkins). When his young helper, Charlie (Ed Nelson), arrives, they go to the old Bleaker House to conduct salvage operations. They find nothing at the old house, the home of Van Prinn, and Joe kicks a desk in disgust. A panel swings open, revealing a secret drawer. Joe reaches in and pulls out a pair of spectacles bearing the legend *Veritas*, or truth. Trying them on, Joe discovers he can hear the innermost thoughts of his wife and helper, who are secret lovers plotting to kill him. In a rage, Joe murders both of them. A passing policeman hears Maggie's screams and rushes in. "Cheaters!" Joe screams, trying to smash the spectacles before the policeman's bullets bring him down.

Miriam Olcott (Mildred Dunnock) is the next to obtain the cheaters — she buys them from a demolition sale after shoplifting numerous items from other stores. She is shocked when she hears her daughter, Olive (Barbara Eller), and son-in-law, Edward Dean (Jack Weston), planning to murder her for the inheritance. As soon as she hears that her doctor (Dayton Lummis) has similar plans, she stabs him through the heart with her hatpin. Drinking herself into a stupor, she unknowingly starts a fire and burns to death.

Now members of the *nouveau riche*,

Olive and Edward Dean throw a costume party, with the portly Edward decked out as Benjamin Franklin. During a poker game Edward tries on the spectacles as part of his guise and hears the other players talking about him. Edward blurts out the truth about the glasses and accuses one of the other players of cheating. There is an altercation, and Edward is hit on the head by Sebastian Grimm (Harry Townes). He collapses on the floor, dead.

Grimm is the next link in the chain. An unpublished author fascinated by the spectacles, he decides to work them into his novel in progress, to be titled *The Cheaters*. He has worked out the truth behind the others' deaths, and tells his wife, Ellen (Joan Tompkins), the *real* purpose of the cheaters — self-revelation. "Know thyself," he says. Seeking the proper atmosphere, he goes out to the old Bleaker house and makes his way upstairs. Seated before the very mirror into which Dirk Van Prinn looked, Grimm puts on the glasses. A voice tells him to move the lamp closer. Looking deep, Grimm sees his own reflection — a hideous, rotting face. Screaming in terror, he claws at his face and smashes the cheaters to bits.

"The Cheaters" was first published in the November 1947 *Weird Tales*. In the story there is no introductory scene with Dirk Van Prinn; other than that, the structure is quite similar. The four protagonists apparently relate their stories in the first person, though it is actually a ventriloquial act by Grimm, the true author of the story. When he himself dons the cheaters he sees "the unutterable foulness beneath all the veneer of consciousness and intellect, and knew it for my true nature. Every man's nature." This shattering revelation induces him to blow his brains out. This is less clear in the adaptation, in which his hideous

visage seems a grossly disproportionate punishment for his actual sins: Grimm is merely an unpublished author (hardly the gravest of crimes) and a bit full of himself, but hardly a monster and not even a murderer (his killing Edward Dean, after all, was an accident). In addition, one might question the likelihood of three consecutive owners of the glasses being threatened with, or involved in, murder, particularly in what seems a short space of time.

These minor cavils aside, "The Cheaters" is one of *Thriller*'s genuine classics, beautifully and atmospherically directed by John Brahm, perhaps best remembered for the werewolf film *The Undying Monster* (1942) and the two 1940s Laird Cregar thrillers *The Lodger* and *Hangover Square*. Although he was often saddled with routine scripts, his acute visual sense and gift for injecting genuine Gothic atmosphere usually served him well. He proved to be an inspired choice to direct *Thriller*, and his episodes are among the series' all-time best. Film critic Andrew Sarris said of him: "His quiet virtues of visual tastefulness and dramatic balance were unable to sustain his career." He died in 1982.

The acting is splendid throughout, perhaps the best ensemble acting in any *Thriller*. Henry Daniell makes the first of his five series appearances, setting the mood instantly, albeit in a minor role. With his icy demeanor and cold, clipped voice, Daniell was perhaps the quintessential *Thriller* actor. He was largely wasted in Hollywood throughout his 35-year screen career, during which he effortlessly rose above his material. Although he matched wits with Garbo in *Camille* (1935) and crossed swords with Errol Flynn in *The Sea Hawk* (1940), his most famous performance is probably his leading role, appropriately opposite

Boris Karloff, in *The Body Snatcher* (1945): his frosty imperiousness and supercilious manner made him the perfect "Toddy" MacFarlane in that Val Lewton classic. He also managed to steal scenes from Chaplin in a rare comic turn in *The Great Dictator* (1940), and he was enjoyable, as always, as a head shrinking medico in *The Four Skulls of Jonathan Drake* (1959). Veteran character actor Ian Wolfe recalled that a young man researching a biography of Daniell shied away from the project after he "ran into rumors of Daniell's bisexuality," even though Wolfe himself recalled that the actor "certainly wasn't flagrant or fey, not at all." Daniell died on Halloween 1963 while making *My Fair Lady*. As Bill Warren notes, "His slimy suaveness helped every film he was ever in."

As the slightly dotty Mother Olcott, Mildred Dunnock is humorous and sympathetic, thankfully not overstepping the line into bathos or out and out comedy. Dunnock, who also made appearances on "Way Out" and "The Web," had a successful career on stage and screen, and is best remembered as Willy Loman's wife in the screen version of *Death of a Salesman* (1951). She received Oscar nominations for both *Salesman* and *Baby Doll* (1956). She died in 1991.

As Edward Dean (curiously, Karloff's introductory spiel misidentifies him as *Percy* Dean, the character's name in Bloch's story), Jack Weston is something of a surprise. He plays the role perfectly straight, with no attempts at humor and none of the mannerisms that sometimes crept into his acting. He is particularly effective in denouncing his fellow card player for cheating, and his overall performance is in marked contrast to his rather tedious acting in the much later episode "Flowers of Evil." Weston was a ubiquitous presence in

films and television throughout the sixties, starring in his own series, *The Hathaways*. He usually played comic villains or henchmen, though he was memorable playing it straight in the *Twilight Zone* episode "The Monsters Are Due on Maple Street." His films include *It's Only Money*, *Mirage*, *Wait Until Dark*, *The Thomas Crown Affair*, and *Fuzz*.

Harry Townes, as the *soi-disant* writer Sebastian Grimm, was a familiar face on television, appearing on *The Twilight Zone*, *Perry Mason*, *Alfred Hitchcock Presents*, and many other shows. He seems a peculiar choice for the cynical, self-mocking Grimm: one envisions a more aristocratic, auctorial type — Murray Matheson, perhaps. But Townes is a good enough actor to pull it off. There's more than a whiff of Dorian Gray in the nightmarish summation in which Townes sees his mirror revealed self, so it's no surprise that Jack Barron's ghastly makeup is similar to Dick Smith's scabrous creation done for the 1961 telecast of the Oscar Wilde story (even though Smith's makeup, renowned for its supreme hideousness, is seen so briefly in this version that it's virtually tossed away). Not so Barron's sulphurous masterpiece, which took two weeks to create. This memorable payoff scene is rightly remembered as one of the highpoints of televised horror.

"The Cheaters" is equally impressive in its other creative aspects. Besides remaining faithful to its source, Donald S. Sanford's teleplay is remarkably inventive, ringing every change on the word "cheaters" in all its myriad meanings (Maggie and Charlie are cheating on Joe, Thorgenson is cheating at cards, etc.). Even the names (Grimm, the Bleaker House) are appropriately mournful. Equally appropriate is Jerry Goldsmith's lovely, graceful theme for Mother Olcott (referred to as "Shopper" and

"Shoplifter" on the music cue sheet), first heard during her shoplifting spree, and returning as a sinister violin solo when she is preparing to murder her doctor.

In sum, "The Cheaters" shapes up as one of *Thriller*'s best episodes; after the passage of 30 years it has lost little of its capacity to chill, and in its literacy, unity and terseness of narrative, it remains one of television's true classics of the macabre.

"The Hungry Glass" (airdate: January 3, 1961). Produced by William Frye. Directed by Douglas Heyes. Teleplay by Douglas Heyes, based on the short story by Robert Bloch. Director of Photography: Lionel Lindon, A.S.C. Music: Pete Rugolo. Edited by Michael R. McAdam. Art Director: Howard E. Johnson. Assistant Director: Carter DeHaven III. Set Decorators: John McCarthy and George Milo.

Cast: William Shatner (Gil Trasker), Joanna Heyes (Marcia Thrasher), Russell Johnson (Adam Talmadge), Elizabeth Allen (Liz Talmadge), Donna Douglas (Young Laura Bellman), Ottola Nesmith (Old Laura Bellman), Clem Bevans (Obed), Pitt Herbert (Storekeeper), Duane Grey (Bearded Man).

William Shatner gives a fine performance in "The Hungry Glass," one of the finest early *Thriller*s, and another of William Frye's notable successes.

Amid a roomful of mirrors, lovely Laura Bellman (Donna Douglas) pauses constantly, admiring her reflection and fanning herself. But when a man with a hook raps at the door, an old woman (Ottola Nesmith) answers, saying, "Leave me alone, can't you — leave me alone with my mirrors."

Some years later two new arrivals appear in the New England town of Cape Caution: Gil Trasker (William Shatner) and his wife, Marcia (Joanna

Heyes). They have come to move into the old Bellman place. "That location property comes fully equipped with visitors," one of the locals warns. What's more, the Traskers are warned that there are no mirrors in the house. Adam Talmadge (Russell Johnson), the realtor who sold them the place, arrives with his wife, Liz (Elizabeth Allen), to drive them to the house. "What's this about no mirrors?" Gil asks. Adam explains that there were some nasty accidents — some people killed by shattered glass — and the locals worked the stories into a series of murders.

They drive to the house, which overlooks the water. As they are getting acquainted, Liz suddenly lets out a scream, saying she saw someone in the glass reaching for Marcia. Alarmed by the sound, Adam cuts his hand on a glass. Liz explains that she saw a man in the glass — a man with a hook for a hand. "Fine, next time we'll get *him* to open the champagne," Adam says. But after the Talmadges leave, Gil, too, sees a ghostly figure. He does not tell his wife.

The next day Gil cuts himself shaving when Marcia pops her head into the bathroom. But when he complains about it later, she tells him she hasn't left the other room. Gil, growing fearful, senses that whatever presence is in the house is somehow involved with the mirrors. "It's as if somebody doesn't want us here," Marcia says. "I never felt so — unwelcome."

Gil, a photographer, sets up a darkroom in the basement. Developing a photograph he took in the house, he sees the face of a child, which he cannot account for, and hides the photograph. Marcia, meanwhile, in exploring the attic, has found a locked room. Forcing the lock, she finds a room filled with mirrors. She tells Gil. He asks if she snapped a picture of a little girl with his camera; when she says no, he decides it must have been a double exposure. But when Gil looks in the mirror room, he sees the same ghostly figure and collapses.

Later, Marcia asks Gil what he saw. He explains that it's the old trouble, a result of his war experiences in Korea. "Ever since we got to this place last night, my mind's been working overtime, playing tricks," he says. He tells her it looked like an old woman with a fan.

Adam and Liz come over with a bottle of champagne. Gil asks Adam why the house has stood vacant for 20 years. Adam explains that a man named Jonah Bellman built it in the 1860s for his bride, Laura. She had all the mirrors installed in order to admire her beauty. After his death she was alone with the mirrors, but never saw herself as anything but young and beautiful. When her nephew brought a doctor, she appeared at the door (the scene depicted in the prologue), very old and quite insane. She danced toward the window glass and was killed by falling into the mirror. Her nephew, the man with the hook, was also killed by a mirror. And a little girl disappeared near the house — the same one seen in Gil's photograph. Gil asks Adam if he is losing his mind. "Gil, please — get out of this house," Adam begs. "Don't stay another night." But before Gil can leave, he learns that Marcia is alone in the room with the mirrors. Hearing her scream, he rushes up to the attic. He sees Marcia being pulled into the mirror by the old woman. Gil smashes the mirror to bits with a poker. Adam grabs him; Gil struggles, but when Adam tells him to look down at the floor, he sees Marcia's body. She lies dead amid the broken glass, her head smashed in. Gil breaks down.

Later, Gil tells Adam and Liz: "You see how it was. There was this madwoman, and she saw herself in the glass. It was vanity, all vanity, nothing but vanity, and you can see she danced herself into the glass and died there, but somehow she stayed on and pulled others in there with her, into the glass, and that's how it happened. That's how I happened to — kill my wife."

Gil suddenly stands up; he sees Marcia in the glass, beckoning to him, and he jumps through the window to his death on the rocks below. Liz faints, and Adam carries her out of the house, but just before he leaves, he sees the ghostly figure beckoning to him. Resisting the impulse to return, he carries Liz to their car.

Producer William Frye followed the success of "The Cheaters" with one of *Thriller*'s most chilling ghost stories. Author Jay Allen Sanford thought "The Hungry Glass" was "the episode that truly turned the critical and popular tide, a pivotal ghost story."

Robert Bloch's original short story, "The Hungry House," a curious haunted house story with little dialogue and two unnamed protagonists, was published in the April 1950 issue of *Imagination*. In adapting it, writer-director Douglas Heyes made several changes. Most notably, he expanded the story without padding it, making Gil Trasker a veteran of the Korean war — which causes him to doubt his sanity — and by enlarging the characters of the realtors, the Talmadges, and making their friendship an important element in the story. Additionally, by making Gil a photographer, he enlarged the obsession with visual imagery.

The mirror motif is employed throughout. Mirrors are, of course, not only objects of vanity, but reminders of mortality. As Karloff remarks in the prologue: "Every time you look in one you see death at work." Heyes draws on our fascination with mirrors, and our reluctance or avidity to gaze into them. Sometimes this visual assault is stunning: when Marcia stumbles into a room full of mirrors, we see a multitude of reflections, almost like a multi-screen image. This may evoke memories of *The Lady from Shanghai*, or the scene in *The Fly* (1958) shown from the insect's point of view.

In addition to this visual cleverness, the dialogue crackles with wit and verbal ingenuity, and the light-hearted banter between the Traskers and the Talmadges makes a nice contrast to Gil's later grim soliloquy. (Looking over the house, Marcia comments: "You'll see — it'll be a showplace." "Like Madame Tussaud's?" Liz replies.) Heyes also indulges in Bloch's characteristic wordplay. When Adam comments that Gil seems to be in a reflective mood, Gil snaps, "Reflective? That's a funny word to use. I mean, this house has a reputation for reflections, hasn't it?"

William Shatner gives arguably the best performance of his career as Gil Trasker. Whether relating his experiences in Korea, learning the truth about the mirrors, or accepting the guilt for the death of his wife, he is believable throughout and never indulges in the mannerisms that affected his later acting. Indeed, at times his emoting became a little *too* realistic. Co-star Russell Johnson remarked: "I remember having one hell of a struggle with Shatner to keep him from going into that mirror. And he was a strong guy ... I mean, it was all out. He doesn't hold anything back. It was all I could do to restrain him!"

The Canadian-born Shatner did a few films (including *The Brothers Karamazov* [1958] and *Judgment at Nuremberg* [1961], but seemed more at home on television. Besides appearing in the most memorable *Alfred Hitchcock Presents* ("The Glass Eye"), he did two notable *Twilight Zone*s: "Nick of Time" and the well-remembered "Nightmare at 20,000 Feet." He also did a later *Thriller*, "The Grim Reaper." He's best known, of course, as Captain James Kirk on *Star Trek* and in the successful film series which followed. More recently he served as the host for *Rescue 911*.

The other actors don't have such showy parts. Joanna Heyes (the wife of Douglas Heyes, previously seen in "The Purple Room") is believable as Marcia, and Elizabeth Allen (later seen in "The Grim Reaper") is likewise effective as Liz Talmadge.

But the real surprise is Russell Johnson, who does a fine job as Adam Talmadge. Although he's best known for his stint as the Professor on *Gilligan's Island*, Johnson was a veteran of several well-remembered fifties sci-fi classics, namely *It Came from Outer Space* (1953), *This Island Earth* (1955) and *The Space Children* (1958). He also appeared in two memorable *Twilight Zone*s, "Back There" and "Execution."

"The Hungry Glass" remained a pleasant memory for Johnson, as he recalled:

> It was a powerful show, and I enjoyed very much working with Douglas [Heyes] and Bill Shatner. I'd worked with Shatner before, a number of times, and he's always a good actor to work with, for me, anyway; I really enjoyed the give and take with Bill.
>
> I thought it was a good script, I really did, and Douglas is a good director. I thought the cast was really good: his wife was one of the women in the show, and the other was Elizabeth Allen, who had been one of the poster girls for Jackie Gleason — a good actress.

That aired, as a matter of fact, on Thanksgiving night one particular year when everybody was home watching television, and everybody was home in Hollywood, too. So the next day my agent called me and said, "My God, the phone is ringing off the hook, and I've got more people, more offers ..." It was amazing, it really was. So it produced a lot of work for me.

It was a wonderful show, wonderful for me, and I'm very proud of it. It's good work, I think. Some years ago someone sent me a copy of it.

Another memorable member of the cast was little-known Donna Douglas (later to play Elly May on the long-running *The Beverly Hillbillies*) as the young Laura Bellman. Douglas also appeared in Heyes' memorable *Twilight Zone* episode "The Eye of the Beholder." Appearing as the hideously aged Laura Bellman was screen veteran Ottola Nesmith, later to make an appearance as another withered hag in the most celebrated *Thriller* of all, "Pigeons from Hell."

Once again, much of the credit must go to writer-director Heyes. His sense of the dramatic never falters, neatly balanced by his splendid visual touches. Asked about "The Hungry Glass" many years later, Heyes recalled: "Most people that remember 'Thriller' remember that episode. A lot of people told me that, for weeks afterward, they couldn't look in their mirrors. They were afraid of their mirrors."

"The Poisoner" (airdate: January 10, 1961). Produced by William Frye. Directed by Herschel Daugherty. Written by Robert Hardy Andrews. Director of Photography: Benjamin H. Kline, A.S.C. Music: Jerry Goldsmith. Art Director: Howard E. Johnson. Edited by Richard Belding. Assistant Director: Carter DeHaven III. Set Decorators: John McCarthy and Julia Heron.

Cast: Murray Matheson (Thomas Edward Griffith), Sarah Marshall (Frances Griffith), Brenda Forbes (Mrs. Abercrombie), Jennifer Raine (Helen Abercrombie), David Frankham (Proctor), Richard Peel (Justin), Maurice Dallimore (George Griffith), Seymour Green (Sir John Herbert), Sam Edwards (Charles Larrimore), Keith Hitchcock, Nelson Welch, Donald P. Journeaux.

The first *Thriller* to use a real-life figure as a protagonist, "The Poisoner" is the stylish account of a multiple murderer far more charming and witty than his victims, and features a showcase performance by Murray Matheson as this aesthetic assassin.

In 19th-century England, Thomas Edward Griffith (Murray Matheson) pours his wife, Frances (Sara Marshall), a glass of brandy. To this he adds a dash of poison — tasteless and nearly impossible to detect — kept in his Borgia ring. She understandably refuses to drink with him. In anger, he mutilates the portrait of her he had painted.

Karloff tells us in the introduction:

> Thomas Edward Griffith, who made this lovely picture and then destroyed it, really lived. He was a writer, a painter, and a critic. In each of these arts he displayed talent. But his real genius lay elsewhere. We have the testimony of Charles Lamb, Charles Dickens, Oscar Wilde, and other famous witnesses that Griffith was the master of the gentle art of murder — a dabbler in the occult, and a connoisseur of the exotic. Griffith was far ahead of the medical men of his time in the lethal science of toxication. In simple terms, Griffith was a poisoner.

At some point before the events depicted in the prologue, Griffith is seen presiding over the unveiling of his wife's portrait. The gathering is disrupted by the arrival of her mother (Brenda Forbes) and wheelchair-bound sister, Helen (Jennifer Raine), two working class women very different in tone and breeding from the aristocratic Griffith. "I didn't expect them until tomorrow," Frances says. "I didn't expect them at all," Griffith sniffs. He is further outraged by the discovery that his new wife is not rich. He storms out of the house. "What kind of man did you marry, anyhow?" Mrs. Abercrombie asks. "He's a murderer," Helen says.

The two women make themselves at home in Griffith's house. Griffith returns and, by means of his Borgia ring, poisons Mrs. Abercrombie's drink. He tells her that he is not wealthy, despite his upper class appearance and manners, but that he expects to profit from the reputation he is building. Threatening to destroy his reputation, she finishes her drink as Helen watches from upstairs. A moment later a scream rings out, and Mrs. Abercrombie is dead.

Helen accuses Griffith of murder, but there is no evidence of poison. Proctor (David Frankham), Mrs. Abercrombie's legal representative, arrives and tells Griffith that the dead woman's estate goes to Helen.

"I didn't know," Frances says, "I really didn't know."

"My perfect wife," Griffith remarks bitterly.

Griffith's Uncle George (Maurice Dallimore) arrives, having been summoned by Frances. He has always denied Griffith his money, and now accuses him of having forged his name on a bank draft. Griffith asks him for money; George refuses. Shortly afterward he appears to succumb to a heart ailment, and a doctor is summoned. After the doctor leaves, Griffith finishes the job.

Helen, ever the busybody, is eavesdropping as usual, and when Griffith advances on her, she falls down the stairs in her wheelchair and is killed. Griffith tries to explain away the dual tragedies, but Frances is unconvinced. "Murderer!" she shouts. "You poisoner!" She runs from the house, only to return with Proctor and police officials, but Griffith brazens it out, saying, "I sent my dear wife to fetch you hours ago." When they accuse him of the murders, he calmly points out that a wife cannot testify against her husband.

Griffith is taken into custody. Larrimore, his attorney (Sam Edwards), comes to see him in prison, expecting to find him in deep distress, but Griffith seems to be enjoying the experience, calling it interesting, and telling him, "As a matter of fact, I am much respected here, not because I am called a poisoner, but because the other prisoners think my crimes earned me £10,000. That makes me their hero, since their own crimes were so much less profitable." He sends Larrimore away and prepares his own defense.

During the preliminary trial, Griffith scoffs at the idea that he possesses an undetectable poison. He avers that there is reasonable doubt as to his guilt; accordingly, he is released. He signs a bank draft, ordering it to be distributed among his fellow prisoners. Avoiding an angry mob in the streets, he returns home to his wife, where he destroys her painting. He brings her a poisoned drink, but before she can down it, the police arrive to arrest Griffith, not for murder but for the forged bank draft drawn on his uncle's account. The penalty is transportation to Australia and a lifetime of hard labor. Rather than accept this, Griffith drinks his own poison and dies, an aristocrat to the end.

The real life counterpart of "The

Poisoner" was Thomas Griffiths Wainewright (1794-1847), art and literary critic (and occasional murderer). In his book *Intentions*, Oscar Wilde defended Wainewright in his critical essay "Pen, Pencil, and Poison: A Study in Green," depicting him as a conscious and misunderstood artist, and supplying the memorable epigram: "The fact of a man being a poisoner is nothing against his prose."

The *Thriller* adaptation of Wainewright's career is hardly a classic, but it's a polished entertainment, witty and all of a piece. Technically a crime episode, the label hardly seems apropos; it's really a character study of an aesthete who happens to be a murderer.

Taking his cue from Wilde, Robert Hardy Andrews' script makes Griffith the hero of the piece: since the so-called good people (Griffith's uncle and in-laws, as well as the police) are so bourgeois, Griffith comes off as the most appealing character. The concept of an aristocratic killer was used for comic effect in *Kind Hearts and Coronets*, and indeed "The Poisoner" is a similar (if less obvious) black comedy. There's an air of "let's see how much we can get away with," and since Griffith's victims are invariably bourgeois, greedy or just plain annoying, it's difficult to fault him, at least on aesthetic grounds. Moreover, Griffith is no mere dilettante: he's an accomplished painter and author, and some of his Wildean asides are so witty and epigrammatic that it's hard to feel much empathy for Frances and Proctor, who seem doltish by comparison. Inevitably, of course, Griffith is hoisted on his own petard; this is the single most unbelievable element in the teleplay, dictated more by censorial ukase than from any internal logic. It's an easy out, though Griffith is at least allowed to die in character. (The real-life Wainewright

was not so fortunate—he did time on an Australian penal colony on a lesser charge.)

There's little of visual interest in "The Poisoner," aside from Helen's fall down the stairs, which is patterned after Arbogast's fall in *Psycho*, and features similar rear projection. For the most part, the episode is left to its actors.

Murray Matheson works wonders in the role of Thomas Edward Griffith. An English actor who worked mostly in American films and television, he is by turns enraged, mocking, even heroic— and always masterful. His film appearances include *Botany Bay* (1953), *Assault on a Queen* (1966), and *Twilight Zone— The Movie* (1983). He was impressive as the clown in the memorable *Twilight Zone* telecast "Five Characters in Search of an Exit." He is also featured in a later *Thriller*, "Letter to a Lover." He died in 1985.

The other actors are, quite properly, overshadowed by Matheson. Sarah Marshall, a beautiful blonde seen to good advantage in "God Grante That She Lye Stille," seems a simpering scatterbrain, and even David Frankham, making the first of his four *Thriller* appearances, comes off as an ineffectual do-gooder. (For more on Frankham, see the entry on "The Closed Cabinet.")

Lastly, and perhaps most notably, "The Poisoner" marked the debut of Herschel Daugherty as a *Thriller* director. He would go on to direct more episodes than anyone else (15, to John Brahm's 11 and Ida Lupino's nine). A television veteran, he directed the pilot for *Wagon Train*, and individual episodes of such series as *Alfred Hitchcock Presents*, *Checkmate*, *The Tall Man* and *General Electric Theater*. He was honored as best director by the Screen Directors' Guild. His film credits are less extensive: *The Light in the Forest* (1958), a Walt Disney feature with James MacArthur, and a western, *The Raiders* (1963). Much of his work for *Thriller* is exemplary ("Waxworks," "The Grim Reaper," and "The Prisoner in the Mirror" are among the finest in the series), and if he had a less distinctive individual style than John Brahm or Ida Lupino, his episodes were no less distinguished for their craftsmanship.

"The Poisoner" provides polished entertainment of an altogether different sort than television viewers have become used to over the past 30 years. It offers a bold, if perfidious, protagonist, and it dares to make sport of death. It may not be among the top rank of *Thrillers*, but it's certainly a memorable and entertaining minor episode.

"Man in the Cage" (airdate: January 17, 1961). Produced by Maxwell Shane. Directed by Gerald Mayer. Teleplay by Maxwell Shane and Stuart Jerome, from the story by John Holbrook Vance. Director of Photography: John L. Russell, A.S.C. Music: Pete Rugolo. Edited by Howard Epstein. Art Director: Russell Kimball. Assistant Director: William Dorfman. Set Decorators: John McCarthy and George Milo.

Cast: Philip Carey (Darrell Hudson), Diana Millay (Ellen), Theo Marcuse (Arthur Upshaw), Barry Gordon (Slip-Slip), Eduardo Cianelli (Inspector), Guy Stockwell (Noel Hudson), Al Ruscio (Allah El Kazim), Daniele Aubry, Than Wyenn, Jonathan Kidd, Pat Sexton, Naji Gabbay, Lilyan Chauvin, Russ Bender, Robert Stevenson, Booth Colman, Arlette Clark, Pedro Regas, Joe Abdullah.

"Man in the Cage" is one of producer Maxwell Shane's livelier outings, a reasonably diverting melange of smuggling, drugs and murder set in an exotic locale.

In Morocco, soldier of fortune Noel Hudson (Guy Stockwell) is running guns. Against his wishes, drugs are being smuggled as well. When a guard pulls a gun on Noel, a struggle ensues and the gun goes off, killing the guard. Noel gets rid of the body and then drives on.

In Tangier some time later Noel's brother, Darrell (Philip Carey), arrives, looking for him. He has not heard from him for weeks. A small boy named Slip-Slip (Barry Gordon) takes him to Noel's apartment. The room has been broken into. Darrell finds a photograph of Noel with a woman on the beach. Shortly afterward Darrell meets Arthur Upshaw (Theo Marcuse) and a girl named Ellen (Diana Millay). Darrell tells Upshaw that Noel sent him a letter telling him he was in trouble and needed money. Upshaw tells him Noel was working for him, smuggling cargo, and disappeared. But Darrell refuses to show him the letter from Noel. "Tangier is a very dangerous city — a stranger on such a quest as yours might make a fatal error," Upshaw tells him.

Darrell spots the girl in the photograph, but she can tell him little of Noel's whereabouts. He gets a call from an unknown man and arranges a meeting at the man's apartment. But when he arrives, he finds the man strung up, dying from being tortured. Darrell cuts him down, but he dies before he can tell him anything. Later, Darrell is visited by an inspector from the Tangier police force (Eduardo Cianelli) who asks about the dead man. Darrell denies any knowledge of him. The inspector tells Darrell he has him booked on a flight out of Tangier leaving in 48 hours.

Having received a message from Ellen, Darrell goes to see her. She tells him the package Noel disappeared with contained $1 million worth of heroin. She proposes that they work together.

But the boy, Slip-Slip, approaches Darrell, telling him a man has sent a message claiming he knows where Noel is. It turns out to be a trap, sprung by two men who want the letter from Noel. They lock Darrell in a cage used for penning animals, then go off to find the letter. He manages to free himself, then locates the two men. One explains that Upshaw was to deliver weapons for the heroin, but they only received two shipments out of a promised 20.

Disillusioned, Darrell returns to his hotel room. After a run-in with Upshaw, he decides to join forces with Ellen. Using her car, they drive to the Hotel Gide d'Etape, where Noel was last seen. He disappeared somewhere on the road between there and Tangier. He sent the heroin ahead by parcel post from the hotel.

Driving along the road, they find the missing truck with ridiculous ease. It went off the side of the road at the spot where Noel was ambushed. Darrell climbs down and finds Noel's body in the cab; he was shot through the head. "The world was just a merry-go-round for Noel; he was always reaching for the brass ring," Darrell remarks, in one of the more egregiously bad lines of dialogue.

Back in Tangier they head for Noel's apartment. In the basement they find the boxes of heroin, which arrived two days after Noel left. Burdett, an American car dealer, turns out to be in on the racket. He prepares to shoot Darrell and Ellen, but the police arrive in the proverbial nick of time, having been summoned by Slip-Slip.

"Man in the Cage" is a fast-paced tale of foreign intrigue with an enticing locale (even if the whole thing was shot on Universal's sound stages), and although it's pretty standard stuff, at least the action is lively and the actors

reasonably proficient. There's one jarring lapse of credibility: after establishing that his brother Noel was ambushed and his truck forced off the road, Darrell Hudson admits that searching for it might be useless. "A truck could stay hidden down there for years," he says, only to find it a few seconds later lying in plain sight, even though the area had been thoroughly searched previously.

The acting is adequate. Philip Carey was a rugged, good looking performer who played Philip Marlowe in the fifties and appeared on the NBC series *Laredo* in the sixties, but for a generation of TV viewers, he is best remembered as the man who asked the immortal question, "Are you man enough for ... Granny Goose?" in a commercial. He's a competent if unexciting actor, playing the stalwart hero with little style; he's a generic hero type in the mold of Peter Graves or Leslie Nielsen, and like many over the hill actors, found gainful employment in soap operas. Since 1979, he has played Asa Buchanan on *One Life to Live*.

Barry Gordon was a busy child actor in the sixties. He wasn't cute, and he isn't particularly appealing as Slip-Slip, the money-grubbing little beggar who attaches himself to Darrell Hudson. Gordon's most memorable role was in *A Thousand Clowns* (1966).

Diana Millay was an attractive blonde. She doesn't have much to do in "Man in the Cage" aside from using her womanly wiles on the hero. She appeared on *Dark Shadows* for a time in the sixties.

Theo Marcuse, a shaven-pated heavy, provides a few moments of stylish villainy as Arthur Upshaw, but he isn't on screen long enough to make much of an impression. He died in 1967.

One actor who manages to rise above the material (if only briefly) is old, reliable Eduardo Cianelli. He makes the most of his limited opportunities, and the episode could have used much more of him. He had a more substantial role in the much later episode, "The Bride Who Died Twice."

"Man in the Cage" is hardly an outstanding episode; it doesn't even stand comparison with the better crime entries such as "The Watcher" or "The Merriweather File." But it's easy to take, tells an interesting (if frankly unoriginal) story, and is by no means as taxing as something like "The Big Blackout." Small praise, perhaps, but the average viewer could do worse.

"Choose a Victim" (airdate: January 24, 1961). Produced by Maxwell Shane. Directed by Richard Carlson. Written by George Bellak. Director of Photography: Lionel Lindon. Music: Pete Rugolo. Editing: John Blunk. Assistant Director: John Bowman. Art Director: Howard E. Johnson.

Cast: Larry Blyden (Ralph Teal), Susan Oliver (Edith Landers), Vaughn Taylor (Phil), Guy Mitchell (Hazlett), Tracy Roberts (Fay), Billy Barty (Sam), Henry Corden (Sid Benajain), Henry Hunter.

"Choose a Victim" is an adequate, if unexceptional, *Thriller* that looks more like an episode of *Alfred Hitchcock Presents.*

Ladies' man Ralphie Teal (Larry Blyden) spots an attractive young girl named Edith Landers (Susan Oliver) drive up in an expensive sports car. He tampers with her engine, then "happens" along just in time to fix it. He has coffee with her, then meets her later on the beach, and invites her over to his place. Edith lives with her uncle, with whom she does not get along, in a big house. Ralph notes Edith's expensive jewelry.

Edith's uncle Phil (Vaughn Taylor) is anxiously trying to marry her off to a suitable young man. Ralph sneaks into their home, intending to burgle it, but Edith awakens. Ralph admits his intentions, and turns to leave, promising never to see her again, but Edith calls him back. "I understand ... honestly I do, how you feel about my having things, and you just don't." They presumably spend the night together.

The next day at the beach, Edith gives Ralph an expensive cigarette lighter as a gift. Later, she also presents him with a sweater, but tells him she can't be seen in public with him; her uncle is looking for an excuse to fight and drive her from the house, which belonged to Edith's parents and is rightfully hers.

They go on meeting under the pier. Ralph suggests they do away with Uncle Phil; after all, no one has seen them together. Edith refuses. "We work it so it looks like an accident," Ralph suggests; otherwise he will leave her. Edith reluctantly agrees.

Ralph arranges for Phil to have a fatal "accident" caused by Edith nudging him over a cliff, but at the last moment, she freezes. "I wanted to do what you said, but I couldn't," she says. Ralph resolves to try again, this time by himself. After an aborted second attempt, Ralph knocks Phil unconscious, then puts him in his car and sends him over the cliff.

The next morning the police take Ralph in for questioning. They accuse him of murder. Edith is brought in; Ralph denies knowing her. Edith claims that he bothered her on the beach, then followed her home and met her and her uncle on another occasion. Stung, Ralph blurts out the truth. "You set it all up from the very beginning, didn't you, so that I'd do it for you?" Ralph says, "Can't you see it was her?" he shouts at the police. "Can't you see it?"

Leaving, Edith discovers she has lost a glove. She returns to Ralph's place to retrieve it, but Ralph's ex-girlfriend, Fay (Tracy Roberts), has picked it up. When Edith tries to grab it back, her wrist is encircled by a policeman's hand. He tells her they suspected her for some time. If Edith had never known Ralph, as she claimed, why did his shirt smell so strongly of her expensive perfume?

Though "Choose a Victim" is competently directed and acted, there's really little or nothing to distinguish it from the numerous murder for profit playlets presented so regularly on Hitchcock's show, giving it a slightly shopworn, seen-it-before quality. Even the final twist, while clever, smacks of irrelevance. In addition, the characters are clichéd, and the actors, though adequate, can do little to enliven them.

Larry Blyden (spouting outdated hipster jargon, calling his car a "heap" and looking for someone to "swing" with) is unappealing as Ralph (although this was presumably intentional). A familiar presence on TV throughout the fifties and sixties, Blyden was perfectly cast as go-getter Sammy Glick in a 1959 NBC production of *What Makes Sammy Run?* He also played in a 1960 *Moment of Fear* dramatization of *Conjure Wife* that Fritz Leiber claimed was the best adaptation of his novel. Blyden guested on *The Twilight Zone* and *The Alfred Hitchcock Hour,* and emceed numerous game shows during the sixties and seventies. In an ironic postscript, he died in 1975 in an auto accident strikingly similar to the one he tries to arrange for Vaughn Taylor in "Choose a Victim."

Susan Oliver, a beautiful green-eyed blonde, plays Edith adequately. Oliver appeared frequently on television throughout the sixties; she played Ann Howard on the long-running *Peyton Place.* She died of cancer in 1990.

Vaughn Taylor hasn't much to work with as her uncle Phil: he's simply there to act disagreeable and get bumped off. Taylor was frequently seen on TV and in movies, and is perhaps best remembered as Marion Crane's boss in Hitchcock's *Psycho* (1960). He can also be seen in a much later *Thriller,* "Cousin Tundifer." He died in 1983.

"Choose a Victim" is a resolutely average episode, certainly not the best Maxwell Shane was capable of producing, but still mildly enjoyable, even if it lacks real distinction.

"Hay-Fork and Bill-Hook"

(airdate: February 7, 1961). Produced by William Frye. Directed by Herschel Daugherty. Written by Alan Caillou. Director of Photography: Benjamin H. Kline, A.S.C. Music by Jerry Goldsmith. Edited by Danny Landres. Art Director: Howard E. Johnson. Assistant Director: Edward K. Dodds. Set Decorators: John McCarthy and Hal Gausman.

Cast: Kenneth Haigh (Detective Inspector Harry Roberts), Audrey Dalton (Nesta Roberts), Alan Napier (Constable Evans), Alan Caillou (Sir Wilfred), Doris Lloyd (Mrs. Evans), J. Pat O'Malley, Lumsden Hare, Ronald Long, Basil Howes, Kendrick Huxham, Richard Peel, Gil Stuart, Barry Bernard, Iris Bristol.

An atmospheric but curiously unsatisfying episode, "Hay-Fork and Bill-Hook" promises a good deal more than it delivers. Still, it's not entirely without interest.

In the small village of Dark Woods, near some Druidic stones deep in the mountains of the Welsh borders, a lone man is stalked and killed by some unseen presence wielding a hay-fork who then carves a cross on the body with a bill-hook — methods used in the ritual killing of witches.

Detective Inspector Harry Roberts of Scotland Yard (Kenneth Haigh) arrives at the village. He is on his honeymoon with his bride, Nesta (Audrey Dalton). As they look over the ancient stones, he remarks, "They say the spirits of the slaves who brought them here still watch over them." He also tells her that ritual sacrifices on St. Valentine's Day are performed to appease the harvest gods. They are confronted by Constable Evans (Alan Napier), armed with a hay-fork. "There are evil spirits about," the superstitious constable remarks. "Evil spirits and evil people." He stares suspiciously at Nesta.

During the drive to the village, Nesta nearly causes an accident, telling Harry he's about to hit a black dog. But after he runs off the road, there is no sign of the animal. They continue on foot to the home of Sir Wilfred (Alan Caillou). When Nesta tells him of the dog, Sir Wilfred informs them there are no such animals in the village — a black dog is considered an omen of death. Forty years ago, he tells them, a villager said he saw a black dog that changed into a headless woman. Since that time the man was bewitched; he was the one who was ritualistically murdered. When Sir Wilfred learns his wicker hamper is missing, Nesta remarks that it is just the kind the Druids used in executing their victims. What's more, she can foresee the exorcising of a witch, even feeling the flames. Harry protests that the Druids have been gone for a thousand years. Still, Sir Wilfred advises the Robertses not to mention the black dog to the villagers. "The hidden forces here, Mr. Roberts, are powerful forces because the people believe in them," he says. He reminds Harry that no one but his wife saw the black dog, and that she is young, beautiful — and bewitching. Nesta, meanwhile, sees a fire burning near the stones, and they rush to the scene.

In the village pub the locals are discussing Nesta. The barman comments on the light in her eyes. Constable Evans tells them she has seen the black dog. The Robertses and Sir Wilfred arrive at the pub. An old woman has been burned as a witch and taken to the druidic stones in the wicker basket stolen from Sir Wilfred's house. Harry maintains that they are dealing with madness, not witchcraft. Sir Wilfred confesses that his own father died in a mental institution.

Alone in their room at the inn, Nesta again sees the black dog and calls for Harry, but when he comes running in, the dog is gone.

The following day Harry sends Nesta to the county seat to look up the local archives. The librarian tells her that Sir Wilfred's father was in love with a village girl, but never married her; she later married Constable Evans' father. The loss drove Sir Wilfred's father out of his mind. Nesta asks to see the records of births for the past 40 to 50 years.

Harry, meanwhile, has men with metal detectors combing the grounds for a watch belonging to the murdered man. Nesta arrives and tells him that Constable Evans is actually Sir Wilfred's brother. They locate the watch and Harry announces that he will take it to the post office; from there it will be sent to Scotland Yard to be examined for fingerprints. He hopes the murderer will try to steal the watch during the night.

Back at the inn, Mrs. Evans (Doris Lloyd) accuses Nesta of being a witch. "You killed him, didn't you?" Nesta asks. "Yes," the old woman says. Nesta tries to escape, but is taken captive by Constable Evans. "Take her to the burning place," his mother orders. They bind and gag her, and carry her off in the basket. Harry, meanwhile, is keeping his vigil outside the post office.

Sir Wilfred, armed with a scythe,

confronts Evans, telling him to let the girl go. They fight, and Sir Wilfred is run through with a hay-fork. Harry, meanwhile, having seen the black dog, rushes to the inn, only to find Nesta gone. Seeing the fire amid the stones, he hurries back. He and Evans fight; he overpowers the older man and rescues Nesta, then takes Constable Evans and his mother into custody.

The major fault with "Hay-Fork and Bill-Hook" is that the stage is so beautifully set for a story replete with witchcraft and druidic rites that it's doubly disappointing when nothing much happens and the episode culminates with the killer's arrest. The appearance of the black dog (and Karloff's potent introduction) leads one to suspect the supernatural may be involved, but the ambiguity that *Thriller* thrived on is present only fleetingly. Almost from the beginning, it is obvious that it's strictly a murder case, and all the promising hints of witchcraft remain firmly in the background.

That's not to say that "Hay-Fork and Bill-Hook" is without interest. Alan Caillou's teleplay contains some interesting local lore and insights into country folk: Sir Wilfred shows Harry a hand warmer used by the locals — a small cylinder into which live coals are placed, a useful item on the cold moors. In another scene, men with metal detectors find a mole spike on the grounds. And when Nesta remarks to the librarian that the druidic stones are ancient, she's told they're quite modern — less than 1,100 years old.

Kenneth Haigh was an appealing young British actor who originated the stage role of Jimmy Porter in John Osborne's *Look Back in Anger*. His film career was undistinguished; he appeared in *Cleopatra* (1963) and *A Hard Day's Night* (1964), and was in "Banquo's

Chair," a memorable episode of *Alfred Hitchcock Presents* actually directed by Hitchcock. He's quite good as Harry Roberts.

Alan Caillou and Audrey Dalton had worked together previously in "The Prediction." Of the two, Caillou comes off far better as Sir Wilfred, even though he's obviously a red herring. Audrey Dalton, unfortunately, fails to come off at all. She's inept in all three of her *Thriller* appearances; here, as Nesta, she isn't believable at all, and her inadequate playing is thrown into sharper relief by the actors around her.

Alan Napier, on the other hand, seems to be having a fine time as Constable Evans. Napier was also in three *Thrillers*, but this is his largest part. Normally seen in dignified roles, here he's a grubby-looking backwoods constable, somewhat similar to the tramp he played in *The Invisible Man Returns* (1940). A friend of James Whale's, Napier was usually seen as a butler or a noble lord. His genre films include *The House of the Seven Gables* (1940), *The Uninvited* (1944), *House of Horrors* (1946), and *Journey to the Center of the Earth* (1959), but he's probably best known as the loyal butler Alfred on television's *Batman*. He died in 1988.

Special praise must be accorded Jerry Goldsmith for his outstanding score. As Randall Larson notes in his book *Musique Fantastique*, "Goldsmith wrote a pretty Irish folk tune alternately played by woodwind and viola over rhythmic strings, balanced by atonal, conflicting string figures." And reviewer John Caps, in *Filmmusic Notebook*, writes that "While the murder mystery on screen was pedestrian and pedantic, the music immersed us in the atmosphere of the setting and built up a frightful mood of unpredictable tension."

"The Merriweather File" (airdate: February 14, 1961). Produced by Maxwell Shane. Directed by John Brahm. Teleplay by John Kneubuhl, from the novel by Lionel White. Music: Pete Rugolo. Director of Photography: John L. Russell, A.S.C. Edited by Richard Belding. Art Director: Russell Kimball. Assistant Director: Frank Losee. Set Decorators: John McCarthy and Julia Heron.

Cast: Bethel Leslie (Ann Merriweather), James Gregory (Howard Yates), Edward Binns (Lieutenant Giddeon), Ross Elliott (Charles Merriweather), K. T. Stevens (Virginia Grant), Bernard Fein, Nesdon Booth, Richard Reeves, Gil Perkins.

"The Merriweather File," based on the novel by Lionel White (author of *Clean Break*, which became Stanley Kubrick's *The Killing*), is one of *Thriller's* more satisfying crime entries, due to its ingeniously twisted plot.

A mysterious figure breaks into a suburban home and turns on the gas, intending to kill its occupant, and leaves a child's rubber ball as a calling card. Ann Merriweather (Bethel Leslie) awakens, smells the gas and cries out for help. Her neighbor, Howard Yates (James Gregory), comes running in; when he asks about the rubber ball, Ann explains that it belonged to her dead boy, Billy. Ann's husband, Charles, is away at work, and will not return until the following day. When Howard tries to call the police, Ann dissuades him. She tells him this wasn't the first attempt on her life; three years before, just after Billy was killed due to her negligence, Ann tried to kill herself. But tonight is different. Howard tells Ann to have her husband buy her a dog for safety and companionship.

Charles Merriweather (Ross Elliott) arrives home with the dog. Later he goes to his club while Ann stays home with a headache. The next day Charles has a blowout on the road; when a garageman arrives to change the tire, a policeman happens along just as the car's trunk is opened, revealing a dead body.

Lieutenant Giddeon (Edward Binns), questions Charles, but he insists he doesn't know the dead man's identity. Charles confides to Howard, his attorney, that he was out with another woman and didn't get home until 6 a.m. Howard tells him to contact the woman for an alibi, but Charles refuses; he won't subject Ann to the disgrace, and he tells Howard he wants the woman left out of it, if possible. Lieutenant Giddeon shows Charles' trunk key to Howard; Charles apparently lied about not having it when the police arrested him. When Ann goes home that night, the intruder is back, going through the bureau drawers. The figure grabs Ann, then runs out of the house. Ann screams; Howard comes running, but there is no sign of the mysterious figure.

The next day the police, combing the grounds outside the Merriweather house, find Charles' gun hidden in the garbage. Howard tells Charles that he will have to contact his woman friend; Charles reluctantly agrees. In the meantime, the dead man has been identified as Jay Carver, tout, bookie, petty thief.

Howard drops by to see Virginia Grant (K. T. Stevens), the woman who was with Charles that night. She agrees to provide Charles with the alibi he needs. But when Howard goes through one of Virginia's photo albums, he finds pictures of her with Jay Carver. He returns to see Ann, who tells him that Charles made a withdrawal of $3,000 from their bank account, possibly to pay off Carver. "Every move I make just seems to get him deeper into this thing,"

Howard laments. "I want to believe he's innocent, I know he's innocent, and yet…" He hires a private investigator, who finds that Charles owed Jay Carver gambling debts. "You've practically hanged your client by making Virginia Grant talk," the investigator tells Howard. Carver deposited $3,000 in his account. What's more, Virginia is being held by the police as Charles' accomplice.

Despite all this, Charles still insists he's innocent. He is tried, found guilty, and electrocuted.

Sometime later, Howard is home, trimming the Christmas tree when he receives an unexpected visitor: Lieutenant Giddeon. He tells Howard that Virginia Grant, who is dying, has revealed the truth behind the Merriweather case: Charles Merriweather didn't kill Jay Carver, but he was behind the attempted murder of his wife, committed by Virginia while disguised as a man. Charles blamed Ann for the death of their son. He then hired a professional killer — Carver — and paid him $3,000. Carver tried to kill Ann: instead, she killed him with Charles' gun. Wanting revenge on Charles, she put the body in the trunk of his car and planted his gun in the garbage. Charles couldn't tell the truth, as it would implicate him and Virginia Grant. Ann had her revenge, watching the law destroy Charles.

Just then a figure enters the house, laden with holiday gifts. "This is my wife, Ann," Howard says.

"Congratulations," Lieutenant Giddeon replies, "and a Merry Christmas."

"The Merriweather File" ranks as one of the better crime episodes of *Thriller*. There are surprises aplenty, and even if one foresees the final twist (that Ann Merriweather has become Howard's wife) there are still ample shocks in store. Some are petty contrivances: when

Charles Merriweather's car trunk is opened, the police happen along at just the right moment to see the body. In addition, some characters' motivations (particularly Ann Merriweather's) seem arbitrary. But these are minor quibbles: events unravel so swiftly that one hardly has time to notice, much less object; only on a second viewing does one have a chance to spot inconsistencies. John Brahm has little time to create an atmospheric *mise en scène* (the plot simply moves too swiftly), but the action is effectively managed. There are numerous clever instances of foreshadowing: before we learn that Ann has married Howard, for example, we see her dog in his living room, and their growing affection is subtly delineated through gestures and asides.

The acting is remarkably consistent. Bethel Leslie, a lovely blonde who appeared in "Child's Play," is fine as Ann Merriweather. James Gregory likewise does a fine job as Howard Yates. Gregory was a familiar face in movies and television (he played the McCarthyite senator John Dierkes Iselin in *The Manchurian Candidate* [1962], and was a regular on "Barney Miller"). Edward Binns, for some reason done up in obtrusive (and unconvincing) makeup as Lieutenant Giddeon, is good, as always. Binns was one of the *Twelve Angry Men* (1957), and was a frequent guest on television throughout the sixties. Ross Elliott, too, is believable as the beleaguered Charles Merriweather. Elliott played minor roles in movies and was a regular for three years on TV's long-running *The Virginian*. Buffs may recall him from *Tarantula* (1955), *The Indestructible Man* (1956) and *Monster on the Campus* (1958).

One of Maxwell Shane's best episodes, "The Merriweather File" deserves greater acclaim for its ingenious story line and effective acting. It may not be top-notch *Thriller*, but it is a diverting crime entry with some effective shocks for the unwary viewer.

"The Fingers of Fear" (airdate: February 21, 1961). Produced by William Frye. Directed by Jules Bricken. Written by Robert H. Andrews. Director of Photography: Benjamin Kline. Edited by Danny Landres. Music: Pete Rugolo. Assistant Director: Donald Baer. Art Director: Russell Kimball.

Cast: Nehemiah Persoff (Lieutenant Jim Wagner), Robert Middleton (Ohrback), Kevin Hagen (Spivak), Thayer Roberts (Merriman), Robert J. Stevenson (Dr. Lascoe), H. M. Wynant (Sid), Dick Wessel (Zimmer), Sam Gilman (Officer Dutton), Ted deCorsia.

"The Fingers of Fear," like "The Watcher," is a strong crime drama once again emphasizing that appearances can be deceptive and leading to an unexpected and frightening finale.

An elementary school teacher goes after a ball knocked out of the playground, and finds a dead little girl's body in the park, the latest in a series of child murders. The police are looking for an overweight, brutish looking man, a description that fits Ohrback (Robert Middleton), a simple-minded dishwasher who works nearby.

Lieutenant Jim Wagner (Nehemiah Persoff) finds a fragment of something he cannot identify in the park. Nearby, a rare type of blood is found on the scene. Ohrback, meanwhile, drives to a nearby lake and throws a knife in the water. Unbeknownst to him, a small boy fishing nearby retrieves it from the water and takes it to the police. He gives a description of Ohrback and his car. Another man who saw Ohrback in the park at the time of the killing reports his license number to the police. Ohrback

paints his old car and trades it in for another, then asks his friend, Zimmer (Dick Wessel), to lie, setting up an alibi.

Wagner, meanwhile, has traced Ohrback to his job at the Sunrise Diner. Ohrback makes a run for it, but Wagner stops him. The boy and the man in the park both pick Ohrback out of a lineup. Zimmer then tells the police that Ohrback's alibi is phony. There is one setback: the rare blood type does not match Ohrback's. He is arrested anyway, but Wagner isn't satisfied. "The pieces don't fit together right," he says. Shortly afterward a friend of Wagner's small daughter Kathy is picked up by a man with a talking doll.

Wagner's partner, Spivak (Kevin Hagen), has identified the fragment Wagner found in the park: it is from the foot of a doll, a very expensive type made by only one toy factory in Italy. They find a shop that sells the dolls; only three have been sold in the past six months. When Wagner shows Ohrback the doll, he says he saw a man in the park with one of the same design. The police psychiatrist explains that the psychopath may lavish his love on an inanimate figure; if he reaches for reality and a little girl rejects him, something snaps. Wagner finds the doll with the broken foot in a doll hospital, but there is no description of the owner. They eventually track him down: his name is Merriman. In the meantime the little girl in the park is saved when she runs into a teacher and the man with the doll runs away.

At home, Merriman (Thayer Roberts), the man with the doll, is living in a fantasy world, with the doll seated at the dinner table, where he serves her a meal. Wagner and Spivak are watching from the doorway. "We're happy together," Merriman tells the doll. "We love each other, don't we?" The two policemen walk in and tell Merriman he is under arrest, but when they try to take the doll, he stabs it repeatedly with a knife rather than surrender it, then breaks down in tears.

"The Fingers of Fear," aside from its irrelevant title, is a disturbing episode, more topical now than when initially telecast. Once again, it is a warning to look beyond the surface of things, particularly people. Ohrback, the overweight, feeble-minded man repeatedly described as looking like a monster in a movie, is innocent; the real killer is a respectable-looking man in a suit who can afford the finer things in life, such as an expensive talking doll.

A taut little drama, filmed in a gritty, hard-edged style, "The Fingers of Fear" takes on the trappings of fantasy at its climax as we enter the fetishistic world of the killer. His attack on the doll he loves so much has a sick fascination; it's more disturbing than if he actually attacked another little girl.

The performances are excellent. Nehemiah Persoff, who trained at the Actors' Studio, is especially good as Lieutenant Wagner. His films include *On the Waterfront* (1954), *This Angry Age* (1957), *Some Like It Hot* (1959), *Fate Is the Hunter* (1964), *The Power* (1968) and *Psychic Killer* (1975).

Robert Middleton has the showy part—a feeble-minded man described as a monster, and he plays it sympathetically. Alternately touching and pathetic, he's at his best in the scene in which he caresses the doll like a small boy. Middleton, who was somewhat similar to Robert Strauss, was nearly always cast as a villain, and was seen in such films as *The Desperate Hours* (1955), *The Court Jester* (1956), and *A Big Hand for the Little Lady* (1966). He's in a later *Thriller*, "Guillotine." He died in 1975.

Kevin Hagen is adequate but unexceptional as Spivak. He would be seen in

a later (and lesser) *Thriller*, "Flowers of Evil."

"The Fingers of Fear" can only be described as one of the more disturbing *Thrillers*; unlike the horror episodes, there's no solace in any supernatural trappings—its setting is, all too clearly, the real world.

"Well of Doom" (airdate: February 28, 1961). Produced by William Frye. Directed by John Brahm. Teleplay by Donald S. Sanford, based on the short story by John Clemons. Music: Jerry Goldsmith. Director of Photography: Lionel Lindon, A.S.C. Edited by Richard Belding. Art Director: Howard E. Johnson. Assistant Director: Edward K. Dodds. Editorial Supervisor: David J. O'Connell. Musical Supervision: Stanley Wilson. Sound: John W. Rixey. Set Decorators: John McCarthy and Hal Gausman.

Cast: Ronald Howard (Robert Penrose), Henry Daniell (Squire Moloch), Torin Thatcher (Jeremy Teal), Fintan Meyler (Laura Denning), Richard Kiel (Styx), Billy Beck (Cyril), Molly Glessing, Diana Bourbon.

"Well of Doom" is one of *Thriller*'s creepiest first season classics. It's so loaded with fine performances and an overpowering atmosphere of gloom that it's easy to overlook its faults, particularly the ending, in which the seemingly supernatural events we have witnessed are none too convincingly rationalized.

A car is sweeping through the English countryside in the fog. In the back are Robert Penrose (Ronald Howard), on his way to a bachelor party being thrown for him, and Jeremy Teal (Torin Thatcher), the overseer of his late father's estate. Suddenly the car comes to a halt in front of a huge man dressed in 17th-century garb (Richard Kiel). The figure drags the chauffeur out of the car and begins crushing the life out of him.

A weird figure (Henry Daniell) materializes out of the fog. "Call your brute off, man — he's killing him," Teal says. "No power on earth can help your chauffeur now, Mr. Penrose," the figure announces. "Who are you?" Penrose asks. "What do you want?" "Some call be Beelzebub," the figure replies. "Some call me Belial; you may call me Moloch — Squire Moloch." He orders the huge man, named Styx, to dragoon the others into the car.

A few hours before, in Hardwick Castle, Penrose had been surprised to receive a visit from Teal, since they were not on speaking terms. Deciding to bury the hatchet, they drank to Penrose's fiancée, Laura Denning (Fintan Meyler). Teal also agreed to accompany Penrose to a stag party that night.

But while Laura was lying in bed that night, Styx entered the room and clamped a huge hand over her face.

Back in the present, Squire Moloch is keeping two pistols trained on Penrose and Teal. Penrose offers Moloch money — half a million pounds. "It's not enough," Moloch declares. Abandoning the car, Moloch begins leading his captives across the moors. At one point he snaps his fingers and Styx's torches burst into flame. They reach the ruins of a Gothic stronghold, part of Penrose's estate. Teal makes a grab for Moloch's pistols, and Penrose keeps Styx at bay with a torch. But when Teal makes a run for it, Moloch points his finger at him and Teal falls dead. Penrose attacks Moloch, but is knocked unconscious.

When he awakens, Penrose is inside a prison cell — the place was once a dungeon. "What do you want?" Penrose asks Moloch. "Vengeance," Moloch answers. He shows Penrose a well in the center of the cell. "In that well your father

drowned the rightful owner of this estate and usurped his property and position," he says. "Who?" Penrose demands. "He killed — me," Moloch says, then explains: "I could not come back during your father's lifetime; I had not earned the right. But I was permitted to return on the eve of your marriage to take my rightful place as master of Hardwick." He tells Penrose that Laura will be his bride; she has been bound and gagged, and lies helpless in another cell. Moloch shows Penrose a paper that will confer all of Penrose's property and money upon him. But Penrose refuses to sign it; he fears they will kill him and Laura if he does.

After Moloch leaves, Penrose manages to loosen one of the bars on his cell. He tries to free Laura, but the bolt on her cell door is jammed. Returning to his cell, he rips his coat apart to make a rope from the jagged lengths of cloth. He lowers this rope into the well, securing one end to a peg which he drives into the side.

Moloch returns, threatening to send Styx to call on Laura. Penrose signs the paper. "Now, keep your part of the bargain," Penrose says. "Release us." "Your release is only seconds away," Moloch says. Styx begins to advance on Penrose; the giant picks him up and throws him into the well. They leave him to drown.

Penrose climbs up the rope, despite a loosened peg, and leaves his cell. There is no sign of Laura. He heads upstairs, where he overhears Moloch and Styx laughing together. "Just shows you how costume and the right atmosphere can let you fake anything," Moloch says. He is actually a stage magician named Riley. He tells Styx, whose real name is Joe, to finish off Laura. But Joe worries about the chauffeur. "What if he talks?" he asks. "Cyril's my problem," says Teal, alive and hearty. "You two just finish what you were hired to do." Teal intends to say that Penrose and Laura eloped; he will stay on as overseer and bleed the estate white. But Riley and Teal have a falling out over the money and, in a dual shootout, manage to kill each other. Penrose walks into the room, stalking Joe, who screams, "No, you're dead! Go away!" and then falls to his death from the top of the stairs.

Penrose finds Laura, bound and gagged but unharmed, in another room.

"Well of Doom" is a memorable adventure in the macabre. Even though, as expected, the seemingly supernatural events witnessed are no more than a magician's tricks, the episode exudes a disturbing miasma from first to last. John Brahm was an inspired choice as director, and his gift for atmosphere is perhaps better exemplified here than in any other episode. Moloch and Styx, two "netherworld creatures," as Karloff calls them, parade through fog enshrouded moors, past gnarled trees, their torches flaming in the dense fog, and the eerie photography makes the most of their nocturnal prowling. In addition, the slow, deliberate pacing gives the episode a curiously dreamlike, disturbing quality ("I must be dreaming," Penrose comments at one point). And Brahm adds imaginative touches whenever possible: when Styx bends over Laura's bed to abduct her, we see him from her perspective, upside down.

Everything about the story line takes advantage of the weird possibilities inherent in the basic material. (There's a particularly eerie moment when Moloch tells Penrose that he drowned in the well and returned from the dead; it's enough to make one suspend disbelief in the supernatural after all.) Donald S. Sanford's teleplay, based on John Clemons' short story, bears a resemblance to the Lon Chaney film *London After Midnight* (1927). In that long-lost silent classic (remade as *Mark of the Vampire* in 1935) Chaney played a detective who dressed up as a weird vampire skulking around an abandoned dwelling in order to frighten a murderer into confessing. Here things are switched around a bit, with the masqueraders being the villains, but Henry Daniell's bizarre appearance strangely resembles Chaney's — they both wear beaver hats with white hair jutting out underneath, and both have strange-looking sidekicks (in Chaney's case, a vampirish young woman).

There's another reading of "Well of Doom" suggested by Greek mythology. Penrose, whose name is very suggestive, is in effect taken to the land of the dead; after surviving various tortures and refusing to succumb to temptation, his Orphic descent into the underworld is complete when he is "killed" by being thrown into the well. After his immersion, which can be read as a kind of baptism, he is "reborn" a stronger man for all his experiences — no longer the trusting dupe he was at the beginning — and reunited with his lover.

The acting is first-rate, for the most part. Ronald Howard is quite believable as the bedeviled Robert Penrose. Howard, the son of noted screen star Leslie Howard, played Sherlock Holmes in a syndicated television series during the fifties. He appeared in such films as *The Queen of Spades* (1948) and Hammer's *The Curse of the Mummy's Tomb* (1964). Doug Benton remembers him as "just someone who was along for the ride. He really didn't take acting seriously. He was better looking than his father, and bigger. He was a competent actor, but he could have been a lot more." He also appears in two other *Thrillers*, "God Grante That She Lye

Stille" and "The Specialists." He seems to have retired from acting.

Henry Daniell has the best role of his five *Thriller* appearances, and the veteran actor makes the most of it. With his Mephistophelian appearance (conspicuously missing a front tooth), he's equipped with first-rate dialogue ("Hark to this dandy: the wine must be a potent brew to fire such courage in such a lily liver"), and hisses his line with diabolic relish. Hollywood made poor use of Daniell's talents; as John and Michael Brunas and Tom Weaver point out in their book *Universal Horrors*:

> Daniell's film career seemed doomed for the outset by his rigid, unyielding demeanor (ironically, in his younger days, Daniell frequently complained to interviewers of his resentment towards being typecast as a juvenile) ... Daniell's stylish villainy insured him of a busy career right up until his death in 1963, but his contempt for Tinsel Town wasn't entirely justified; he simply had neither the stature nor the flexibility of a Claude Rains or Cedric Hardwicke.

(For more on Daniell, see the entry on "The Cheaters.")

Torin Thatcher, one of the screen's great villains, has an unusually benevolent role (at least until the climax), but he invests it with his usual gruff authority and even arouses a measure of sympathy for the perfidious Teal. Afflicted with a limp in private life (it's particularly evident in several scenes in "Well of Doom"), Thatcher normally played heavies and figures of authority. He made his film debut in 1934; his films include *Great Expectations* (1946), *The Crimson Pirate* (1952) and *Witness for the Prosecution* (1957). He's probably best known as the evil magician in *The Seventh Voyage of Sinbad* (1958); he played

virtually the same role in *Jack the Giant Killer* (1962). He died in 1981.

Richard Kiel makes an impressive appearance as the giant Styx. (It's a nicely ironic touch that after posing as a supernatural menace throughout, he's frightened by Penrose's apparent return from the dead; although it's a bit difficult to accept that three of the leading characters — Teal, Moloch and Styx — all die within the space of less than a minute.) Kiel, of course, has been a familiar presence for more than 30 years, starting out on television and then appearing in low-budget films like *The Phantom Planet, Eegah!* (both 1962) and *House of the Damned* (1963). Unfortunately, at the time he made "Well of Doom" he wasn't much of an actor (he was only 21 years old), and this is evident in his dialogue scenes with Henry Daniell and Torin Thatcher. He improved greatly later on, making an impression as the steel-toothed "Jaws" in two James Bond films, *The Spy Who Loved Me* (1977) and *Moonraker* (1979). He was a regular on the short-lived TV series *The Barbary Coast*, and turned up frequently on *The Wild, Wild West* as Michael Dunn's giant henchman. Doug Benton recalls that "Kiel had some sort of medical condition, and he had very little stamina. If you worked him too hard he had to sit down and rest. He must have built himself up later on, because by the time he did the James Bond pictures they had him doing all kinds of incredible things."

Fintan Meyler has little to do as Laura Denning. She spends much of her time bound and gagged in a dungeon.

"Well of Doom" commands a special place among the list of *Thriller* classics. It may not be supernatural, but it's (once again) a fine example of crisscrossing genres, a style that works to the episode's (and the viewer's) advantage.

"The Ordeal of Dr. Cordell"

(airdate: March 7, 1961). Produced by Maxwell Shane. Directed by Laszlo Benedek. Written by Donald S. Sanford. Director of Photography: Benjamin Kline. Music: Morton Stevens. Edited by Danny Landres. Art Director: Howard E. Johnson. Assistant Director: Frank Lossee. Set Decorators: John McCarthy and William L. Stevens.

Cast: Robert Vaughn (Dr. Frank Cordell), Kathleen Crowley (Dr. Lois Walker), Robert Ellenstein (Dr. Brauner), Russ Conway (Lieutenant Boutaric), Marlo Thomas (Susan Baker), Helen Brown, Lorrie Richards, Norm Williams.

One of the most compelling of the first season *Thrillers*, "The Ordeal of Dr. Cordell" may well be producer Maxwell Shane's best episode ever. Buoyed by fine acting (particularly by Robert Vaughn), it's a chilling account of one man's descent into madness.

A man working in the lab at Pendleton College has an accident in which test tubes break. He puts out the resultant fire with an extinguisher, but his gas mask does not work, and he collapses after inhaling the fumes. Upon examination, he has no heartbeat.

Dr. Cordell (Robert Vaughn) revives after an injection of adrenaline. Other than having a splitting headache, he feels all right. Cordell tells Dr. Brauner (Robert Ellenstein) that a new kind of gas was generated by the fire, which occurred while he was seeking an antidote to nerve gas.

His fiancée, Dr. Lois Walker (Kathleen Crowley), drives him home. When a bird in a cage tolls a bell, the sound affects Cordell, almost driving him out of his mind. His heart begins to pound and any sound is amplified. Lois comforts him, telling him it's an aftereffect of the accident. But once he is alone, he hears the bell again, setting him off.

Cordell sleeps late the next day. His landlady's screams bring him running; her bird has been killed, presumably by neighborhood boys.

Later that day Cordell comments to Lois: "Despite the job we're facing, I feel positively stimulated." Reaching for matches, he finds the bird's bell in his pocket.

For the next three weeks they try to recreate the gas. One night, after Lois has left, Cordell stays late to check over his notes. A young student named Susan Baker (Marlo Thomas) enters by mistake, looking for the library. She is wearing earrings with bells. The sound sets Cordell off; he pursues her across the campus and kills her. The next morning he wakes up with one of her earrings on his nightstand.

Driving over to the college, Cordell sees a police car parked outside the chemistry building. Lois is being questioned by Lieutenant Boutaric (Russ Conway) of the homicide squad. He asks Cordell if he has heard of the murder of a young coed on campus. "Poor thing — what he did to her," Lois comments.

Dr. Brauner gives Cordell a physical examination, but finds nothing wrong with him. Afterward he hears Lieutenant Boutaric telling Brauner the killer tore off Susan's earrings, dropping one near the scene of the crime. "What kind of psycho would ignore her wristwatch and the money in her purse and just take a worthless little thing like this?" Boutaric asks. Dr. Brauner explains that a sudden change in brain chemistry could turn a normal man into a killer.

Cordell is becoming obsessed with his work, not leaving the lab for days, searching desperately for an antidote to the gas. He and Lois quarrel. "Ever since that accident you've been on a one man rampage." she says, storming out of the lab. When Cordell goes after her, he runs into Lieutenant Boutaric. He tells him the killer will go on the prowl again — "that type has to."

"Type?" Cordell asks.

"You didn't see what he did to that girl, did you?" Boutaric asks. "I wish I hadn't."

Dr. Brauner suggests Cordell take a vacation. When he refuses, Brauner offers him a choice: hand in his resignation or marry Lois and go on his honeymoon. "The day you became personally involved in this problem you ceased being a scientist," he tells Cordell.

That night the school is having a bonfire. Students are cheering their team, but one of the rooters, a coed, has a bell. The sound sets Cordell off. He pursues her and kills her.

Cordell wakes up in a hotel. On the floor is the bell and a newspaper with the headline STRANGLER STRIKES AGAIN. He calls the lab and talks to Lois, telling her to give up the experiments. She tries to tell him they've isolated the element in the gas, but Cordell isn't listening. He tells her he's got to speak to her alone. She suggests meeting at a chapel. Meanwhile, Lieutenant Boutaric tells Dr. Brauner he suspects Cordell of the crimes. He has found the dead girl's earring in Cordell's room.

Cordell waits for Lois at the chapel. But the bell in the tower begins to chime, setting him off; screaming in agony, he runs up the tower, trying to stop it. Lois arrives and, hearing his screams, follows him. He attacks her, then falls to his death.

Although "The Ordeal of Dr. Cordell" was produced by Maxwell Shane (and is therefore a crime episode), it has the look and feel of a horror entry with a soupçon of science fiction. Frank

Cordell, in fact, is a figure made familiar by many sci-fi movies: the tragic hero contaminated by exposure to science. But instead of transforming into a scaly monster, his metamorphosis into a sadistic killer is more subtle and horrifying (although the murders are not graphically depicted or described, their brutality is alluded to). Cordell's predicament is somewhat reminiscent of Laird Cregar's in *Hangover Square*, in which Cregar, a noted composer, goes mad and commits murder whenever he hears discordant sounds. There are even more distant echoes of Stevenson's *Dr. Jekyll and Mr. Hyde*. There is one troubling aspect: our sympathy for Cordell is lessened by his failure to turn himself in to the police; it seems irresponsible, to say the least, for him to go on after finding Susan Baker's earring in his room after her death.

That aside, "The Ordeal of Dr. Cordell" is a particularly vivid episode. Cordell's bouts of madness are imaginatively staged, with blurred images of Cordell shrieking in agony, and shots of his intended victims seen from his distorted perspective, followed by a whirling, blinding camera spinning around and around. His gradual descent into complete madness is compellingly and convincingly depicted.

Most of the acting burdens fall on Robert Vaughn's shoulders, and he's more than up to the challenge. An intense, intelligent performer (Vaughn is one of the few actors to have received a Ph.D.), he's coolly controlled, gifted at clever repartee, yet finally obsessed and desperate as he feels sanity slipping away. Vaughn is much more believable here than in his usual roles, where he's so unctuous and overbearingly slick that he becomes a caricature of intellectual villainy. Vaughn received an Oscar nomination for his performance in *The Young*

Philadelphians (1959); he also appeared in *The Magnificent Seven* (1960) and *Bullitt* (1968), but, of course, he's best known for his television role as superspy Napoleon Solo on *The Man from U.N.C.L.E.* (1964-68), where his oily facade was put to good use. His most recent appearances have been restricted to selling hairpieces on late night television.

The rest of the cast is capable, including a very young Marlo Thomas (five years away from *That Girl*) as the unfortunate Susan Baker. Genre fans may recall Kathleen Crowley, who plays Lois Walker, as the heroine of several fifties sci-fi and horror films, including *Target Earth* (1954), *The Flame Barrier* (1958) and *Curse of the Undead* (1959). Robert Ellenstein was a familiar face on television all through the sixties, and Russ Conway, who plays Lieutenant Boutaric, was a familiar supporting actor in the fifties; he had a larger than usual role in *The Screaming Skull* (1958).

"The Ordeal of Dr. Cordell" ranks as one of the most harrowing *Thrillers* ever; it's also one of the most uncompromising, with no happy ending, no reassurances of normality anywhere. It shows that Maxwell Shane was capable of producing a first-rate episode that stands comparison with the series' best.

"Trio for Terror" (airdate: March 14, 1961). Produced by William Frye. Directed by Ida Lupino. Written by Barre Lyndon, from stories by Stephen Grendon (August Derleth), Wilkie Collins, and Nelson Bond. Director of Photography: Lionel Lindon, A.S.C. Editor: Richard Belding. Art Director: Russell Kimball. Music: Morton Stevens. Assistant Director: Ben Bishop.

Cast: (Story One) Richard Lupino (Simon), Terence De Marney (Uncle Julian), Iris Bristol (Kitty), Gil Stuart

(Train Guard), Nelson Welch (Doctor). (Story Two) Reginald Owen (Hussar), Robin Hughes (Collins), Peter Brocco (Majordomo), Jacqueline Squire (Old Woman), Reginald Plato (Croupier). (Story Three) John Abbott (Kriss Milo), Michael Pate (Shanner), Noel Drayton (Superintendent), Richard Peel (Inspector).

"Trio for Terror," the first of *Thriller's* multi-part episodes, suffers from the problem endemic to all such short story compendiums: unevenness. One episode usually stands out, while the others pale by contrast. Even in the classic *Dead of Night*, the standard for all horror compendiums, the ventriloquist episode makes the others seem slight. In "Trio for Terror," one segment is pure gold, while the others appear tarnished. With more attention to detail, all three segments might have comprised a noteworthy horror anthology. There is no obvious thematic link, though all three stories take place in London (and appropriately are introduced by Karloff in a pub). Unfortunately, "Trio for Terror" puts its best story first, and the inevitable feeling of anticlimax soon sets in.

"The Extra Passenger": Simon (Richard Lupino) tells his girlfriend, Kitty (Iris Bristol), of his plan for murdering his rich uncle to obtain his inheritance. She tells him she will leave him if he fails to carry it out. Simon takes the train to an area near his uncle's home, establishing an alibi by locking himself in his compartment, then letting himself out the other door. He makes his way to his uncle's home, and finds the old man (Terence De Marney) amid a welter of black magic artifacts, including skulls, a strutting rooster, and burnt offerings. Simon sneaks up on his uncle and bludgeons him to death.

Simon re-boards the train unseen,

but finds to his horror that somehow an extra passenger has entered his compartment: a man dressed in black with a hat pulled down over his face. When Simon tells him he's in the wrong compartment, the man says, "I am not" and expresses knowledge of Simon's uncle. He tells him the old man was a warlock and had his own familiar, and that he could send a lich — a corpse — about for a special purpose, "like now." Simon is about to strike the figure when he raises his head. It is his uncle. "Come to me, Simon," he says. "Bring your face closer." He reaches for him and Simon's face is encircled by the talon of a gigantic bird.

The police find Simon's body in the compartment, his throat torn out, even though both doors are locked. The doctor says the wounds were made by a fighting cock, and that its claws penetrated Simon's throat.

"A Terribly Strange Bed": At Royster House, a gambling establishment, Collins (Robin Hughes), an off duty guard officer, wins at roulette over and over. He bets on impulse and gets the right number. He also gets a glass containing a drugged drink (and we see the game through the lens of a wobbly, roving camera). Collins puts everything he has on number two — and wins, breaking the bank. Reeling from the effects of his drinking, he is led upstairs to a room with a canopied bed; he puts his money under the pillow and goes to sleep. Sometime later that night the top of the bed begins to descend. Waking at the last possible second, he barely escapes being smothered. Some time later the top of the bed begins to rise. Collins grabs his money, wrapped in a cloth, and exits through the window, climbing down a drainpipe. He rushes to his friend, Ashton, to tell of his experience and show him his fortune — but all he has is a cannonball left by the Hussar (Reginald Owen).

"The Mask of Medusa": The police are searching for the Leighton Strangler (Michael Pate), who takes refuge in a wax museum. They have his trademark, a black kid glove left at the scene of his latest strangling. The killer, named Shanner, thinks he is alone until a little man named Mr. Milo (John Abbott) appears. Shanner compliments him on the lifelike qualities of his statues. Milo explains that before he opened his waxworks his primary interest was in Greek mythology. Shanner notices that one figure — the notorious murderer Dr. Hartwell — is very cold and very hard, yet looks a bit grey. Tumbling to Milo's secret much too soon, Shanner asks if the statue *is* the missing doctor. Milo admits that it is indeed the real Dr. Hartwell, just as the other figures are actually the real murderers. "You killed them," says Shanner. "You took it upon yourself to kill them, and petrify them somehow, and then to exhibit them here in this freak shop. You're a worse murderer than any of them ... What did you do? Poison them? Shoot them? Drop them alive in a vat of plaster?" Milo says that they killed themselves, all in the same way, then asks if Shanner has ever heard of Medusa. Milo located the marketplace where Perseus buried her head and dug there, unearthing it. When Shanner expresses disbelief, Milo indulges in a bit of sophistry, comparing the effect of the Gorgon's head to petrified wood, Lot's wife, and radio transmissions.

The police arrive, looking for the strangler. Milo lets them in, but keeps mum about his visitor. Shanner poses as a statue while the police search the museum. After the police leave, Milo notices Shanner's black kid glove and finally catches on to his visitor's identity.

Saying he does not want to do this, Milo whips open a box and says, "Look, you murderer — look on the mask of Medusa!" The Gorgon's eyes open wide as Shanner is turned to stone, and — voila! — Mr. Milo has added another figure to his museum.

"Trio for Terror" is a mixed bag indeed. The first segment, "The Extra Passenger," is a minor classic of the macabre. Supposedly the work of "Stephen Grendon," "The Extra Passenger" was actually one of 17 stories all written within *one month* by the amazing August Derleth. As Derleth notes in his introduction to *Mr. George and Other Odd Persons*, it was written "specifically to swell the log of *Weird Tales*. Since that estimable and lamented magazine already had enough stories by August Derleth in its files, the byline of Stephen Grendon was used." Derleth's choice of a pseudonym was hardly mystifying: he had used the name in several of his mainstream novels, such as *Evening in Spring*, in which "Steve Grendon" was the narrator.

In the story, published in the January 1947 *Weird Tales*, Simon (called Mr. Arodias) has no girlfriend, and the murder of his uncle (called Thaddeus) is passed over in a single sentence. The extra passenger is a more grisly specter: his head is smashed in and blood is running down his face. The *Thriller* segment omits this, but the murder is effectively showcased: we see Simon's uncle through a glass case, his features distorted: and after Simon bludgeons him, he is seen swiveling madly in his chair, his head at an angle.

The actors are perfectly cast. (For the record, this is the only *Thriller* not to feature Karloff introducing the individual cast members.) Richard Lupino (the director's brother) makes an effective, cunning Simon, and Terence

De Marney is properly menacing as Uncle Julian. De Marney, the brother of English actor Derrick De Marney, appeared with Bela Lugosi in a early Hammer film, *The Phantom Ship* (1936), and with Karloff in *Die Monster Die!* (1965). He appears in a similar role in a later *Thriller*, "The Return of Andrew Bentley."

The second segment is based on Wilkie Collins' well-known and oft-reprinted story. For most of its length it's a reasonably effective adaptation: the bed lowering soundlessly in the middle of the night, propelled by a giant wooden screw, is nightmarish. And Robin Hughes (seen as the Devil in the *Twilight Zone* episode "The Howling Man" and as the ubiquitous head in the ridiculous *The Thing That Couldn't Die*) is effective as the gambler, Collins (a nod to the author, since the narrator of the original story remains unnamed). But it makes the mistake of tacking on a humorous ending, replete with sitcom-style musical backing, shattering the ominous mood that has been so carefully built up. And Reginald Owen, as the Hussar, plays his role for broad comedy, distracting attention from Collins and making the proprietors of Royston House seem less fearsome than frolicsome.

The final segment is more problematic. Like "A Terribly Strange Bed," it, too, is let down by the ending. As Jay Allen Sanford wrote in his article "Karloff Through the Looking Glass: Horror on 'Thriller,'" "The actual mask of Medusa looks like a high school student slapped it together from papier-mâché and jiggled it for the camera." (The Gorgon's head in the otherwise fine Hammer film *The Gorgon* [1964] is a similar letdown.) This is unfortunate, since this segment is truly creepy and well-directed by Ida Lupino. There is one particularly clever directorial touch: when Shanner sees the Gorgon's head, the camera moves from him over to Milo and the head, then follows Milo back to where Shanner was standing, to hold on a statue dressed in Shanner's clothes (presumably Shanner himself, gorgonized), all in one smooth movement.

Unfortunately, the original story by Nelson Bond begs several questions that the adaptation never attempts to answer. For one thing, why does Milo (called Cavendish in the story) reveal his amazing (and criminal) story to a complete stranger? For another, how did he manage to track down the murderers, fugitives from justice whom the police were unable to lay their hands on? And for that matter, just how did Milo locate the Gorgon's head without looking upon it himself and being turned to stone? Under the weight of so many questions, the story collapses.

These problems to one side, the segment is well cast, and the actors do their best to put the story over. John Abbott (once described as "the poor man's Basil Rathbone") makes a creepy Kriss Milo. Perhaps best known as the vampiric Webb Fallon in *The Vampire's Ghost* (1945), Abbott made occasional forays into the horror and mystery genres, appearing in *The London Blackout Murders* (1942), *Cry of the Werewolf* (1944), and *Pursuit to Algiers* (1945). He was also in the TV movie "The Cat Creature" (1976), scripted by Robert Bloch.

Michael Pate is believable as Shanner (called Milo Shaner in the original story). Whether expressing disbelief in the legend of the Gorgon or smiling as his hands encircle the neck of one of Milo's statues, Pate is everything the role calls for. Pate, an Australian, is usually cast in villainous parts. His best-known genre role may be as the vampire in the

bizarre horror-western *Curse of the Undead* (1959). His other credits include *The Strange Door* (1951), *The Black Castle* (1952) and *The Maze* (1953). In the 1954 telecast of *Casino Royale* he appeared as James Bond's friend Felix Leiter (mysteriously Anglicized and rechristened Cedric Leiter). Pate later wrote *The Film Actor* (1970), a book on performing.

Perhaps the most notable aspect of "Trio for Terror" is the debut of Ida Lupino as a *Thriller* director. British-born, she was the daughter of comedian Stanley Lupino. She started in films as an actress in 1933, and appeared in many notable productions, including *The Adventures of Sherlock Holmes* (1939), *They Drive By Night* (1940), and *High Sierra* (1941). She continued on into the fifties, entering into a tempestuous marriage with Howard Duff, with whom she appeared in a television series, *Mr. Adams and Eve*. While her film career was still going strong, she moved into writing and directing — a career move almost unheard of for a woman at that time. Her first two efforts as director — *Never Fear* (1950) and *Hard, Fast and Beautiful* (1951) — passed without notice, but her third film was probably her best. *The Hitch-Hiker* (1953), which she also wrote, features an unnerving performance by William Talman as the murderous hitchhiker picked up by two unsuspecting men. It is tautly directed, and holds up well as a minor suspense classic. Lupino followed this up with *The Bigamist* (1953), the only one of her directorial efforts in which she appears.

By the fifties she had moved into television, and directed many episodes of such then-popular series as *77 Sunset Strip*, *Have Gun, Will Travel*, *The Untouchables*, *Hong Kong*, and others. She was one of the stars of *Four Star Playhouse*, where she met William Frye. Years later, he would recall her to work on *Thriller*. (Some years after *Thriller* had left the air, Frye hired her to direct a theatrical film, *The Trouble with Angels* [1966], which would prove a popular, if not a critical, success.) Lupino died in 1995.

"Trio for Terror" ranks somewhere around the middle of Lupino's eight *Thriller* episodes. (Her best is probably "La Strega" or "Guillotine.") It is noteworthy chiefly for its first, and best, segment. As a compendium it is let down by inattention to detail and the inevitable curse of unevenness, a bane that would similarly plague the later multi-part episode "Dialogues with Death."

"Papa Benjamin" (airdate: March 21, 1961). Produced by Maxwell Shane. Directed by Ted Post. Teleplay by John Kneubuhl, from the short story by Cornell Woolrich. Music: Pete Rugolo. Director of Photography: Lionel Lindon, A.S.C. Edited by Danny Landres. Art Director: Howard E. Johnson. Assistant Director: Carter DeHaven, III. Editorial Supervisor: David J. O'Connell. Musical Supervision: Stanley Wilson. Sound: Vernon W. Kramer. Set Decorators: John McCarthy and William L. Stevens.

Cast: John Ireland (Eddie Wilson), Jeanne Bal (Judy), Robert H. Harris (Jerry Roberts), Henry Scott (Tommy Statts), Jester Hairston (Papa Benjamin), Peter Forster (Inspector Daniels), Alex Finlayson, Caleb Peterson, Cora C. Lang, Alibe Copage.

The first of *Thriller*'s three Cornell Woolrich adaptations, "Papa Benjamin" is the least effective of the three. It's a rather conventional voodoo entry, with some mood but little suspense.

On one of the islands in the Caribbean, Eddie Wilson (John Ireland) runs into a police station. He hands his gun to Inspector Daniels (Peter Forster) and tells him he has just killed a man named Papa Benjamin. He says he acted in self-defense because the other man was killing him with voodoo.

In flashbacks we learn that Eddie, an orchestra leader, was appearing with his band at the Caravan Hotel. Inspired by the sights and sounds of the Caribbean, he tries to compose something with the flavor of the islands, without success. "It'll happen, Eddie," his girlfriend, Judy (Jeanne Bal), tells him, but he is unconvinced. When he hears his drummer, Tommy Statts (Henry Scott), playing a strange rhythm, he recognizes it as the music he has been seeking. He also finds a talisman near his piano. Later, he sees Statts retrieve the talisman, then follows him. "I didn't know it then," Eddie says, "but that rhythm was driving me to my death — a slow, horrible death."

Eddie follows Statts to an old house, where he is admitted after showing a guard the talisman. Eddie sneaks in through an open window. He sees natives performing voodoo rites, driven by the music. One of them is Statts. Eddie is discovered and nearly killed by Papa Benjamin (Jester Hairston), but Statts saves his life by telling the voodoo chieftain that Eddie will remain silent about what he has seen and heard. "Or you die," Papa Benjamin declares. Eddie is initiated into the cult, and released. Later, Eddie tells Statts he plans to use the music he heard in the act. Statts warns him not to. When Eddie refuses, Statts says, "Goodbye, dead man." Eddie never sees Statts again.

Soon afterward, Eddie begins writing the "Voodoo Rhapsody." He works around the clock, commenting, "It was like the music owned me." Two weeks later, it is finished. Eddie's agent, Jerry Roberts (Robert H. Harris), flies down for its initial performance, along with a delegation of musical publishers and recording executives. But Eddie collapses during the performance. When he revives, he says it was like someone stuck a knife in his back. The doctor diagnoses it as nervous tension; but after he has gone, Eddie finds a voodoo doll in his bed with a pin in its back.

It happens again when Eddie returns to New York. Eddie hasn't the energy to work; he doesn't show up for half of his engagements. Jerry Roberts suggests it may be due to a mental condition. But Eddie now believes he is cursed. When he tells Judy this, she walks out on him. Eddie realizes he must return to see Papa Benjamin and beg him to remove the curse. He flies back to the island and makes his way to the old house. Inside he finds Papa Benjamin. "You had your chance — you was warned," he tells Eddie. When Eddie offers him money, he shakes his head. "What has been done cannot be undone," he says. Eddie shoots him repeatedly, then takes off running.

The flashbacks end. Eddie takes the policeman, including Inspector Daniels, back to the house, but there is no sign of Papa Benjamin.

Back home, Eddie finds that Judy has returned and Jerry has secured a booking for Eddie and his band. During the performance, a number of patrons shout to Eddie to play "Voodoo Rhapsody." Eddie obliges, and all seems to go well, but when the performance is over, Eddie falls dead. The doll with the pin in its back lies beside him.

Cornell Woolrich must have seemed a natural choice for *Thriller's* producers: The characteristic bleakness of his best stories fit in well with *Thriller's* penchant for downbeat melodramas.

Woolrich's own life was as downbeat as any of his fictional works. Born

Cornell George Hopley-Woolrich in New York in 1903, he spent a large part of his childhood traveling in Latin America with his father, a civil engineer. He entered Columbia College in the early twenties, but never graduated. His first novel was published in 1926; five more followed, as well as numerous short stories, none of which he liked. "It would have been a lot better if everything I'd done until [the thirties] had been written in invisible ink and the reagent had been thrown away," he wrote in his autobiography.

In the mid-thirties he began writing a different kind of story. His new market was the pulps — *Dime Detective* and *Dime Mystery*. By the end of that decade his work was appearing in nearly all the pulps, including *Argosy* and *Black Mask*, and even such general fiction magazines as Whit Burnett's *Story*. His fiction was characterized by certain settings (the seedy hotel and dance hall) and themes (the race against the clock, the little man trapped by fate). His first mystery novel, *The Bride Wore Black*, published in 1940, was followed by five more over the next eight years, each with the word "black" in the title. He also wrote under several pen names: he published *Phantom Lady* (1942) as William Irish, and *Night Has a Thousand Eyes* (1945) as George Hopley.

Woolrich was an introvert, living alone with his mother in a hotel, under her domination. She died in 1957. Woolrich had become a diabetic and an alcoholic, and was obsessed with the idea that he might be homosexual. His condition deteriorated. He developed gangrene in one leg; by the time doctors examined it, it had worsened and had to be amputated. Woolrich remained in isolation, finally dying of a stroke in 1968, leaving an estate of nearly $1 million. "I was only trying to cheat death," he wrote in a fragment found among his papers. "I was only trying to surmount for a little while the darkness that all my life I surely knew was going to come rolling in on me some day and obliterate me." An excellent biography of Woolrich, *First You Dream, Then You Die,* by Francis M. Nevins, Jr., was published in 1988 by the Mysterious Press.

Woolrich's work was adapted by Hollywood scriptwriters with varying degrees of success. *Phantom Lady, Rear Window* and *The Leopard Man* (from his novel *Black Alibi*) rank among the more successful, but many of the others are mediocre or worse. His classic story "Three O'Clock" was done as an hour-long episode of the television series *Suspicion,* directed by Alfred Hitchcock.

During 1961 Revue Productions paid Woolrich $4,600 for television rights to three of his stories, filmed as "Papa Benjamin," "Late Date," and "Guillotine" on *Thriller.* "Papa Benjamin" fails to do justice to Woolrich's characteristically bleak story, originally published in 1935 under the title "Dark Melody of Madness." John Kneubuhl's teleplay moved the setting from New Orleans to the Caribbean, but kept fairly close to the original plot (one minor change involved altering the protagonist's name from Eddie Bloch to Eddie Wilson, for obvious reasons). Nevertheless, the ominous mood and sense of impending doom found in the original story is present only fleetingly, due to Ted Post's unimaginative direction. There are minor compensations: the milieu (though it differs from that of Woolrich's story) is adequately evoked, and the voodoo rites are convincingly staged. There is also some effective intercutting from the natives, dancing and chanting, to Papa Benjamin's face, then to Eddie Wilson, all to the accompaniment of voodoo drums. But the climax

is disappointing, and little of Woolrich's fatalistic world view seeps in. The basic story line was used four years later in the Amicus anthology film *Dr. Terror's House of Horrors.*

John Ireland, an underrated actor, is, as usual, very good in the lead. One of Hollywood's more offbeat leading men, Ireland always projected intelligence and a degree of cynicism, appropriate attributes for Eddie Wilson. His career seems to have been sabotaged: his supporting role in Howard Hawks' classic western *Red River* (1948) was drastically cut, and he disappears for a long stretch in the middle. Hawks said it was because Ireland was smoking marijuana and showing up late on the set; others claimed it was because Ireland had a romance going with "Howard's girl," Joanne Dru (whom he later married). Ireland had one of his best roles as the cynical reporter in *All the King's Men* (1949); after this, his career declined with remarkable (and baffling) rapidity. He appeared in 1951's *The Scarf* (a mystery bearing a suspicious similarity to Robert Bloch's supposedly unrelated novel of the same title), and then drifted into supporting parts in such films as *Spartacus* (1960) and *The Ceremony* (1963). He played a wife murderer in William Castle's enjoyable *I Saw What You Did!* (1965), and then wound up in low-budget junk: *Guyana* (1980) and *The Incubus* (1982). He died in 1992.

Jeanne Bal is adequate as Judy. She has little to do but sit around and cheer Eddie on, but she's acceptable. She was a regular on a short-lived TV series *Love and Marriage,* and after a season on *Bachelor Father,* became a regular on *Mr. Novak.*

It's nice to see Robert H. Harris turn up on a *Thriller,* albeit in a small role. One of Hollywood's more easily recognizable character actors, he was usually officious and beaky, but in "Papa Benjamin" he's surprisingly sympathetic as Jerry Roberts. He was a regular on the early television series *The Goldbergs*, and had a rare leading role as a mad makeup man in the 1958 film *How to Make a Monster*. His other film credits include *Mirage* (1965) and *Valley of the Dolls* (1967). He died in 1981.

It's unfortunate that "Papa Benjamin" was the first of *Thriller*'s Woolrich adaptations (as well as the last of Maxwell Shane's episodes). Better things lay ahead.

"Late Date" (airdate: April 4, 1961).

Produced by William Frye. Directed by Herschel Daugherty. Teleplay by Donald S. Sanford, based on the story by Cornell Woolrich. Director of Photography: Ray Rennahan, A.S.C. Music: Jerry Goldsmith. Edited by Richard Belding. Art Director: Russell Kimball. Assistant Director: John Clarke Bowman. Set Decorators: John McCarthy and William L. Stevens.

Cast: Larry Pennell (Larry Weeks), Edward Platt (Jim Weeks), Jody Fair (Helen), Chris Seitz (Gordon), Stuffy Singer (Art Brinkerhoff), Steve Mitchell (Sid), Stuart Randall (Deputy Crowell), Richard Reeves (Truck Driver), Judy Crowder, Ruth Warren.

A cop out ending seriously damages "Late Date," an otherwise exceptionally suspenseful *Thriller*, the second (in a row) to be adapted from a story by Cornell Woolrich.

In a seaside resort town, muscular Larry Weeks (Larry Pennell) comes home from a day at the beach, only to find the body of his sister-in-law, Doris, murdered by his brother, Jim (Edward Platt). Larry knew Doris was seeing another man, but never had the nerve to tell Jim. Jim wants to phone the police, but Larry tells him not to. "She got what

she deserved, Jim, she's not worth your life," Larry tells him. Larry arranges an alibi for his brother, saying he owes it to him. "I remember how you took care of me after mom and dad died," he says. Jim is reluctant, but Larry convinces him to stick to the story they have concocted. "Now you've got your job," Larry tells him. "Mine's upstairs."

Helen (Jody Fair), Doris' daughter, arrives home. Jim sneaks out of the house while Larry hides the body so Helen won't see it. He waits until nightfall; Doris' lover, Gordon (Chris Seitz), calls. Larry tells him Doris left a message to meet her at the Paradise Club at 8:30. "It was your party, mister — you're going to pay for it, not Jim," Larry says.

Wrapping the body in a rug, Larry puts it in the trunk of his car, then sets out for the Paradise Club, but has a flat tire on the way. He gets a lift from a truck driver, but the man throws him off when he thinks Larry stole the rug. Despite other setbacks, Larry manages to hide the body in the back seat of Gordon's car. Not knowing it's there, Gordon takes off, drinking and driving too fast.

When Larry gets back home, he finds Jim there. He has changed his mind and wants to confess. But just then policemen arrive with the news that Gordon's car went over an embankment — both he and Doris are dead. Larry and Jim are home free. But Jim refuses Larry's pleas to remain silent, and gets in the police car; Larry reluctantly follows.

"Late Date" was based on Woolrich's 1935 story "The Corpse and the Kid," also known as "Boy with Body." For most of its length, it's a terrifically suspenseful crime story concerned with the problems of disposing of a body. As usual with Woolrich, it's a race against the clock, with events conspiring to thwart Larry's goal of reaching his destination by 8:30, and Jerry Gold-smith's nerve-wracking score, with its clock-like ticking, reminding us of the remorseless progression of time. Despite the setbacks fate keeps putting in his way, Larry finally succeeds, so it's not merely disappointing but also dispiriting when his brother has a sudden change of heart, thanks to the network's censorial attitude. Kindred wife murderers got away free on *Alfred Hitchcock Presents* via Hitch's jokey, tongue-in-cheek assurances, in the epilogues, that justice was done. No such latitude was permitted here, and the fine acting and suspenseful direction can do little to alleviate the situation.

The actors are very good. Larry Pennell appeared mostly in B movies; he was the hero on a short-lived TV series, *Ripcord*, and a semi-regular on *The Beverly Hillbillies*. He was a decent actor, judging from "Late Date," and his muscular build makes him a believable protagonist, even if it's a little hard to accept him as Ed Platt's brother.

Edward Platt was a solid performer who often played stern authority figures; it's a little surprising to find him playing a murderer, even if the crime was justified, but he pulls it off, giving his usual intense performance. His films include *Rebel Without a Cause* (1955), *North by Northwest* (1959) and *Atlantis, the Lost Continent* (1961), though of course he's best remembered as the Chief on *Get Smart*. He died in 1974.

The other actors, including Jody Fair as Helen and Richard Reeves as the surly truck driver, are competent.

"Late Date" is a problematic episode. It's undeniably suspenseful and unnerving, but the last minute compromise mitigates against its effectiveness. In addition, although Woolrich's distinctively cynical world view is present, the bleakness seems assumed and unjustified.

"Yours Truly, Jack the Ripper" (airdate: April 11, 1961). Produced by William Frye. Directed by Ray Milland. Screenplay by Barre Lyndon, based on the short story by Robert Bloch. Photography by Kenneth D. Peach, A.S.C. Edited by Danny Landres. Art Director: Loyd S. Papez. Music: Jerry Goldsmith. Assistant Director: James Hogan. Art Decorators: John McCarthy and Joseph Kish. Paintings courtesy of the Martin Lowitz Galleries.

Cast: John Williams (Sir Guy), Donald Woods (John Carmody), Edmond Ryan (Captain Jago), Adam Williams (Hymie Kralik), Nancy Valentine (Arlene), Ransom Sherman, Sam Gilman, Pamela Curran, Jill Livesey, Gloria Blondell, J. Pat O'Malley, Miss Beverly Hills.

"Yours Truly, Jack the Ripper" does not rank as one of the more successful *Thrillers*. Although based on Robert Bloch's famous short story, the episode suffers from padding. Bloch himself feels that the story was better adapted elsewhere, and thought that "the gratuitous changes [made by screenwriter Barre Lyndon] conventionalized it."

In the teaser, a woman hurries home through the dimly lit streets of London, circa 1888. "Is he about tonight?" she fearfully asks a constable. She makes it home, enters her flat, and is preparing for bed when a figure with a knife approaches and a black-gloved hand clamps over her mouth. In the street outside, a singer (J. Pat O'Malley) croons the ballad of Jack the Ripper.

Many years later, in a unidentified big city, Sir Guy (John Williams) is explaining his theory regarding a series of murders to the police: according to him, there will be another in three nights, six in all. John Carmody (Donald Woods), a consulting psychiatrist with the police department, listens to Sir Guy's theory sympathetically, but Captain Pete Jago (Edmond Ryan) has only scorn for the Englishman. Jago thinks the killer is a psychopath imitating Jack the Ripper; Sir Guy thinks it is the Ripper himself. Captain Jago objects to this, saying that if the Ripper were alive he would be 90 years old or more. Sir Guy suggests that the Ripper has not aged because of the pattern of the killings and the dates — all ritual sacrifices at the proper time with the proper ceremonies, in return for which the gods grant the boon of eternal life and youth. Needless to say, the police do not believe him, but stake out the areas he suggests, anyway.

Sir Guy thinks the Ripper may be associated with the avant-garde. Carmody admits that he was associated with similar groups during his younger days. Despite their precautions, the Ripper strikes again, killing a young girl. The mutilations are the same. Sir Guy then tells Captain Jago that there will be another murder on the night of the 22nd.

Sir Guy pursues his theory of the Ripper being an artist living among unconventional types. He tells a group of painters that there was a gap of 126 days between the first and second murders, and then 63 days between the second and sixth, the last. One of the artists, Hymie Kralik (Adam Williams), has a morbid imagination, associating his model Arlene (Nancy Valentine) with the dead girl.

At the funeral, one of the pallbearers drops the casket and the corpse stares with open eyes at the mourners.

During a party attended by the avant-garde, Sir Guy tries to spot the Ripper, without success. That night, despite the precautions of the police, Arlene becomes the Ripper's next victim.

One more victim is due, but with the previous murder sites forming the sign of a broken cross, the police are able to predict where the next killing will occur. They stake out the area, a strip joint, while Sir Guy and Carmody wait inside, but nothing happens. Sir Guy describes the Ripper as "a vampire who fattens not on blood but on life itself — a ghoul, nourished by death." He tells Carmody that he will turn over all he has on the Ripper to Interpol if they do not catch him that night. Carmody suggests that they go outside to get some air.

In the alley, Carmody tells Sir Guy that they've missed him. When Sir Guy asks for a match, Carmody pulls out a knife instead and stabs him. Sir Guy calls out "John!" "Not John — Jack," Carmody says, disappearing into the night.

Unlike most of *Thriller*'s resident ghouls, Jack the Ripper was a very real person. From August 31 to November 3, 1888, he cut a bloody swath through London's East End, slaughtering five prostitutes. These atrocities drew widespread attention to Whitechapel's poverty and unsanitary living conditions, prompting George Bernard Shaw to observe sardonically: "Whilst we conventional Social Democrats were wasting our time on education, agitation and organization, some independent genius has taken the matter in hand, and by simply murdering and disembowelling four women, converted the proprietary press to an inept form of Communism."

After the murder of Mary Kelly, in which the organs and appendages of her body were laid out in a row on a table, the Ripper's activities abruptly — and mysteriously — ceased. Inevitably, speculation over his identity continues even today, more than a century later. The leading suspects include a Russian

Doctor named Pedachenko; a poet-tutor named J. K. Stephen, who was losing his mind as a result of a fall from a horse; a British doctor named Stanley; and the notorious wife poisoner Neill Cream (whose last words, as he stood on the gallows, was "I am Jack the..."). The most sensational theory tagged the Ripper as the Duke of Clarence, heir to the throne of England. This is a rather dubious theory, considering that Clarence was shooting game in Scotland when two of the murders were committed.

A far more plausible suspect, and "the firm favorite among Ripperologists," as author Donald Rumbelow puts it, is Montague John Druitt, a cricket-playing barrister. Druitt was going slowly insane; his body was found floating in the Thames, his pockets weighted with stones, on December 31, 1888.

Dramatization of the Ripper's exploits began almost immediately. Rumbelow points to a music hall performance of 1889, based on Mary Kelly's murder, as the first of these. Additionally, the first work of fiction involving the Ripper was published in Finland in 1892. Probably the best known fictionalization, Marie Belloc-Lowndes' The Lodger, was originally a short story published in 1911 and expanded into a novel two years later. Hitchcock's silent version of the novel was filmed in 1926 and remade several times, most notably in 1944 by Thriller's own John Brahm.

Among short stories, the best-known and most frequently anthologized is almost certainly Bloch's. First published in Weird Tales' July 1943 issue, the story made its 26-year-old author a name to be reckoned with, and despite certain dated aspects, it remains memorable for its shock ending, similar to that of Agatha Christie's The Murder of Roger Ackroyd. As Randall Larson points out in his study of Bloch's work, "The story

was a pivotal one for Bloch. It reinforced his move away from the cosmic Lovecraftian terrors into the more disturbing horrors of human reality." The story was adapted for radio several times, the most memorable being Laird Cregar's reading on The Kate Smith Hour. Bloch later wrote a novel, The Night of the Ripper (1984), but this had nowhere near the impact of his original story.

One problem in putting the story on film is that much of its impact comes from the final revelation that the narrator himself is the Ripper. Thankfully, director Ray Milland did not seek to duplicate this effect by using a subjective camera technique, which would have been awkward and intrusive; nevertheless, the filmed ending has nowhere near the impact of the story's conclusion.

Milland's direction is effective in some scenes (the killings) but drags in others (the party, the striptease). Too much time is devoted to the artists, and the avant-garde milieu is sketchily and unconvincingly evoked. And Adam Williams, best known for playing villainous roles such as the thug, Valerian, in North by Northwest, seems an odd choice to play a sensitive artist. Actually, with its emphasis on detection and police stakeouts, "Yours Truly, Jack the Ripper" plays more like a crime episode. (Ironically, it was reportedly the most widely viewed episode of the series.)

Jerry Goldsmith's score, on the other hand, is wonderfully apt and evocative, an obvious precursor of his music for John Huston's The List of Adrian Messenger (1963), which it closely resembles.

The performances are adequate. John Williams is appropriately cast as Sir Guy (in the story, his mother was one of the Ripper's victims, making his vendetta against the killer more meaningful). Williams was one of Hollywood's favorite Britishers, best known as

Chief Inspector Hubbard in Hitchcock's *Dial M for Murder* (in which he tangled with Ray Milland). He also appeared in *Sabrina* (1954), *To Catch a Thief* (1955), *Witness for the Prosecution* (1957), and *Midnight Lace* (1960), among other films. He died in 1983.

Donald Woods is likewise suitably cast as John Carmody. He was a familiar face in films and television, beginning with featured roles in *A Tale of Two Cities* (1935) and *Anthony Adverse* (1936); he later drifted into B films. He turned up in William Castle's *13 Ghosts* (1960) as the lead.

In all, "Yours Truly, Jack the Ripper" must be judged a disappointment, considering its famous source, and one of the few times Bloch was poorly served by *Thriller*. It also marks the last time a Bloch story would be adapted by someone else; beginning with the next episode, Bloch would do the scripting himself—with far more satisfying results.

"The Devil's Ticket" (airdate: April 18, 1961). Produced by William Frye. Directed by Jules Bricken. Teleplay by Robert Bloch, from his short story. Director of Photography: John L. Russell, A.S.C. Music: Morton Stevens. Musical Supervision: Stanley Wilson. Edited by Danny Landres. Art Director: Howard E. Johnson. Editorial Supervisor: David J. O'Connell. Sound: Frank H. Wilkinson. Associate Producer: Douglas Benton. Assistant Director: Ben Bishop. Set Decorators: John McCarthy and William L. Stevens. Paintings courtesy of the Martin Lowitz Galleries.

Cast: Macdonald Carey (Hector Vane), Joan Tetzel (Marie Vane), Patricia Medina (Nadja), John Emery (The Pawnbroker), Robert Cornthwaite (Spengler), Hayden Rorke (Dr. Frank), Bartlett Robinson (Art Critic), Audrey Swanson (The Nurse).

Another certifiable *Thriller* classic, "The Devil's Ticket" was the first episode adapted by Robert Bloch. The result is a chilling horror tale, a switch on the venerable deal with the devil ploy, bolstered by fine acting and a genuinely nightmarish denouement.

In a pawnshop, the greedy Spengler (Robert Cornthwaite) sits counting his money. From behind a closed door a mysterious voice beckons him to approach. "I can't see you," Spengler says. "Where are you?"

"Here, you miserable little miser, waiting for you," the unseen figure says. "I've been waiting a whole year." Spengler is compelled to approach the door. When he passes through it, the door closes behind him and clouds of smoke billow up from underneath it.

Impoverished artist Hector Vane (Macdonald Carey) sits with his wife, Marie (Joan Tetzel), bemoaning his lack of success. "The critics said I was a finished artist — how right they were," Hector laments. He prepares to visit Spengler to pawn one of his paintings.

When he arrives at the pawnshop, Hector finds no sign of Spengler. Another man (John Emery) has taken his place. He refuses to take the painting, telling Hector, "You should be rich — famous." "Who are you?" Hector asks. "Your benefactor — the one who can give you all that you desire," the man says. "What the devil d'you mean?" Hector says. "Now, now," the man replies, "let's not mention any names." He proposes to pawn Hector's soul for 90 days in exchange for fame and riches. At the end of that time Hector must present him with a painting. Hector signs a contract and receives a ticket, redeemable by sundown on April 5th.

When Hector returns home, he finds that a powerful art dealer is planning a one man show of his paintings. At the show Hector's work is snapped up by wealthy patrons. When Hector returns to the pawnbroker to offer him a landscape, the man refuses it, insisting on a portrait revealing the model's soul. "So it's your soul against another," the pawnbroker says. "That would be murder — worse than murder," Hector says. "Perhaps there's someone you would like to get rid of," the pawnbroker points out. "Paint his portrait and satisfy us both."

At the studio, Hector is carrying on with his beautiful model, Nadja (Patricia Medina). She wants him to leave his wife and marry her. Hector, unsure of his sanity, visits a psychiatrist (Hayden Rorke). He tells him of his dealings with the pawnbroker, but the psychiatrist explains that the man played on Hector's gullibility, and that his success would have happened anyway. He agrees to visit the pawnbroker. But when Hector returns to the psychiatrist's office, the pawnbroker has taken his place. "You owe me a painting — remember?" he says. "You have only 13 days left, Mr. Vane."

Nadja asks Hector to paint her. Horrified, he refuses, then hits on the idea of painting his wife. When she questions his motivation, he tells her, "For the picture I have in mind, I wouldn't paint anyone but you." He finishes the portrait on April 3rd. But when he shows it to Nadja, she is horrified. In a jealous rage she slashes it to ribbons. He now has 48 hours left.

After sundown on April 5th Hector has an unexpected visitor — the pawnbroker. "You know why I'm here," he says. "Is it ready?" Hector shows him the portrait — a perfect likeness of the pawnbroker. "What the — what trickery is this?" he exclaims. "You thought you had me, didn't you?" Hector says. "Take your hideous soul and get out of here."

The pawnbroker admits defeat and asks for the pawn ticket. Marie brings Hector his overcoat — but it is a new one, not the shabby one he had always worn. When Hector asks Marie what she did with the old one, she blurts out, "I — burned it." The pawnbroker laughs. "I told you women are often my allies," he says. He pushes Marie away, locks the door, and advances on Hector. As Marie pounds on the door outside, thick clouds of smoke billow up from underneath.

One of the all-time best *Thrillers*, "The Devil's Ticket" benefits from Robert Bloch's first-rate adaptation of his own short story. First published in *Weird Tales* in September 1944, it is remarkably similar to Bloch's teleplay. One of the few differences is that, in the story, Nadja burns the portrait of Marie, along with most of Hector's studio; in the *Thriller* adaptation, she slashes the portrait while Hector simply stands there, not lifting a finger to stop her, despite the fact that she's not merely threatening his life, but consigning his soul to eternal damnation. On the plus side, Bloch's teleplay is taut, with a good deal of foreshadowing: Marie comments on Hector's old coat twice, and the sign in the pawnshop — "No article redeemed without ticket" — is visible in the first shot. Nor is there much padding: even Hector's visit to the psychiatrist, which seems unnecessary at first, has a sinister payoff. In addition, the memorable opening scene, in which the miserly Spengler is called to his doom by an unseen figure, is an eerie vignette.

Macdonald Carey at first seems an odd choice for the role of Hector Vane. Conventional casting would have dictated a younger man, but Carey's maturity adds a layer of desperation to Vane's quest for success. Carey gives a memorable performance throughout: he's quite believable as an artist, and his final, terrified expression as the Devil advances on him is truly haunting.

Carey, of course, was one of Hollywood's most notable leading men (and one of *Thriller*'s biggest catches). His films include Hitchcock's *Shadow of a Doubt* (1943), *The Lawless*, *Copper Canyon* (both 1950), *Stranger at My Door* (1956), and *The Damned* (1963), among others. From 1965 until his death in 1994 he was a regular on the popular soap opera *Days of Our Lives* (he was also the star of a short-lived syndicated series, *Lock-Up*, several episodes of which were scripted by Robert Bloch). Viewing "The Devil's Ticket" after the passage of more than 30 years, the veteran actor remarked:

> I had forgotten the show entirely, and I had forgotten how good it was. It's very seldom that I can look at a show and look at myself, and I was able to sit through this without a flinch. I was quite pleased.
>
> Joanie Tetzel, who played my wife, had been in my life in other ways. She was the best friend of my now ex-wife. The first argument I had with my ex-wife was when I slept through Joanie Tetzel's wedding. I was quite surprised when she divorced the guy later and married Oscar [Homolka]. But Joan worshipped at the altar of the theater, so it was only natural.
>
> I had forgotten Pat [Medina] being the sort-of slut. Pat and I did a movie together called *Stranger at My Door*, and it was one of the best movies I ever did. Pat was always good luck for me.
>
> John Emery was never really as popular as he should have been. He was married to Tallulah Bankhead. He was one of the last of the leading men who toured the United States.
>
> [Overall] I thought ["The Devil's Ticket"] was one of the best things I

ever did. I'm very proud of it. Bob Bloch came up to me at the Vagabond Bookshop when I was first being published, and he couldn't have been more flattering, couldn't have been nicer, and he talked about this show, and I didn't know what he was talking about. I can see now why he was so pleased with it, why he spoke of it so highly. I liked everything about it. The tag is enough of a surprise. There's enough foreshadowing; it doesn't tip its hand completely — you think right away he's going to paint the Devil.

> It's too bad they can't bring [*Thriller*] back. It's a hell of a good show. They don't make them like that any more! Everybody is good in it — it's done impeccably, it's written well, it's produced well. It should be revived, but I don't know how you would do it.

Hector Vane's temptress is played by beautiful, British-born Patricia Medina. She appeared mostly in routine films, including *The Three Musketeers* (1948), *Magic Carpet* (1951), *Phantom of the Rue Morgue* (1954), *The Beast of Hollow Mountain* (1956), and *The Killing of Sister George* (1968), before retiring from movies. She was married to actor Joseph Cotten. She also appears in a later *Thriller*, "The Premature Burial."

Joan Tetzel is adequate as Marie Vane. For more on her career, see the entry on "An Attractive Family."

John Emery is in good form as the Devil. He's impeccably cast, although considerably more youthful than the figure described in Bloch's story: "His hair was the color of yellowed ivory, and his skin had the parchment texture of incunabula." Although he's attired in a business suit, and doesn't have horns, hooves or a tail, there are subtly suggestive details in Emery's performance that underline his satanic nature, most notably the hand gestures he makes after replacing Vane's psychiatrist: they are remarkably similar to those of Christopher Lee in the Hitchcock segment "The Sign of Satan." Emery was an American stage and screen actor sometimes cast (as Leslie Halliwell puts it) as "Mephistophelian types." His films include *Here Comes Mr. Jordan* (1941), *Spellbound* (1945), *Rocketship X-M* (1950), *The Mad Magician* (1954) and *Kronos* (1957), though he's probably best remembered as Tallulah Bankhead's only husband. He was one of the actors considered for the role of Dr. MacFarlane in *The Body Snatcher*, along with Alan Napier, Albert Dekker, George Coulouris and Philip Merivale (they all lost out to Henry Daniell). Emery died in 1964.

Robert Cornthwaite makes a welcome cameo appearance as the unfortunate Spengler. Cornthwaite is of course best remembered as Professor Carrington in the original version of *The Thing* (1951). One of his most recent film credits was Joe Dante's *Matinee* (1993). He also appears in a later *Thriller*, "The Grim Reaper."

"The Devil's Ticket" can hardly be faulted. It is first-class in all departments, a truly memorable deal with the devil yarn that happily marks Robert Bloch's advent as a *Thriller* scriptwriter.

"Parasite Mansion" (airdate: April 25, 1961). Produced by William Frye. Directed by Herschel Daugherty. Teleplay by Donald S. Sanford, based on the short story by Mary Elizabeth Counselman. Director of Photography: John L. Russell, A.S.C. Music: Morton Stevens. Assistant Director: Edward K. Dodds. Art Director: Russell Kimball. Associate Producer: Douglas Benton. Edited by Danny Landres. Set Decorators: John McCarthy and William L. Stevens.

Cast: Pippa Scott (Marcia Hunt), James Griffith (Victor Harrod), Jeanette Nolan (Granny), Tommy Nolan (Rennie), Beverly Washburn (Lollie).

Replete with a moody opening and a wonderfully atmospheric "old dark house" setting, "Parasite Mansion" could have been one of the all-time best *Thrillers*, but its blithe acceptance of the supernatural lessens its effectiveness. Still, it's an above average episode with some truly creepy moments.

Marcia Hunt (Pippa Scott), a young teacher, comes to a detour in the road during a thunderstorm. Up ahead she sees an old mansion illuminated by flashes of lightning. The sudden sounds of gunshots terrify her and she drives her car off the road into a tree.

Awakening some time later, she finds herself a prisoner in the strange mansion, home of the Harrod family. Victor (James Griffith), a drunken ex-doctor, has applied stitches to her head wound. When Marcia reacts to a strong odor, Granny (Jeanette Nolan), a hideous old hag, cackles unpleasantly. "You might as well get used t' the smell o' corn liquor, honey," she says. She tells her that Rennie (Tommy Nolan), Victor's younger brother, shot at her. Victor tells her there was a sign reading PRIVATE PROPERTY, which she didn't see, and informs her that she will have to remain in the house until her car is fixed: the nearest neighbor is 10 miles across the swamp. Marcia soon learns the Harrods are concealing a secret; to prevent her from learning it, they warn her to stay in her room.

Sometime later Marcia tries to leave. She notices a locked door atop a short flight of steps. Venturing outside, she is nearly killed when Rennie shoots at her. Victor wrestles the gun away from the boy, then locks Marcia in her room. Marcia says she wants to help the boy;

Victor dismisses her claims, telling her he could show her "things that'd shake your sanity — things that you'd see in nightmares!" "Why don't you show her, Victor?" Granny asks. When Marcia suggests that the secret of the house consists of Rennie's mental illness, Granny laughs. "You can't begin to imagine the things this house is hidin'!" she tells her.

Soon afterward Marcia notices a hidden door behind a chest of drawers. Pushing the chest aside, she pulls the door open. Brushing aside cobwebs, she ascends a flight of stairs that lead to a lighted room. Inside is a young girl named Lollie (Beverly Washburn). She fears that Marcia has come to take her away and lock her up. "I want to be your friend," Marcia tells her. When she hands the girl a brooch that she admires, it begins to levitate; it floats through the air and blood suddenly wells up on Lollie's arm. Granny appears, cackling; she takes the brooch herself, then proposes to tell Victor. Marcia pleads with her not to and offers her engagement ring as a bribe.

Marcia returns to her room. Victor comes in. Granny reveals that Marcia saw Lollie and tells him of the attempted bribe. "Now you can *never* leave," Victor tells Marcia. He explains that Lollie lives in terror that she will be taken away from them. Marcia tells Victor that Lollie is afflicted with stigmata. Victor snorts at this explanation and shows her shelves full of books on the phenomenon, then reveals the real secret of the house: "We're afraid of *it*— the thing that snatched your pin and threw it — the thing that scratched Lollie." *It* is a poltergeist, an invisible parasite that has been in his family for three generations and has attached itself to Lollie, tormenting her at every opportunity.

Later that night they sit down to dinner. To her horror, Marcia sees that a sixth place has been set. But they have just begun to eat when streaks of blood appear on Lollie's face. A mug floats through the air, then comes flying at the girl's head as Granny cackles with laughter. Lollie runs screaming from the room.

"You don't seem to be afraid," Marcia says to Granny.

"Why should I be?" the hag answers. "*I'm* no Harrod."

Marcia questions Victor about the demon. He tells her it has plagued the Harrods ever since Granny married his great-uncle. Shortly afterwards, Granny tries to convince Victor to do away with Marcia, but he refuses. While Marcia is sleeping, Rennie stands over her with a knife. "Kill her," Granny commands, but the boy cannot do it. Marcia awakens; she and Granny struggle. The knife floats through the air and into Granny's hand. "This is the real secret of this house — my power to do *this*," Granny says. She advances on Marcia with the knife, but when she upsets a kerosene lamp, the flames set fire to her dress. Enveloped by fire, she runs screaming out of the house.

"It was Granny all the time," Marcia explains. "She knew the secret of levitation ... and she was using it to destroy you and your family." She had always nursed a grudge against the "high and mighty" Harrods, and had used it to maintain the upper hand over them all these years. Now the curse has ended.

Mary Elizabeth Counselman, author of "Parasite Mansion," is best remembered for her grim, haunting tale "The Three Marked Pennies." After its appearance in *Weird Tales* in 1934 the story attained legendary status and is now considered a classic of the supernatural. This bleak allegory is in sharp contrast to her other stories, which display an attitude exemplified by her views on horror fiction in general:

> The Hallowe'en scariness of the bumbling but kindly Wizard of Oz has always appealed to me more than the gruesome, morbid fiction of H. P. Lovecraft, Clark Ashton Smith, and those later authors who were influenced by their doom philosophies. My eerie shades bubble with an irrepressible sense of humor, ready to laugh with (never *at*) those earthbound mortals whose fears they once shared.

This philosophy, while not necessarily incompatible with the writing of horror fiction, nonetheless indicates the primary weakness of "Parasite Mansion," first published in the January 1942 *Weird Tales*. Its protagonist, Marcia Trent, is an assistant professor of abnormal psychology, and it's infuriating (and not a little unbelievable) to hear her dismiss claims that a poltergeist is haunting the Mason family (called the Harrods on *Thriller*) while glibly asserting the existence of levitation and telepathy as though they were everyday occurrences. Rather than being terrified by the events at Parasite Mansion, she goes at them like an occult Sherlock Holmes, dismissing the terrors out of hand and putting everything in its place with a smug rightness that deflates all the atmosphere of weird menace. (It's likewise unbelievable that Granny, after revealing her secret, simply dies of a heart attack in a *deus ex machina* ending; the *Thriller* denouement, in which she meets a fiery fate, is marginally more believable.)

Thankfully, Donald S. Sanford's adaptation avoids this matter of fact approach, though it's still hard to take Marcia's summary dismissal of the poltergeist, blithely asserting that it's only a case of levitation and stigmata. It's also

unbelievable that this young woman would succeed in solving, in one evening, a mystery that has plagued the Harrods for three generations.

Apart from these drawbacks, the episode is gripping and suspenseful. The opening scenes of the car in the rain and Marcia's first glimpse of Parasite Mansion are splendidly atmospheric. Her ascent to the hidden room in which Lollie is being kept is obviously patterned after Lila Crane's exploration of the Bates cellar in *Psycho*, and is similarly suspenseful.

The acting is variable. Pippa Scott, an attractive young actress seen in such films as *Petulia* (1968) and *Cold Turkey* (1971), struggles with her Southern accent, but for the most part is acceptable as Marcia Hunt.

James Griffith, as the whiskey sodden Victor Harrod, plays another of the weak characters that were his stock in trade. He's an aristocrat gone to seed, an ex-doctor reduced to squalid surroundings, and Griffith manages to suggest the man's degradation and self-loathing without overdoing it (though he seems a little old to be Rennie's brother; he looks more like the boy's father). For more on Griffith, see the entry on "The Storm."

Jeanette Nolan, on the other hand, is over the top as Granny. Admittedly, the role calls for a broad performance, but with her cackling and muttered asides, she makes the old hag more eccentric than evil. Nolan played a similar role in the later episode "La Strega." A noted character actress who was married to actor John McIntire, Nolan's films include Orson Welles' version of *Macbeth* (1948, as Lady Macbeth), *The Big Heat* (1953), and *The Rabbit Trap* (1958). She appeared frequently on television, and was a regular on several series, including *The Richard Boone Show* and *The Virginian*.

Tommy Nolan was a child actor popular during the early sixties. He's adequate as Rennie. He also appears in the *Thriller* episode "Child's Play."

Overall, "Parasite Mansion" is a grim and suspenseful entry that just misses being a classic. It has some very effective moments and a good cast, and, like most *Thrillers*, can be viewed more than once with little diminution of interest.

"A Good Imagination" (air-date: May 2, 1961). Produced by William Frye. Directed by John Brahm. Teleplay by Robert Bloch, from his short story. Director of Photography: Benjamin Kline, A.S.C. Associate Producer: Doug Benton. Art Director: Howard E. Johnson. Assistant Director: Frank Losee. Set Decorators: John McCarthy and Julia Heron. Music: Morton Stevens.

Cast: Edward Andrews (Frank Logan), Patricia Barry (Louise Logan), Ed Nelson (George Parker), William Allyn (Randy Hagen), Ken Lynch (Joe Thorp), Britt Lomond (Arnold Chase), Jim Bannon (Sheriff), Grace Canfield (Celia Perry).

An amusing but slight murder tale, "A Good Imagination" shows Robert Bloch in a lighter mood.

After cuckolded husband Frank Logan (Edward Andrews) dispatches his wife's paramour, Randy Hagen (William Allyn), she is surprised to find him at home reading a book. He tells her he has been attending a booksellers' convention in Philadelphia. He then taunts her with the key to Hagen's apartment. Shocked, Louise (Patricia Barry) tells her brother, Arnold Chase (Britt Lomond), that Frank has killed Randy, but he tells her there isn't enough evidence to convict Frank. He suggests they hire a private investigator named Joe Thorp to look into the matter.

Thorp (Ken Lynch), posing as a collector, visits Logan's bookshop. Logan sees through his ruse. Thorp accuses him of flying back from the convention to murder Randy Hagen, then offers to keep quiet for $10,000. Logan agrees to meet Thorp at a fishing cabin with the money. But when Arnold shows up there, he finds Logan waiting for him. Logan poisons him, then dumps his body in the lake, along with that of Thorp, whom he previously poisoned.

Logan relocates his errant wife in an isolated house. She is visited there by George Parker (Ed Nelson), a handyman. They are immediately attracted to each other, and are soon meeting clandestinely — although Logan, as usual, is quick to suspect the truth. He invites George over to seal up a hole in the basement wall. When George finishes, Logan tells him Louise is sealed up within, bound and gagged. George, who has a morbid fear of death, runs off and subsequently suffers a breakdown. He babbles his story to the police, but the sheriff interviews Louise, who is hale and hearty. Afterward, Logan walls up his wife for real.

Some time later the sheriff arrives with George Parker in tow, explaining that he might regain his reason if he sees Louise alive. "We just want to have a look at Mrs. Logan now," the sheriff says. "Where is she?"

For "A Good Imagination," Robert Bloch adapted his own short story, which originally appeared in the January 1956 *Suspect*, and expanded it considerably. The story, which bears a similarity to John Collier's classic "De Mortuis," begins with Logan instructing Parker to seal up the hole in the wall (and ends with the murderer getting away with his crime — a denouement television censors would have frowned on, hence the added twist with the sheriff's arrival). *Thriller's* hour length necessitated additional mayhem, making Logan a multiple murderer. Even with these additions the story seems better suited to *Alfred Hitchcock Presents*, although Bloch provides some amusing in-jokes: after dispatching Randy Hagen, the bookish Logan is seen perusing *Lady Chatterley's Lover*; after disposing of two bodies in a boat he turns to *An American Tragedy*. And when Thorp poses as a book collector, he's seeking *The Insider and Others* by "J. P. Morgenstern," a rare book published in 1939 — an obvious reference to *The Outsider and Others* by H. P. Lovecraft, published by Arkham House the same year.

Edward Andrews, making the first of his three *Thriller* appearances, is amusing as Logan. The plump, bespectacled Andrews was a familiar character actor. His film appearances include *The Phenix City Story* (1955), *The Unguarded Moment* (1956), *Elmer Gantry* (1960), *Advise and Consent* (1962), and many others. He was a regular on TV's *Broadside* and *The Doris Day Show*. One problem with his three *Thriller* episodes is that they all resemble one another: in "Cousin Tundifer" he is planning to murder his uncle, in "A Third for Pinochle," his wife, and in "A Good Imagination," his wife's inamoratos. Andrews died in 1985.

Patricia Barry was a strikingly beautiful actress seen to best advantage in the memorable *Thriller* episode "A Wig for Miss Devore." She later appeared in the soap opera *The Guiding Light* and *Days of Our Lives*.

Ed Nelson, making the third of his four *Thriller* appearances, is adequate as the unfortunate George Parker. For more on Nelson, see the entry on "Dialogues with Death."

"A Good Imagination" is a slight, amusing murder fable; it's hardly a classic *Thriller*, but is sufficiently entertaining.

"Mr. George" (airdate: May 9, 1961). Produced by William Frye. Directed by Ida Lupino. Teleplay by Donald S. Sanford, from the short story by "Stephen Grendon" (August Derleth). Music: Jerry Goldsmith. Director of Photography: John F. Warren, A.S.C. Associate Producer: Doug Benton. Edited by Danny Landres. Art Director: Loyd S. Papez. Assistant Director: Wallace Worsley. Editorial Supervisor: David J. O'Connell. Musical Supervision: Stanley Wilson. Sound: William Lynch. Set Decorators: John McCarthy and Julia Heron.

Cast: Gina Gillespie (Priscilla), Virginia Gregg (Edna), Howard Freeman (Jared), Lillian Bronson (Adelaide), Joan Tompkins (Laura Craig), John Qualen (Conductor), Ruth Perrott.

"Mr. George" is a gentle ghost story dealing with a child's (so-called) imaginary playmate, and his efforts to protect her. It's a somewhat atypical *Thriller*, but still well directed and acted.

Three relatives — Edna (Virginia Gregg), Jared (Howard Freeman) and Adelaide (Lillian Bronson) — find they have been left very little by their late cousin. What's worse, little Priscilla (Gina Gillespie) has been left in their care. Priscilla goes to see Mr. George, an imaginary playmate, and leaves a note beside the grave of George Craig.

The three relatives find that the entire estate, worth $500,000, has been left in trust to Priscilla. They attempt to break the will, without success. "What do we know about raising children?" sniffs Edna. "Only Priscilla stands between us and half a million," she observes later on. She suggests that something could happen to Priscilla, but Jared is reluctant. Priscilla, meanwhile, is in bed talking with Mr. George; he rocks back and forth in a chair.

Sometime later, Mr. George tells

Priscilla not to be afraid, no matter what happens. Edna suggests that Priscilla could have an "accident" by getting locked in a trunk and suffocating, and Adelaide hurries to put the plan into effect. But Mr. George intervenes, saving Priscilla's life, but causing the closing trunk lid to break Adelaide's neck.

Laura Craig (Joan Tompkins), George's sister, arrives unexpectedly to take care of Priscilla. Jared and Edna decide to arrange another "accident." Jared tries to kill Priscilla by hitting her with a swing, but once again Mr. George intervenes, and Jared is killed instead.

Edna learns that Laura, who is to be given custody of Priscilla, intends to take her away. Edna stretches a wire across the top step, but again Priscilla is warned by Mr. George, and Edna falls down the stairs instead. Mr. George tells Priscilla that Laura will look after her from now on.

"Mr. George" is an adaptation of a short story by August Derleth, published under his pen name Stephen Grendon in the March 1947 issue of *Weird Tales*. Although he may be best known as an anthologist and publisher (he founded Arkham House, which published the first works of Ray Bradbury, Robert Bloch and Fritz Leiber, among others), Derleth (1909-71) also wrote a staggering number of short stories, novels, books of poetry and nonfiction works. He published 137 stories in *Weird Tales* alone, more than any writer other than Seabury Quinn, and his total output includes more than 100 books. Much of his work in the genre is slight (particularly his Cthulhu Mythos tales, pseudo-collaborations with H. P. Lovecraft), but some of his ghost stories are effective. "Mr. George" is one of his better efforts. It was originally filmed by Revue in 1953, but Donald Sanford's adaptation is far superior, and Ida Lupino's direction

shows a distinct feel for its milieu and characters. There's a lot of fluid camera work (in one scene the camera is attached to a swing arcing back and forth over Jared's dead body).

The actors are competent, if little-known. Virginia Gregg was a radio actress who appeared frequently in films and on television. Her screen credits include *All the Fine Young Cannibals* (1960), *Joy in the Morning* and *Two on a Guillotine* (both 1965). She was evidently a favorite of Jack Webb's, for she appeared frequently on *Dragnet*. She's appropriately harsh and overbearing as Edna.

Gina Gillespie was a popular child actress of the late fifties and early sixties, thankfully not prone to cute antics or histrionics. She's quite believable as Priscilla. She appeared on two TV series—*Law of the Plainsman* and *Karen*, and appeared in such films as *Andy Hardy Comes Home* (1958).

Howard Freeman was a character actor usually seen in comic roles. His films include *Once Upon a Time* (1944), *House of Horrors* (1946), and *Dear Brigitte* (1965). He died in 1967.

Lillian Bronson was a character actress who appeared in *Walk on the Wild Side* (1962) and *The Americanization of Emily* (1964), among other films. She's adequate as Adelaide.

"Mr. George" is a deceptively gentle ghost story, pleasant enough but hardly one of *Thriller*'s finer hours.

"The Terror in Teakwood"

(airdate: May 16, 1961). Produced by William Frye. Directed by Paul Henreid. Teleplay by Alan Caillou, based on the short story by Harold Lawlor. Director of Photography: John F. Warren, A.S.C. Original Music: Jerry Goldsmith. Piano solos composed and performed by Oscar Giovannini. Edited by Edward Haire.

Art Director: Howard E. Johnson. Associate Producer: Douglas Benton. Assistant Director: John Clarke Bowman. Set Decorators: John McCarthy and Julia Heron.

Cast: Guy Rolfe (Vladimir Vicek), Hazel Court (Leonie Vicek), Charles Aidman (Jerry Welch), Reggie Nalder (Gafke), Vladimir Sokoloff (Papa Glockstein, "Glocky"), Linda Watkins (Sylvia Slattery), Bernard Fein (Stage Manager), George Kane (Photographer), John Craven, Monica Henreid.

One of the undeniable *Thriller* classics, "The Terror of Teakwood" suffers only from a fundamental incongruity necessitated by network censorship. Apart from this, the episode is first-rate in every way — dark, moody, and admirably atmospheric. In the words of Jay Allen Sanford, "Terror in Teakwood" may (arguably) be *Thriller*'s absolute scariest episode.

In a Polish graveyard, the macabre figure of the cemetery keeper, Gafke (Reggie Nalder), opens the gates to admit a mysterious figure (Guy Rolfe), who pays him off. Gafke leads the figure to a crypt, saying, "Your accent is strange to me. What are you doing here?" "A pilgrimage," the figure answers, then gives instructions: "Wait for me outside; leave me alone," "Alone in here?" Gafke asks. "What kind of a man are you?" "A man with money," the stranger replies. "Now go."

Gafke watches from outside and reacts in horror at what he sees — the stranger desecrating the grave.

Some time passes. Musician Jerry Welch (Charles Aidman) receives a visit from his old flame, Leonie (Hazel Court). She is now married to the famous pianist Vladimir Vicek. But there is trouble in the household: she is convinced someone is trying to murder her husband. The night before, some-

one broke into the apartment; cold hands were clutching her throat and there was blood all over Vicek's body. Moreover, it was not the first time she had found him like this. She wants Jerry to come and live with them as Vicek's manager; Vicek is just beginning his American tour.

Jerry goes to see Papa Glockstein, nicknamed "Glocky" (Vladimir Sokoloff), to ask his advice; Glocky tells him to take the job. He also tells Jerry that Vicek has but one passion: his music, and a mania to surpass the great composer-pianist Czarnowitz. "But Czarnowitz is dead," Jerry points out. Just then he receives a phone call from Leonie: Vicek is locked in his room, playing the piano and screaming at the top of his lungs. When he emerges from the locked room, he is bleeding profusely; he collapses on the floor.

When he revives, Vicek refuses to see a doctor. He accepts Jerry in his employ and entrusts him with a small teakwood box shaped like a casket; he tells him to keep it always in sight. When Vicek is gone, Leonie explains that the trouble began when Czarnowitz supposedly died — she thinks he is still alive. One night Vicek went to the cemetery where he was buried; Leonie believes he found that the body was missing. What's more, the music Vicek was playing was the Czarnowitz Sonata — Czarnowitz was the only one physically capable of playing it with such mastery. Leonie believes Czarnowitz is in New York and trying to kill Vicek.

While Jerry and Leonie are out walking, they are followed by a man with a cane: Gafke. He explains to Jerry that he was once a caretaker in a cemetery. "What I know is worth a lot more than what I have," he says. When Jerry asks if Czarnowitz is still alive, the skull-faced Gafke laughs. He has followed

Vicek all the way to America, and if he tells what he knows, they will put Vicek in prison. "Put him in prison?" Jerry asks. "For what?" Gafke laughs. "What happened in that graveyard?" Jerry demands. "The money first," Gafke says.

Jerry goes back to Vicek's apartment and opens the teakwood box. Inside are a pair of hands.

In the meantime, music critic Sylvia Slattery (Linda Watkins) receives tickets to Vicek's concert. She thinks the concert will destroy Vicek's reputation: Vicek is scheduled to play — or attempt to play — the Czarnowitz Seventh. He will make himself a laughingstock and be booed off the stage, and Sylvia is laughingly anticipating his ruin. "He must be out of his mind," Jerry comments. Czarnowitz wrote a sonata no one else could play, because no one could match the phenomenal spread of his hands, thus explaining Vicek's pathological hatred of Czarnowitz, centered on a pair of hands. "Did you ever see them?" Sylvia asks. "Yes, Sylvia — I have seen them," Jerry says.

Jerry returns to Leonie and tells her that Vicek opened Czarnowitz' casket and made a cast of the dead man's hands. The cast is now in the teakwood box.

That night at the concert Sylvia is waiting for Vicek. "A lot of people in there have come to watch him die ... I'm one of them," she says. "I want to see their mockery tear him apart." Vicek begins the seventh sonata, playing brilliantly. "He can do it," Leonie says. "Jerry, he's going to make it." Sylvia listens in disbelief. When Vicek finishes, the audience breaks into rapt applause, the loudest cheering coming from Sylvia Slattery. Vicek rises to accept their tribute, and Leonie faints as she sees blood dripping down Vicek's gloved hands.

Back at the apartment, Leonie has been put to bed. A strange figure enters

via the window: Gafke, brandishing a large knife. He tells Vicek he wants money. "You miserable scum," Vicek says. "Do you think I'm afraid of you? Do you think I'll let you ruin my triumph?" They struggle, and Vicek throws him over the balcony to his death many floors below.

Shortly afterward he hears Leonie calling Jerry's name in her sleep. He confronts Jerry and tells him to open the teakwood chest. Jerry does; it is empty. Vicek takes out Gafke's knife. He admits he stole his rival's hands. "But even in death I found a way to conquer him," he says. "I won." Vicek tells Jerry that in time the hands came alive; he put them on, like gloves, and played the sonata with them. But the spirit came back into them and tried to kill him while he was sleeping. "I know what those hands are capable of in the night," Vicek says. "I placed them on her bed, close beside her on the pillow, while she slept." Leonie screams; Vicek and Jerry fight, with Jerry getting the upper hand. He breaks down Leonie's door and finds her lying unconscious. The hands crawl along the floor, out of the room. There is a terrifying scream from Vicek. They find him lying on the floor dead, the hands around his throat.

In adapting Harold Lawlor's short story (which appeared in the March 1947 *Weird Tales*), writer-actor Alan Caillou made several changes, few for the better. In the story the pianist (named Ondia Hurok) cut off the hands of his hated rival — something the *Thriller* episode hints at but never makes clear. When Gafke reacts in horror (and when Jerry later tells Leonie what happened in the cemetery that night), his anguished expression suggests the defilement of Czarnowitz' corpse, and it's a distinct disappointment when Jerry reveals that all Vicek did was make a cast of the dead man's hands. Another matter left unclear in the *Thriller* version is the power and motivation of the hands; in the original story they took on a life of their own only at night, and were docile the rest of the time. Conversely, Caillou improved matters by expanding Gafke's role. In the story he's a loose end, cheated out of money by the pianist and scared off by Jerry (called Giles in the story). Here he manages a confrontation with Vicek, only to be thrown to his death.

But these are minor quibbles. For most of its length, "The Terror in Teakwood" is an engrossing horror tale, from its atmospheric opening in a fog choked cemetery to its macabre but logical conclusion. There are some unforgettable images: the cynical, hardened Sylvia Slattery reduced to a sobbing, credulous believer by Vicek's piano mastery; Vicek rising to accept his acclaim, blood dripping down his hands; and the hands themselves crawling across the floor with a life of their own. (Admittedly, this image is reminiscent of Robert Florey's *The Beast with Five Fingers*). Actor Paul Henreid (best remembered as Victor Laszlo in *Casablanca*) is a surprising choice as director, particularly since he was screenwriter Curt Siodmak's original choice for the role Peter Lorre played in *The Beast with Five Fingers*. (According to Siodmak, Henreid demurred, saying, "I won't play opposite some goddamned hand!") Hands, of course, are a common motif in horror fiction, the two best known being *Beast* and *The Hands of Orlac*.

The actors are excellent. Guy Rolfe, a tall, aristocratic Englishman with more than a hint of cruelty, is perfectly cast as Vicek. Rolfe is best known to horror fans as the eponymous protagonist of William Castle's disappointing *Mr. Sardonicus* (1961), though he's played in many other kinds of films, including *King of the Khyber Rifles* (1954), *The Stranglers of Bombay* (1960), *Snow White and the Three Stooges* (1961) and *Nicholas and Alexandra* (1971).

Hazel Court was, of course, one of the most active horror heroines of the fifties and sixties, appearing in *Devil Girl from Mars* (1954), *Ghost Ship* (1957), *The Curse of Frankenstein* (1957), *The Man Who Could Cheat Death* (1959), *Dr. Blood's Coffin* (1961), *The Premature Burial* (1962), *The Raven* (1963), and *The Masque of the Red Death* (1964). After *Red Death*, she married director Don Taylor and retired from films. One of her last appearances on TV was in the *Wild, Wild West* episode "The Night of the Returning Dead" (1968). As Bill Warren comments, she was "better served by villainous roles than ones in which she has to be the menaced maiden. She always looks like she could clobber whatever it is that's out to get her, but also as if she could easily fall victim to her own schemes."

Charles Aidman is described in the entry on "Knock Three-One-Two."

Reggie Nalder is impeccably cast as the skulking graveyard rat Gafke, and Henreid inserts frequent closeups of Nalder's leering face with its unique skull-like physiognomy. For years rumors persisted that he had been disfigured in a fire, but a reader of *Video Watchdog* wrote in to explain that the disfigurement occurred when Nalder was 14 and being treated for a severe case of acne. While he was undergoing ultraviolet treatment, the nurse left the room and forgot to return in time; Nalder was scarred for life. The disfigurement became more noticeable as he grew older: evidently the most damage was done to his lower lip and chin.

Nalder got his start playing macabre characters as the assassin in Hitchcock's second version of *The Man Who Knew Too Much* (1956). His other genre appearances include *The Manchurian Candidate* (1962), *Mark of the Devil* (1970), the TV movie *The Dead Don't Die* (1975), *Dracula's Dog* (1978), the TV movie *'Salem's Lot* (1979), and *The Devil and Max Devlin* (1981). He also appeared in a *Wild, Wild West* episode, "The Night of the Gruesome Games," and turns up in a larger role in a later *Thriller*, "The Return of Andrew Bentley." He died in 1991.

Vladimir Sokoloff gives a fine supporting performance as Papa Glockstein, referred to as "Glocky" throughout. A solid character actor who always added verisimilitude even in the smallest of roles, Sokoloff was memorable in such films as *For Whom the Bell Tolls* (1943), *Cloak and Dagger* (1946), *I Was a Teenage Werewolf* (1957, as the lycanthrope-fearing janitor), and *Mr. Sardonicus* (1961, as Guy Rolfe's father). On television he gave a touching performance as the grieving father in the *Twilight Zone* episode "Dust"; he can also be seen in a later *Thriller*, "Flowers of Evil."

Linda Watkins, in her second *Thriller* appearance, makes a vivid impression as the acid-tongued Sylvia Slattery. The scene in which her contempt for Vicek turns into adoration is especially memorable. Watkins specialized in these bitchy characterizations; she plays similarly acidulous figures in "The Cheaters" and "A Wig for Miss Devore."

It would be unfair to pass over "The Terror in Teakwood" without taking note of Jerry Goldsmith's memorable score, as well as the piano solos composed and performed by Oscar Giovannini. Of all *Thrillers*, this has perhaps the most impressive soundtrack, an aural feast well designed to complement a grisly tale of ambition and revenge.

"The Prisoner in the Mirror"

(airdate: May 23, 1961). Produced by William Frye. Directed by Herschel Daugherty. Written by Robert Arthur. Music: Morton Stevens. Director of Photography: Benjamin Kline. Art Director: Alex Mayer. Set Decorators: John McCarthy and Julia Heron. Associate Producer: Douglas Benton. Assistant Director: George Bisk.

Cast: Lloyd Bochner (Harry Langham), Marion Ross (Kay), Jack Mullaney (Fred Forrest), Henry Daniell (Count Cagliostro), Pat Michon (Yvette Dulaine), Peter Brocco (Professor Thibault), David Frankham (Marquis de Chantenay), Pamela Curran, Walter Reed, Frieda Inescourt, Erika Peters, Louis Mercier.

Continuing the tradition that by now had become a hallmark of *Thriller*, "The Prisoner in the Mirror" is another first-rate episode.

In 1910 Paris, the Marquis de Chantenay (David Frankham) is dining with a lovely young woman. He dazzles her with demonstrations of legerdemain, producing flowers and birds seemingly out of thin air. "I am the world's greatest magician — the only real magician left," he announces. After making diamonds appear he says "The real magic is yet to come. The most stupendous trick of all. Look into my eyes." The young woman, spellbound, stares into his face, which turns into a skull. She screams as skeletal hands encircle her throat.

As the police are pounding on the door of the Marquis' flat, he is busy painting over the surface of a large mirror. They announce that they have a warrant for his arrest. The Marquis swears he is not guilty of the girl's murder and, finished painting over the mirror, jumps out a window to his death.

In modern-day Paris, Professor Thibault (Peter Brocco) is telling Harry

Langham (Lloyd Bochner) to give up his interest in the 17th-century magician Cagliostro. He tells him he once wrote a thesis on the magician but destroyed it. When Langham protests that Cagliostro has, after all, been dead for nearly 200 years, Thibault replies, "Evil never dies." Langham asks the professor about a particular mirror that Cagliostro apparently considered very important; Langham has been searching antique stores for it, without success. Thibault warns him not to continue his researches, and accompanies him to the tomb of a woman named Yvette Dulaine. He lifts the coffin lid; the girl is still young and beautiful. "She has lain exactly as you see her since the year 1780," Thibault says. Cagliostro desired her, she repulsed him, and she has remained in this death-like state all these years. Thibault implores Langham to go home to America.

Instead, Langham goes to an antique shop and finds a mirror, covered with paint, that belonged to the Marquis de Chantenay. Scraping off some of the paint, he sees a young woman's face in the glass.

Back in Boston, the mirror is delivered to Langham's home, where his fiancée, Kay (Marion Ross), is planning to celebrate his return from Paris. Langham ignores her; alone with the mirror, he begins scraping away all the paint. Kay notices a change coming over her fiancé. Langham sees a figure with a candelabra — "Yvette," he calls. The girl nods; she cannot speak. Kay interrupts; when Langham asks her to look into the mirror, she sees nothing. Returning to see Yvette once again, Langham instead encounters a man dressed in 17th-century garb (Henry Daniell); he identifies himself as a victim of Cagliostro. Referring to Yvette, he says: "We are both, alas, prisoners within the mirror of that

infamous magician Count Alessandro Cagliostro. We exist in a dark dimension that is neither life nor death." When Yvette rejoins him, he repeats one of Cagliostro's spells. "Now it is time for you to join us," he announces. "Rise and join us in the world of the mirror." Langham's spirit rises and enters the glass, leaving his body still seated in a chair. "Au revoir, monsieur," the other man says. "It is 50 years since I last left the world of the mirror. I am hungry for the taste of life again." He steps out of the mirror and enters Langham's body. "Now his spirit is free — and he has taken your body for his evil purposes," Yvette says. "Who is he?" Langham asks. "Count Alessandro Cagliostro," she replies.

Cagliostro (in Langham's body) meets a young girl. The next day he is questioned by a detective who says an officer saw him enter his house at 4:15 a.m. He tells Cagliostro/Langham he fits the description of the man who strangled the young girl the night before, but the glib magician manages to convince him that he's mistaken.

Cagliostro/Langham is suddenly much more attentive to his fiancée; when Kay comments on this he replies, "Today I am a different man." Kay's brother, Fred Forrest (Jack Mullaney), arrives with the paper in his hand, but his sister and her fiancé are going out to dinner. In the mirror Yvette tells Langham that only Cagliostro can shatter it, and that as long as they are trapped inside they cannot die. Fred enters the room and examines the mirror. Langham screams at him, but Fred cannot hear.

When Cagliostro/Langham and Kay return, she reaches for matches in his coat pocket and finds the dead girl's earrings (in a contrived incident, she happens to see, at that very moment, a photograph of the dead girl wearing the earrings). Cagliostro/Langham is forced to kill Kay. Fred comes downstairs, finds his sister dead, and chases Cagliostro/Langham upstairs. They fight, and Cagliostro/Langham is thrown against the mirror, breaking it. He dies with a look of ecstasy on his face, and his handsome features dissolve into a skull.

In a way, it's a shame that writer Robert Arthur chose a historical personage as his protagonist; in "The Prisoner in the Mirror," Count Cagliostro is invoked as such an evil presence that it's a letdown to learn that the real Cagliostro was the 18th-century's greatest charlatan, a predecessor of that latter-day faker, Aleister Crowley.

Alessandro di Cagliostro (1743-95) was born Giuseppe Balsamo in Palermo, Sicily, and grew up as a street urchin. Admitted to a monastery, he was expelled when he substituted the names of well-known harlots for those of the martyrs. He visited Greece, Egypt, Arabia, Persia and Rhodes, and studied alchemy (always a useful pursuit) and the occult sciences. He married Lorenza Feliciani in 1768, and became a forger of documents, meanwhile selling love philtres and the "elixir of long life." He also claimed to be adept in sommoning up the dead (whom he said revealed the future to him). He and his wife traveled from town to town throughout Europe, performing feats of prestidigitation. He succeeded in capturing the imaginations of some of the most important men of the era, including Goethe, Schiller and Tieck.

In 1785, implicated in the Affair of the Diamond Necklace, Cagliostro was imprisoned in the Bastille for nine months, then banished from France. Upon his release, he and his wife visited London, then traveled again on the Continent. In 1789 he was arrested in Rome for heresy and condemned to death by the Inquisition; the sentence was later commuted to life imprisonment, and he died in confinement at San Leone in 1795.

He was a favorite subject of silent film makers. Georges Méliès made *Cagliostro's Mirror* (!) in 1899, and there were various versions of his exploits in 1910, 1912, 1920, and 1928 (two). For years Orson Welles wanted to direct a version; he wound up playing him in an undistinguished 1949 programmer called *Black Magic*.

All of this leads up to "The Prisoner in the Mirror" and its author, Robert Arthur. A noted radio and pulp writer, he worked for MGM in the thirties while he wrote for magazines such as *Unknown* and *Weird Tales*. Besides working for the radio series "The Mysterious Traveler," he edited the magazine spun off from it. His best-known work may be the anthologies he ghost-edited for Alfred Hitchcock, such as *Bar the Doors, Twelve Stories for Late at Night* and *Stories My Mother Never Told Me*. Among his teleplays is the *Thriller* two-parter "Dialogues with Death." He died in 1969.

"The Prisoner in the Mirror," Arthur's finest *Thriller* adaptation, has a marvelous fairy tale ambience accented by Morton Stevens' graceful score. There are a few discrepancies: Why does Yvette not warn Langham of Cagliostro's intentions when she has the chance? Why does she pretend to be mute, only to speak later? And why do we see so little of the world of the mirror? (Admittedly, this may have been necessitated by budget considerations.) Audiences accustomed to state of the art visual effects may find the mirror illusions primitive: Langham simply steps through an empty frame to join the prisoners on the other side; there's nothing like the poetic translucency of the imagery in Jean

Cocteau's *Orpheus*. Likewise, when Cagliostro finally dies, there's simply a dissolve to a skull rather than the expected dissolution of his features (although his smile is a clever touch: for a man who has lived so long, death must come as a relief).

Other aspects of the production are well up to standard, notably Benjamin Kline's imaginative cinematography. And the teaser, in which Cagliostro, in the body of the Marquis de Chantenay, performs magic, is an impressively eerie, mystifying prologue that sets the tone for what is to follow.

The performances are fine. Lloyd Bochner, normally a rather stiff actor, plays two parts convincingly. Genre fans may recall him as "The Dream" in William Castle's *The Night Walker* (1965), and he was the protagonist of the memorable *Twilight Zone* episode "To Serve Man."

Marion Ross makes little impression as Kay. A familiar television presence, she was a regular on *Mr. Novak*, but is probably best known as Marion Cunningham on the long-running *Happy Days*.

Henry Daniell, as always, is suitably suave as Cagliostro, though his actual screen time is limited. Even so, he makes his presence felt. He would have much larger roles in the later episodes "Well of Doom" and "God Grante That She Lye Stille." (For more information on Daniell, see the entry on "The Cheaters.")

Jack Mullaney was a regular on several television series, including *My Living Doll* and *It's About Time*. He died in 1982.

David Frankham makes a brief but unforgettable appearance in the prologue, the second of his four *Thriller* performances. (He had previously been seen in "The Poisoner," and would later appear in "The Closed Cabinet" and "The Specialists.") For more on Frankham, see the entry on "The Closed Cabinet."

"The Prisoner in the Mirror" is an eerie episode that succeeds despite its minor inconsistencies and primitive visual effects, and can be enjoyed straightforwardly for its compelling story. On another level, it can be read as an apt metaphor for all of us who sit gazing into our television screens. In a very real sense *we* are the prisoners in the mirror, leaving behind our shells to enter an unreal existence, a world that is neither alive nor dead, the realm of long-deceased actors playing out the same dramas again and again, a world both unreal and timeless.

"Dark Legacy" (airdate: May 30, 1961). Produced by William Frye. Directed by John Brahm. Written by John Tomerlin. Director of Photography: John F. Warren, A.S.C. Music: Jerry Goldsmith. Musical Supervision: Stanley Wilson. Edited by Edward Haire, A.C.E. Art Director: Loyd S. Papez. Associate Producer: Doug Benton. Assistant Director: Ben Bishop. Editorial Supervision: David J. O'Connell. Set Decorators: John McCarthy and Frank Tuttle.

Cast: Harry Townes (Mario Asparos/Radan), Ilka Windish (Monika Asparos), Henry Silva (Toby Wolfe), Alan Napier (Attorney), Richard Hale (Lars Eisenhart), Doris Lloyd (Mrs. Pringle), Ned Glass (Vince Fennaday), Milton Parsons (Butler).

Although "Dark Legacy" has a first-rate premise, it fails to sustain it, and finally falls apart due to a weak ending, though there are compensations in John Brahm's stylish, atmospheric direction.

In a forbidding old mansion (the same one seen as Sir Wilfred's house in

"Hay-Fork and Bill-Hook"), an old magician lies dying. Downstairs, the old man's relatives have gathered. They include Lars Eisenhart (Richard Hale), Mrs. Pringle (Doris Lloyd) and Mario Asparos (Harry Townes). The butler (Milton Parsons) dismisses them, after first having each of them inscribe his name on a parchment strip. These he gives to his master, Radan (Harry Townes, again). He casts a spell in order to choose his successor. After he throws the other names in the fire, one strip of parchment clings to the pages of his grimoire. It bears the name of his nephew, Mario Asparos. Having accomplished his task, Radan climbs into his coffin.

Mario is a professional magician appearing in a small club with his wife Monika (Ilka Windish), who is also his assistant. After failing to wow his unappreciative audience, Mario is told by his employer, Vince Fennaday (Ned Glass), that he needs new routines. Mario and Monika are visited by an old friend, former magician Toby Wolfe (Henry Silva). During their conversation Mario receives word that his uncle has died. He returns to his home for the reading of the will. The lawyer (Alan Napier) announces that one item, a book of unusual properties, is to be left to one of the heirs. Lars Eisenhart is enraged that Radan's greatest tricks have not been willed to anyone.

Mario is called away to the phone. His wife is on the line; she is frightened by the storm and has a premonition of danger. After she goes to close a window, she finds a book suddenly and inexplicably atop Mario's desk. "Radan has chosen you as his heir," Toby Wolfe explains. "He could have revealed his secrets to Lars. You must admit that Lars is the only first-class magician left in the Asparos clan. Radan designated you. I'm sure he had a reason for it." Monika seems disturbed by the book, but Mario

examines it, finding rituals, incantations and conjurations, including spells for summoning Aztoroth. Toby explains that Aztoroth is a satanic messenger. "Well, we know Radan was pretty far gone in this stuff," Toby says. "I guess he meant to make you a great magician by passing along one of his pet demons."

Monika advises Mario to get rid of the book, but he refuses. He reminds her that she could have married Toby. When Mario speaks of his ambition to be as great a magician as his uncle, Monika tells him that Radan was evil. "Just to be around him made me feel — violated. He was the only truly evil man I have ever met," Monika says.

Mario pores over the book. He finds that his dog will not enter the room while the book is present. Attempting to cast one of the spells, he draws a chalk circle on the floor while a storm rages outside. A thick smoke emerges from the fireplace and disembodied eyes float through the air. "Princes of darkness, I salute you," Mario says. But the dog is dead.

Sometime later Mario is playing to bigger and more appreciative audiences. He performs the highlight of the act, in which he fires a pistol at Monika through a glass; she remains unharmed, catching the bullet in her teeth. After the act, Mario tells Vince Fennaday they are leaving to open in Las Vegas. But Monika is badly frightened; she calls Toby and asks him to come to the club. Toby accuses Mario of using Radan's tricks. When he asks about the bullet stunt, Mario says, "Don't you understand? It isn't a trick. Nothing of what I do anymore is a trick. You thought that Radan left me a worthless book ... I tell you, I possess the power that was Radan's!" When Toby suggests that Mario's magic is a form of self-hypnosis, Mario tells him he will show him things.

"I'm going to show you ... Aztoroth!" he says.

Back at home, Mario prepares to cast a spell. "No one can perform black magic," Toby scoffs. "Merlin could; Cagliostro could; pharaohs' magicians could," Mario declares. Monika, terrified, runs for the door; Mario brings her back, locking it. He casts the spell. Smoke arises as before. Aztoroth appears. "Send it back!" Toby yells. "In the name of heaven, send it back!" Suspecting Toby and Monika of being lovers, Mario orders the demon to destroy them. But Toby grabs the book and hurls it into the fire. Mario screams.

When Toby awakens sometime later, he finds Mario dead and Monika unconscious. "I saw something," he tells her. "Sometimes a twisted mind can affect all those people around it. I only know the book wouldn't have been enough. The demon that destroyed Mario was within him, and we've got to think of it that way."

For about half its length, "Dark Legacy" is an enjoyable excursion into the realm of black magic and demonology, but it's ultimately let down by conventional plot development and a disappointing ending. The story line begs several questions. Why does Radan's spell indicate that Mario is the proper person to receive the book? He seems a questionable choice, particularly since all he does with his arcane knowledge is use it to spruce up his magic act. And what is the purpose of the two other claimants to Radan's estate, Miss Pringle and Lars Eisenhart? They seem to be present for a confrontation with Mario that never occurs. In terms of plot, they could have been dispensed with entirely.

The opening, with the old dark house and an anxious family awaiting the word of a dying magician, promises

vintage *Thriller* chills, and the story line seems rich in possibilities. Horror films of that era rarely dealt with black magic, and the exceptions (such as *Curse of the Demon* and *Burn, Witch, Burn*) tended to be excellent, so one's expectations are naturally heightened. But Mario Asparos fritters away his dark legacy. And the denouement, in which he summons the demon, only to have it destroy him, is predictable and disappointing (compare it to the fiery and exciting train climax of *Curse of the Demon*). John Brahm's atmospheric touches are helpful (the floating eyes hovering amid the smoke is a startling, almost surreal, image), but "Dark Legacy" just doesn't live up to its initial promise.

The actors can hardly be faulted. Harry Townes, previously seen in "The Cheaters," is quite believable as the obsessed Mario Asparos (though there's an extended shot of his leering, frenzied face that's more comical than frightening). He's not helped by the makeup man: he looks ridiculous in a fright wig and old-age makeup as Radan.

As Monika, Ilka Windish is adequate, though her screaming and overdone reactions to everything (including an electrical storm) are hard to take. It's difficult to believe she would stay as Mario's assistant after he began using real magic in their act, much less that she'd agree to witness the climactic summoning of Aztoroth.

As Toby Wolfe, Henry Silva is fine, though Wolfe himself is a contradictory character. He keeps jabbering about self-hypnosis, yet when the demon appears he's screaming at Mario to send it back, all his self-possession gone. (And the minute the danger is past, he's back to rationalizations). The rest of the time he's as smug as Marcia Hunt in "Parasite Mansion." Nothing is made of his former profession of magician, nor is he the least bit surprised when Radan's book mysteriously appears, laughingly attributing it to Radan despite the fact that the man is dead.

The other actors are familiar faces to *Thriller* viewers. They include Richard Hale (from "The Incredible Dr. Markesan"), Doris Lloyd (from "Hay-Fork and Bill-Hook"), and Alan Napier (from "The Purple Room" and "Hay-Fork and Bill-Hook"). Additionally, it's nice to see Milton Parsons as Radan's butler, even though it's a small role. Parsons, one of the most cadaverous-looking actors ever to set foot in a horror film, made a career of playing macabre characters, usually undertakers, and was seen in *Dead Men Tell* (1941), *The Hidden Hand* (1942), *Cry of the Werewolf* (1944) and *The Monster That Challenged the World* (1957). His best role was probably in Roger Corman's *The Haunted Palace* (1963), and he was creepy as ever in the *Dick Van Dyke Show* episode, "The Ghost of A. Chantz." He died in 1980.

"Dark Legacy" is a frustrating episode, mainly because the initial premise is so intriguing; and it's so full of that distinctive *Thriller* atmosphere that, when the inevitable letdown occurs, it's doubly disappointing. It's still a handsome episode to look at, and boasts the services of a fine cast, but leaves one with the inevitable sense of an opportunity wasted.

"Pigeons from Hell" (airdate: June 6, 1961). Produced by William Frye. Directed by John Newland. Teleplay by John Kneubuhl, from the short story by Robert E. Howard. Music: Morton Stevens. Director of Photography: Lionel Lindon, A.S.C. Associate Producer: Doug Benton. Film Editor: Danny B. Landres, A.C.E. Art Director: George Patrick. Assistant Director:

Charles S. Gould. Editorial Supervision: David J. O'Connell. Musical Supervision: Stanley Wilson. Sound: Lyle Crain. Set Decorators: John McCarthy and Julia Heron.

Cast: Brandon DeWilde (Tim Branner), Crahan Denton (Sheriff Buckner), David Whorf (John Branner), Ken Renard (Jacob Blount), Guy Wilkerson (Howard), Ottola Nesmith (Eula Lee Blassenville).

"Pigeons from Hell" is probably the most recognized episode of *Thriller*. Its impact was so strong that many who saw it when it was initially telecast more than 30 years ago remember it with an uncomfortable vividness to this day. It is a tour de force of horror, with an intensity and singleness of purpose that make it a standout even among such memorable episodes as "The Purple Room," "The Hungry Glass" and "The Grim Reaper." In sum, it's the single greatest *Thriller* of all.

Two young brothers, Tim (Brandon DeWilde) and John Branner (David Whorf), are driving through the American south when their car goes out of control. "You and your shortcuts," Tim says. John goes in search of a pole with which to pry the car loose from a ditch, but instead finds a forbidding old plantation house overrun by pigeons. "It was like they ... were attacking me," John says when the birds take flight. "The trouble with us is we're both tired," Tim tells him.

As they prepare to enter the old house, Karloff intones:

> "The swamp is alive, crawling with creatures of death, creatures that lurk camouflaged in the undergrowth, waiting patiently for an unsuspecting victim ... and our young friend was alarmed by a flight of pigeons. Harmless, you say? Well, you'll find he has good reason for

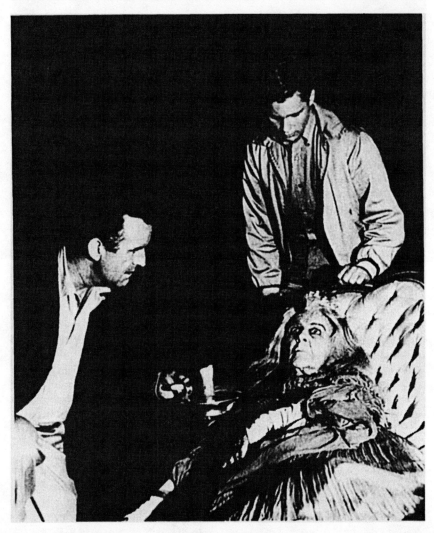

Perhaps television's all-time scariest excursion into horror: Crahan Denton, left, and Brandon DeWilde examine the zuvembie (Ottola Nesmith) in the celebrated "Pigeons from Hell" (Ronald V. Borst/Hollywood Movie Posters).

alarm, for those were no ordinary pigeons — they were the pigeons from hell. That is both the title and the substance of our story. Spirits come back from the dead to guard their ancestral home against intruders, spirits that in life fed on evil, and now in death return to feed upon the living, return each night, driven relentlessly by the spell of a terrible curse."

Tim and John enter the house. There is no sign of anyone. "Nobody's been home for quite a while," Tim says. Spider webs overhang everything; a spiral staircase leads upstairs. Despite their cheerless surroundings, the two decide to spend the night. They bring in their sleeping bags and start a fire to keep warm. John notices the portrait of a woman, covered by spider webs, in the main room.

The two spread out their sleeping bags and lie down to sleep. John is still disturbed by the sounds of pigeons.

Sometime later that night John is awakened by an eerie wailing. In a trance, he rises and ascends the stairs. Tim awakens and, finding his brother gone, goes to look for him. He hears a bloodcurdling scream from the second floor. He runs up the stairs and sees the shadow of a man with a hatchet approaching him. It is John: his face is covered with blood, as is the hatchet. He swings it at Tim, burying it in the wall. Tim runs from the house. John descends the stairs, walking with a zombielike gait, the bloody hatchet in his hand. Tim runs through the woods until he collapses.

Tim awakens to find Sheriff Buckner (Crahan Denton) peering over him. He tells him old Howard (Guy Wilkerson) found him and brought him to his cabin. "We found this old house," Tim tells the sheriff. "It was deserted. We were going to spend the night. And I woke up. He wasn't there. I heard him scream. I ran to the stairs and I saw him. His head ... his head was smashed, but he was walking with a hatchet in his hand. He was walking down the stairs to me. His head was *split*, but he was walking. He was dead. I know he was dead."

Buckner recognizes the deserted house as the old Blassenville place, and announces they are going back there. At the sound of the name, old Howard takes off running. Taking Tim with him, Sheriff Buckner returns to the house in his station wagon. Inside, Buckner finds blood on the stairs and John's body in the main room. The hatchet is buried where Tim's head would have been.

The sheriff does not believe Tim's story. When Tim mentions the pigeons, Buckner scoffs; he's lived around the house all his life and has never seen a single pigeon. He tells Tim he will have to arrest him for murder: "You and your brother had an argument, and you killed him!"

"No!" Tim shouts. "If I had, don't you think I could make up a better story than the one I told you?"

"Maybe," Buckner snaps.

The two go upstairs. On the second floor they find more blood. They continue along the corridor. As they enter a room, the light in Buckner's lantern dims and goes out. "What's wrong with it?" Tim asks. "Nothing," Buckner says. When they leave the room, the light comes on again.

"Do you still believe I killed my brother?" Tim asks.

"No, I don't," the sheriff says.

They take John's body out to the station wagon, then return to the house to wait for something to happen. Tim notices the painting and asks about it. "One of the Blassenville sisters, I think," Buckner says. "The last Blassenville sister left here over 50 years ago." They go upstairs again. They find an organ; dust lies heavy over everything but the keys. "It's as though somebody plays it," Tim says. "Maybe somebody does," the sheriff replies. He finds a diary in Elizabeth Blassenville's handwriting. She fears that someone is after her: "All the help has run away," one of the entries runs. "My sisters gone. I am here alone."

Buckner notices a door that has mysteriously shut; when he tries to enter the room beyond, the lantern goes out, only to grow bright again when the door is shut.

"We'll see Jacob Blount," Buckner

says, referring to a former servant who worked for the Blassenvilles.

They find old Jacob (Ken Renard) in his cabin, aged and infirm. "Jacob, who's in that house?" Buckner demands. Jacob tells him that Eula Lee, a servant, was a Blassenville like the others, a half-sister. Buckner asks if Eula Lee is in the house, still alive. Jacob says that, if he told, the big serpent would send a little brother to kill him. He tells Buckner that he was a maker of zuvembies; Eula Lee came to his hut and drank the holy drink. Time means nothing to a zuvembie, Jacob says; they can command the dead as well as snakes, birds, and fowl, and only lead bullets can kill them. Hearing pigeons, Jacob fears for his life. As he pokes the fire, a snake encircles his hand. He screams in agony; Buckner kills the snake and prepares to make an incision to drain the poison, but Jacob is dead.

When they return to Buckner's station wagon, it is covered with pigeons. "They've come back," Tim says.

Back at the old house Buckner sits loading his gun. He suggests that Tim stretch out and get some rest. Tim falls asleep and awakens later that night, screaming John's name. There is no sign of the sheriff. Tim hears the weird wailing and, hypnotized, ascends the stairs. An old hag emerges from the room upstairs and raises a hatchet to split his head. Four shots ring out. Buckner emerges from the shadows and slaps Tim into reality. He reveals a hidden room behind a wall; inside are the rotting skeletons of the three murdered Blassenville sisters, along with the corpse of Eula Lee.

"Pigeons from Hell" was the work of Robert E. Howard, the creator of sword and sorcery fiction. Howard's own short life was a grim contrast to those of his stalwart heroes. Born in 1906 in Peaster, Texas, the only son of Dr. Isaac M. and Hester Howard, he was a frail boy often left in the company of his mother while his father, a general practitioner, was away on calls. The family later settled in the small town of Cross Plains in Central Texas. The teenaged Howard, bullied by other boys, began devoting himself to physical fitness, becoming a highly competitive boxer and horseman and building himself into a six foot, two-hundred pound muscleman similar in physique to his fictional alter egos Conan the Barbarian, King Kull and Bran Mak Morn.

After finishing high school he took a few courses at Brownwood College before beginning his career as a freelance writer. In 1924, after "three years of writing without selling a blasted word," he sold three stories to *Weird Tales*. Discouraged by his lack of success, he went off to study bookkeeping at Howard Payne College before returning to writing. He was a natural storyteller, and his most memorable stories were sword and sorcery tales featuring the giant Cimmerian, Conan, and the grim Solomon Kane.

Meanwhile, his private life was in turmoil. He and his mother had developed a tightening bond, virtually shutting out his father, and Howard had little contact with women. As the years passed, his attachment to his mother grew.

He continued to sell fiction, gradually expanding his markets. By the time of his death he was writing for virtually all the pulp magazines, turning out fantasy, detective, oriental adventure, horror, western and boxing stories. He had finally cracked *Argosy*, a prestige market, after trying for years, and was on the verge of escaping the pulp ghetto altogether: his first book, *A Gent from Bear Creek*, was about to be published in England.

In June 1936 his mother lapsed into a coma; she had been ill for some time, and there was no hope for recovery. Howard, who had talked of suicide for several years, borrowed a gun and shot himself on June 11, 1936. His mother died the following day. (Howard's life was the subject of the full-length biography, *Dark Valley Destiny*, by L. Sprague de Camp, Catherine Crook de Camp, and Jane Griffin, published by Bluejay Books in 1983.)

Howard's chief legacy may be his Conan stories, which continue to be reprinted year after year. Some critics, notably August Derleth and E. Hoffman Price, considered his broadly humorous westerns his best work. Others felt that poetry was Howard's true métier. But the general consensus is that as a supernaturalist he lacked the cosmicism of his *Weird Tales* contemporaries H. P. Lovecraft and Clark Ashton Smith. His macabre fiction was, moreover, an apparent concession to the marketplace and, in part, an attempt to emulate Poe, Machen, and Blackwood. As Dennis Rickard points out in his study, "Through Black Boughs: The Supernatural in Howard's Fiction,"* his chief drawback as a writer of weird fiction was his predilection for a larger than life hero who would vanquish the supernatural menace at hand:

> In the bulk of the stories where the protagonist encounters a being or force beyond human ken, no matter how dangerous it appears to be ... it ultimately falls before the hero, whose aggrandizement seems to be paramount to Howard...[w]hatever the uncanny ingredient, it most often proves to be a means to an end — the triumph of the superhero or the downfall of a malfeasant. The occasional exceptions to these structures are his best stories in the genre.

The most notable such exception is "Pigeons from Hell," easily Howard's best macabre story, published posthumously in the May 1938 *Weird Tales*. Stephen King has called it "one of the finest horror stories of our century." In his study *The Last Celt*, Glenn Lord recounts the genesis of the story in a quotation from Howard:

> No Negro ghost story ever gave me the horrors as did the tales told by my grandmother. All the gloominess and dark mysticism of the Gaelic nature was hers, and there was no light and mirth in her ...
> As a child my hair used to stand straight up when she would tell of the wagon that moved down the wilderness roads in the dark of the night, with never a horse drawing it — the wagon that was full of severed heads and dismembered limbs...[a]nd in many of her tales, also, appeared the old, deserted plantation mansion, with the weeds growing rank about it and the ghostly pigeons flying up from the rails of the veranda.

Appropriately, "Pigeons from Hell" has the quality of a folktale handed down over the years. As Rickard notes, Howard's literary style was part of the tradition of oral storytelling associated with the Celts (Howard was inordinately proud of his Celtic heritage). Even here, however, Howard's chief failing as a horror writer is present: Sheriff Buckner shows few qualms in the presence of the supernatural, and his stoicism and raw courage make him Conan's psychological, if not physical, equal. ("The Southerner must have nerves of steel," the protagonist thinks as they lie waiting in the darkness of Blassenville Manor.)

Interestingly, the story lay dormant

Published in The Dark Barbarian, *a collection of critical essays edited by Don Herron (Greenwood Press, 1984).*

for 23 years, unknown to all but aficionados of weird fiction, before *Thriller*'s adaptation (the first film version of any of Howard's works). John Kneubuhl's teleplay is reasonably faithful to its source, save for omitting Howard's final revelation that the thing in the house is not the servant girl but Celia Blassenville herself. Kneubuhl also makes the two young men brothers.

Some *Thriller* fans have found fault with "Pigeons from Hell," declaring that the pace slackens around the middle. Others object to the title, seeing the pigeons as jarringly irrelevant and even inappropriate (in the story the pigeons are, according to legend, the souls of the dead Blassenvilles let out of hell), but such cavils seem minor indeed compared with the episode's cumulative power. For one thing, it's exhilarating to see a horror story played for all its full-blooded potential with little regard for censorial ukase (though some care was exercised in the scene with John Branner after the zuvembie's attack: his face, covered with blood, is kept in shadow; this actually works to the episode's advantage, making his half-seen injuries seem even more fearful). For another, it represents *Thriller*'s artisans working at their absolute peak; of all 67 episodes, this was the most economical to produce, costing a mere $118,000, as opposed to the average episode cost of $125,000. It also took only three and one half days to shoot, as compared to the usual five or six. "Nobody wanted to do it," recalls William Frye. One reason was the recalcitrance of its avian cast: "We had hundreds of pigeons flying off in every direction," Frye says. "As I remember, we paid 50 cents for each pigeon."

Brandon DeWilde gives perhaps the best performance of his career as Tim Branner (named Griswell in the story). Beginning as a carefree young wayfarer,

he becomes a haunted man by episode's end, shattered by his brush with the supernatural. His fevered soliloquy, recounting his brother's death, is filmed in close-up, and DeWilde is affectingly vulnerable, his voice breaking as he cries out, "Oh, Johnny!" It's one of the strongest performances in any *Thriller*, on a par with Rip Torn's in "The Purple Room" and William Shatner's in "The Hungry Glass."

DeWilde, a child star, made his film debut in *The Member of the Wedding* in 1952 at the age of 10. His other films include *All Fall Down* (1961) and *Hud* (1963), but for a generation of filmgoers, he is remembered as the small boy who pursued Alan Ladd, shouting, "Come back, Shane!" in the classic western of that title. He did an early television series, *Jamie*, in 1953, and was memorable in Robert Bloch's *Hitchcock* segment "The Sorcerer's Apprentice," an episode never seen in syndication because of its (mostly off-screen) bloodshed. DeWilde played the impressionable juvenile so long that it hurt his chances for adult stardom. He died in 1972 in an automobile crash at the age of 30 (Robert E. Howard's age when he committed suicide).

Crahan Denton makes an interesting contrast to DeWilde. Where Tim is youthful and tentative, the sheriff is weathered and dogmatic. Although he initially rejects superstition ("That's bunk!" he shouts when Tim suggests Jacob's death may have been caused by the zuvembie), he's willing to confront the supernatural on its own terms, displaying exemplary courage. (His very name, Buckner, hints at his heroic stature: Howard used it for the hero in his story "Black Canaan," and the protagonist of his western tales was named Buckner J. Grimes.) Denton, with his leathern face and backwoods voice, is perfectly suited to the role. Doug Benton recalls that "Crahan Denton had a tendency to drink. He drank himself to death, in fact. Cirrhosis. He was big in live television. Had a tremendous career." A solid but underrated actor, Denton was fine in such films as *Bus Riley's Back in Town* (1965), in which he played a homosexual undertaker!

David Whorf, unfortunately, gives the weakest performance in "Pigeons from Hell." He's simply not a talented actor, and plays John Branner in a monotonal daze throughout. Although his part is the smallest of the three principals, it's still a glaring deficiency. The son of actor-director Richard Whorf, David soon left acting and became an assistant director. He's visible in a small part in a much later (and lesser) *Thriller*, "Flowers of Evil."

Ken Renard gives a convincing performance as Jacob Blount, late of Barbados. It's a role that could seem ridiculous through careless inflection or gesture, but he is compelling and believable as the maker of zuvembies. His death scene, a danse macabre, is a memorably eerie vignette. Renard was seen in a later *Thriller*, "The Return of Andrew Bentley."

Ottola Nesmith (previously seen as the aged Laura Bellman in "The Hungry Glass") reveals a horrifying visage as the undead Eula Lee. Rather amazingly, Doug Benton recalls, "She was a great beauty in her day. She looked a lot like Gladys Cooper. She was British — a music hall performer." She made small appearances in films, including *The Wolf Man* (1941), *The Invisible Ghost* (1941), *Return of the Vampire* (1944) and even *Sunset Boulevard* (1950) before becoming a horror hostess on television. "She had two sons," Benton said. "One was a producer. I don't think she was any relation to Mike Nesmith of the Monkees, but

you never know; he could have been her grandson." Nesmith died in 1972 at the age of 83.

Other aspects of the production are well up to standard. Lionel Lindon's photography is notably atmospheric. Blassenville Manor is every inch the haunted plantation house of Howard's story. And Morton Stevens' score lends the appropriate doom chords; the zuvembie's wailing is also a notably eerie effect.

But it's John Newland's direction that elevates "Pigeons from Hell" to classic stature. It's almost a textbook example of how to create scenes of unease. From our first view of the Blassenville home to the final shot of the lifeless Eula Lee, Newland's direction never falters. He employs shadows to memorable effect, and when he finally shows us Eula Lee, he begins with an out of focus close-up of her gnarled hand, providing a memorable *frisson*. The focus gradually sharpens to reveal a hideous hag lusting for blood.

Born in 1917 in Cincinnati, the son of a newspaper drama critic, John Newland began his cinematic career as an actor, appearing as "Algy" in the Bulldog Drummond films starring Tom Conway. He directed such films as *That Night* (1957) and *The Violators* (1957), and was kept busy during the fifties, appearing on numerous anthology shows such as *The Loretta Young Show*, *The Web* and *Robert Montgomery Presents*. He played the doctor in *Tales of Tomorrow*'s 1952 adaptation of *Frankenstein* starring Lon Chaney, Jr., as the Monster. (The inebriated Chaney, thinking the live performance was a dress rehearsal, went through the show gingerly handling the props and breakaway furniture). But it is, of course, as host and director (and occasional star) of *One Step Beyond* that Newland is best remembered. The show ran for three seasons, a total of 94 episodes, and, amazingly, Newland directed *every* one. The series had ended by the time Newland joined *Thriller*. Following "Pigeons from Hell," he went on to direct three more episodes ("The Return of Andrew Bentley," "Portrait Without a Face" and "Man of Mystery"), each memorable in its own way.

Doug Benton recalls:

> John Newland was an absolute genius at staging things. He'd come on the set and say, you stand there and you do this and you do the other thing, and all of a sudden it would be four o'clock and you'd be going home. Actors liked working for him, because they thought they were doing what they liked, when they were actually doing exactly what *he* wanted. And then, at other times, John would get bored. He was like the little girl in that rhyme: "When he was good he was wonderful, and when he was bad he was horrid."

Newland was evidently well pleased by "Pigeons from Hell." Asked about it many years later, he remarked: "That is probably the one I most enjoyed. The highlight of the ones I did. Brandon DeWilde was ... quite a good choice. Did an amazing job." Asked about censorship and the lack of interference from NBC, Newland told *Filmfax*: "They were much more lenient in those years than they are now. There was much, much less concern with jeopardy to young people and things like that. You couldn't make that. You couldn't make that episode today."

Newland's pride is justified, for "Pigeons from Hell" remains a high watermark, not only among *Thriller* episodes but among video adaptations of horror classics in general. Even after the passage of 32 years, it remains televi-

sion's most memorable excursion into the macabre.

"The Grim Reaper" (airdate: June 13, 1961). Produced by William Frye. Directed by Herschel Daugherty. Teleplay by Robert Bloch, from the short story by Harold Lawlor. Original Music: Jerry Goldsmith. Director of Photography: Bud Thackery, A.S.C. Associate Producer: Douglas Benton. Film Editor: Edward Haire, A.C.E. Art Director: John J. Lloyd. Assistant Director: Carter DeHaven, III. Editorial Department Head: David J. O'Connell. Musical Supervision: Stanley Wilson. Set Decorators: John McCarthy and Julia Heron.

Cast: William Shatner (Paul Graves), Natalie Schafer (Bea Graves), Elizabeth Allen (Dorothy Linden), Scott Merrill (Gerald Keller), Henry Daniell (Pierre Radin), Fifi D'Orsay (Toinette), Paul Newlan (Sergeant Bernstein), Robert Cornthwaite (Phillips).

Almost any episode following "Pigeons from Hell" should by rights come as a severe anticlimax, but "The Grim Reaper" is no disappointment: on the contrary, it's one of the most frightening *Thriller*s ever, a near perfect exercise in terror.

In 19th-century Paris, Pierre Radin (Henry Daniell) goes to see his son, Henri, who has locked himself away in a room. "Radin — he paints monsters," says the concierge, Toinette (Fifi D'Orsay). "He sketches at night, in graveyards." They knock at Henri's door; there is no answer. They open the door, only to find the young man's body hanging from the ceiling. "Why would he kill himself?" his father asks. The answer lies on the canvas: the angel of death — the grim reaper, holding a scythe. "His last picture — and he finished it," Pierre says. "Perhaps the picture finished him," Toinette adds.

More than 100 years later, young Paul Graves (William Shatner) arrives at Graves' End, the estate owned by his eccentric Aunt Bea (Natalie Schafer), a successful — and wealthy — mystery writer. "Who designed this place — Charles Addams?" Paul asks. Bea introduces him to her fifth husband, Gerald Keller (Scott Merrill), a television actor. Paul asks Gerald for his autograph. He also meets Bea's secretary, Dorothy Linden (Elizabeth Allen). Bea then shows Paul her newest acquisition: Henri Radin's painting of the Grim Reaper. Paul explains that the painting is the reason he has come. He advises her to get rid of it, and tells her its history: since its creation in 1849, it has had 17 owners, 15 of whom have met with violent or mysterious deaths. Paul warns her there is a curse on the painting. Bea laughs it off, but Paul reminds her of the stigmata — the picture bleeds every time someone is about to die. Paul reaches up and touches the painting, and his fingers come away dripping blood.

Gerald, meanwhile, is making a play for Dorothy. Bea knows about her husband's unfaithfulness, and takes solace in liquor. Paul meets with Dorothy and tells her his aunt's life is in danger. "We must destroy the picture before it destroys her," he says. He tries to convince Bea, but she refuses to listen, telling him that Gerald and Dorothy are planning to get rid of her. Paul warns her about the painting, reminding her of the stigmata, but Bea goes on drinking.

Later that night Dorothy awakens Paul. They find Bea's lifeless body sprawled on the stairs; she apparently drank and fell, hitting her head. When a police sergeant (Paul Newlan) arrives on the scene Dorothy mentions the painting. The sergeant explains that a lab man went over the picture with x-

rays and microphotography; there wasn't a trace of blood. Dorothy tells Paul she suspects Gerald had something to do with his wife's death. Bea's lawyer, Phillips (Robert Cornthwaite), arrives to read the will: Bea has left everything to Gerald.

Dorothy leaves Graves' End. Gerald, unable to sleep since his wife's death, visits Paul and asks him for a sedative. They discuss the picture; Paul reveals that the blood was on his finger and he never touched the painting. When Gerald expresses bewilderment, Paul tells him he needed money; he used the picture as an excuse to visit Bea. He shows Paul the autograph he asked for earlier; he has attached a confession and suicide note to it. Paul reveals that the sedative should be taking effect soon. And with Gerald dead, Paul will inherit everything. Gerald collapses.

Paul is now alone at Graves' End. He sees his victims' faces superimposed over the skull of the Reaper. Understandably nervous, he prepares to leave, only to run into Dorothy; she has returned to destroy the painting. Trying to stop her, Paul blurts out the truth: "There's no curse!" Paul shouts. "You — you're the one," Dorothy says in disbelief. She distracts Paul and runs to the door, locking him in. Paul turns to look at the picture, only to see an empty frame. Hearing the sound of a scythe approaching him, he tries to escape, but is cut down by an unseen figure.

Dorothy returns with the police. She unlocks the door to the study and they find Paul's body, his throat cut to ribbons. "What kind of weapon could have done that?" the sergeant asks. "The picture — look at the picture," Dorothy screams. The reaper's scythe is dripping blood.

Like so many other *Thriller* classics, "The Grim Reaper" mixes genres with wholly successful results, veering from the supernatural to rationalized crime drama and back again. From its moody beginning in a French garret to its macabre finale, "The Grim Reaper" is an atmospheric tour de force of terror, with everything contributing to its powerful overall effect, including its clever dialogue, liberally seasoned with double entendres, and Jerry Goldsmith's eerie score, with its sinister violin strokes.

"The Grim Reaper" began life as a short story by Harold Lawlor titled "The Black Madonna," published in the May 1947 *Weird Tales*, though it served only as a prelude to Bloch's teleplay. Asked about his contributions, Bloch responded:

> "The Grim Reaper" (in the short story, it's a Madonna portrait that sheds tears) was, as you say, just a taking-off point for what ended up as my teleplay. Somehow the original concept didn't fit my image of what a *Thriller* episode should be, so I replaced the sad Madonna and her sighs with the Grim Reaper and his scythe.
>
> And to anyone who affects to sneer at the pun, let me say that this is exactly how I got the idea — by word (or in this case, sound) association. I'm susceptible to influence from rhyme or assonance, and think this is true of most writers.

Despite the script's cleverness, there is one major lapse in credibility when Paul, the methodical murderer, blurts out his guilt to Dorothy. It's simply not believable that, after plotting the deaths of his aunt and her husband with such cold-blooded thoroughness, this Machiavellian villain would stumble so badly. To its credit, the script does provide a rationale of sorts for his uncharacteristic behavior: he's understandably jittery after seeing his victims' faces reflected in the portrait.

The other aspects of the production are first-rate. The acting, for one, is a major asset. William Shatner, previously seen in "The Hungry Glass," once again turns in a fine performance. His transformation from clean-cut young man (he's understandably embarrassed around his dotty aunt, who refers to him as "the world's oldest eagle scout") to scheming killer is nicely handled (though there's one overdone shot with him shaking his fist at the painting and grinning maniacally that rather tips the scales). The character itself is a recurrent figure in Bloch's fiction: the apparently ordinary, even sedate, individual who conceals his murderous impulses behind a facade of normalcy. As in many other *Thrillers* where evil masquerades as virtue, there's an implicit warning to look beyond the surface. (For more on Shatner, see the entry on "The Hungry Glass.")

Natalie Schafer is enjoyably over the top as Aunt Bea in a slightly theatrical but amusing turn. She seems to be enjoying her role, relishing Bloch's clever and cynical dialogue, and makes the most of her drunk scenes. Schafer's film work includes *Caught* (1949) and *The Law and the Lady* (1951), but she is, of course, best known as Mrs. Howell on the long-running *Gilligan's Island*. She died in 1991 at the age of 90.

Elizabeth Allen, her dark hair dyed blonde, is fine as Dorothy Linden, though the role isn't very demanding. Her expressions of fright are effective without being overdone; interestingly, the expected romance between her and Paul never blossoms. Allen was a regular on *The Paul Lynde Show* and *C.P.O. Sharkey*, but is perhaps best remembered as the "Glea-girl" who used to say "And *away* we go!" on the old *Jackie Gleason Show*. She was previously seen with Shatner in "The Hungry Glass."

Scott Merrill doesn't make much of

an impression as the womanizing fortune hunter Gerald Keller. He's unpleasantly aggressive, and his death by poisoning is agonizingly prolonged.

The rest of the cast, albeit confined to minor roles, is surprisingly strong. It's always nice to see Henry Daniell exuding the proper Gothic atmosphere, even in the minor role of Pierre Radin. Fifi D'Orsay, a Canadian leading lady of the early thirties, makes a brief appearance as Toinette. Paul Newlan makes his third *Thriller* appearance, appropriately cast as a dour policeman. And, finally, it's enjoyable to see Robert Cornthwaite in the small role of a lawyer. Cornthwaite was previously seen in "The Devil's Ticket."

Over the years a rumor has grown that the Reaper was seen walking out of the portrait when the episode was first telecast. Jay Allen Sanford claimed that "A few seconds of this scene were subsequently clipped for reruns and syndication, though the piece may actually be more effective without them." Unfortunately, as with the spurious "Tamara, the Georgian Queen" episode, this supposed footage does not exist. As Ken Kaffke, President of the *Thriller* Fan Club, puts it:

> There's now no doubt that there never was any actual shot of the skeleton/Reaper, though even Robert Bloch vaguely recalls it. I suspect memories become twisted with a scene or two from *13 Ghosts* or even *Metropolis* which briefly features the Reaper, though due to [the episode's] relative obscurity until recently, I suspect a lot of childhood memories added the screaming painting/burning skeleton scenes from *13 Ghosts*.

This proves, once again, how swiftly an unchecked rumor can take on the dimensions of fact.

SECOND SEASON, 1961-1962

"What Beckoning Ghost?"
(airdate: September 18, 1961). Produced by William Frye. Directed by Ida Lupino. Teleplay by Donald S. Sanford, from the short story by Harold Lawlor. Director of Photography: John F. Warren, A.S.C. Music: Jerry Goldsmith. Art Director: Howard E. Johnson. Edited by Danny Landres. Musical Supervision: Stanley Wilson. Associate Producer: Doug Benton. Assistant Director: Charles S. Gould. Set Decorators: John McCarthy and Julia Heron.

Cast: Judith Evelyn (Mildred Beaumont), Tom Helmore (Eric Beaumont), Adele Mara (Lydia Adler), Frank Wilcox (The Detective).

Thriller thrived on ambiguity, but never more so than in "What Beckoning Ghost?," the series' second season opener. Nothing is as it seems, and the result is a satisfying murder plot-cum-ghost story that never quite tips its hand.

Eric Beaumont (Tom Helmore) tells his wife, Mildred (Judith Evelyn), to go downstairs to get champagne. Hearing an organ playing a requiem, she enters the drawing room, only to find a coffin with a wreath bearing the message: MY DEAR WIFE REQUIESCAT IN PEACE. The shock is nearly too great for her; the room begins spinning, and she collapses.

When she recovers, she finds Eric and her sister, Lydia Adler (Adele Mara), at her bedside. There is no sign of the coffin. Eric tells her she imagined it; what's more, he's had a doctor in to examine her and she doesn't even remember his visit. Lydia tells her she was overtired and had a nightmare. Eric and Lydia quarrel, but he assures his wife, "You simply buried a very frightening memory in your subconscious. It will come to the surface eventually." He tells her that her heart has not improved the way they had hoped. Mildred is suspicious of her husband's assurances and the doctor's visit, and tells him, "I know I saw a coffin. I know I saw a funeral wreath. And I did hear music!" After Eric leaves, Mildred, still unsure, finds a box of pills with the doctor's name on it.

When Mildred awakens sometime later, Lydia offers her champagne. "Champagne for breakfast?" Mildred asks. "Breakfast? It's seven o'clock," Lydia informs her. After Eric tells her the doctor has visited her again, Mildred has doubts about her sanity. "You're just as sane as I am," Lydia assures her. After they leave, Mildred listens in on Eric's phone conversation with the doctor. Eric tells him that Mildred has had another memory lapse. The doctor tells him she may have to be institutionalized. When Eric sees Mildred again, she apologizes "for the horrible things I've been thinking."

Eric plans to leave on a business trip. He tells her he's having a piano installed in her room. He makes her

120

promise not to go into the drawing room until she's well. When Mildred is signing over some checks to Eric, Lydia advises her to cut her bank account down the middle, giving Eric half with no strings attached. Mildred decides to take her advice.

But when Eric returns from his trip, he telephones his lawyer and tells Mildred he can't accept the property settlement. He also allows her the run of the house — even the drawing room, saying she can now recognize anything not real as an illusion. But that night Mildred awakens and goes downstairs, hearing the requiem. She enters the drawing room and sees the coffin. "Not — real," she says to herself. Approaching it, she looks down — and sees herself inside. She collapses.

A figure approaches. It is Eric. Beside the coffin stands Lydia, with a lifelike mask of Mildred in her hand. "Darling — you mustn't forget her precious pink camellias," Lydia tells Eric.

After the funeral Lydia receives a condolence note remarking on the loss of Mildred's dear husband. Lydia laughs it off, but Eric is disturbed. Later that night, drunk, he staggers up the stairs, hearing the same requiem Mildred heard. When he asks Lydia if she heard to music, she says, "Don't be ridiculous."

Sometime later the doorbell awakens Eric. He goes to answer it and finds a wreath inscribed MY BELOVED HUSBAND/REST IN PEACE. "Who brought it?" Eric demands. Lydia says she didn't see anyone deliver it. In an envelope attached to the wreath is Mildred's wedding ring. It was buried with her. Lydia suggests someone had a copy made, but Eric is unconvinced.

Eric goes to the mausoleum where Mildred is buried. He finds his own date of death inscribed in the stone beside his intended burial place. He tells Lydia,

adding that the date is that very day. She accuses him of arranging everything himself, suffering from an attack of conscience. "There's one other possibility," Lydia points out, "and I don't believe in ghosts."

Eric drinks himself into a stupor. Hearing the requiem again, he staggers out, only to run into Lydia. "She's come back," he tells her. Lydia maintains that she hears nothing. Eric goes downstairs to the drawing room and sees the coffin. Lydia cannot see it. Just then the doors close, locking Lydia out. Reacting to something (or someone) off camera, Eric falls through the window to his death.

Police officials question Lydia. She explains that it was all in Eric's imagination. When the detective (Frank Wilcox) accuses her of pushing Eric — the police found a piece of lace in the button of his coat — Lydia denies it. Just then she hears the requiem, but the detective does not. "It's Mildred — she's playing," Lydia says. She runs toward the window, but the detective leads her away. Atop the piano are pink camellias and a portrait of Mildred.

Donald S. Sanford's teleplay is a faithful adaptation of Harold Lawlor's short story, published in *Weird Tales'* July 1948 issue. The basic idea (a man and woman cause the death of a third party, then receive cryptic warnings that the dead person has come back) had been used before in "The Purple Room" and would become a house theme, reused on several occasions, but not with as much ambiguity. The piece of lace in the button of Eric's coat is very suggestive, and the final, haunting shot of Mildred's portrait is likewise rich in ambivalence. Cunningly, the episode plays on our expectations (and perhaps our memories of Clouzot's *Les Diaboliques*) by suggesting that Lydia is behind it all, only to undercut this by hinting that

Eric is doing it (as Lydia suggests) to punish himself, then shifting gears once more with Lydia's (presumed) descent into madness. Many *Thrillers* toyed with this concept of crisscrossing genres, but none is as richly ambiguous or sinisterly suggestive as "What Beckoning Ghost?"

The acting is uneven. Judith Evelyn is fine as Mildred. She looks frail enough to succumb to a heart attack, and her final collapse is disturbingly realistic. Primarily a stage actress (her real name was J. E. Allen), she's best remembered as Miss Lonely Hearts in Hitchcock's *Rear Window* and as the deaf mute wife in William Castle's *The Tingler* (in which she also played a character frightened to death by her husband, only to return from the dead in an ambiguous finale). She died in 1967.

Tom Helmore is equally believable as Eric Beaumont. He makes the most of his alcoholic binges, and his drunken ascent of the stairs is well acted (and imaginatively photographed). Helmore's film appearances include *The Tender Trap* (1955) and *The Time Machine* (1960), though he's probably best remembered as Gavin Elster, the sophisticated villain of Hitchcock's *Vertigo* (1958). (Coincidentally, Helmore was the former husband of Boris Karloff's fifth wife, Evelyn ["Evie"] Karloff.)

Adele Mara, unfortunately, is not nearly so convincing as Lydia. Most of her line readings ring hollow, and she brings little conviction to her role. A Spanish American dancer who appeared in many B films during the forties, she played the female lead in *Curse of the Faceless Man* (1958) and was also in *The Vampire's Ghost* (1945) and *The Catman of Paris* (1946).

Many years after *Thriller's* adaptation, "What Beckoning Ghost?" was done as a motion picture, *Dominique* (a.k.a. *Dominique Is Dead*), starring Cliff Robertson and Jean Simmons. The result was an idiotic mishmash, with little of the suggestiveness of the *Thriller* version, which remains perhaps the most ambiguous of all of its crisscrossing episodes.

"Guillotine" (airdate: September 25, 1961). Produced by William Frye. Directed by Ida Lupino. Teleplay by Charles Beaumont, based on the short story by Cornell Woolrich. Music: Jerry Goldsmith. Director of Photography: Benjamin H. Kline, A.S.C. Art Director: Howard E. Johnson. Editorial Department Head: David J. O'Connell. Edited by Danny Landres. Musical Supervision: Stanley Wilson. Set Decorators: John McCarthy and Julia Heron. Associate Producer: Doug Benton. Assistant Director: Carter DeHaven, III. Sound: Frank H. Wilkinson.

Cast: Alejandro Rey (Robert Lamont), Danielle DeMetz (Babette Lamont), Robert Middleton (Monsieur DeParis), Gregory Morton (The Prison Director), Marcel Hillaire (The Barber), Gaylord Cavallaro (The Cabbie), Janine Grandel (Madame LeClerc), Peter Brocco (The Assistant Director), Louis Mercier (The Wall Guard), Peter Camlin (Louis), Ted Roter (The Prisoner), Guy De Vestel (The Priest), David P. Cross (Guard #1), Charles LeTorre (The Doctor), Vance Howard (The Gendarme), Jacques Villon (The Waiter).

The best of *Thriller's* three Cornell Woolrich adaptations, "Guillotine" is a memorable exercise in mounting suspense. It also has one of the best-remembered endings of any episode.

In 1875 France, prisoner Robert Lamont (Alejandro Rey) watches in horror as his cellmate (Ted Roter) is seized by guards, taken to the guillotine, and executed. He swears he will not share his fate.

Robert's wife, Babette (Danielle DeMetz), comes to see him. He was found guilty of *le crime passionnel*: he found Babette in the arms of another man, and killed him. For this crime he has been sentenced to death. Babette asks him to forgive her. "Don't blame yourself; blame fate," he says. He tells her there is one way of escaping: there is a tradition — an unwritten law — that if the headsman dies and there is no time to name his successor, the next man in line for execution is given his freedom. No hand but the executioner's must lower the blade.

Babette meets Monsieur DeParis (Robert Middleton), the executioner, and makes a date to see him at his home. He admits his profession to her, expecting her to be repelled by it. "You are to be thanked for doing such an unpleasant job," Babette replies. "I am sure you don't enjoy it." DeParis invites her to stay for dinner, over the objections of his housekeeper, Madame LeClerc (Janine Grandel). They drink a toast; later, Babette slips poison into his pancake mix. She sends Robert a note telling him, "The assignment has been completed."

The next morning Robert is seized by the guards and prepared for his execution. They tell him his appeal has been refused. "Be brave," he is told. "Why not?" Robert replies. "It costs no more." Meanwhile, Monsieur DeParis is finishing his breakfast of pancakes. He dresses and sets out for the prison. On the way he begins to feel the effects of the poison, but continues on, staggering through the streets. Babette, waiting outside the prison, is horrified to see DeParis being half carried to the courtyard by a gendarme. DeParis recognizes Babette and has her arrested.

When Robert sees DeParis staggering into the courtyard he is understand-

ably shocked, but confident the dying man will not be able to go through with the execution. "He'll never make it! He'll never make it!" he screams as DeParis drags himself up the steps and onto the scaffold. Robert's head is put in the stock while DeParis crawls with his last breath toward the lever. But just as he is about to pull it, he dies. "He's dead — I win!" Robert cries. The doctor takes the pulse of the headsman; he is indeed dead. But when the doctor lets go of his hand it trips the lever and Robert is decapitated.

"Guillotine" is the only one of *Thriller*'s three Cornell Woolrich adaptations that does full justice to its source. Charles Beaumont's teleplay, based on Woolrich's 1939 story "Men Must Die," is relentless and gripping to the very last. As usual with Woolrich, there is a race against the clock: Robert Lamont's execution is to take place at dawn, and Monsieur DeParis (showing a dedication to duty above all other concerns) refuses to be taken to a doctor even though he is dying, consulting his watch and staggering through the early morning streets of Paris.

Ida Lupino directs with her customary skill. She intercuts throughout the entire episode, emphasizing the connection between Robert Lamont and Monsieur DeParis (even though they do not actually meet until the very end): DeParis asks, "And what is the date, monsieur?" and Lupino cuts to Lamont in his cell, saying, "I don't know the date." Madame LeClerc hands her recipe to Babette; a message is simultaneously handed to Lamont. The camera holds on a sign advertising cognac, only to cut to Lamont savoring a snifter filled with the stuff. Some of her cuts seem merely capricious: when a man comments that Monsieur DeParis would not harm a cockroach, there's a direct cut to one of the insects on its back, struggling furiously to right itself. But, for the most part, "Guillotine" does credit to its grim source.

The acting is above average. Alejandro Rey, an Argentinean, makes an acceptable Frenchman, playing Robert Lamont with the appropriate blend of cunning and desperation. Rey's film career was hardly distinguished: he appeared in *The Swarm* (1978), *Cuba* (1979) and *The Ninth Configuration* (1980), among many others, almost always in supporting parts. He also appeared in another of Lupino's *Thrillers*, "La Strega," but he's best known to television viewers for his role in *The Flying Nun*. He died in 1987.

Danielle DeMetz, the only one of the three principal players to sport a genuine French accent, was a remarkably beautiful if limited actress; fortunately, in "Guillotine" she isn't called upon to do anything beyond her abilities, hence she's acceptable as Babette. Her other genre appearances include *Return of the Fly* (1959), *Valley of the Dragons* (1961) and *The Magic Sword* (1962).

Robert Middleton seems a peculiar choice to play the executioner, Monsieur DeParis. He doesn't overdo his French accent, and he's very effective in his scenes with Babette and when he realizes he's been poisoned. For more on Middleton, see the entry on "The Fingers of Fear."

"Guillotine" was redone as an episode of the feeble anthology series *Darkroom*, which had a brief run on ABC in 1981-82. Michael Constantine played the executioner, and the episode was notable only as an example of the ineptitude by then endemic to any horror-suspense series. It seemed slight, indeed, compared to *Thriller's* version, which (along with Hitchcock's TV version of "Three O'Clock") is rightly regarded as the finest adaptation of Woolrich ever filmed.

"The Premature Burial" (airdate: October 2, 1961). Produced by William Frye. Directed by Douglas Heyes. Teleplay by William D. Gordon. Story by Douglas Heyes, from the works of Edgar Allan Poe. Music: Morton Stevens. Director of Photography: Bud Thackery, A.S.C. Art Director: George Patrick. Editorial Department Head: David J. O'Connell. Edited by Danny Landres. Musical Supervision: Stanley Wilson. Set Decorators: John McCarthy and Julia Heron. Associate Producer: Doug Benton. Assistant Director: John Clarke Bowman. Sound: David H. Moriarty.

Cast: Boris Karloff (Dr. Thorne), Patricia Medina (Victorine Lafourcade), Sidney Blackmer (Edward Stapleton), Scott Marlowe (Julian Boucher), William D. Gordon (Dr. March), Richard Flato (The Friar), Lillian O'Malley (The Housekeeper), Pat O'Malley (The Butler).

One of the most chilling *Thrillers* ever, "The Premature Burial" is first-rate in every way, a memorable horror-suspense entry with some splendid macabre touches.

Victorine Lafourcade (Patricia Medina) attends the funeral of Edward Stapleton (Sidney Blackmer). His physician, Dr. Thorne (Boris Karloff), has doubts about Stapleton's demise, since he was in excellent health, and determines to examine the body. After the mourners leave, the coffin rocks back and forth, then tips over. A hand claws its way out.

Dr. Thorne and his colleague, Dr. March (William D. Gordon), examine the body. Dr. Thorne decides to use a galvanic battery in an attempt to revive Stapleton. The supposedly dead man gets up, takes a few steps, and collapses. When he revives, Thorne explains that he was the victim of a cataleptic trance. Stapleton tells him that he has been conscious since the moment they pronounced him dead. "In the casket, alive — and aware!" Thorne marvels. "Put the knife in my heart!" Stapleton shrieks. "Don't let this happen again! Help me to die!"

Victorine, meanwhile, is making love to Julian Boucher (Scott Marlowe), an impoverished artist whom she had hoped to make rich with Edward's money. Dr. Thorne tells her that Edward has survived but now will live in terror of being buried alive. Unbeknownst to Thorne, Victorine intends to marry Edward for his money. "I suppose I'll never be happy until he's truly dead," Julian says.

Edward marries Victorine. He shows her his vault, built to his specifications, which includes a supply of food and a coffin that opens automatically should he exert the least pressure from the inside. He explains that he is to be buried with his fingers tightly closed around a cord that will ring the bell above the door outside so that everyone will hear it. "Promise me that you will bury me here and that you will listen for the bell!" Edward demands.

While on vacation, Edward and Victorine are out hunting when he suddenly collapses from too much excitement. Victorine removes a necklace and bracelet given to Edward by Dr. Thorne and buries them under a large rock. Edward is, to all appearances, dead.

After Edward's burial Victorine visits Dr. Thorne. He notes that the necklace and bracelet were missing. "In your own mind, were you certain that Edward was dead?" Thorne asks. He has the body brought home, and Edward is buried in the vault in the garden, his hand on the bell cord.

That night Victorine and Julian are together when the bell begins to toll. The door to the vault opens and a shroud wrapped figure is seen walking across the grounds. Julian tells Victorine that Edward has been under the ground for six weeks. "That's enough to kill anyone," he says. He tells her it is Thorne, trying to frighten them into confessing. Victorine finds Edward's necklace lying on her bed. She is beginning to lose her mind. When Dr. Thorne arrives, she says, "It was never you — it *was* Edward," and faints. "He can't be alive," Julian says, but Thorne tells him some men have survived long periods of catalepsy. The figure appears at the front door and climbs the stairs to where Victorine lies in bed. Terrified, Julian confesses his guilt to Dr. Thorne. Victorine emerges from her bedroom, her sanity gone. The figure removes its death mask to reveal the features of Dr. March. Dr. Thorne reveals he went to the spot where Edward died, and found the necklace under the rock, along with evidence of a murder he could not prove.

Although Poe's "The Premature Burial" is more of an essay on the perils of being buried alive than a short story, a number of the elements present in *Thriller's* adaptation are derived from it: the names of several characters, the use of the galvanic battery to restore life, and the description of the vault door, coffin, and bell rope, which "should extend through a hole in the coffin, and so be fastened to one of the hands of the corpse." In addition, Karloff's opening narration is derived from Poe, and sets the ominous mood:

> The boundaries which separate life and death are shadowy and vague. Who is to say where exactly the one ends and the other begins? In certain mysterious maladies all functions of vitality in the human body seem to stop. And then some unseen force sets the magic pinions and the wizard wheels in motion once again. The

silver cord has not been cut, the golden bowl has not been broken. And the soul? One wonders. What, meantime, has happened to the soul?

The actual story is rather more conventional, and it's a disappointment when the "it's all a fiendish plot" ending is exposed, but for most of its length "The Premature Burial" is a serviceable horror tale. There are borrowings from other sources: the bell tolling in the dead of night may have been taken from an early horror film, *Murder by the Clock* (1931); likewise, the "corpse's eye view" of gravediggers shoveling earth directly into the camera lens may have been inspired by the subjective camera work in Dreyer's classic *Vampyr* (1932). There are some startling images: the long shots of Edward Stapleton (actually Dr. March wearing Stapleton's death mask) dressed in his shroud passing by the gates or standing in an open doorway are splendidly macabre.

The actors are competent, for the most part. Karloff returns to form after his off-putting appearance in "The Prediction." Thankfully, he plays Dr. Thorne straight, with none of the tongue-in-cheek posturings that affected his performances in the later episodes "The Last of the Sommervilles" and "Dialogues with Death." Thus, the viewer is kept agreeably off balance as to whether Thorne is in on the plot.

Patricia Medina, previously seen in "The Devil's Ticket," makes a welcome return. She is, as expected, beautiful as the perfidious Victorine, with a hint of sensual cruelty, and her gradual descent into madness is effectively staged. (William Frye recalls that Medina was reluctant to appear in a coffin for the teaser, in which Karloff introduces the cast.) For more on Medina, see the entry on "The Devil's Ticket."

Sidney Blackmer is quite believable

as the unfortunate Edward Stapleton. An American actor with a distinct theatrical flair, he was a capable performer who appeared mostly in routine films. He was the last man left alive after a tidal wave in the legendary lost film *Deluge* (1933). His other films include *Little Caesar* (1930), *My Girl Tisa* (1948) and *Rosemary's Baby* (1968). He died in 1973.

Scott Marlowe, a competent if slightly unlikable actor, is well cast as the scheming Julian. His air of juvenility and weak facade single him out as the culprit almost from the start. Marlowe's film appearances were comparatively few, though he was notable in *A Cold Wind in August* (1961), in which his youthful appearance was used to good effect.

William D. Gordon, who adapted Douglas Heyes' story (and also wrote the teleplay for a later episode, "The Storm") is, unfortunately, no actor. He's very wooden as Dr. March. Thankfully, he has few lines; much of his screen time is spent prowling about the estate.

A few months after *Thriller's* version was telecast, a film adaptation of *The Premature Burial* was released as the third in American-International's Poe series. Although it featured *Thriller* veterans Ray Milland, Hazel Court, and Alan Napier, the screenplay by Charles Beaumont and Ray Russell bears little relation to Poe's essay, and the film is chiefly memorable for Roger Corman's atmospheric direction and Floyd Crosby's sweeping camerawork.

"The Weird Tailor" (airdate: October 16, 1961). Produced by William Frye. Directed by Herschel Daugherty. Teleplay by Robert Bloch, from his short story. Music: Jerry Goldsmith. Director of Photography: Benjamin H. Kline, A.S.C. Art Director: Howard E. Johnson. Editorial Department Head: David

J. O'Connell. Edited by Danny Landres. Musical Supervision: Stanley Wilson. Set Decorators: John McCarthy and Julia Heron. Associate Producer: Doug Benton. Assistant Director: Charles S. Gould. Sound: Joe Lapis.

Cast: Henry Jones (Erik Borg), George Macready (Mr. Smith), Sondra Kerr (Anna Borg), Abraham Sofaer (Nicolai), Iphigenie Castiglione (Madame Roberti), Gary Clarke (Arthur Smith), Stanley Adams (Mr. Schwenk), Dikki Lerner (Hans).

An unjustly neglected episode, "The Weird Tailor" is one of the creepiest *Thrillers* ever, with a memorably macabre denouement.

Young Arthur Smith (Gary Clarke), arriving home drunk one night, hears someone chanting. Stumbling into a room, he finds his father (George Macready) performing black magic rites. Mr. Smith advises Arthur to leave before it is too late, but Arthur stumbles forward, into the magic circle. There is a puff of smoke, and Arthur falls dead.

Mr. Smith goes to see Madame Roberti (Iphigenie Castiglione), a blind psychic. She knows he is seeking his son. "I've got to find a way to bring him back," Smith says. He tells her he will pay anything: "I'm a wealthy man; I'll give my entire fortune." "A man who defies God and nature has no fortune," Madame Roberti replies. "You're playing with words," Smith complains. "You are playing with damnation," she warns. She directs him to see a certain man, who may be able to help.

At "Honest Abe's" used car lot, Smith finds Nicolai (Abraham Sofaer), a most unlikely used car salesman. Smith is skeptical as to whether he's the man he seeks. "Who ever heard of a car dealer named Honest Nicolai?" the other asks. When Smith tells him what he is seeking, Nicolai presents him with a copy of

De Vermis Mysteriis—"Mysteries of the Worm." There are only three copies left in the world; the price is $1 million. Smith is reluctant, but finally agrees to pay for it.

He soon finds the spell he is seeking. "Now, all I have to do is find the right tailor," he says.

At Erik Borg's tailor shop Mr. Schwenk (Stanley Adams) comes to tell Borg (Henry Jones) he has one week to pay his bills. Just after Schwenk leaves, Mr. Smith enters the shop. He explains that he wants a suit cut to his exact specifications: he has his own material — a strange, colorless fabric Borg has never seen before — and the sewing must be done by hand, at certain dates and hours. He tells Borg the suit is for his son, and that he will pay him $500 when it is ready.

Erik sets to work, meanwhile ignoring his wife, Anna (Sondra Kerr), who goes running to her only companion, a discarded dressmaker's dummy with a cracked head. She calls the dummy Hans and tells him, "You are the only friend that I have in the whole world." When Borg shows her the material for the suit, she tells him there is something unholy about it, but Borg pays no attention.

Smith, meanwhile, learns that Nicolai has been killed in a plane crash. Madame Roberti is not surprised. "When he sold you that book he did an evil thing," she says. "He deserved this fate, Mr. Smith." When Smith asks her to forecast his future, the image of a skull appears in her crystal ball.

The suit is finished. Erik takes it to Smith's current place of residence, a cheap room in a downtrodden section of town. He asks for his money, but Mr. Smith is temporarily without funds, having sold his house and liquidated his assets to pay for the book. Erik notices a brand new icebox in his room; opening it he discovers the frozen body of Smith's son. "*Murderer,*" Erik says. "I had to preserve his body, can't you see that?" Mr. Smith replies. He tries to take the suit away from Erik, threatening him with a knife; they struggle, and Erik stabs him. He leaves the room, taking the suit with him.

He returns home, telling Anna to burn the suit. Repairing to a tavern, he encounters Schwenk but, seeing the faces of Smith and his dead son superimposed over Schwenk's, he runs out. When he returns home, he finds that Anna has put the suit on Hans. Erik reveals that he killed Mr. Smith; Anna says she must call the police. Erik begins to strangle her; she cries out to Hans to help her. The dummy begins to move with rapid, jerky movements. It advances on Erik. He screams and runs; the dummy pursues him and kills him, then re-enters the room and speaks in a strange, inhuman voice. "It's all right, Anna," it says mechanically. "I'm here. From now on, just you and I will be together."

"The Weird Tailor" is an outstanding episode often taken for granted, even by *Thriller* fans. In adapting his own short story (published in the July 1950 *Weird Tales*), Robert Bloch expanded the story line and added characters, including Nicolai and Madame Roberti (and also worked in his own forbidden volume *De Vermis Mysteriis*). The title is actually a misnomer: there's nothing particularly weird about the tailor, but then, "The Weird Customer" doesn't have quite the same ring.

There are a few minor inconsistencies. Why, for example, does Mr. Smith sit, practicing black magic at home with his door unlocked, making it possible for his son to interrupt the ceremony? And why does he do so little to stop

Arthur from stepping into the magic circle? In addition, where does he get the material for the suit? And why isn't Erik surprised that, when he tries to sew during the day, his needle won't even enter the material?

Admittedly, these are minor concerns. The important thing is that "The Weird Tailor" exudes a compelling atmosphere from beginning to end. There are some bizarre visual effects, notably the repeated shots of a spider spinning its web, weaving its silklike thread as Erik is simultaneously weaving his otherworldly material. Later, Erik looks at Schwenk and sees a spider's web with Schwenk's face in the middle; it dissolves to the face of Mr. Smith, and then to his dead son's. The eeriest scenes involve the dummy Hans, played by an actor posing as a dummy. It's not a totally convincing illusion — in some shots the dummy's arm and head can be seen moving — but it's a bizarre touch, and the climax, in which the dummy comes to life and murders Borg, only to return to pledge undying love for Anna, is simultaneously creepy and poignant.

The casting is somewhat curious. Henry Jones as Borg (Erik Conrad in the original story) seem slightly uncomfortable sporting a German accent, but for the most part is quite acceptable. Jones, a noteworthy character actor, is equally at home playing downtrodden little men or college professors. He was a regular on several television series, including *Channing* and *Phyllis*, and guested on numerous anthology shows, including *Tales of Tomorrow*, *Alfred Hitchcock Presents*, and *Way Out*. His film credits include *The Bad Seed* (1956), *Will Success Spoil Rock Hunter?* (1957), *Vertigo* (1958), and *Nine to Five* (1980).

George Macready is somewhat miscast as the erstwhile millionaire Mr. Smith. He suggests the man's hauteur and aristocratic bearing quite well, but is less successful showing paternal concern. As Bill Warren notes, "His hard, scarred face lent him mostly to villainous parts, and he was sometimes at a loss to project sympathy, usually settling for a kind of frowning weariness." Macready appeared with reasonable frequency in genre films, including *Soul of a Monster* and *The Monster and the Ape* (both 1945), *The Alligator People* (1959), *Seven Days in May* (1964), *The Human Duplicators* (1965), and *The Return of Count Yorga* (1971). He died in 1973.

Abraham Sofaer does an amusing turn as Nicolai. "You from the fuzz?" he asks when he first meets Mr. Smith. "The bulls — you know. The boys in blue. New York's finest." A Burmese actor who made his film debut in 1931, his screen credits include *Elephant Walk* (1954), *King of Kings* (1961), *Twice Told Tales* and *Captain Sinbad* (both 1963). He's also in another *Thriller*, "The Prediction."

Sandra Kerr is quite affecting as Anna, though her attraction to the middle-aged Borg is a little difficult to fathom. (In the story she was a refugee only too eager to consent to marriage and working in his shop.) It's a difficult role, but she manages to evoke sympathy without sacrificing believability.

Gary Clarke, on the other hand, is quite bad as Arthur Smith (fortunately, his part is mercifully brief). Clarke appeared as the teenage werewolf in *How to Make a Monster* (1958), his main claim to fame, and also appeared in *Missile to the Moon* (1960). He was a regular on the television series *The Virginian*.

But perhaps the most notable performance in "The Weird Tailor" is given by the actor playing the living dummy, Hans. Though he receives no listing in the credits, the role was played by Dikki Lerner (who also appears in a later episode, "The Innocent Bystanders"). Doug Benton recalls that Lerner was a professional mime who used to make money by standing in store windows, daring passersby to catch him moving. His is a faultless performance, suggesting the dummy's newborn sense of mobility and purpose, and providing a memorably creepy conclusion. Robert Bloch was among those impressed by the mimetic accuracy of Lerner's portrayal, though he confessed ignorance of the actor's identity, saying: "I too wish I knew the name of the actor who played the dummy — he was marvelous. Unless, of course, they animated a *real* dummy. I wouldn't put *anything* past those *Thriller* people!"

"God Grante That She Lye Stille" (airdate: October 23, 1961).
Produced by William Frye. Directed by Herschel Daugherty. Teleplay by Robert Hardy Andrews, from the short story by Lady Cynthia Asquith. Director of Photography: Benjamin H. Kline, A.S.C. Music: Jerry Goldsmith. Musical Supervision: Stanley Wilson. Art Director: Howard E. Johnson. Edited by Danny Landres. Editorial Department Head: David J. O'Connell. Associate Producer: Doug Benton. Assistant Director: James Hogan. Sound: Lyle Cain. Set Decorators: John McCarthy and Julia Heron.

Cast: Sarah Marshall (Lady Margaret), Ronald Howard (Dr. Edward Stone), Henry Daniell (Vicar Weatherford), Avis Scott (Nurse Emmons), Madeleine Holmes (Sarah), Victor Buono (Dr. Van de Velde).

An eerie episode involving witchcraft and vampirism, "God Grante That She Lye Stille" is a quietly chilling ghost story.

In 1661 Elspeth Clewer, having been tried and found guilty of both witchcraft and vampirism, is about to be burned at the stake. "You cannot destroy that which will not burn," she warns. "I curse all those who follow me. What I have lost, no woman of my clan will ever have ... first fire, then death — so it shall always be, until my body is restored to me." She is put to the torch.

Three hundred years later Lady Margaret (Sarah Marshall) has returned to her ancestral home. She is to receive the Clewer inheritance when she reaches her 21st birthday. She sees the spectral form of Elspeth Clewer beckoning to her, and also notices that her own form casts no reflection in the mirror. Dr. Edward Stone (Ronald Howard) is summoned to the estate. Lady Margaret tells him of the apparition; he gives her a sedative and prescribes rest. While out searching for her dog, which has apparently run away, he stumbles into the cemetery and sees the grave of Elspeth Clewer with its inscription: God Grante That She Lye Stille. As he turns around, he runs into John Weatherford (Henry Daniell), the local vicar. When Weatherford tells him that Elspeth Clewer confessed to witchcraft, Stone replies she must have been mad. "Can you diagnose from a distance of three centuries, doctor?" Weatherford asks. He tells Stone that Lady Margaret's 21st birthday falls on the same day Elspeth Clewer was burned at the stake.

Sarah (Madeleine Holmes), Lady Margaret's maid, calls Dr. Stone to tell him that Lady Margaret has run off. He finds her lying prostrate over Elspeth Clewer's grave. Shortly afterward, Lady Margaret's dog is found with its throat cut, and the caged birds in her room have had their heads torn off. What's more, Lady Margaret's mouth is smeared with blood.

Dr. Stone engages a nurse named Emmons (Avis Scott) to look after Lady Margaret. Reading over the records of Elspeth's trial for witchcraft, Stone finds that Elspeth was accused of killing birds and beasts and drinking their blood.

During the night Lady Margaret awakens and approaches Nurse Emmons' bedside, plunging a knife into her arm. Dr. Stone summons Van de Velde (Victor Buono), a noted psychiatrist. He diagnoses Lady Margaret's problem as schizophrenia. He also tells Stone that her heart has deteriorated; any shock may prove fatal.

Vicar Weatherford arrives at the estate; he tells Stone that he wishes Lady Margaret well, but that he fears the other — Elspeth Clewer — and reveals that he is the descendant of the man who condemned her to be burned at the stake. Meanwhile, Elspeth has been trying to lodge herself in Lady Margaret's body. When Stone goes upstairs to check on her, she says, "I've won, I've won," just before she dies.

Weatherford tells Stone that Lady Margaret was the last of the Clewer line, and Elspeth has lost her final chance to return to the world of the living. "In death, Lady Margaret has defeated her," he tells Stone, then shows him Elspeth's ghost returning to the grave, condemned to lie suspended between heaven and hell for eternity.

"Eternity is a long, long time," Stone says.

"God grant that she lie still," Weatherford replies.

A quiet ghost tale like "God Grante That She Lye Stille" provides something of a relief to the viewer accustomed to the violence- and special effects-saturated horror stories of today. Although there's little visual horror (mostly superimpositions of Elspeth's ghostly form beckoning to Lady Margaret) it's a satisfying episode, well acted and intelligently scripted and directed. Robert Hardy Andrews' teleplay is reasonably faithful to the short story by the doyenne of ghost story writers, Lady Cynthia Asquith.

There are few dramatic close-ups or striking compositions, but Herschel Daugherty's direction is quietly effective. One shot is subtly disturbing: after the caged birds in Lady Margaret's room have been beheaded, we see her face, with blood smeared across her lips. It's a disquieting image, more effective than any sudden shock or special effect.

The actors are impressive. Sarah Marshall, previously seen in "The Poisoner," is strangely affecting as Lady Margaret and Elspeth Clewer (a role reportedly originally intended for Barbara Steele). She seems a bit healthy for the desperately ill Lady Margaret, but her evident sincerity and classic features help her carry it off. Marshall, the daughter of actors Herbert Marshall and Edna Best, was in a few films in featured roles (such as *The Long Hot Summer* in 1958), but appeared mostly on television.

It's enjoyable to see Ronald Howard and Henry Daniell together again after "Well of Doom," this time as allies rather than antagonists. Both give capable performances and play off each other well, though it's a surprise to see Daniell in clerical garb, considering his propensity for cold-blooded villainy.

The other players are capable. As Van de Velde, Victor Buono adds a nice touch in his second and last *Thriller* appearance (his first was in "Girl with a Secret"), even though his role is limited to one scene. Likewise, Avis Scott (the treacherous nurse in "Letter to a Lover") is quite good in her minor role as Nurse Emmons.

"God Grante That She Lye Stille" is hardly a classic *Thriller*; it's really par for the course, but its unassuming virtues of atmosphere, taste, literacy and intelligence (not to mention a lovely, graceful score by Jerry Goldsmith) should not be judged lightly.

"Masquerade" (airdate: October 30, 1961). Produced by William Frye. Directed by Herschel Daugherty. Teleplay by Donald S. Sanford, based on the short story by Henry Kuttner. Director of Photography: Benjamin H. Kline, A.S.C. Music: Jerry Goldsmith. Art Director: Howard E. Johnson. Edited by Danny Landres. Associate Producer: Doug Benton. Assistant Director: James Hogan. Set Decorators: John McCarthy and Julia Heron.

Cast: Tom Poston (Charlie Denham), Elizabeth Montgomery (Rosamond Denham), John Carradine (Jed Carta), Jack Lambert (Lem Carta), Dorothy Neumann (Ruthie Carta).

"Masquerade," a tongue-in-cheek spoof of old dark house stories and vampire tales, is a reasonably amusing send-up, though its twist ending can be easily foreseen.

Writer Charlie Denham (Tom Poston) and his wife, Rosamond (Elizabeth Montgomery), are on their second honeymoon in the South. When they are caught in a thunderstorm one night, they stop at an old house (the *Psycho* house, in fact) to seek shelter. The door is opened by Jed Carta (John Carradine). "We don't get many visitors here," he says. "You must get awfully hungry in between," Roz comments.

"Make yourselves t' home," Jed tells them. When Charlie asks if they're the only guests, Jed tells them they used to have many more, but they were scared away by talk of vampires in the area. He tells them only a fool would take such talk seriously. "I think he plans to keep us here," Roz says. Charlie suggests that old Jed might be a vampire himself. "People have certain preconceived ideas about vampires," Roz points out. "You sound just like a story editor," Charlie says.

They meet Jed's brother, Lem Carta (Jack Lambert); he has green eyes, like Jed. He tells them that Ma will be coming down. "Putting on a fresh shroud, no doubt," Roz says. Shortly afterward they are attacked by a bat. Jed and Lem, in another part of the house, are meanwhile planning to kill their new guests, just as they did the last ones. "When it comes to slittin' a throat, there ain't no substitute for experience," Jed tells Lem. When Charlie and Roz run into them, Jed tells them about the history of the Henshawe Vampires. "You'd think a vampire'd change with the times," Jed says. "I figure if they acted more or less like other people, they wouldn't suspect what he was." Jed offers them dinner, but Roz tells him she has lost her appetite. "Besides," Charlie says, "Roz is a vegetarian."

They try to escape, but the front door is locked. They hear an eerie laugh. "I hate bats," Roz complains. "If we ever get out of here, I'm going to send you to a psychiatrist," Charlie tells her. Exploring the house, they find Ruthie Carta (Dorothy Neumann) in chains, locked in a cell. She tells them she's no kin to the other Cartas, and implores them to set her free. Charlie locates the key and lets her loose, but the old woman locks them both in the cell. "I'll be back for you," she cackles.

Charlie manages to get them out. They find a secret passageway behind a wall. "I hate dark places," Roz says. "You know, I'm really beginning to worry about you, Roz," Charlie says. He finds a bottle of corn liquor, which he drinks, and a guest book, which lists the Cartas' guests over the years — along with what they stole from each of them. "You two don't scare easy," Jed comments when he and Lem come downstairs. He shows

Charlie and Roz to a bedroom. She finds the clothes of the Cartas' last victim. They fall asleep, but Roz gets up sometime later and goes downstairs, walking as if in a trance.

Charlie awakens later to find Jed kneeling over the dead body of Lem, victim of the "Henshawe Vampires." Charlie goes down to the cellar, despite Jed's pleadings. Ruthie sneaks up on him with a knife, but Charlie seems unconcerned.

Backing out of the cellar sometime later, Charlie runs into Roz. "You *didn't*," she says. "It was either her or me," Charlie declares. Roz has the key to the front door, having knocked Jed out to get it. They hurry out of the house, get in their car, and drive to a nearby trailer park. "Let's not take any more drives in the picturesque back country," Roz says. A cock crows; they prepare to bed down. "I'd give anything to see old man Carta's face when he wakes up and finds Ruthie with those two puncture marks in her throat," Charlie says. He and Roz get in their coffins, close them, and go to "sleep."

As horror comics go, "Masquerade" isn't bad; it hasn't the wit or sophistication of a classic like James Whale's *The Old Dark House*, but it's still leagues away from the heavy-handed spoofing of *Night Gallery*. A faithful adaptation of Henry Kuttner's humorous short story, which originally appeared in the May 1942 *Weird Tales*, the main problem with "Masquerade" is that its ending can easily be foreseen. The Denhams don't seem particularly frightened by their surroundings, and their repartee is liberally peppered with double entendres which rather give the show away. Tom Poston and Elizabeth Montgomery (of *Bewitched*) are amusing as the unfazed couple, and it's always nice to see John Carradine, though the role of Jed Carta hardly taxes his skills. (Jay Allen Sanford complains of his unconvincing hillbilly accent, but under the circumstances this hardly seems distracting.) Lean Jack Lambert (once called "the meanest-looking man in movies") seems an odd choice to play Lem Carta (described in the story as "a gross, obese mountain of a man"), but at least he's properly menacing. The Carta mansion has some of the ambience of the household in *The Texas Chainsaw Massacre*, and Jerry Goldsmith's lively score keeps the whole thing moving.

It's often-remarked that the effective horror spoof (such as *Abbott and Costello Meet Frankenstein* or *The Ghost Breakers*) must be a successful example of the thing it's spoofing. In this regard "Masquerade" comes up short. For all the talk of missing guests and slitting throats, there just isn't anything intrinsically frightening about the Carta mansion (although Ruthie's intended assault on Charlie in the cellar comes close), and the episode suffers as a result. This seems doubly disappointing when one considers that it's the only *Thriller* to deal with vampires, admittedly in a humorous fashion (although "God Grante That She Lye Stille" touched on the subject). It also seems odd that Carradine, famed for his portrayal of Dracula, should be playing a non-vampiric murderer, but then that's part of the joke.

Donald S. Sanford, who adapted the story, remembers that "Masquerade" was shot quickly:

> "Masquerade" was fun. Something fell through, and they gave me the short story, and we had to move fast. They shot the first draft, really; we cut a few lines out, and we had to get off the stage [quickly].
>
> We all loved it. The contact producer from NBC — we always had a contact, somebody from NBC that

would come and read the scripts, make certain there wasn't too much violence, and alert us: "Be careful about so and so," particularly in the shooting — they didn't like "Masquerade" at all. I don't know why, but they just didn't like it. [Fortunately] they didn't have the authority to say, "You can't shoot this." Because I wanted to do another one, a sequel to that — I had an original idea, and I got shot down. Anyway, the show wasn't renewed for the third year, so that solved that problem.

"The Last of the Sommervilles" (airdate: November 6, 1961).

Produced by William Frye. Directed by Ida Lupino. Written by Ida Lupino and R. M. H. Lupino. Director of Photography: John F. Warren, A.S.C. Music: Jerry Goldsmith. Art Director: Howard E. Johnson. Edited by Danford B. Greene. Associate Producer: Douglas Benton. Assistant Director: Ben Bishop. Set Decorators: John McCarthy and Julia Heron.

Cast: Boris Karloff (Dr. Albert Farnham), Phyllis Thaxter (Ursula Sommerville), Martita Hunt (Celia Sommerville), Peter Walker (Rutherford Sommerville), Chet Stratton (Harvey Parchester).

"The Last of the Sommervilles" is an intriguing episode that builds up a fair amount of suspense, only to be let down by a disappointing ending and over acting by most of the principals, including Karloff.

We first see the figure of Ursula Sommerville (Phyllis Thaxter) burying a body in the dead of night. Sometime later her cousin Rutherford (Peter Walker) comes calling at Sommerville Manor to see Aunt Celia (Martita Hunt), whom he has not seen in 15 years. He is the last of the Sommervilles, and has come seeking money, having squandered his inheritance, but his slightly dotty aunt has other ideas. "Not a penny. He won't get a penny," she decides.

Rutherford plots with Ursula. She suggests they arrange a fatal "accident" for dear Aunt Celia. "Murder?" Rutherford asks. "That's a nasty word," Ursula replies. "Murderers are occasionally hanged," he points out. "So are Christmas stockings," she ripostes. She suggests that Rutherford carry out the deed; as she, Ursula, is the sole beneficiary of Celia's will, she'll need an alibi. Then, when she comes into the money, she can give Rutherford the $20,000 he needs.

There is an interruption: Dr. Farnham (Boris Karloff), an old friend of Celia's, arrives. He provides an alibi for Ursula by driving her into town. Celia goes upstairs to take one of her nightly baths, followed by Rutherford. He arranges for her to be electrocuted in the bathtub.

After the funeral Ursula shows Rutherford a note left in the letter box. It reads MURDER IS NOT CHEAP NOR SILENT. Rutherford suspects Dr. Farnham. Ursula proposes that they arrange a similar accident for him; when Rutherford balks at a second murder Ursula reveals that she has already taken care of Aunt Sophie, the body we saw her disposing of at the beginning.

Dr. Farnham pays a visit to the house, alarming Rutherford with his veiled suggestions and cryptic hints implying he knows who killed Celia. That night Ursula wakes Rutherford, telling him someone is outside, watching the house. There is a light in the nearby woods. Taking a pistol, they go out to investigate. Rutherford gets caught in the bog. Ursula stands watching, making no move to help. "You tricked me!" Rutherford shouts. "I had to, dear," Ursula replies. "It was the only

way. I never could have trusted you, Rutherford, not really, and you just aren't worth twenty thousand dollars." Rutherford slips beneath the surface of the bog, and Ursula retrieves the lantern she left hanging on a nearby tree.

Aunt Celia's money, along with Sommerville Manor and all Celia's jewelry and paintings, has been left to Harvey Parchester (Chet Stratton), who happens to be Ursula's husband. But in a surprising twist, Dr. Farnham appears to explain that Ursula and Harvey were killed in an accident, their bodies recovered from the bog alongside Rutherford's.

"The Last of the Sommervilles" has several things going for it: a moody opening, some splendid photography, a marvelous Victorian mansion with ornate furnishings, and some clever directorial flourishes by Ida Lupino. It's a shame the episode is let down by such broad acting totally out of sync with the rather macabre story line. Everyone seems to be trying to outdo everyone else, with the result that only Phyllis Thaxter's understated performance stands out.

The story line itself reuses the familiar house theme of a man and woman disposing of a third party and then suffering the consequences, but here there's hardly a hint of the supernatural. Admittedly, this theme worked better in "The Purple Room," "What Beckoning Ghost?" and "The Premature Burial," at least partly because it seemed fresher at the time. This time around it seems shopworn.

Ida Lupino's direction is stylish, but for the most part it seems wasted effort. Still, there are clever touches, notably Aunt Celia's death in the bathtub; at the moment the old lady is electrocuted, there's a close-up of her hand squeezing a sponge, then relaxing in death while bath water begins spreading across the floor.

The over acting is perhaps the episode's biggest problem. Karloff, sporting a bizarre hairstyle and Coke-rim glasses, seems to be enjoying himself hugely as Dr. Farnham, but his forced gaiety soon becomes annoying; it's one of his most mannered performances.

Martita Hunt is initially amusing as Aunt Celia, but her eccentricities are never as amusing as the Lupinos evidently intended. Her overstated performance contrasts sharply with the grim reality of her sudden death, leaving the viewer unsure of whether the episode is meant to be taken as black comedy or convoluted murder mystery. In any event, she's over the top. Although she's probably best remembered as Mrs. Havisham in David Lean's production of *Great Expectations* (1947), Hammer fans will recall her as the Baroness Meinster in *The Brides of Dracula* (1960). Doug Benton remembers her as being every bit as eccentric as her character:

> Martita Hunt had done something — *The Madwoman of Chaillot*, I think — and we got her to do an episode. Before she got here her agent told me she was a very peculiar person — eccentric was the word. He said the dressing room she would use had to be antiseptic, so we had the cleaning department go over it, twice. And within an hour, we got a screaming call from her agent saying Martita wasn't happy, and to get over there right away. So I hopped on my bicycle, which was how most of us got around back then, and pedaled over to her dressing room. I knocked on the door, it opened, and Martita was standing there starkers, screaming that she had found mouse droppings in the bathroom. We managed to calm her down, and after that she was fine.

Martita Hunt's other films include *The Ghosts of Berkeley Square* (1947), *Treasure Hunt* (1952) and *Bunny Lake Is Missing* (1965). She died in 1969.

Peter Walker is much too broad as Rutherford. Whether he's drinking too much or overreacting to Dr. Farnham's suggestive hints, he's unbelievable. Rutherford, in addition, comes across as rather a dunce, letting Ursula get the better of him all the way down the line. It's only fitting that he should perish through her trickery, since he doesn't seem to have the wits to see through anyone.

Phyllis Thaxter, on the other hand, gives an understated performance. She's as malevolent as she is greedy, and there's a wicked gleam in her eyes as she plots the demise of each succeeding Sommerville. It's rather disappointing (and not a little unbelievable) to learn that she has shared the fate of her victims, in a coda obviously tacked on to appease the censors. Nonetheless, Thaxter's acting stands out due to its welcome restraint. She was a leading actress during the forties, appearing in such films as *Bewitched* (1945) and *Blood on the Moon* (1948), but spent the remainder of her career as a character actress; her later films include *The World of Henry Orient* (1964) and *Superman* (1978).

Overall, "The Last of the Sommervilles" must be counted as a disappointment. It had potential, but it goes sadly unfulfilled.

"Letter to a Lover" (airdate: November 13, 1961). Produced by William Frye. Directed by Herschel Daugherty. Teleplay by Donald S. Sanford, based on the play by Sheridan Gibney. Director of Photography: Benjamin Kline. Music: Morton Stevens. Art Director: Howard E. Johnson. Editor: Danford Greene. Assistant Director:

James H. Brown. Associate Producer: Doug Benton.

Cast: Ann Todd (Sylvia Lawrence), Murray Matheson (Andrew Lawrence), Felix Deebank (Donald Carver), Avis Scott (Estelle Weber), Jack Greening (Inspector Rogers), Richard Peel (Sergeant Lathrop), Brendon Dillon (Coggins).

An unexpectedly effective (but little-heralded) episode, "Letter to a Lover" has so many twists and turns in its plot that a second viewing seems essential.

In present day England a man enters a doctor's office, then ducks out before Nurse Weber (Avis Scott) can identify him, leaving behind the corpse of Dr. Harold Evans. Nurse Weber removes all evidence, then calls the police.

Sylvia Lawrence (Ann Todd) runs to Donald Carver (Felix Deebank) for solace, and to escape from her husband Andrew (Murray Matheson), the man seen fleeing the doctor's office. Sylvia returns home; Andrew tells her she must face facts, and that they need six to eight months in the country for her to be well again. They pull up in front of a country estate, where Sylvia is frightened by the dog which Andrew keeps to guard against prowlers.

Andrew goes to meet Nurse Weber in a pub. "When someone does you a favor, surely it's usual at least to say 'thanks'," she says, referring to the purloined evidence. Andrew offers her money, but she wants a permanent position in Andrew's household. She knows that he came to the office expecting to find his wife with the doctor; there is a record of Sylvia's appointment at 2 P.M., the very hour Dr. Evans was murdered.

Meanwhile, Donald Carver arrives at the estate, having received a letter from Sylvia. She tells him Andrew is

keeping her prisoner, and that if she doesn't get away, she will go out of her mind. Andrew arrives and tells Donald that Sylvia has been under a strain and cannot stand any excitement. When Andrew goes out, Donald searches through his desk and calls a newspaper friend for information on the murdered doctor, who went by several aliases. Andrew returns and admits to Donald that he was in the doctor's office. He also tells him that Sylvia killed Dr. Evans. A few moments later Sylvia tells Andrew that the doctor was dead when she was in his office and then accuses Andrew of doing the deed himself.

Later on, Donald returns to the estate, entering surreptitiously. But Andrew is at home, with a gun. Andrew locks himself in his study; a shot rings out. Donald tells Sylvia that Andrew has killed himself and warns her not to summon the police, but to let Nurse Weber find the body the following day. But when she goes to the study the next morning, the door is open and there is no sign of Andrew. What's more, his car is gone.

Sylvia goes to see Donald in London, but he is not at home. Instead she finds Inspector Rogers of Scotland Yard (Jack Greening). He had a tip that Sylvia and Donald were leaving the country. When they go out to the estate, the place is closed up. Nurse Weber arrives and accuses Sylvia of murdering her husband, Dr. Evans. Inspector Rogers gets a call: they have found Andrew's car in the river. But Andrew is alive; he shoots a constable and prepares to fix the blame on Sylvia. Andrew offers to drink a toast, meanwhile slipping something into one of the glasses. But the police arrive and arrest the real murderer of the doctor — Nurse Weber. "We've been onto you a long time," says Inspector Rogers. "Ever since we discovered you removed certain evidence from the scene of the crime — false evidence, which you planted, then changed your mind about." "You mean my wife is innocent?" Andrew asks. The constable he shot is alive, and Sylvia is forgiving, telling Andrew, "You haven't killed anyone." But it is too late for Andrew — he has poisoned himself.

"Letter to a Lover" comes as something of a surprise, for the episode is rarely discussed, even among *Thriller* fans, and the title leads one to expect an innocuous trifle. Instead, "Letter to a Lover" is a complex, tightly plotted mystery that invites comparison with Agatha Christie or John Dickson Carr. Based on a play by Sheridan Gibney, it keeps the finger of suspicion pointing in all possible directions, and the plot has so many twists and turns that even the most alert spectator may admit to confusion on a first viewing. Additionally, it's nice to see a mystery replete with the distinctive *Thriller* horror atmosphere: Morton Stevens' ominous score, a lonely country estate setting, and plenty of fog. Anyone seeking true horror may come away disappointed, but the fair-minded fan will admit it's a first-class exercise in misdirection.

The actors are all well above average. Ann Todd, a leading actress in British films, is perhaps best known for *The Seventh Veil* (1945), though genre fans will recall her from Hammer Films' *Scream of Fear* (1961), which has a similarly twisted plot. She died in 1993.

Murray Matheson is discussed in the entry on "The Poisoner." Although he doesn't have as effective a showcase for his skills here, he's quite believable as Andrew Lawrence.

"Letter to a Lover" may disappoint those seeking *Thriller*'s usual fare, but for those willing to sample something different, it's a delicious (albeit confusing) soufflé of mixed identities, scrambled motives and fresh red herrings.

"A Third for Pinochle" (airdate: November 20, 1961). Produced by William Frye. Directed by Herschel Daugherty. Written by Mark Hanna and Boris Sobelman. Music: Morton Stevens. Director of Photography: Benjamin H. Kline, A.S.C. Art Director: Howard E. Johnson. Editorial Department Head: David J. O'Connell. Edited by Danny Landres. Musical Supervision: Stanley Wilson. Set Decorators: John McCarthy and Julia Heron. Associate Producer: Doug Benton. Assistant Director: James H. Brown. Sound: David H. Moriarty.

Cast: Edward Andrews (Maynard Thispin), Ann Shoemaker (Mrs. Thispin), Doro Merande (Melba Pennaroyd), June Walker (Deirdre Pennaroyd), Barbara Perry (Babs Dawson), Ken Lynch (The Lieutenant), Vito Scotti (Buddy Welsh), Tommy Farrell (The Messenger), Burt Mustin (The Redcap).

The second of Edward Andrews' three murder with a twist episodes, "A Third for Pinochle" is probably the least interesting of the three. It's cleverly done and competently plotted, but lacks any real distinction.

Two old women dispose of a man by hitting him over the head with a meat cleaver. One of the women chides the other: "We hardly knew him."

These two women, Melba (Doro Merande) and Deirdre Pennaroyd (June Walker), are the neighbors of henpecked husband Maynard Thispin (Edward Andrews) and his tightwad wife (Ann Shoemaker), whom they are constantly observing through powerful binoculars.

Mrs. Thispin has made out her will in Maynard's favor, and he can't wait to get rid of her. When he orders cyanide to kill some weeds, she comments that cyanide is a bad poison. "Well, it's good *and* bad," Maynard says. "Depends on who gets it." Unbeknownst to his wife,

Maynard is carrying on a romance with Babs Dawson (Barbara Perry), promising her a mink coat. He finally kills his wife as she is preparing to leave for a trip. He drives off with a dummy in the front seat of his car, under the observation of his neighbors. His wife's body is actually in the trunk. At the station he makes certain he is seen boarding the train with a woman resembling his wife, then disposes of the body in a ravine.

After destroying the dummy, he is visited by a police lieutenant (Ken Lynch). He suspects Mrs. Thispin never got on the train. But when they question the two ladies across the street, Maynard's story is confirmed. After Maynard gives Babs the brush-off he receives a call from the two old ladies. They know it wasn't Mrs. Thispin in the car, and plan to blackmail Maynard by forcing him to play pinochle with them; they frequently play right around the clock. "Two-handed pinochle is so dull, Mr. Thispin, you can't imagine," Deirdre says. "Dear Mr. Thispin will never leave us," Melba says.

"A Third for Pinochle" is a resolutely routine black comedy featuring Edward Andrews, once again, as a scheming protagonist with murder on his mind. It's competently handled, but derivative. There are distinct echoes of *Arsenic and Old Lace* in the two homicidal old ladies. (In one of the less successful scenes, they attempt to add a salesman [Vito Scotti] to their list of victims, only to have him take off running, the whole scene accompanied by hokey music.)

There are one or two nice touches. There's a hint of wit in the cat and mouse dialogue between Maynard and the police lieutenant (Ken Lynch, in a role similar to the one he played in "A Good Imagination"), and a macabre moment when Maynard burns the

dummy's head in the fire and the face melts away. Aside from these scenes, there's very little that's distinctive. It's an amusing *divertissement*, nothing more.

Edward Andrews plays the hen-pecked husband with his usual acerbic élan. He evidently enjoyed these roles, for he told *Starlog's* interviewer: "I did three or four segments. There was a wonderful guy named [Boris] Sobelman, and he wrote one for me. Then, it was so successful, they wrote a few more. I wish they did that kind of tongue-in-cheek stuff now." (For more on Andrews, see the entry on "A Good Imagination.")

The other players are competent but unexceptional. Doro Merande was frequently seen as "acidulous, eccentric and whimsical spinsters," to quote Leslie Halliwell. Her films include *Our Town* (1940), *Sullivan's Travels* (1941), and *The Cardinal* (1963). She died in 1975. Ann Shoemaker was a character actress, appearing in *Conflict* (1945), *Sunrise at Campobello* (1960) and *The Fortune Cookie* (1966), among other films.

There's little to be said about "A Third for Pinochle." Once seen, it tends to fade from memory, unlike most *Thriller*s, and is simply too similar to both "A Good Imagination" and "Cousin Tundifer" to stand on its own.

"The Closed Cabinet" (airdate: November 27, 1961). Produced by William Frye. Directed by Ida Lupino. Teleplay by Kay Lenard and Jess Carneol, from the story "The Closed Cabinet." Director of Photography: Benjamin Kline, A.S.C. Music: Jerry Goldsmith. Art Director: Howard E. Johnson. Edited by Danford B. Greene. Associate Producer: Douglas Benton. Assistant Director: John Clarke Bowman. Set Decorators: John McCarthy and Julia Heron.

Cast: Olive Sturgess (Evie Bishop), David Frankham (Alan Mervyn), Jennifer Raine (Lucy Mervyn), Peter Forster (George Mervyn), Patricia Manning (Lady Beatrice), Doris Lloyd (Dame Alice), Myra Carter (Maid), Kendrick Huxham (Andrews), Molly Glessing (Agnes).

"The Closed Cabinet," based on an anonymous Victorian ghost story, is an eerie but not altogether satisfying effort more notable for its fine Gothic atmosphere and superb photography than for the merits of its plot.

In Mervyn Castle a young woman, Lady Beatrice (Patricia Manning), takes a knife from a cabinet and plunges it into the heart of her cruel husband, Hugh Mervyn, then kills herself with it. When Hugh's mother, Dame Alice (Doris Lloyd), discovers the bodies, she decrees that in each generation there shall be a Mervyn who will bring shame and death to the family for eternity — "an end there shall be, but it will be beyond the limit of man to discover it. Who fathoms the riddle shall lift the curse and end Mervyns' strife." With that, she returns the knife to the cabinet.

Three hundred years later Evie (Olive Sturgess) arrives at Mervyn Castle, and is greeted by her lover, Alan (David Frankham), his brother, George (Peter Forster), and George's wife, Lucy (Jennifer Raine). She insists on staying in the castle's haunted room, where several Mervyn ancestors suffered violent deaths. Inside the room Evie notices the exquisite cabinet; according to legend, the curse will remain until someone finds a way to open it.

Downstairs, Alan and George are arguing. Alan insists that neither of them has the right to marry and thus endanger the life of the woman he loves. They nearly come to blows. "You know, Alan," George comments, "anyone would think

you were trying to provoke me enough to make that curse come true." In the meantime Evie has seen the spectral form of a woman at the far end of the corridor. When she mentions the woman to Alan, thinking it's a houseguest, he shows her a portrait and explains that the woman she saw was Lady Beatrice, dead for 300 years.

That night, during a fierce thunderstorm, Lady Beatrice again appears to Evie. The next morning, when Evie mentions the storm to the maid, the girl tells her they haven't had a storm in a week. Evie comes to believe that the storm somehow haunts the room and tells Alan, "If I can solve the mystery of the room, I think it will help you to be happy here."

Evie and Alan set out to explore the castle. When they come to a locked door, Alan sets out to find the key. But the door mysteriously swings open, and Evie enters the dungeons. She finds a bust of Hugh, Lord of Mervyn, and a hidden room containing the missing coffin of Lady Beatrice. The specter appears but vanishes when Alan intrudes on the scene. He tells Evie that no one knew where Lady Beatrice was buried for 300 years. He also tells her that he and George are the last of the Mervyns. George's sentiments on the subject are harsh: "I believe the cabinet will open when the last of the Mervyns is dead," he says.

Alan tells Evie that if life were different he would ask her to marry him. That night a storm arises outside Evie's room. Once again Lady Beatrice's ghost appears. In a trance, Evie turns the figure of a knight on the cabinet; it opens, and she finds the knife. She is about to plunge it into the figure of Hugh, lying on her bed, when she cuts her hand with it instead. She shows Alan the cabinet. A sliding panel opens, and Alan finds a parchment with the legend:

Pure blood stained by the blood-stained knife
Ends Mervyn shame, heals Mervyn strife.

Evie has brought peace to Lady Beatrice at last, and an end to the curse of the Mervyns.

Based on a Victorian ghost story handed down over the years (and reworked by editor-anthologist Basil Davenport), "The Closed Cabinet" is a gentle ghost story that takes place entirely within Mervyn Castle. It is one of the most atmospheric settings for any *Thriller*, and it's rather a pity the story doesn't allow for the trappings to be used for their full, macabre effect. The dungeons are enmeshed in cobwebs, and there's some wonderfully moody photography similar to Mario Bava's striking compositions in *Black Sunday* taking full advantage of the dank surroundings. Likewise, the spectral appearances of Lady Beatrice are suitably eerie and unnerving, but for the most part, she evokes, not fear, but sadness.

The same could be said for the episode itself. There's little suspense in the story: the ghost is not malevolent, so there's no need to be concerned for Evie's safety. It's just a matter of time before she solves the riddle and lifts the curse. Likewise, none of the other principals are ever menaced, and the expected conflict between Alan and George never develops into anything more than a nasty argument, so there's an undeniable feeling of letdown.

Linked to this are weaknesses in the acting. Olive Sturgess and Jennifer Raine are simply not believable in their roles, and the dialogue scenes between them are especially weak. David Frankham, on the other hand, gives a solid, convincing performance, the best in the episode. In addition to his four *Thriller* appearances, Frankham's genre films include *Return of the Fly* (1959), *Master of the World* (1961), and *Tales of Terror* (1962). One of his last films before his apparent retirement was *King Rat* (1965). Peter Forster is adequate, if unmemorable, as his brother George, but the most striking member of the cast is Patricia Manning as Lady Beatrice. Though she never speaks while in her spectral form, she makes one of the most beautiful — and believable — ghosts in television history.

"Dialogues with Death" (airdate: December 4, 1961). Produced by William Frye. Directed by Herschel Daugherty. Written by Robert Arthur, based on his own short stories. Director of Photography: Bud Thackery, A.S.C. Art Director: Howard E. Johnson. Music: Morton Stevens. Musical Supervision: Stanley Wilson. Edited by Danny Landres. Editorial Department Head: David J. O'Connell. Associate Producer: Doug Benton. Assistant Director: Ronnie Rondell. Set Decorators: John McCarthy and Julia Heron.

Cast: Boris Karloff (Pop Jenkins and Colonel Jackson Beauregard Finchess), Ed Nelson (Tom Ellison and Daniel Lejean), Estelle Winwood (Aunt Emily), Ben Hammer (Harry), William Schallert (Professor MacFarland), Norma Crane (Nell Lejean), George Kane (Harry Jervis), Jimmy Joyce (Ambulance Attendant).

"Dialogues with Death," another multi-part episode, suffers from the same unevenness that plagued "Trio For Terror": one episode peters out disappointingly, while the other, despite some unconvincing Southern dialects, has a grandly grisly climax.

"Friend of the Dead": Old Pop Jenkins (Boris Karloff), a morgue attendant, talks to his "clients," carrying on long conversations with the recently deceased. "It's hard to get used to being dead, isn't it?" he says to his most recent arrival. "Now, the first thing to do is to be calm, tell yourself it's perfectly natural to be dead. Oh yes, later you'll be going on somewhere else, but right now it might help if we talked a little. Tell me anything you want to. When you have things on your conscience it sometimes helps to tell someone about them."

Reporters Tom Ellison (Ed Nelson) and his associate, Harry (Ben Hammer), decide to drop by the morgue to take pictures of the recently deceased Dan Gordon for a newspaper story. They hear Pop conversing with the corpse. "Been on the job a long time, Pop. You need a change," Harry says. Tom asks Pop if Gordon knows who killed him. Pop inadvertently lets slip the name of Gordon's murderer: Professor MacFarland. The professor shot him in a dispute over his sister, who was appearing at Gordon's nightclub.

Tom and Harry go to see Professor MacFarland (William Schallert). They ask about his sister, and when the professor's attention is diverted, Tom finds the gun in his drawer, just where Pop Jenkins said it would be. Taking the gun as evidence, they leave. Driving back to town, Tom swerves to avoid a man standing on the road. The car goes over the side. Tom manages to escape, but can't get the door open to save Harry. He walks back to town, arriving at the morgue. Pop Jenkins tells him an ambulance is already on its way to rescue Harry. But after two more deliveries Pop shows Tom one of the bodies — Harry's. "He was killed in the wreck," Pop explains. But then he shows him the second body. It is Tom's. "You'd already started trying to come for help," Pop says. "So you just kept on trying till you got here." "Then I'm ..." Tom begins. "I'm sorry," Pop says. Tom disappears,

and Pop has two new clients to converse with.

"You see, boys," Pop says, "that information you got me to give you — it just wasn't meant for anyone living to make use of. And that hitchhiker you saw — you know who he was. Now, boys, you mustn't be frightened. Tell yourself this is all perfectly natural. Yes, of course, I know it's hard at first to realize that you're dead. But you'll get over it in time."

"Welcome Home": In a decaying Southern mansion (the same one seen in "Pigeons From Hell") Colonel Jackson Beauregard Finchess (Boris Karloff) and his sister, Emily (Estelle Winwood), receive some unexpected visitors: nephew Daniel Lejean (Ed Nelson) and his wife, Nell (Norma Crane). They are on the lam; Daniel is wanted for murder. When he seems surprised that Aunt Emily doesn't recognize him, she has a simple explanation: "We didn't recognize you because you're dead," she says. Colonel Jackson tells him he read that he (Daniel) was killed in a holdup. Emily assumes that Nell is dead as well. Daniel's real purpose in returning home is to look for a large sum of money he knows is hidden somewhere on the estate.

Upstairs they find Daniel's old room filled with dust and cobwebs. "What a cute family I married into," Nell complains. "We have got to get out of this fleabag."

"The swamp does things to houses," Daniel points out, "and the people too."

The next day Daniel shows Nell the family mausoleum. He tells her of a family member who suffered from catalepsy and was buried alive, and of the time he locked Aunt Emily in the mausoleum overnight. Back at the house Colonel Jackson tells Nell the story of Daniel's father, who insisted on being buried with a telephone in his coffin just in case he was buried during a similar cataleptic seizure.

During a rainstorm Colonel Jackson tells Daniel the money he's looking for is in his coffin. "Since you weren't using it, seemed a safe place no one'd look for it," he says. With thunder and lightning overhead, Daniel and Nell enter the mausoleum, which is rapidly filling with water. He finds his own crypt, complete with a date of death. Opening it, he finds the money — all $50,000. Just then the door of the mausoleum is bolted shut by Aunt Emily. Daniel and Nell try to open it, without success. The water level continues to rise. But Nell remembers the telephone buried in his father's coffin. Daniel pries the lid off, reaches in, and finds it. He calls the operator and asks to be connected with the sheriff. He tells him they're locked in the mausoleum. The sheriff tells him to be patient: he'll be there in an hour.

Back inside the house Colonel Jackson hangs up the phone. "I don't believe he recognized our voices," he says. "He thought you were the operator and I was the sheriff." "I don't suppose he realizes the telephone only connected here with the house," Aunt Emily says.

"Dialogues with Death," based on two short stories by Robert Arthur, is, as usual with multi-part episodes, uneven.

The first begins promisingly, but soon turns into what Jay Allen Sanford calls "one of those shopworn 'Whoops, I'm dead' tales." The story line changes direction in midstream, just when it's beginning to get interesting. (Was Professor MacFarland ever arrested for killing Dan Gordon? The segment doesn't bother to let us know.) The hitchhiker on the road is an eerie image, but from then on we're in familiar territory, and

Tom's body appearing on the slab comes as no surprise, rather a confirmation of a cliché. Karloff's sympathetic performance as Pop Jenkins is a minor saving grace, but overall the conventionality of the tale soundly defeats it.

The second segment is more successful, despite its semi-spoofing approach. Both Karloff and Estelle Winwood give histrionic performances as two dotty Southerners, but the macabre atmosphere and the grisly final twist are nicely handled. The overdone Southern dialects are a drawback (Ed Nelson's is particularly vexing), but overall the grim mood of the story remains intact.

The actors are generally effective. Estelle Winwood had an amazingly long career in films and on stage. She appeared with Bela Lugosi in *The Red Poppy* on Broadway in 1922, and was featured in such films as *The Swan* (1956), *The Magic Sword* (1962) and *Camelot* (1967). When she died in 1984 at the age of 101, she was the oldest member of the Screen Actors Guild.

Ed Nelson, who had previously appeared in "The Fatal Impulse" and "The Cheaters," appeared in such fifties horror and sci-fi films as *The Brain Eaters* and *Night of the Blood Beast* (both 1958). He's a decent actor, projecting both energy and intelligence. He played Dr. Michael Rossi on TV's long-running *Peyton Place*.

"Dialogues with Death" does not rank among the better *Thrillers*; it's not even on the level of "Trio for Terror," which, for all its unevenness, has one classic segment. But it's adequate enough, providing a few macabre moments along the way.

"The Return of Andrew Bentley" (airdate: December 11, 1961). Produced by William Frye. Directed by John Newland. Teleplay by Richard

Matheson, based on the short story by
August Derleth and Mark Schorer.
Music: Morton Stevens. Director of
Photography: John F. Warren, A.S.C.
Art Director: Alex Mayer. Editorial
Department Head: David J. O'Connell.
Edited by Danny Landres. Musical
Supervision: Stanley Wilson. Set Deco-
rators: John McCarthy and Julia Heron.
Associate Producer: Doug Benton.
Assistant Director: Frank Losee. Sound:
Earl Crain, Jr.

Cast: John Newland (Ellis Corbett), Antoinette Bower (Sheila Corbett), Philip Bourneuf (Dr. Weatherbee), Oscar Beregi (Reverend
Burkhardt), Reggie Nalder (Andrew
Bentley), Terence DeMarney (Amos
Wilder), Ken Renard (Jacob), Ton Hennesy (The Familiar), Norma Crane.

One of the grimmest yet most satisfactory *Thrillers* ever, "The Return of
Andrew Bentley" is a memorable tale of
graverobbing and black magic.

Ellis Corbett (John Newland) and
his bride, Sheila (Antoinette Bower), are
summoned to the home of Ellis' uncle,
Amos Wilder (Terence DeMarney).
Amos tells them he is about to die; he
will leave everything to Ellis, on the condition that he continue to live in the
house and examine Amos' sealed burial
vault. If anyone is discovered tampering
with the vault, Ellis will find written
instructions he must follow. Staring out
the window, he suddenly shouts: "I'll
block him yet. Amos Wilder is still a
match for you. Do you hear me,
Andrew?" Shortly afterward, he is found
dead, having drunk poison.

He is laid to rest in the cellar.
Afterwards Ellis seals the vault, then
draws runic symbols over the door, in
accordance with Amos' instructions.
Later, Ellis asks Dr. Weatherbee (Philip
Bourneuf) about Andrew; the doctor
replies that Andrew Bentley died two

years ago. Ellis and Sheila go down to
check on the vault; unbeknownst to
them, they are being observed by a mysterious figure (Reggie Nalder).

Ellis finds a message left by his
uncle instructing him to look up a particular book, *The Rites of Protection*; he
also receives a visit from the Reverend
Burkhardt (Oscar Beregi). He warns
Ellis not to read from the book, but Ellis
does; the book warns against demons
who haunt the places of the dead, seeking to possess the dead and use them.
Ellis goes down to examine the vault
again. He finds the mysterious figure
standing in front of the vault, along with
his familiar (Tom Hennesy). Ellis collapses. Sheila finds him, and helps him
upstairs. When Ellis tells his servant
Jacob (Ken Renard) about his experience, it is obvious the latter knows the
identity of the figure. "Who is he,
Jacob?" Ellis asks. "He is — Andrew
Bentley," Jacob screams before running
for the door, only to find Bentley waiting outside. Jacob dies from the shock.

Dr. Weatherbee explains that
Andrew Bentley was a sorcerer, a practitioner of black magic. Everyone feared
him. He had a familiar, a demon summoned to do his bidding. Ellis finds the
written instructions left by his uncle;
they direct him to find Bentley's corpse
and destroy it. Amos killed him two
years earlier with a hunting knife; what
they have seen is Bentley's ghost. Bentley wants Amos' body so it can be inhab-
ited by the familiar.

They decide to seek out Reverend
Burkhardt. But on the road they
encounter the familiar; the carriage loses
a wheel and they are forced to continue
on foot. The familiar attempts to follow,
but cannot cross water. Reaching
Burkhardt's home, they double back,
descending to the vault, where they
encounter Bentley. Burkhardt repels him

with a cross, and he disappears into another room. They find a secret room just beyond, and in it a skeleton with a knife through it. "Burn it quickly," Burkhardt says. Ellis sets fire to the skeleton, and as it burns the familiar vanishes. Andrew Bentley is, at last, truly dead.

"The Return of Andrew Bentley" was one of a number of short stories written during the summer of 1931 by August Derleth and Mark Schorer. ("Colonel Markesan," done on *Thriller* as "The Incredible Dr. Markesan," also resulted from this collaboration.) They worked together in a rented cottage. Derleth set down the basic outline of each story, and the first draft was written by Schorer. Derleth then did a final revision. As they recounted in the introduction to the Arkham House collection *Colonel Markesan and Less Pleasant People*:

> In our meetings we seldom found it necessary to talk very much about methods or plots. Our collaborative conversation usually concerned theme and setting. "Let's see — we did the werewolf theme yesterday — how about a zombie story tomorrow?" Or, "Well, how would you like to spend tomorrow in New Orleans after today in the Sahara?"

Most of the stories were published in *Weird Tales* or *Strange Stories*. "The Return of Andrew Bentley," which appeared in the September 1932 *Weird Tales*, is one of the more memorable. It was selected for inclusion in Bennett Cerf's Modern Library anthology *Famous Ghost Stories*, and is remarkably similar to Richard Matheson's *Thriller* teleplay. One grisly detail left out is an incident in which the narrator makes a grab for Andrew Bentley's hand just before being knocked unconscious. He awakens later to find a fragment of human bone in his hand, clearly showing the first two joints of the little finger.

Thriller's adaptation is appropriately enshrouded in gloom from first to last. John Newland's direction seldom falters: he makes the most of Amos Wilder's house, from the study containing books of esoteric knowledge to the cobweb festooned cellar. Many of the shots are angled to show the characters through the omnipresent cobwebs, and Newland extracts every last drop of atmosphere from these dank surroundings. As usual, there's very little in the way of visual effects: the familiar is seen wearing a grotesque mask (described by Jay Allen Sanford as looking "like an *Outer Limits* castoff") and seen through a vaseline smeared lens. Surprisingly enough, it works quite well.

John Newland, doubling as director and actor, makes a somewhat stolid hero. The role makes few demands on him: most of the time he's simply carrying out his uncle's instructions. He's rather bland, but then the role is simply not that interesting. For more on Newland, see the entry on "Pigeons from Hell."

As Sheila, Antoinette Bower also has little to do. This is not surprising, since her character didn't appear in the original story, but was added, presumably because a female lead was deemed necessary. She's beautiful, but that's about all; from a dramatic standpoint, her character could have been dispensed with entirely. (For more on Bower, see the entry on "Waxworks.")

Philip Bourneuf provides adequate support as Dr. Weatherbee. A reliable (if little-noticed) character actor, Bourneuf's career was spotty. His films include *Joan of Arc* (1948), *Hemingway's Adventures of a Young Man* (1962), and *The Molly Maguires* (1970). He died in 1979.

Oscar Beregi is something of a surprise as Reverend Burkhardt, since we're so used to him playing sinister characters. (You almost expect him to be in league with Andrew Bentley.) He was memorable in the *Twilight Zone* episode "Death's-head Revisited," but his film appearances tended to be unremarkable.

Of course, it's Reggie Nalder who is the center of attention throughout the entire episode. Even though he never says a word, it is difficult to take your eyes off him, whether he's unfurling his black cape or staring with his hypnotic gaze in close-up (a startling effect). His sinister form and ratlike physiognomy made him the perfect choice for Andrew Bentley. Nalder played this kind of role often, in movies and on television. As Tom Weaver points out in his book *Poverty Row Horrors!*:

"Through what seems like divine intervention, Hollywood was never without a ghoulish [Dwight] Frye-type for their horror films. Frye ruled the graveyard roost from 1930 until his death in 1943, when the pockmarked, emaciated Skelton Knaggs made his horror debut in Val Lewton's *The Ghost Ship*. Knaggs turned up in many horror films between 1943 and his death ... in 1955 — the year Reggie Nalder had his first prominent role as the assassin in Hitchcock's *The Man Who Knew Too Much*. Nalder carried the baton until his recent death. Next?

(For more on Nalder, see the entry on "The Terror in Teakwood.")

Surprisingly enough, one person less than thrilled with "The Return of Andrew Bentley" is its scriptwriter, the famed fantasy author Richard Matheson. It is his only *Thriller* teleplay, and although it's a perfectly satisfactory episode, Matheson has little regard for it. Apparently his script was revised by someone higher up, and Matheson was displeased. Matheson later spoke of it during an interview with Jay Allen Sanford:

RM: "What I had done ... I don't know if you're familiar with a *Twilight Zone* of mine called 'Nick of Time'?"

JAS: "Sure. Bill Shatner, the fortune telling machine with the bouncing devil's head."

RM: "Well, I put that couple into a bantering thing. I did a similar thing [for *Thriller*] with that sort of bandying about, gradually becoming involved in genuine fear. And, uh, they played it pretty heavy from the start."

JAS: "It was a rather dark episode."

RM: "Which is not really my cup of tea."

"The Remarkable Mrs. Hawk" (airdate: December 18, 1961).

Produced by William Frye. Directed by John Brahm. Television story and teleplay by Donald S. Sanford, based on the short story by Margaret St. Clair. Music: Morton Stevens. Musical Supervision: Stanley Wilson. Director of Photography: Ray Flin. Edited by Danny Landres. Art Director: Frank Arrigo. Sound: Earl Crain, Jr. Editorial Department Head: David J. O'Connell. Associate Producer: Doug Benton. Assistant Director: Chuck Colean. Set Decorators: John McCarthy and Julia Heron.

Cast: Jo Van Fleet (Mrs. Hawk), John Carradine (Jason Longfellow), Hal Baylor (Pete Grogan), Paul Newlan (Sheriff Thomas Ulysses Willetts), Martin Eric (Larkin), Donald Elson (Clemins), Bruce Dern (Johnny Norton), Raymond Cavaleri (Billy), James Parnell (Al), Kevin Enright (Al's Helper), Hurley Bell (The Drifter).

A definite change of pace, "The

Remarkable Mrs. Hawk" ranks as one of the cleverest episodes. It's not particularly frightening, but then it doesn't really try to be.

Johnny Norton (Bruce Dern) tells Mrs. Hawk (Jo Van Fleet) that he is quitting his job on her farm. He proposes to bludgeon her and steal her money, but she is too quick for him. "I told you you could have anything you want," she says. "All you had to do was ask." He steals her money and runs, but doesn't get far; a moment later he is screaming in agony from some unseen complication. Mrs. Hawk smiles in satisfaction.

"That's Johnny, he's in trouble," Pete Grogan (Hal Baylor) tells his fellow tramp, Jason Longfellow (John Carradine). Longfellow tells him it's too late, and knocks Pete cold. "I'm afraid Johnny is beyond our aid—or anybody's," Jason says. When Pete awakens, Jason—a Latin scholar—tells him of the hobo rumor that has drawn him across the country: an advertisement for a husband for the remarkable Mrs. Hawk. Lonely young men, Jason says, are not likely to have inquiring family members come looking for them after they disappear. Jason plans to blackmail Mrs. Hawk.

Mrs. Hawk, meanwhile, is winning all the hog prizes at the county fair. She welcomes Jason and Pete, posing as uncle and nephew, to her home. That night Pete hears pigs squealing outside and sees Mrs. Hawk transform one of the pigs into Johnny.

Sheriff Willets (Paul Newlan) comes inquiring about Johnny, mentioning the young man's companions, Jason and Pete, who are wanted for assault. Pete returns to Mrs. Hawk's abode. While he sits eating her pancakes he begins to grunt uncontrollably. "And this little piggy ..." Mrs. Hawk recites.

Jason comes to visit, and tells Mrs. Hawk he knows the Greek translation of her name: Circe. He says he knows her husband Ulysses was protected from her witchcraft by a remarkable herb. When she accuses Jason of sacrificing Johnny, he admits that he used him as a kind of guinea pig. Jason blackmails her, asking for her money and farm. But when he uses her feather pen to sign a deed, he licks the tip. He asks where Pete is. "Changing," Mrs. Hawk replies. Jason soon learns that he, too, has been altered—it was on the tip of the feather. "Just a little pinch of powder, that's all it takes," Mrs. Hawk tells him.

Sheriff Willetts comes to look around Mrs. Hawk's farm. He has stumbled upon her secret, but refuses to believe it. She serves him donuts. "You disappoint me," she says. "I thought you were different." Sheriff Willets transforms into a pig. Mrs. Hawk then sends the lot of them off to the slaughterhouse, only to encounter another young man at her front door.

Margaret St. Clair's "Mrs. Hawk" was published in the July 1950 *Weird Tales*. A very brief story with a surface resemblance to John Collier's "The Lady on the Grey," it involves a contest of wills between Mrs. Hawk and the sheriff. He suspects the truth when he sees a pig with a harelip, an affliction suffered by one of her lonely hearts correspondents, but is transformed himself when he eats one of her donuts.

In adapting and expanding the story for *Thriller*, Donald S. Sanford added several characters, including the beguiling tramp with a PhD, Jason Longfellow (his name links him with both a leading American poet and a hero of classical mythology). The result is one of the more unusual *Thrillers*: the customary Gothic mansion and fog-shrouded catacombs have been temporarily replaced by a pig farm and county fair. Sanford also indulges in some clever wordplay: the sheriff's middle name is Ulysses, the same as Circe's husband. And Mrs. Hawk herself, who reminds him that her husband was a seafaring man, is known as C. Hawk ("Sea Hawk"). The C. stands for Cissy, an updating of Circe. There are other amusing gambits: when we first see Johnny Norton, the tattoo on his arm is immediately noticeable; we later see the selfsame tattoo on the pig being led off to the slaughterhouse.

Sanford's most amusing conceit is the addition of the scholarly tramp. Sanford recalls, "on that one I suggested John Carradine as a character. The story is based on the legend of Circe, and I suggested Carradine as sort of a bum." Carradine was quoted some years later as saying "[both *Thrillers*] were very good ones, particularly ... 'The Remarkable Mrs. Hawk'. I enjoyed that. The man who wrote it was well acquainted with Greek mythology." Sanford himself was equally impressed with Carradine's erudition: "Boy, this guy knew his Latin," he recalled. "All the Latin I used in the script I learned in school. I had an expert at UCLA check it — and Carradine corrected *him!*"

This unorthodox character was a departure for the hard-working Carradine. Whether quoting Shakespeare or engaging in cat and mouse games with Mrs. Hawk, Carradine is a delight, playing the character to the hilt (but without indulging in his usual hamminess) and even upstaging Jo Van Fleet in their scenes together. He comes off far better here than in his similarly eccentric role in "Masquerade."

It seems unnecessary to enumerate more than a few of Carradine's extensive credits. He made his film debut in 1930 in *Tol'able David*, and acted in well over

200 more until his death in 1988. His best non-genre roles were probably in two John Ford films: *Stagecoach* (1939) and *The Grapes of Wrath* (1940). For years he denied being a horror actor, but in truth he may have appeared in more genre films (over 75) than any other performer, including Karloff. He gave fine, understated performances as Dracula in *House of Frankenstein* (1944) and *House of Dracula* (1945); his all-time best performance may have been as *Bluebeard* (1944) under Edgar Ulmer's direction. Unfortunately, he did his best genre films in the forties; later dreck such as *Astro-Zombies* (1969) and *Blood of Dracula's Castle* (1969) made his name virtually synonymous with low budget trash, a sad comedown for a once great trouper.

The other actors are equally at home in their unconventional roles. Jo Van Fleet is particularly amusing as Mrs. Hawk. She isn't quite as attractive as the character in the original story, but she's appropriately domineering, and manages to suggest Mrs. Hawk's sinister side. In one of the few atmospheric flourishes at which he excelled, director John Brahm uses low key lighting to suggest this in a close-up at the end of the prologue; it's an effective shot, sinister yet slightly comic, like the episode itself. An accomplished performer, Van Fleet won an Oscar for her role as James Dean's estranged mother in *East of Eden* (1955). She is also seen in *Wild River* (1960), *Cool Hand Luke* (1967) and *The Tenant* (1976).

Paul Newlan is his usual gruff, non-smiling self as Sheriff Willets in his fourth *Thriller* appearance (he was also seen in "The Big Blackout," "The Cheaters" and "The Grim Reaper"). Perhaps best remembered as Lee Marvin's boss on the TV series *M Squad*, Newlan is quite amusing as the unwilling beneficiary of Mrs. Hawk's attentions.

Hal Baylor is adequate as Pete Gro-gan. He was a regular on *The Life and Legend of Wyatt Earp* in the fifties.

The supporting actor most people remember from "The Remarkable Mrs. Hawk" ,is, of course, Bruce Dern. Although he's only seen in the prologue (and once again, briefly, later on), he gives his usual quirky, distinctive per-formance, the kind that helped to single him out as a character actor. He was very busy throughout the sixties, usually in small but memorable parts: he was the unfortunate sailor clubbed to death in Hitchcock's *Marnie* (1964), and the equally unfortunate suitor deprived of his hand and then his head in *Hush ... Hush, Sweet Charlotte* (1965). In the sev-enties he became a bona fide star, with leading roles in *The Cowboys* (1972), *Silent Running* (1972), *The Great Gatsby* (1974) and Hitchcock's *Family Plot* (1976). After a while his career faltered, and he went back to character roles. His daughter Laura has appeared in such films as *Wild at Heart* (1990) and *Juras-sic Park* (1993).

"The Remarkable Mrs. Hawk" is a most peculiar *Thriller*. Although there's a certain macabre fascination in the idea of transforming men into pigs, it hasn't the usual accoutrements one has come to expect from the series: there are no *frissons* and none of the haunted house atmosphere that worked so well in pre-vious episodes. What it lacks in tradi-tional appurtenances it makes up for in originality of conception. Thankfully, it never quite descends into comedy, though its tongue is obviously planted in its cheek. It may qualify as one of the more memorable *Thrillers* through the sheer novelty of its presentation.

"Portrait Without a Face"

(airdate: December 25, 1961). Produced by William Frye. Directed by John Newland. Written by Jason Wingreen. Director of Photography: Lionel Lin-don. Editor: George Nicholson. Art Director: Howard E. Johnson. Music: Morton Stevens. Assistant Director: Carter DeHaven, III. Associate Pro-ducer: Doug Benton. Paintings courtesy of the Martin Lowitz Galleries.

Cast: Jane Greer (Ann Moffat), Robert Webber (Arthur Henshaw), Katharine Squire (Agatha Moffat), George Mitchell (Sheriff Pete Brown-ing), Brian Gaffikin (Nat Fairchild), John Newland (Robertson Moffat), John Banner (Martin Vander Hoven), Gage Clarke (Dr. Josiah Grant), Alberta Nel-son (Marie Browning).

"Portrait Without a Face" stands as one of the best examples of crisscrossing genres. It begins with a seemingly super-natural situation, drops suggestive hints that there is indeed a spectral presence at work, then shifts gears by positing a per-fectly rational explanation for every-thing, only to undercut this with its final revelation that the supernatural is pres-ent after all. For some narrow-minded fans who want ground rules laid down well in advance, this can be annoying, but for more open-minded viewers, this exercise in misdirection is part of what makes *Thriller* unique.

Robertson Moffat (John New-land), an egocentric, obnoxious artist, is seen antagonizing heavy-drinking reporter Nat Fairchild (Brian Gaffikin), jeering at him and declaring his inten-tion to paint the Angel of Death. When Fairchild asks if he intends to paint at night, Moffat replies, "I do my best work at night. I love the night. It excites me. You know, I've often thought death must be like the night. I mean, it's so absolutely still. Nothing stirs."

Moffat throws Fairchild out of his studio, then receives a phone call from a woman; he taunts and insults her into hanging up, then prepares to begin the painting. He is interrupted by a masked figure, a phantom archer who fires an arrow from a crossbow through the skylight, striking Moffat down before he can paint a brushstroke.

Six months later Arthur Henshaw (Robert Webber), an appraiser from the Janus Galleries, arrives at Moffat's home to do the catalogue for the gallery's exhibit of his paintings. He encounters the eccentric Agatha (Katharine Squire), Moffat's aunt, who says that the artist's death was "a judgment ... from on high." He also meets Moffat's widow, Ann (Jane Greer). She takes him to the artist's studio, located in a separate building, which hasn't been opened since the murder. She shows Henshaw the blank canvas, but something has been added: Moffat's face, with an arrow through his head. Ann faints.

Sometime later Henshaw questions her doctor (Gage Clarke), who suggests that someone had a duplicate key to the studio and added Moffat's face as a macabre joke. When Henshaw suggests a supernatural explanation, the doctor says, "This is the 20th century, man, not the 16th." "You know, doctor," Henshaw ripostes, "back in those days, if two men were having a conversation like this, one of them would probably be saying, 'This is the 16th century, not the 12th.'"

Ann awakens and insists on going to the studio, saying she must destroy the painting. Henshaw asks if there could be a duplicate key; Ann denies the possibility. In the studio they find Agatha cackling — and more detail added. Someone is filling in the portrait, bit by bit. What's more, the style is unmistakably Robertson Moffat's. "He's dead," Ann says, "but Robbie is painting this picture ... of his murderer."

Pete Browning (George Mitchell), the sheriff who investigated Moffat's

murder, arrives. Henshaw tells him a distinguished art critic is coming to authenticate the painting. The reporter, Fairchild, also drops by, having heard talk of the ghost in the studio. "You know," Fairchild remarks, "it wouldn't surprise me in the least if a man who loved life as much as Robbie Moffat did wasn't able to come back from the grave for more." Browning throws Fairchild out, then plants himself in front of the picture to watch for any further changes. He falls asleep, only to awaken when Agatha lets out a scream, having seen a figure at the window. Browning runs back to the house, but it is only the art critic (John Banner) who has come to authenticate the painting. Browning returns to the studio to find most of the painting completed. "The only thing left is the ... face of the murderer," Henshaw says.

The art critic finishes his examination of the picture and pronounces it unmistakably a genuine Robertson Moffat — despite the paint being still wet. Browning wants to impound the picture, but Henshaw tells him something supernatural is afoot. Browning scoffs at this, declaring, "If all the fiends in Hell came out and marched by me, I wouldn't believe my own eyes." Henshaw decides to spend the night in the studio.

Sometime later Ann enters the studio, knife in hand, and attempts to destroy the painting, but Henshaw stops her. He asks her if she killed her husband. She tells him she hated Moffat because of his monstrous ego and wanted to kill him but didn't; what's more, she doesn't want to know who did. Henshaw lets her in on a secret: he has always had a most peculiar talent — he can imitate the style of any painter, a talent he has made little use of before now, in order to lure the murderer out of hiding. There is a sound from outside the studio. Henshaw climbs up to the skylight and intercepts the murderer, who is preparing to fire a flaming arrow at Ann. They struggle, and the murderer falls through the skylight, breaking his neck.

Fairchild arrives with Browning's wife, whom Moffat painted in the nude. Moffat promised her the painting, then withheld it to blackmail her. Then, as they watch, the painting fills in its last detail — the face of Sheriff Browning.

The main strength of "Portrait Without a Face" is its ingenious plot by writer-actor Jason Wingreen. Echoes of *Dorian Gray* abound, though here the portrait fills itself in rather than aging; actually, in some ways, the story might be considered a companion piece to "The Grim Reaper," which also featured a supernatural painting and crisscrossing genres. The episode plays fair in its rational resolution: Henshaw is always nearby when the additions occur (though he must be a remarkably fast painter as well as a master forger). This central situation generates so much suspense that one can excuse the implausibilities. For example: why don't the characters simply take turns watching the painting, since the alterations occur only when no one is present? The portrait itself is a more serious flaw; Robertson Moffat is supposedly a dazzling artist, yet judging from the picture, his talents seem meager indeed. This makes Moffat's egocentrism and boastful arrogance even more disagreeable.

John Newland's direction demonstrates once again, just as in "Pigeons from Hell" and "The Return of Andrew Bentley," his affinity for the macabre. Despite the geographical limitations (the action is confined to the house and grounds and Moffat's studio) the situation never becomes static, and the exteriors, choked with thick fog, provide a

suitably eerie background. Although the episode hardly rivals "Pigeons from Hell" in terms of suspense of hackle-raising horror, it is sufficiently engrossing in its own right.

The acting is variable. Jane Greer is quite restrained and believable as the troubled Ann Moffat, though her attempted assault on the painting with a large knife seems out of character, inserted for an extra thrill. Best remembered as the *femme fatale* in the film noir classic *Out of the Past*, Greer was a familiar face in films of the forties, fifties and sixties, including *The Big Steal* (1949), *The Prisoner of Zenda* (1952), and *Man of a Thousand Faces* (1957).

As the mysterious Arthur Henshaw (presumably no relation to the "Henshaw vampires" in "Masquerade"), Robert Webber gives a fine, understated performance. Webber was an underrated actor who delivered solid performances over the years in films like *Twelve Angry Men* (1957), *Harper* (1966), *The Dirty Dozen* (1967), *10* (1979) and *S.O.B.* (1981), but never became firmly fixed in the public mind. He died in 1989.

The other actors are a mixed bag. John Newland (doubling as actor) overplays Robertson Moffat, making him such an overbearing ogre it's hard to imagine anyone marrying him. He's loutish and lacking even a hint of silky charm (our first view of Moffat is him strangling Nat Fairchild!). On the other hand, George Mitchell as the prosaic Sheriff Browning and Brian Gaffikin as the inebriated reporter are both acceptable (though the latter character verges on cliché). It's nice to see Gage Clarke, veteran of many a B science fiction and horror film, this time as a doctor rather than in his usual role as a priest. And TV viewers may recognize the late John Banner (the impenetrable Sergeant Schultz of *Hogan's Heroes*) as the art expert. But Katharine Squire overdoes her role as the dotty Agatha. Constantly running through the house and studio, and given to repeating herself incessantly ("Dead ... as a mackerel!" she scoffs of Moffat), she has red herring written all over her. It doesn't help that the actress is so heavily and unconvincingly made up to look older; it adds another layer of theatricality to her already overdone performance. Her constant cackling, meant to be comic, quickly becomes annoying.

Other aspects of the production are well up to standard, from Morton Stevens' moody score to Lionel Lindon's photography, which gives Moffat House the creepy ambience of Baskerville Hall. Overall, even though "Portrait Without a Face" is not top drawer *Thriller*, it is distinctly above average; as an episode of almost any other horror suspense anthology series, it would be a standout.

"An Attractive Family" (airdate: January 1, 1962). Produced by William Frye. Directed by John Brahm. Teleplay by Robert Arthur, from his own short story. Director of Photography: Henry Freulich, A.S.C. Music: Morton Stevens. Musical Supervision: Stanley Wilson. Editorial Department Head: David J. O'Connell. Art Director: Howard E. Johnson. Edited by Danny Landres. Associate Producer: Doug Benton. Assistant Director: Carter De-Haven, III. Set Decorators: John McCarthy and Julia Heron.

Cast: Richard Long (Dick Farrington), Joan Tetzel (Marion Farrington), Otto Kruger (Burt Farrington), Leo G. Carroll (Major Downey), Joyce Bulifant (Jinny Wells), Will Wright (Constable Walker), William Mims (George Drake), Paul Barselow (Mr. Lamb), Deirdre Owen (Alice Wells).

An amusing comedy of murders, "An Attractive Family" is stylishly

directed by John Brahm with his customary eye for striking images and shadowed compositions.

Young Jinny Wells (Joyce Bulifant) approaches an old mansion. The gates mysteriously swing open to admit her. She does not want to enter the old house, but voices impel her to go in. Once inside (it's the old *Psycho* house again), she ascends the stairs. She enters a room with a noose hanging from the ceiling. Three voices cry out to her, telling her to hang herself; then there will be no more nightmares. She steps up onto a chair, puts the noose around her neck, and plunges into darkness.

The foregoing is, of course, only a nightmare. In short order we are introduced to the Farringtons, the attractive family of the title. Dick (Richard Long) and Marion (Joan Tetzel) go canoeing with Marion's husband, George Drake (William Mims). The canoe overturns, and George, who never learned to swim, cries for help. Dick obligingly swims over, only to drown him. "He panicked, just like you said he would," Dick tells his sister, who now will inherit George's wealth.

In Mexico, Uncle Burt (Otto Kruger) barges in on Dick's honeymoon with wealthy young Alice Wells (Deirdre Owen). When Burt prepares to take her picture posing on the edge of a cliff, he asks her to take a step backwards — with the inevitable result. It is hardly coincidental that Dick and his wife made out joint wills just the day before.

Sometime later, in New England, the Farringtons are visited by Major Downey (Leo G. Carroll), who has come to take Jinny, who is Alice's sister, on a bird watching expedition. Jinny has recently been plagued by nightmares; Marion invites the Major to Jinny's 21st birthday party. They plan a nice gathering, especially since Jinny isn't going to live to enjoy her money.

Jinny and Major Downey approach the house she's seen in her nightmares. The house is supposedly haunted — one of the heirs hanged herself in the room Jinny saw in her dream. The rope he used is still hanging from the ceiling.

The Farringtons are meanwhile discussing Jinny. Dick cannot take any more money out of her estate. If she doesn't die before her 21st birthday, Dick, as executor, will have to give an accounting of Alice's will; he has already spent Jinny's half.

Major Downey inadvertently picks some poisonous mushrooms. Marion prepares them for Jinny's dinner, but the girl spills them on the floor. Mario reminds the others there will be ample opportunity to murder Jinny during the picnic the next day. After her death Dick will automatically inherit the remainder of her estate.

After another nightmare Jinny wakes up screaming. She was about to hang herself with the rope in the Merriview house. Marion calls a psychiatrist to suggest that Jinny is developing suicidal tendencies. "In an hour this whole town will know about my call to Boston," she tells Uncle Burt, "and you know what this town thinks about anyone who has to see a psychiatrist."

Dick takes Jinny to the old Merriview house while Marion and Burt follow. He forces Jinny to go upstairs, telling her, "The only way to get rid of your fears is to face them. Now I'm going to show you that there's nothing to be afraid of." They enter the room with the noose, the room in Jinny's dream. Dick compels Jinny to put the noose around her neck while standing on a chair. Marion and Burt tie her hands. "You're going to kill me," Jinny says. "Nonsense, dear, you're going to kill yourself," Marion replies. Dick admits killing Alice.

Just then Constable Walker (Will Wright) and Major Downey break in. "I thought you were going to be too late," Jinny says. "I'm sorry, Jinny," the major says, "but I had to get every word recorded." He is actually Jinny's godfather; the mushrooms and the dreams were simply ruses to trap the Farringtons. As they are led away by the constable, Major Downey remarks, "I think we can call a halt to our bird watching now. After all, how can we ever top three vultures?"

For most of its length, "An Attractive Family" coasts along quite agreeably. John Brahm's visual sense serves him well, as always, though by this time the *Psycho* house is perhaps too familiar a background. In addition, it isn't difficult to foresee the ending, though Brahm caps it neatly with Major Downey's description of the Farringtons as vultures — at which point a group shot complete with sinister shadows and low key lighting reveals the three at their vulturine worst.

Although "An Attractive Family" aspires to be a heartless black comedy in the tradition of *Kind Hearts and Coronets*, some genuine poignancy comes through. The Farringtons' first victim, George Drake, is presented as a pompous buffoon, but Alice Wells is a more sympathetic victim. Consequently there's a more emotional tug when Jinny describes her. "She wrote to me the morning she died, about how wonderfully happy she was ... she was so plain and awkward and shy ... you were the only man who ever realized how nice she actually was," she tells Dick, and for a moment the Farringtons' murderous expediency takes a more personal toll.

One of the nicest things about "An Attractive Family" is to see its cast of veteran actors working together. Leading man Richard Long never quite achieved stardom; he appeared mostly in second features. His smooth, handsome features seemed almost a handicap, as they limited him to light leading roles, though he invariably handled these with flair and assurance. Noted film critic James Agee singled him out for praise for his supporting role in Orson Welles' *The Stranger* (1946). His other films include *The Egg and I* (1947), *Cult of the Cobra* (1955) and *House on Haunted Hill* (1958). He found steady employment on television as a regular on several series, including *The Big Valley* and *77 Sunset Strip*. He died in 1974 at the age of 47.

Joan Tetzel was a stage actress who appeared in occasional films, such as *Duel in the Sun* (1946) and *The Paradine Case* (1947). She was married to Oscar Homolka, the star of "Waxworks," and appeared in a previous episode, "The Devil's Ticket." She died in 1977.

Otto Kruger was a polished actor adept at suave villainy, though he played sympathetic roles as well, usually avuncular types. He was the swinish Nazi villain in Hitchcock's *Saboteur* (in the role originally intended for Harry Carey). His other films include *Dracula's Daughter* (1936), *Jungle Captive* (1945), *Colossus of New York* (1958) and *The Wonderful World of the Brothers Grimm* (1962). He died in 1974.

Leo G. Carroll is amusing, as always, as Major Downey. He usually played his roles for humor, though he could be sinister on occasion, as in Hitchcock's *Spellbound* (1945). He actually appeared in six Hitchcock films, more than any other performer (apart from the director himself). He may be best remembered as the ghost-ridden "Topper" in the popular TV series; he also appeared on both *The Man* and *The Girl from U.N.C.L.E.* He died in 1972.

Joyce Bulifant is properly ingenuous as Jinny. A regular on several TV series through the seventies, she's prob-

ably best known as Marie Slaughter on *The Mary Tyler Moore Show*.

Overall, it's hard to dislike "An Attractive Family." It's certainly no classic, but as a smooth, polished entertainment — a comedy of murders — it's crisp and enjoyable.

"**Waxworks**" (airdate: January 8, 1962). Produced by William Frye. Directed by Herschel Daugherty. Teleplay by Robert Bloch, based on his short story. Music: Morton Stevens. Director of Photography: Benjamin H. Kline, A.S.C. Art Director: Howard E. Johnson. Editorial Department Head: David J. O'Connell. Edited by Danny Landres. Musical Supervision: Stanley Wilson. Set Decorators: John McCarthy and Julia Heron. Associate Producer: Doug Benton. Assistant Director: Donald Baer. Sound: Earl Crain, Jr.

Cast: Oscar Homolka (Pierre Jacquelin), Antoinette Bower (Annette Jacquelin), Ron Ely (Mike Hudson), Alan Baxter (Sergeant Dane), Booth Colman (Lieutenant Bailey), Martin Kosleck (Colonel Andre Bertroux), J. Pat O'Malley (The Morgue Attendant), Amy Fields (Irene Colton), George Spicer (The Young Man), June Kenney (The Girl).

Another true *Thriller* classic, "Waxworks" is arguably the finest episode of the second season.

Pierre Jacquelin (Oscar Homolka) is giving a group a tour of his wax museum, showing off his chamber of horrors featuring the figures of famous murderers. A young woman (Amy Fields), engrossed in sketching one of the figures, accidentally stays past closing time. The lights go out. The young woman tries to find her way out of the building, unaware she is being stalked by a man with a club foot. The figure corners her and raises an axe while the young woman screams in terror.

Lieutenant Bailey (Booth Colman) and Sergeant Dane (Alan Baxter) are assigned to the young woman's murder after her body is found in an alley, along with her sketch of the wax figure. Dane goes to see Pierre Jacquelin; he identifies the sketch as that of Varnac, a French murderer guillotined in Paris. He introduces Dane to his niece, Annette (Antoinette Bower), a beautiful young woman who helps her uncle with the wax figures, which he sculpts. She vouches for his whereabouts on the night of the murder, and explains her uncle has only been in America for about a month. Dane takes a romantic interest in Annette, and invites her to dinner. But on the way to the restaurant, he is run down and killed by a car; the driver is one of Jacquelin's wax figures!

After testifying at police headquarters, Annette is taken to dinner by Mike Hudson (Ron Ely), a young policeman. Jacquelin, meanwhile, is being questioned by Lieutenant Bailey; he suggests that the killings might be the work of a frustrated suitor who is following Annette. At that very moment Annette and Mike are being shadowed by a mysterious figure. The figure confronts them outside the wax museum, but is taken captive by Bailey. "It's all right now — we've got our murderer," Bailey declares, a trifle prematurely.

The mysterious figure turns out to be Colonel Andre Bertroux (Martin Kosleck), late of the French Sûreté. He is acting as a private citizen, but tells the detectives, "It is happening again — just as it happened in 1946 and 1948 and 1953 and 1959." A traveling waxworks comes to town, and, with it, a series of mysterious deaths. It has happened throughout Europe. Bertroux says he does not suspect Jacquelin or his niece. When Bailey points out that there are no others, Bertroux retorts, "There are

50 others." He suspects that, somehow, the wax figures are responsible; the detectives treat him with skepticism, but provide him with a police guard outside his door.

Later that night Bertroux knocks out the guard and goes to the waxworks. He bangs on the door until Annette lets him in. He explains that he has followed the Jacquelins for 17 years. "When I was not following you I was following *them*," he says, referring to the figures. "There are ways of bringing wax figures to life," he insists, suggesting Jacquelin has used hair from the real murderers to impart life to the figures, just as witches do with wax dolls. He demands to see Jacquelin; Annette tells him her uncle is sleeping. They enter his private quarters, but find only a dummy in the bed. They both hear footsteps coming closer. One of the wax figures enters and slashes Bertroux. He falls into a vat of bubbling wax.

Bailey and Mike Hudson break into the wax museum, armed with a search warrant. The place is apparently deserted. As they are looking for the Jacquelins, Mike is mysteriously stabbed, apparently by one of the wax figures. Pierre Jacquelin emerges from the shadows and pulls a gun on Bailey. The policeman accuses him of committing the murders himself while disguised as the wax figures. He knocks the gun from Jacquelin's hand, then covers him with it. When Bailey asks about Annette, Jacquelin tells him she is his wife. Her body, or a wax image, stands behind a curtain. Jacquelin tells Bailey that she was sentenced to death 30 years before; he made a wax image of her, and disguised himself according to her instructions. He had to kill to nourish her life force with fresh blood. Bailey tells him that it is only a wax figure of Annette; Jacquelin retorts that when he whispers a spell, she will awaken. He makes a grab for the policeman's gun; it goes off, wounding Jacquelin, and in the struggle the wax figure is set afire. "Don't you see?" Bailey asks. "That's only a statue. The real Annette must be alive." "This *is* the real Annette," the dying Jacquelin reveals. "The statue that comes alive — I molded it over her own body." He dies. The flames melt the figure, revealing the skull underneath the wax.

"Waxworks" stands as one of the finest *Thrillers* ever. Robert Bloch adapted it from his own short story, published in the December 1938 *Weird Tales* when its author was 21 years old. The original story concerns a young poet drawn to the wax figure of Salome, modeled after a murderess whose body serves as the frame for the statue. The story was adapted somewhat more faithfully for the multi-part feature film *The House That Dripped Blood* starring Peter Cushing, but this adaptation is sadly inferior to *Thriller's* version.

From its stylish direction to its spendidly eerie and evocative photography, "Waxworks" is first-rate in every department. Bloch's teleplay sets up three different protagonists (Dane, Bertroux and Hudson) and then kills them off in rapid succession, rudely shattering audience identification with each. There's also a soupcon of gallows humor: the morgue attendant (J. Pat O'Malley) calmly removes a sandwich he keeps refrigerated on one of the slabs; and Pierre Jacquelin, reminiscing about one of his wax models, says, "As I recall, he was sent to the guillotine in April. Ah, Paris in the spring — how romantic."

There are many splendidly macabre moments: after Sergeant Dane is run down by a hit and run driver, we see the mysterious wax figure at the wheel of the car; there's a notable shot of the blind murderer advancing on Colonel Bertroux with his hook upraised; and the final shot of Annette going up in flames, the wax melting her features to reveal the gaping skull beneath, is a memorably nightmarish image.

The actors are impressive. Oscar Homolka, one of the great character actors of all time, is alternately sympathetic and sinister as Pierre Jacquelin. Born in Vienna, he made his film debut in 1930 and was a familiar figure in supporting roles for more than 40 years. He was memorable as the villain in Hitchcock's *Sabotage* (1936) and as the sadistic henchman in William Castle's *Mr. Sardonicus* (1961). He died in 1978. (Asked about specific casting choices on *Thriller*, Bloch recalled that "I would have liked to see what Peter Lorre might do in 'Waxworks'.")

Antoinette Bower (previously seen in "The Return of Andrew Bentley") is beautiful and enigmatic as the mysterious Annette. The striking French actress was a frequent guest on such series as *Alfred Hitchcock Presents* and *The Twilight Zone*. She seems to have disappeared into minor supporting roles; one of her later credits is a Charles Bronson film, *The Evil That Men Do* (1984).

Ron Ely makes a colorful hero; it comes as a considerable shock when he's abruptly dispatched. An actor of considerable physical presence and disarming humor, Ely is probably best known as television's Tarzan; he also played Doc Savage in George Pal's disappointing movie adaptation. He later replaced Bert Parks as announcer of the Miss America pageant.

Martin Kosleck, a fine character actor, sports a creditable French accent in his only *Thriller* appearance as the intrepid Colonel Bertroux (in Bloch's original story the Colonel loses his head to the waxen Salome). The Russian-born Kosleck played many slimy Nazis during the war years; he was notable as Goebbels in *The Hitler Gang* (1944). He also found time to carve a minor niche in the horror genre with his roles in *The Mad Doctor* (1941), *The Mummy's Curse* (1944), *The Frozen Ghost* (1945), *House of Horrors* (1946), *She-Wolf of London* (1946) and the notorious cheapie *The Flesh Eaters* (1964). Always a dependable supporting actor, Kosleck makes the most of his scenes in "Waxworks," elevating the character of the Colonel from a mere red herring to a believable (if somewhat foolhardy) investigator. Kosleck died in 1994.

Booth Colman and Alan Baxter (previously seen in "The Watcher") are both rather colorless as minions of the law. And, at the beginning, there's a brief glimpse of June Kenney (heroine of Bert I. Gordon's *Earth vs. the Spider* and *Attack of the Puppet People*) as one of the onlookers at the museum.

Like many other first-rate *Thrillers*, "Waxworks" charts a wavering course between crime and horror before coming down firmly on the latter side. Bloch's twisting story line, with its red herrings and false starts, is a splendid exercise in misdirection, and that, coupled with the waxworks theme (a perennial in horror films), works to the episode's advantage. "Waxworks" is *Thriller* at its best.

"La Strega" (airdate: January 15, 1962). Produced by William Frye. Directed by Ida Lupino. Written by Alan Caillou. Director of Photography: Benjamin H. Kline, A.S.C. Art Director: Howard E. Johnson. Music: Morton Stevens. Editorial Department Head: David J. O'Connell. Edited by Danny Landres. Musical Supervision: Stanley Wilson. Associate Producer: Douglas Benton. Assistant Director: Donald Baer. Sound: Earl Crain, Jr. Set Decorators: John McCarthy and Julia Heron.

Cast: Ursula Andress (Luana), Alejandro Rey (Tonio Bellini), Jeanette Nolan (La Strega), Ramon Novarro (Maestro Giuliano), Frank de Kova (Lt. Vincoli), Ernest Sarracino (Padre Lupari).

One of director Ida Lupino's best efforts, "La Strega" is a chilling account of witchcraft in Italy at the time it was still spoken of as "the old religion."

Around 100 years ago in a small Italian village, a young girl named Luana (Ursula Andress) is set upon by some village men; they call her "Strega" — witch. They throw her into the river to drown. As she floats down the river clinging to a log, a young painter named Tonio Bellini (Alejandro Rey) sees her and rescues her. He takes her home and cares for her. When she awakens she asks Tonio if he believes in witches; he laughs at the suggestion. She tells him the villagers are sure her grandmother is a witch. Tonio is sketching her portrait when she suddenly screams and tells him her grandmother is coming for her. Tonio tells her no one is outside, but when they look out the window they see the fearsome figure of La Strega (Jeanette Nolan). Tonio hides Luana in a trunk, then admits the old woman. "I come for Luana," she says. Tonio tells her he doesn't know where she is. La Strega finds the portrait, and says, "For the last time — where is she?" When Tonio refuses to answer, she puts a curse on him: his blood will boil and his hands will do the work of the devil. She leaves, but when Tonio tries to release Luana, he cannot open the trunk. He somehow manages to get it open, but Luana realizes he is very sick. "She cursed me," Tonio says. Luana puts him to bed and paints a cross above his head to break the spell. When Tonio awakens, his fever is gone. He is falling in love with Luana. But when he looks at the portrait he did of her, the image of La Strega stares back. He throws the portrait in the fire, only to see the ghostly image of a black cat staring at them. "La Strega!" Luana cries.

Maestro Giuliano (Ramon Novarro), Tonio's best friend, comes to see him. Tonio tells him what has happened; Giuliano explains that the black cat is used to keep strangers away from the sabbat held in the woods. That night the three of them view the sabbat from a hiding place. La Strega is presiding over the revelers. Tonio screams at them to stop it. La Strega points her finger and the revelers vanish in a puff of smoke. Tonio hears Luana scream, and rushes back to find Giuliano dead. "I'll go back to her," Luana decides. "If not, the next time it will be you," she tells Tonio. He refuses, telling her he will go to see La Strega and beg her — on his knees, if necessary — to release them from the curse.

They go to see Padre Lupari (Ernest Darracino). Tonio leaves Luana with him, then goes to see La Strega. "I know why you come," the old crone says. "It will do you no good. I knew you would break sooner or later." Screaming in horror, Tonio strangles La Strega, then buries the body.

When Tonio returns to Padre Lupari, he finds the police waiting to arrest him in connection with Giuliano's death. Luana has gone. The padre mentions that he saw La Strega *after* Tonio killed her. Fleeing from the police, Tonio runs back to La Strega's hovel and digs up her grave, only to find the body of Luana. Screaming and in tears, he is led off by police to be arrested for murdering Luana.

"La Strega" is a chilling tale of witchcraft by writer-actor Alan Caillou; as usual with his scripts, it's a well-researched piece with persuasive bits of local lore (La Strega's curse is particu-

larly nasty) and a most cheerless denouement. Ida Lupino's direction rivets the viewer's attention from first to last; there are some startling images, notably La Strega's face superimposed over Tonio's portrait of Luana, adumbrating the transference of personalities. Likewise, the danse macabre commemorating the sabbat is nicely choreographed, although we don't see enough of it to savor its true satanic flavor.

The cast is multinational, and the clash of accents is sometimes jarring, though this is a minor complaint. Ursula Andress, on the cusp of international stardom with the release of *Dr. No* (1962), is beautiful and affecting as Luana. Her Swedish accent seems out of place, but her evident sincerity is sufficient to put the character over. She became an international sex symbol during the sixties in such films as *What's New, Pussycat?* (1965), *The Tenth Victim* (1965) and *Casino Royale* (1967). In virtually all of these she was decorative rather than dramatic. She made an insipid Ayesha in Hammer Films' version of Haggard's *She* (1965), but showed the glimmerings of a comic style in *Perfect Friday* (1970). She's still active in films in Europe.

Alejandro Rey is fine as Tonio, though his Argentinean accent seems incongruous (he explains that he recently arrived in Italy from Spain). Doug Benton recalls that director Ida Lupino thought the two actors were the most beautiful people she'd ever seen, even though "Andress had an accent you could cut with a knife, and Alejandro Rey couldn't speak English." (For more on Rey, see the entry on "Guillotine.")

Jeanette Nolan is alternately terrifying and comical as La Strega. She's weighed down with a very artificial looking makeup that seems designed for the stage rather than television, and in some scenes it's difficult to take her seriously. But she chews the scenery with merciless abandon, whether she's spitefully spelling out the effects of her curse or officiating at the sabbat. Lupino provides her with a memorable introductory shot: as Luana and Tonio stare out the window, seeing only a beggar woman in the street, La Strega looms up out of the shadows and leers up at them in full close-up. (For more on Nolan, see the entry on "Parasite Mansion.")

Ramon Novarro is adequate as Tonio's friend, Maestro Giuliano. Novarro's greatest period of fame was in the silent era: he starred as *Scaramouche* (1923) and as *Ben-Hur* in the 1925 spectacular. After sound came in, his parts grew less prominent, though he found frequent employment as a character actor. In 1968 he became the victim of one of Hollywood's most notorious murders when he picked up two young men and brought them back to his home, apparently for a homosexual liaison. (According to Kenneth Anger's *Hollywood Babylon*, the two young hustlers killed the veteran actor by stuffing a dildo — a present from Rudolph Valentino — down his throat.)

"La Strega" apparently had a smooth production history, though there was at least one minor hitch, as Doug Benton remembers:

Ida Lupino was one of the most conscientious directors around — nothing like the directors today: she was a thoroughgoing professional, and she got there on time, and finished on time. Well, we had built a very elaborate set with hills and stuff, and she would get up a 4 a.m. and walk over to the set, long before the production people got there, to get a feel for that day's shooting. Well, this one day she misstepped and went sliding down the hill and

broke her ankle. She couldn't move, and so she had to wait until someone arrived at 6 o'clock to take her to a doctor. And so she did the rest of the show with her leg in a cast.

"La Strega" tends to be a particular favorite of *Thriller* fans, who routinely rate it near the top in polls of all-time favorite episodes. It's an admittedly chilling and flavorful entry, but it rather palls beside an undeniable classic such as "Pigeons from Hell" or "The Cheaters." Even so, it may well be Ida Lupino's most memorable *Thriller*— a haunting and evocative tale of witchcraft and triumphant evil.

"The Storm" (airdate: January 22, 1962). Produced by William Frye. Directed by Herschel Daugherty. Teleplay by William D. Gordon, based on the story by McKnight Malmar. Director of Photography: John F. Warren, A.S.C. Music: Morton Stevens. Art Director: Frank Arrigo. Edited by Danny Landres. Associate Producer: Douglas Benton. Assistant Director: Edward K. Dodds.

Cast: Nancy Kelly (Janet Willsom), David McLean (Ben Willsom), James Griffith (Ed Brandies).

The basic situation in "The Storm" is classic in its simplicity: a frightened woman alone in a house during a storm. From that simple premise every last drop of suspense has been wrung, and the results are splendidly effective.

During a rainstorm a young woman wearing a diamond ring is pursued by a man whose features we do not see. He catches her and strangles her. The only witness to the murder is a black cat.

Ed Brandies (James Griffith), a taxi driver, drops Janet Willsom (Nancy Kelly) off at home. She has been away for two weeks. He makes unwelcome advances; she warns him that her husband will soon be home. Declining to take the hint, Ed says, "I irritate everyone. Now, at the risk of undermining our relationship, you have neighbors three miles down the lane. Let me take you there until the storm blows over." Janet declines the offer, and Ed drives off.

Thunder rumbles overhead; with only the black cat for company, Janet settles in for the night. She discovers the thermostat isn't working, so she lights a fire and phones to leave a message for her husband to call; he is away on business and wasn't expecting her home till tomorrow morning. The operator calls back to tell Janet that her husband isn't at his office; what's more, if he tries driving up, he may find the roads washed out. After Janet hangs up the lights go off and then on again. She hears a noise outside and goes out to investigate, but it is only the storm doors banging against some cans. When she goes in, the lights go out. Venturing out again into the storm, she goes down into the cellar with a flashlight, looking for the main power circuit. Back inside the house, she finds a letter addressed to her husband; he has received several and told Janet they were from his cousin Agnes. Just then a window breaks. Peering out through the curtains, Janet sees a pair of eyes. It is only an owl. Relieved, she puts the cat out.

The storm continues. Janet hears a rapping sound and goes to investigate, but it is only the mailbox, swinging in the wind. "Oh Ben, oh Ben, please come home," she says. "I'm beginning to act silly." Going down to the cellar again, this time to stop a window from banging, she sees the dead woman's body in her trunk, the diamond ring on her finger. Terrified, she rushes upstairs and calls the operator, but the connection is not clear; the operator cannot hear her plea for help. Janet makes a run for Ben's truck, but as she drives off, one tire gets stuck in the mud. "Oh Ben, what am I going to do?" she cries. Running back to the house through the rain, she grabs a knife with which to defend herself. The cat has mysteriously reappeared and there are wet footprints on the carpet. Just then a figure passes in front of the French doors; Janet unlocks them, then stands ready with the knife. "All right — the door is open!" she screams. "Come in — I want to see you!"

The door opens — only to admit Ben (David McLean). Janet collapses in tears; he comforts her. She tells him about the dead woman in the cellar. Ben, disbelieving, goes down to look; there is no body in the trunk. "What about the diamond ring?" Janet asks, then tells him about the cat and the wet footprints. Ben admits there might have been a prowler. But when Janet tries to call the police, Ben dissuades her. What's more, Janet cannot find the letter addressed to Ben. She says the police might think the letter was from a woman who loved Ben and followed him here; they might also think he killed her. "Ben, did you — did you come in here? Did you take the envelope?" she asks. Ben admits it and takes the envelope from his pocket, but when he unfolds it the diamond ring drops out.

Janet backs away from him, then turns; running out into the storm, she sees the girl's body in the back of the truck. Ben comes after her, but is left screaming her name in the pouring rain.

While not strictly speaking a horror episode, "The Storm" is one of the most suspenseful *Thrillers* ever. Based on McKnight Malmar's frequently anthologized 1944 short story, William D. Gordon's teleplay adds a few things (such as the murder at the beginning and the cat) and the protagonist is somewhat more self-reliant and strong willed (in the story, she considers disposing of the body herself and later accepts without dispute the explanation that she imagined the whole thing). The story's ending is less contrived: Ben is wearing the diamond ring on his finger, whereas in the filmed version it too conveniently falls from the envelope.

These minor changes aside, Gordon's teleplay is faithful to its source, and Herschel Daugherty's direction is expert. As in "The Purple Room," stock devices are trotted out and exploited for all their theatrical worth, and again the focus is on a single person facing the unknown (the main difference being that in "The Storm" there's no suggestion of the supernatural). Just when you begin to relax, the screws are tightened a bit more. Helping to heighten the suspense is Morton Stevens' ominous music, its shrieking violins reminiscent of Bernard Herrmann's *Psycho* score.

The acting is a major asset. Nancy Kelly registers every fearful reaction from a shudder to a scream, and remains believable throughout. The sister of actor Jack Kelly, Nancy appeared in *Tailspin* (1938), *Stanley and Livingstone* (1939) and other films, and was nominated for an Oscar for *The Bad Seed* (1956). She died in 1995.

David McLean's part is much smaller, but he's effective as Ben. McLean was the star of a short-lived TV western, *Tate*, and the lead in the film *X-15*, co-starring Mary Tyler Moore. He also played the detective in *The Strangler* (1964).

James Griffith as Ed Brandies (a character not described in the original story) is an odd character, speaking in quotations and eager to take advantage of Janet Willsom (she describes him as "that weird taxi driver" later on). He's

clearly a red herring, but both the actor and the character are distinctive, quirky presences. Griffith was similarly distinctive in a small part in *The Vampire* (1957). He had a larger role in the *Thriller* episode "Parasite Mansion."

Some sources list David Janssen as being in "The Storm," but he's not in evidence.

Though there's nary a trace of the supernatural, "The Storm" nonetheless delivers its full measure of suspense. It's a gripping and undeniably powerful episode whose influence would be felt three years later in "An Unlocked Window," a similarly compelling episode of *The Alfred Hitchcock Hour*. "The Storm" was more or less remade in 1972 as a TV-movie called *The Victim*, again directed by Herschel Daugherty, and starring *Thriller* alumni Elizabeth Montgomery, Sue Anne Langdon and Ross Elliott. An average suspense film, it had precious little of the impact of *Thriller*'s version.

"A Wig for Miss Devore"

(airdate: January 29, 1962). Produced by William Frye. Directed by John Brahm. Television story and teleplay by Donald S. Sanford, based on the short story by August Derleth. Music: Morton Stevens. Director of Photography: Benjamin H. Kline, A.S.C. Art Director: John Meehan. Editorial Department Head: David J. O'Connell. Film Editor: Danford B. Greene. Musical Supervision: Stanley Wilson. Set Decorators: John McCarthy and Julia Heron. Associate Producer: Douglas Benton. Assistant Director: Les Berke. Sound: Earl Crain, Jr.

Cast: Patricia Barry (Sheila Devore), John Fiedler (Herbert Bleake), John Baragrey (George Machik), Herbert Rudley (Max Quinke), Linda Watkins (Arabella Foote), Ina Victor (Betty), Bernard Fein (Lester Clyne),

William O'Connell (Chester #2), Pamela Searle (Meg Peyton), Maurice Dallimore (Boker #1), Barry Bernard (Chester #1), Kendrick Huxham (Bishop), Jonathan Morris (Boker #2).

One of the most chilling *Thrillers* in the program's two-year run, "A Wig for Miss Devore" is a satisfying mix of witchcraft lore and Hollywood exposé, even if the latter is a bit heavy-handed.

In the 18th century, a beautiful young woman named Meg Peyton (Pamela Searle) is to be hanged for witchcraft and the murder of six men. But when her executioners prepare to remove her wig she reacts in terror. The trap is sprung and her wig falls off, but when the executioners look they see the withered arms of an old woman clutching the wig.

In Hollywood 200 years later Sheila Devore (Patricia Barry), a once popular actress, is intrigued by a script based on Meg Peyton's life and death. She tells her agent, Herbert Bleake (John Fiedler), that the script will make a suitable comeback vehicle, and that she will wear Meg Peyton's own wig for the role; she tells Bleake there was a rumor that she made the wig out of her victims' hair and put a spell on it.

Bleake goes to see Max Quinke (Herbert Rudley), head of the studio. He tells Bleake that Sheila Devore is a has-been, too old for the part. Bleake threatens legal action, since Quinke and others received illegal profits from her films. Quinke reluctantly agrees to Bleake's blackmail terms.

As *The Legend of Meg Peyton* is being readied for production, the wig arrives, sent by a museum in London. When Sheila comes in wearing it, she looks as beautiful as she once did. Later, suspicious gossip columnist Arabella Foote (Linda Watkins) tells Sheila that people are beginning to wonder why she

is never seen without it. Sheila's old director, George Machik (John Baragrey), is directing the film; during a quiet moment off the set, he reveals to her that Max Quinke stole from her. "You're not going to the police?" Machik says. "No, Georgie," Sheila says, "I have a much better idea."

That night she is alone with Quinke. He asks her to take off her wig. Sheila obliges; Quinke reacts in terror as two withered hands reach for him, then drown him in his own pool. Machik arrives and proposes marriage to Sheila; she agrees. A husband, after all, can't testify against his wife.

Bleake tells Sheila he has a letter from the museum in London, but Sheila refuses to listen to him. Arabella Foote goes to see Bleake and steals the letter. Meanwhile, Sheila and Machik are alone together in Machik's apartment. Sheila knows that Machik inherited money from his partnership with Quinke, and reminds him of it. But while they are embracing Sheila removes her wig. Machik reacts in terror and, backing away, falls from the terrace to his death.

The Legend of Meg Peyton is released and scores a great success. When Bleake finally gets in to see Sheila, he tells her that the wig carries a curse; what's more, wearing it has changed Sheila's personality. He knows she has murdered two men, but Sheila seems unconcerned. "You know something, Herbert — after a while, this wig grows on a person," she says. "Just imagine — being able to go on and on and on, always looking beautiful, never growing old."

At a party Arabella Foote waits for Sheila in her dressing room. When she appears Arabella tells her she knows of the wig's demonic powers. "Take off the wig, Sheila," she commands. Sheila refuses, but Arabella rips it off. The withered hands claw at Arabella's face, and a hooded figure runs from the room. Bleake goes after her. The figure runs out of the studio, but is struck by a falling pillar. Her features are illuminated by a truck's lights: Bleake gasps in terror at the hideous creature lying at his feet.

Bleake rushes back to Sheila's dressing room for the wig. A rather plain-looking maid who has been trying it on emerges, transformed into a stunning beauty.

August Derleth's short story "A Wig for Miss Devore" originally appeared in the May 1943 issue of *Weird Tales*. It's a serviceable horror tale, but not much more. Donald S. Sanford's adaptation is an engrossing tale of witchcraft and the quest for eternal youth, and it's easily one of the best episodes of *Thriller's* second season. John Brahm directs with his customary gift for atmosphere and horrific detail: Sheila Devore's withered hands clawing at the camera is a memorable effect, and the final revelation of Sheila's grotesque features is a notably macabre image; Jack Barron's ghastly makeup recalls Dick Smith's superbly putrescent Dorian Gray design.

It's unfortunate that the Hollywood milieu depicted in "A Wig for Miss Devore" is so transparent a caricature: it's the same unreasonable facsimile of Tinsel Town seen in numerous potboilers, and just about as convincing. It's ironic that, of all milieus, Hollywood should be so inept at depicting itself. (As Bill Warren notes: "The real Hollywood just isn't shown in movies.") Sheila Devore's comeback in the unlikeliest of star vehicles is likewise hard to swallow, and the sudden popularity of *The Legend of Meg Peyton* (seen through a montage of theater marquees and headlines in *Variety*) is even more unbelievable. But perhaps it's inevitable;

something about Hollywood seems to evoke this kind of overblown depiction.

The acting is average. Patricia Barry, a stunningly attractive actress previously seen in "The Purple Room" and "A Good Imagination," makes a suitable Sheila Devore. Although at first she seems the stereotypical scatterbrained film star beloved of TV melodramas, she soon becomes a revenge seeking temptress under the influence of the wig. Barry's film career was spotty; she appeared in *Kitten with a Whip* and *Send Me No Flowers* (both 1964), among other films, and was a regular on a short-lived TV sitcom, *Harris Against the World*. More recently, she's been a regular on the soap opera *The Guiding Light*. And, yes, that *is* Barry under the makeup in the chilling denouement.

John Fiedler, invariably cast as a milquetoast, has one of his best roles as Herbert Bleake. Fiedler's most notable film role was as one of the *Twelve Angry Men* (1957). His other films include *The World of Henry Orient* (1964) and *The Odd Couple* (1968). He was a regular on such TV series as *Kolchak: The Night Stalker* and *The Bob Newhart Show*, and a frequent guest star on sixties anthology series. (He was particularly memorable in an episode of *Alfred Hitchcock Presents* called "Incident in a Small Jail," in which his mild-mannered persona was used for sinister effect, and in an episode of *Star Trek* titled "Wolf in the Fold," he was cast very much against type as Jack the Ripper.)

John Baragrey, previously seen in "Worse Than Murder," is suitably suave as George Machik. He was a fairly standard leading man type, and worked frequently on television in the fifties and sixties.

Herbert Rudley is seen briefly as studio head Max Quinke. Rudley, a little-noticed actor, had roles in *Casbah*

(1948) and *Raw Edge* (1956), and played the hero in the execrable *The Black Sheep* (1956). He was a regular on several television series, including *The Californians* and *The Mothers-In-Law.*

Linda Watkins, previously seen as the gossip columnist in "The Terror in Teakwood," has a very similar role here as Arabella Foote, a composite of Hedda Hopper and Louella Parsons (right down to the outlandish hats). Watkins is also seen in "The Cheaters."

"A Wig for Miss Devore" is an effective tale of witchcraft and revenge; if it weren't for its hackneyed depiction of Hollywood, it might well rank among the finest of all *Thrillers*. Even with this handicap, it's an above average episode with some memorably macabre highlights.

"The Hollow Watcher" (airdate: February 12, 1962). Produced by William Frye. Directed by William F. Claxton. Written by Jay Simms. Director of Photography: Benjamin H. Kline, A.S.C. Musical score by Sidney Fine and William Lava. Art Director: Howard E. Johnson. Editorial Department Head: David J. O'Connell. Musical Supervision: Stanley Wilson. Edited by Danny Landres. Associate Producer: Doug Benton. Assistant Director: Chuck Colean. Set Decorators: John McCarthy and Julia Heron.

Cast: Audrey Dalton (Meg O'Danagh Wheeler), Sean McClory (Sean O'Danagh), Warren Oates (Hugo Wheeler), Denver Pyle (Ortho Wheeler), Sandy Kenyon (Mason), Walter Burke (Croxton), Norman Leavitt (Hendricks), Lane Bradford (Boles), Eve McVeagh (Mrs. Curtis), Mary Grace Canfield (Ally Rose).

One of the most bizarre of the second season *Thrillers*, "The Hollow Watcher" has some eerie moments, but suffers from obvious padding and indifferent handling.

In the tiny North Carolina hamlet of Black Hollow, Ortho Wheeler (Denver Pyle), owner of the general store, is irate because his son, Hugo (Warren Oates), has taken a mail-order bride, an Irish woman named Meg (Audrey Dalton). Ortho is beating his son senseless when Meg hits him over the head, killing him, and places his body inside a scarecrow that stands on the property. When Hugo awakens she tells him his father ran off.

A month passes. Townspeople suspect Hugo and his wife did Ortho in. Someone suggests that the hollow watcher — a local demon — might have been responsible. "No, hollow watcher always leaves a corpse — or part of it, as a warnin'," Croxton (Walter Burke) says. Meg's brother, Sean (Sean McClory), arrives in Black Hollow, and promptly gets into a fight with one of the locals. Mason, the storekeeper (Sandy Kenyon), tells Sean of the hollow watcher: "It's a thing that sneaks around in the shadows ... stares at the guilty till their grit gives way ... does 'em in." He tells Sean the hollow watcher may be a bear or mountain lion, or even a man.

Sean and Meg are lovers rather than siblings; Sean has murdered his wife, and asks Meg why she has allowed Hugo to live. She tells him she doesn't know where Ortho's money is. She also explains that Ortho's body is in the scarecrow, but for some reason the carrion birds ignore it, and that the scarecrow keeps getting closer and closer to the house. Sean goes out with a shotgun. The scarecrow approaches him; he fires at it, severing an arm. Protruding from it is a piece of bone. Sean tells Meg that it was Hugo dressed as a scarecrow, perhaps to avenge his father.

Sean searches for the hidden

money. Hugo returns home unexpectedly, his arm intact. Sean tells Meg the hollow watcher will appear that night. Later he encounters Hugo, wielding a shotgun; he says he heard a sound out by the barn, and goes off to investigate. Sean goes out after him, armed with a knife, only to find Hugo's body — and the scarecrow. He sticks his knife in it, but the figure strikes him across the face, then kills him.

Meg remains inside the house, waiting. Hearing footsteps, she looks up, only to see the scarecrow staring in at her. It smashes through the window. She runs upstairs, but the scarecrow follows. Trapped, she thrusts a torch at the figure, setting it afire. The head burns away, revealing the skull of Ortho Wheeler, while Meg collapses in tears, her sanity presumably gone.

"The Hollow Watcher" has a different look and feel than most of *Thriller's* horror episodes, probably because of its director, writer and composer were all new to the series. William F. Claxton's direction is unremarkable. It frequently bogs down: Sean's fight with one of the locals, for example, is merely padding, and resembles a scene from any standard western of that era, replete with stock music. This is surprising, considering that Claxton directed "The Jungle," one of the moodiest, most atmospheric *Twilight Zones* ever (though his film credits are mostly B westerns). It's to Claxton's credit that the pace picks up toward the end: the scene in which the scarecrow takes a vicious swipe at Sean's face is surprisingly bloody, and his final assault on the house is both eerie and suspenseful.

The script, too, has a number of loose ends. Much is made of Meg's propensity for fondling a rag doll, with the implication that Ortho's money is inside, yet surprisingly this isn't the case.

Additionally, how did Meg manage to hoist Ortho's body up onto a ten foot pole by herself? The episode has a desultory, unfinished feel. The author, Jay Simms, is best known to horror aficionados for his screenplays for *The Giant Gila Monster*, *The Killer Shrews* (both 1959), *Panic in Year Zero!* and *Creation of the Humanoids* (both 1962). "None of his films amounted to much," Bill Warren notes, "but all were especially dismal regarding dialogue." Surprisingly, most of the dialogue in "The Hollow Watcher" is quite acceptable, with some of the flavor of the backwoods (though verisimilitude is rudely shattered whenever Audrey Dalton, not the most convincing of actresses, attempts an Irish brogue). There's too much padding in the beginning, but after the scarecrow's initial attack, Simms creates a certain amount of ambiguity as to whether the scarecrow is real or merely a disguise for Hugo. Once again, a rational explanation is offered, only to be undercut by a purely supernatural denouement, after all.

Audrey Dalton, as expected, is not very convincing as Meg. Sadly, an Irish accent is beyond her capabilities, and she gives her usual inadequate performance. She didn't have much of a career in films, appearing in *Titanic* (1953), *Casanova's Big Night* (1954), *Separate Tables* (1958), and a few others. Genre fans may recall her in William Castle's *Mr. Sardonicus* (1961). She was inadequate in that as well.

Sean McClory is a little better as Sean, even though his part amounts to little more than a stock Irishman, glib with his tongue and fast with his fists. At least his brogue is real. McClory had some experience with the Abbey Theater, then went to Hollywood. His films include *The Desert Fox* (1951), *Ring of Fear* (1954), *Moonfleet* (1955) and *Valley of the Dragons* (1961). He was a regular on the TV series *The Californians*, and also appears in the very last *Thriller*, "The Specialists."

Warren Oates is fine, as usual, in the cryptic role of Hugo Wheeler. (For more on Oates, see the entry on "Knock Three-One-Two.")

Denver Pyle is his usual ornery self in his cameo role as Ortho Wheeler, and Walter Burke makes an amusing appearance as one of the locals.

Walking scarecrows do not number among the screen's most popular menaces. The idea for "The Hollow Watcher" may have been suggested by John Metcalfe's creepy novelette *The Feasting Dead*, with its ambiguous presentation of an ambulatory scarecrow. In *Puritan Passions* (1923) a scarecrow is brought to life, and of course there's *The Wizard of Oz*. The closest cousin to "The Hollow Watcher" is probably a dismal 1981 TV movie with a similar plot, *The Dark Night of the Scarecrow*, which went over much of the same ground with little or none of its effectiveness. "The Hollow Watcher" never looked so good.

"Cousin Tundifer" (airdate:
February 19, 1962). Produced by William Frye. Directed by John Brahm. Written by Boris Sobelman. Director of Photography: Bud Thackery, A.S.C. Music: Morton Stevens. Edited by Danford B. Greene. Musical Supervision: Stanley Wilson. Art Director: Howard E. Johnson. Editorial Department Head: David J. O'Donnell. Assistant Director: John Clark Bowman. Set Decorators: John McCarthy and Julia Heron. Associate Producer: Doug Benton.

Cast: Edward Andrews (Miles Tundifer), Sue Ann Langdon (Queenie De Lyte), Vaughn Taylor (Pontifex Tundifer), Howard McNear (Jack Passas-

stroy), Dayton Lummis (Millard Braystone), Chet Stratton (Alfred Marvin), Hallene Hill (Old Woman), Cyril Delevanti (Old Man), Bart Patton (Young Workman), Jim Bannon (Police Lieutenant), Clem Bevans (Old Gaffer), Edgar Dearing (Police Sergeant).

The final episode of the three humorous entries featuring Edward Andrews, "Uncle Tundifer" is arguably the best of the three, a generally amusing mix of murder and time travel.

Miles Tundifer (Edward Andrews) stands outside a burlesque show advertising the performance of Miss Queenie De Lyte (Sue Ann Langdon), then browses at the newsstand, paying particular attention to a book titled *Thirty-three Ways to Get Away with Murder*. He goes to see his attorney, Millard Braystone (Dayton Lummis), who tells him he cannot have his wealthy uncle institutionalized merely because of his penchant for restoring old houses; but Miles is worried because the old man's $1 million has gone down to $400,000. "There are two things to do to your uncle — either kill him or cure him," Braystone tells Miles.

Miles drives over to one of his uncle's houses, complaining about the cost of the reconstruction. "What are the nails made of—platinum?" he asks the workman, Mr. Passasstroy (Howard McNear), who has painstakingly restored the house to what it was 100 years ago. "What's a hundred thousand dollars, Mr. Tundifer, when your heel grinds and pounds on a floor that belongs to another age?" Passasstroy asks. Miles tells him his uncle will rebuild no more houses, on the advice of his psychologist.

Alone in the house, Miles walks across the parlor. The carpet mysteriously rolls up, furniture appears, the fire lights — and Miles is suddenly back in

1890. He looks out the back door and sees a street from that period. But when he rushes to the front door, it is 1962 again. He repairs to a bar, where the bartender tells him it is a clear case of teleportation. Miles goes back to take another look. Sure enough, the second he steps into the parlor the same changes occur — the fire lights and furniture appears. But outside it is still 1962.

Pontifex Tundifer (Vaughn Taylor) tells his nephew that his psychologist has told him to give up on houses and find a young woman instead. One arrives: it is Queenie De Lyte. Pontifex invites her to dinner, and Miles sees his fortune flying away.

Miles returns to the house with Mr. Passasstroy, but when they step into the parlor, nothing happens. He also discovers that if he leaves an object inside the parlor no one from 1962 can see it. But, unbeknownst to Miles, he is being observed by two older people (Cyril Delevanti and Hallene Hill).

Miles and Pontifex drive over to the old house. Once inside, Miles hits him over the head and drags his body into the parlor, depositing it in the window seat. Miles then departs, having left $50,000 with the body.

Pontifex is reported missing. The police search the house and grounds, to no avail. Meanwhile, Miles is romancing Queenie, even though she prefers older men — preferably millionaires with one foot in the grave, like Pontifex. When Miles runs short of cash, he returns to get the money from his uncle's body. But when he steps back into 1890 he finds the window seat empty. The two oldsters emerge with Pontifex in tow, his head bandaged, and two constables, who arrest Miles. Pontifex sees Queenie outside and strolls out to join her while Miles is taken off to an 1890 prison inside a paddy wagon. "Where's Miles?"

Queenie asks. "Oh, they're arresting him for something in there," Pontifex says. "There's something crazy going on. It's a crazy house. I'll have them start tearing it down tomorrow."

Conceivably the best of Edward Andrews' three starring vehicles (none of which is that good), "Cousin Tundifer" benefits from its time travel plot, which adds a touch of novelty (even if it seems like an episode of *The Twilight Zone*). It's the only *Thriller* to deal with time travel, and affords Andrews a unique way of getting away with murder.

There are some good jokes, mostly verbal, but director John Brahm manages a few visual touches: after Andrews solemnly declares, "I never had any intention of murdering my uncle," the scene dissolves to a table full of knives, brass knuckles, blunt instruments, nooses, poisons and guns. Likewise, the scenes of the two old people peering from the shadows in the old house are nicely atmospheric, and the time traveling house itself, with its reappearing furniture and player piano (endlessly repeating "Narcissus," a popular tune from the period) is a nice visual touch.

Edward Andrews, as always, makes the most of his dialogue, alternating between innuendo and pompous conceit. It's a shame that none of his *Thriller*s allowed him to be truly sinister — here, as usual, he's amusing even when preparing to murder his uncle — for, in movies like *The Unguarded Moment*, he could project a very distinctive and persuasive aura of villainy.

The other actors are adequate in lightweight parts. Sue Ann Langdon does her patented dumb blonde bit, and Vaughn Taylor is amusing as Uncle Pontifex, acting more cantankerous than usual. (Taylor can also be seen in an earlier episode, "Choose a Victim.") Howard McNear (familiar to TV viewers as the barber Floyd Lawson on *The Andy Griffith Show*) has some funny lines as the workman.

In all, "Cousin Tundifer" is an adequate if unexceptional entry. Its combination of murder and time travel, while unique, seems unsuited to *Thriller*, and its light tone makes it difficult to take seriously. As an episode of *Twilight Zone*, it might have made an entertaining half hour; here, it seems padded and unnecessarily prolonged. It is certainly watchable, even if it's a lesser *Thriller*; certainly, far worse episodes were to come.

"The Incredible Doktor Markesan" (airdate: February 26, 1962). Produced by William Frye. Directed by Robert Florey. Teleplay by Donald S. Sanford, based on the short story by August Derleth and Mark Schorer. Music: Morton Stevens. Director of Photography: Benjamin H. Kline, A.S.C. Art Director: Howard E. Johnson. Editorial Department Head: David J. O'Connell. Edited by Danford B. Greene. Musical Supervision: Stanley Wilson. Set Decorators: John McCarthy and Julia Heron. Associate Producer: Doug Benton. Assistant Director: John Clarke Bowman. Sound: Corson Jowett.

Cast: Boris Karloff (Doktor Konrad Markesan), Dick York (Fred Bancroft), Carolyn Kearney (Molly Bancroft), Henry Hunter (Professor Angus Holden), Richard Hale (Professor Latimore), Basil Howes (Professor Charing), Billy Beck (Professor Grant).

The last classic *Thriller*, "The Incredible Doktor Markesan" is the frightening story of a man who has found a way of reviving the dead.

In the deep South, Fred Bancroft (Dick York) and his wife, Molly (Carolyn Kearney), are looking for Fred's uncle, Konrad Markesan. They drive up to Oakmoor, an apparently deserted

estate. Entering the house despite a sign warning that trespassers will be shot on sight, they find the place in an incredible state of decay. Apparently no one has lived there for years. Suddenly a figure appears: it is Dr. Markesan (Boris Karloff), looking more dead than alive. Fred and Molly explain that they are flat broke and need a place to stay until they can find jobs. Fred suggests that Dr. Markesan could use his influence to get them jobs at Penrose University. "I severed my connection with the university — years ago," the old man remarks cryptically. He agrees to let them stay in the house, but warns them not to disturb him for any reason. He tells them they must stay in their room from dusk to dawn.

Molly, looking for food, finds some so old that it crumbles in her hands. "How does he exist?" she asks Fred. "What does he eat?" When they retire upstairs, Dr. Markesan locks the door. In the morning the door is unlocked. "What is he hiding? What doesn't he want us to see?" Molly asks.

That night they find their door locked again. Fred hears weird moaning sounds coming from below. Using a wire, he slips the bolt on the door and ventures downstairs. He sees three netherworld creatures seated around a table in the library, with Markesan presiding over some kind of weird ritual. Fred goes back upstairs; looking for old newspapers to throw into the fire, he sees an obituary for one of the men he saw downstairs — but the paper is 11 years old.

The following night he hears the strange sounds again. He goes downstairs and finds Markesan attending the three figures, lying in coffins. He hears their names: Latimer, Charing and Grant, and the name of Professor Angus Holden. He decides to seek out Professor

Holden, who teaches at the university. He tells Molly to stay in the room.

Going to see Holden (Henry Hunter), he blurts out his story. Holden tells him there was an informal trial, with Latimer, Charing and Grant testifying against Markesan. It was decided that Markesan would resign, ostensibly for reasons of health. Fred insists on knowing the reasons for Markesan's forced dismissal; Holden tells him he had claimed to have devised certain chemical techniques with which he could raise the dead. Now Latimer, Charing and Grant, along with Markesan, are all dead.

Molly, meanwhile, using the wire to open the door, goes downstairs to the library. The three dead men, along with Markesan, approach her. She faints. Fred, in the meantime, has been to the crypt and seen Markesan's date of death — 1954, eight years in the past. Going back to the house, he finds Markesan in his laboratory, along with the three dead men. "Where's Molly?" Fred demands. "You will soon be together," Markesan says. One of the dead men upsets a light fixture and it crashes down on Markesan, killing him. Fred searches for Molly and finds her — a living-dead creature like the others, closing her coffin.

"Colonel Markesan" was one of the stories (along with "The Return of Andrew Bentley") written by August Derleth and Mark Schorer during the summer of 1931 and first published in *Weird Tales* in June 1934. In the story, which is set in Massachusetts, Fred Bancroft is hired by Colonel Markesan (no relation) to keep his estate in shape, and Markesan raises the dead not through science but apparently by some weird form of hypnosis. Professor Holden (called Hohlden) plays a more active role, and decapitates Markesan at the

climax, only to be bitten by the head, after which he dies from the virulent poison that gave Markesan his unholy life! It's one of Derleth and Schorer's wilder collaborations, almost uninhibited to the point of parody.

Donald S. Sanford's adaptation is more conventional, but no less satisfying. It's well thought out, and plays fair in most respects, though it begs one major question: even if one accepts that Markesan was able to bring back the three dead professors by himself, who brought back Markesan?

"The Incredible Doktor Markesan" (the title retains the German spelling) is the only *Thriller* directed by Robert Florey. The French-born director's screen credits include *The Cocoanuts* (1929), *The Face Behind the Mask* (1941) and *The Beast with Five Fingers* (1946), but he's perhaps best known for a film he *didn't* direct, the 1931 classic, *Frankenstein*. After collaborating on the script, he was replaced by James Whale and handed the consolation prize of directing *Murders in the Rue Morgue* (1932). To this day, bitter resentments linger over whether Florey's *Frankenstein* would have been an improvement over Whale's. Brian Taves, author of *Robert Florey, The French Impressionist*, argues that it would have, but the authors of *Universal Horrors* (as well as others) take a different view: "Whale lagged behind Florey visually, but was far more at ease with the language, possessed a far sharper wit, and was a far more discriminating judge of actors ... Had [Florey] directed *Frankenstein*, there might not have been a series at all."

Florey's renowned visual sense is present in every shot of "The Incredible Doktor Markesan": slightly tilted camera angles create a vague sense of unease; a hand-held camera records Fred and Molly's ascent of the stairs. Brian Taves, in his study of Florey's films and television work, notes that "Another favorite [composition] was a view of a character through foreground objects that indicate his or her mental condition." Markesan has a number of shots of this kind, mainly those depicting the dead doctor himself.

Florey may have taken a more than casual interest in the story, because, according to Taves, of the attraction of the *outré* story line:

> Probably the most bizarre motif to appear in Florey's films and television shows was that of bringing the apparently dead back to the realm of the living.... It can be found right through to the end of Florey's career, in television films such as *Alfred Hitchcock Presents:* "The Changing Heart" and *Thriller:* "The Incredible Doktor Markesan."

The actors are all fine. Karloff, in the last of his *Thriller* appearances, has perhaps his best television part ever as the incredible Konrad Markesan. He looks ghostly at the very beginning, and the weird makeup suits his sense of the dramatic. "I can tell you how they got Karloff's face to deteriorate," Dick York told interviewer John Douglas in *Filmfax.* "The makeup man [Jack Barron] took Bromo-Seltzer, ground it up real fine and put it on his face with the facial makeup. Then they sprayed him with water and it went pop, pop, pop, and his face just kind of deteriorated. It was a great idea."

Dick York is fine as Fred Bancroft. York, a likeable actor with a flair for light comedy, appeared on television in such series as *Alfred Hitchcock Presents, Twilight Zone,* and *The Untouchables,* and in such movies as *Operation Mad Ball* (1957), *Cowboy* (1958) and *They Came to Cordura* (1959). It was while making *Cordura* that York injured his back, an ailment that would plague him for the rest of his life. "My spine healed incorrectly," he said. "There were long periods when I'd be perfectly all right, and then there were many other times when I wasn't, when my back would give out and throw me down to the floor amid waves of nauseating pain."

He was in great pain during the making of *Inherit the Wind* (1960), his last feature film. He appeared on a short-lived TV series, *Going My Way* in 1962; two years later he became familiar to millions as Darren Stevens on *Bewitched,* co-starring Elizabeth Montgomery. He stayed with the series until 1969, when his continuing health problems forced him to resign.

His last years were desperate ones: hooked up to an oxygen tank, suffering from emphysema, he raised money by phone for the homeless. Apparently York never succumbed to bitterness. He said: "I've been blessed. I have no complaints. I've been surrounded by people in radio, on stage and in motion pictures and television who love me. The things that have gone wrong have been simply physical things." He died in 1992, aged 63.

Carolyn Kearney is acceptable as Molly Bancroft, a character not in the original story. She appeared in the appalling *Thing that Couldn't Die* (1958).

"The Incredible Doktor Markesan" is one of *Thriller's* darkest episodes: it begins and ends on a note of gloom, with little to lighten the mood. It's a favorite of *Thriller* fans, who see it (rightly) as a showcase for Karloff's performance and Robert Florey's directorial style.

"Flowers of Evil" (airdate: March 5, 1962). Produced by William Frye. Directed by John Brahm. Teleplay by Barre Lyndon, based on a short story by Hugh Walpole. Director of Photog-

raphy: Benjamin H. Kline, A.S.C. Music: Morton Stevens. Musical Supervision: Stanley Wilson. Art Director: Howard E. Johnson. Edited by Danny Landres. Editorial Department Head: David J. O'Connell. Associate Producer: Doug Benton. Assistant Director: Carter De Haven, III. Sound: Frank H. Wilkinson. Set Decorators: John McCarthy and Julia Heron.

Cast: Luciana Paluzzi (Madalena), Kevin Hagen (Arno Lunt), Jack Weston (Maurice Reynard), Vladimir Sokoloff (The Janitor), Gregory Gay (The President), David Garcia (First Student), David Whorf (Second Student).

One of the weakest *Thrillers* ever, "Flowers of Evil" falls down in nearly every department, from an uninteresting script to totally unconvincing acting. It may well rank as the series' lowest ebb.

Working alone at the supply house that provides medical supplies for students, Madalena (Luciana Paluzzi) imagines that the skeleton of her late husband is laughing at her. She knocks the skeleton apart.

"Why did you do it?" her lover, Arno Lunt (Kevin Hagen), demands. "Are they or are they not my husband's bones?" Madalena asks. "Did we or did we not get rid of them?" The skeleton has been sold twice, and returned twice. It seems to have a macabre effect on the students: they suffer from broken bones and illnesses, and complain that it screams.

Maurice Reynard (Jack Weston), the President of the Academy, comes calling. He is in love with Madalena. When he asks about her husband, she tells him he has left her for another woman. "Funny how that skeleton keeps coming back," Reynard comments. He asks Madalena for a copy of Baudelaire's *Les Fleurs du Mal.* She says she will bring

it to him. "He knows," Madalena tells Arno as soon as Reynard has left. "That fat devil knows something!" Arno tells her there is no proof, no evidence, but she remains suspicious.

Madalena brings Reynard the book; he points out that the skeleton's arm is broken in the same place as her husband's. "Have you seen the tank, the great cistern in which we put bodies donated for anatomical studies?" he asks her. He tells her that during the past year an unauthorized cadaver was put into the tank. "Do you think it was my husband?" Madalena asks. Reynard hints that he will inform the police unless she begins seeing him.

Later, Madalena hears the skeleton screaming. She tells Arno they must kill Reynard. "Not another disappearance," Arno says. They decide to poison him and make it look like a stroke.

She goes to see Reynard and adds poison to his champagne. She tells him Arno will have two skeletons in his window — her husband's and Reynard's.

Reynard's body is found; he is presumed to have died of apoplexy. Meanwhile, Madalena, eager to be rid of Arno, sprinkles poison into his liquor. Arno is understandably shocked when some medical students bring in Reynard's skeleton, which they position side by side with that of Madalena's husband.

Arno returns to see Madalena. She is preparing to leave to be with another lover. "You are not going with him," Arno says, and strangles her. He takes her body to his supply house. Tired from his exertions, he pours himself a drink from the poisoned bottle, meanwhile carrying on a conversation with the two skeletons. He finally succumbs to the poison, describing himself as a "foolish college clerk, trying to be a man of the world."

After some of the best *Thrillers* in

the program's two-year run ("Wax-works," "A Wig for Miss Devore," "The Incredible Doktor Markesan"), the program veered sharply downhill in its final eight offerings. With but a single exception ("Man of Mystery"), these are largely mediocre efforts, as if to emphasize that life was running out of the series itself. Of the eight, "Flowers of Evil" is probably the low point.

There are so many problems with the episode, it's hard to know where to begin. There's little suspense, and the few promising ideas — such as the eerie opening in which the skeleton seems to take on flesh as it laughs at Madalena — peter out disappointingly. There's no real ambiguity as to whether the events are supernatural or not; in addition, the characters are thorough clichés, so there's little or no audience involvement in their plight. To make matters worse, the milieu of *fin de siècle* France is only intermittently evoked: the art direction and photography are persuasive, but the actors — two of whom are unmistakably American — destroy what little verisimilitude is built up.

The real culprit is the teleplay. Barre Lyndon's adaptation of Hugh Walpole's story is basically unexciting; there's some promise in the story's setting and in the premise of selling skeletons for medical use (and Madalena's fantasy of the laughing skeleton hints at her mental instability), but the promise goes unfulfilled. What we get instead are too familiar situations and characters, and by the time Arno Lunt, having drunk the poisoned liquor, delivers a dying soliloquy, the episode pretty well comes to a dead stop.

The actors are of little help. Luciana Paluzzi, a beautiful, dark-haired Italian actress, is adequate as Madalena, though she's little more than the typical scheming woman undone by her own

treachery. Paluzzi was a regular on the short-lived spy series *Five Fingers* in the fifties; since then she's appeared in numerous films: *The Venetian Affair* (1966), *The Klansman* (1974), and *The Greek Tycoon* (1978), among others. Her best-remembered role is probably the villainous Fiona Kelly in *Thunderball* (1965).

Kevin Hagen, previously seen in "The Fingers of Fear," tries hard, but his accent is noticeably American; it's difficult to imagine him as anything else.

Jack Weston is definitely out of place; few actors are more quintessentially American. Done up in a goatee and greyed hair, he's unconvincing every time he opens his mouth, and the theatricality of his makeup doesn't help matters. For more on Weston, see the entry on "The Cheaters."

Vladimir Sokoloff, as usual, lends adequate support as the janitor, and there's a brief glimpse of David Whorf (seen in better days as John Branner in "Pigeons from Hell") as a medical student.

Nothing seems to work in "Flowers of Evil." It's one of the poorest of all *Thrillers*, on a par with "The Big Blackout" or "Rose's Last Summer." Perhaps saddest of all, it marks John Brahm's last directorial stint — a sad anticlimax after such memorable episodes as "The Cheaters" and "Well of Doom."

"'Til Death Do Us Part" (airdate: March 12, 1962). Produced by William Frye. Directed by Herschel Daugherty. Teleplay by Robert Bloch, based on his short story. Director of Photography: William Margulies, A.S.C. Edited by Danny Landres. Art Director: Howard E. Johnson. Associate Producer: Doug Benton. Assistant Director: Donald Baer. Set Decorators: John McCarthy and Julia Heron.

Cast: Henry Jones (Carl Somers), Reta Shaw (Celia Hooper), Philip Ober (Elmer Hooper), Jocelyn Brando (Myrtle Hooper), Edgar Buchanan (Dr. O'Connor), Eve McVeagh (Bonnie), Jim Davis (Marshal), Frances Morris (Abbie), Walker Edmiston (Jerry), Delores Wells (Flo), Phil Arnold (Curly), Hurly Bell (Cowhand).

"'Til Death Do Us Part" is the least of Robert Bloch's 10 *Thriller* episodes. In adapting his own short story, he added characters and situations, but the result is a padded confection of little interest or appeal.

Undertaker Carl Somers (Henry Jones) is two-timing his wife. She finds out, and he strangles her and disposes of the body.

Carl moves out West to see Celia Hooper (Reta Shaw), the object of a long-range correspondence, only to find that she weighs 200 pounds. He presents her with forget-me-nots, telling her "there are more where those came from." He also meets her brother, Elmer (Philip Ober), and his wife, Myrtle (Jocelyn Brando). Elmer disapproves of Carl.

Celia and Carl are engaged. "All my life I knew my prince would come along. You've no idea how long I've waited," Celia says. Eyeing her ample girth, Carl says, "Well, I can imagine." Celia explains that her strait-laced brother never approved of Celia's other suitors, who were interested only in her money. When Carl learns this, he shows a renewed interest in Celia. When they are getting better acquainted, Elmer says, "I understand you're a Southern planter." "Well, in a manner of speaking, I am," Carl replies. "I'm an undertaker from St. Louis."

Carl and Celia elope in Carl's hearse. But he soon learns that everything — house, stocks, and money — are in Elmer's name, and he said he would disown Celia if she married without his permission.

Celia soon turns into a shrew. Carl begins carrying on with Bonnie (Eve McVeagh), a dance hall performer, but she fears he will never leave his wife. But fortune smiles upon Carl: he recognizes Dr. O'Connor (Edgar Buchanan) as the missing medico sought in a poisoning case. Carl blackmails him; he needs the money because his undertaking business is in a slump. Elmer, however, overhears Carl carrying on with Bonnie, and tells Celia. Finding the situation unbearable, Carl decides to get rid of his wife. He obtains poison from Dr. O'Connor, telling him, "There's an old nag I'd like to get rid of," and puts it in Celia's coffee. But she is still around the next morning. Understandably irate, Carl goes to confront Dr. O'Connor, but finds he has left town.

When Myrtle unexpectedly dies of a heart attack, Carl gets the job of burying her. Celia notes that the coffin is very deep: "Why, it's big enough for two," she says. Carl strangles her, then dumps the body in the casket, underneath a false bottom.

After the funeral, the marshal (Jim Davis) stops by Carl's undertaking parlor. He tells Carl they suspect Elmer poisoned Myrtle because she discovered he was carrying on with a girl from the saloon. To confirm their suspicions they will have to dig up the grave, "and take another good look at what's inside that coffin."

Robert Bloch's "'Til Death Do Us Part" began life as an amusing three-page trifle published in the January 1960 issue of *Bestseller Mystery*. A straight murder yarn with a twist ending, it seems an odd choice for a *Thriller*. In expanding it Bloch added a few twists and set it in the Old West; it's *Thriller*'s only Western episode (unless one counts

"The Hollow Watcher"). It starts out promisingly, and might have made a moderately entertaining segment of a two-parter, but at a full hour it soon wears out its welcome. As usual with Bloch, there's some amusing wordplay, and Henry Jones is wryly amusing as the undertaker, but the padding is noticeable: the scheming doctor played by Edgar Buchanan serves no purpose, and the episode as a whole has a desultory, hangdog quality. Sadly, it demonstrates once again that *Thriller* was running down.

"The Bride Who Died Twice" (airdate: March 19, 1962). Produced by William Frye. Directed by Ida Lupino. Written by Robert Hardy Andrews. Director of Photography: Benjamin Kline. Music: Jerry Goldsmith. Art Director: Howard E. Johnson. Editor: Danny Landres. Set Decorators: John McCarthy and Julia Heron. Associate Producer: Doug Benton. Assistant Director: Donald Baer.

Cast: Mala Powers (Consuelo De La Verra), Eduardo Cianelli (General De La Verra), Joe de Santis (Colonel Sangriento), Robert Colbert (Captain Antonio Fernandez), Carl Don (Sergeant Vibera), Peter Brocco (Pedro Herreto), Alex Montoya (Custodian of the Cemetery), Pepe Hern (Lieutenant Contreros).

One of the least of this latter round of *Thriller*s, "The Bride Who Died Twice" has little to recommend it.

An evil Mexican colonel named Sangriento — known as "The Bloody One" — gives General De La Verra (Eduardo Cianelli) an ultimatum: he can keep his position — and his life — if he will allow Colonel Sangriento (Joe de Santis) to marry his daughter. Consuelo (Mala Powers) is already betrothed to dashing Captain Antonio Fernandez (Robert Colbert). Sangriento commands

the General to send Fernandez on a mission that means almost certain death. The old man reluctantly agrees.

The general orders Fernandez to command a scout patrol in the mountains. "When you come back..." the general begins. "Don't you mean *if* I come back?" Fernandez asks. After he leaves, General De La Verra mutters "God forgive me."

Consuelo tells her father he has broken her heart. She locks herself in her room. De La Verra shows her a report stating that Fernandez was killed in an ambush. Consuelo faints. Sangriento promises De La Verra a reward after the wedding, three weeks from that day.

At the wedding reception Consuelo goes upstairs to wait for Sangriento. A figure dressed as a peasant suddenly appears, frightening her. When Sangriento goes up later, Consuelo is lying in bed. She does not move; to all appearances she is dead.

After the funeral, De La Verra tells Sangriento, "She's safe now — safe from you. You bought her, you thought you owned her. But she's not yours any longer."

"I have been cheated," Sangriento declares. "I have been robbed. I have been made a fool of. I will not forgive. I will not forget."

After the mourners leave, the figure dressed as a peasant appears. It is Fernandez. He orders the coffin opened, then kisses Consuelo on the lips.

Sometime later in the town square, peasants who have come to town to escape the rebels in the mountains pass Colonel Sangriento's car. He recognizes one of the peasants as Consuelo. He pursues her, but she is nowhere to be found. Sangriento orders the coffin opened; it is empty. Sangriento, certain now that both Consuelo and Fernandez are alive, asks De La Verra where they are; when he declines to answer Sangriento has him tortured. Meanwhile, Consuelo and Fernandez are trying to leave the town when they are spotted by Sangriento and placed under arrest. It is revealed that Fernandez gave Consuelo an Indian drug that simulated death. Fernandez explains that he was shot down by one of his own soldiers under Sangriento's orders. Obeying a similar command, Sergeant Vibera (Carl Don) kills General De La Verra, but the old man manages to take him along. Fernandez, meanwhile, is to be executed as a traitor. In prison, a soldier sympathetic to Fernandez slips him a tiny container of poison.

The next morning Fernandez is prepared for execution. Consuelo appears in a wedding dress, and Sangriento calls her "My beautiful bride," slipping on a ring. Sangriento shoots Fernandez. Consuelo runs to him; Fernandez tells her he shall awaken with the touch of her lips on his, the capsule of poison in his hand. They kiss; Fernandez dies. Consuelo returns to Sangriento, saying, "I have brought back to you everything you have ever owned," and dies in his arms, dropping the poison.

There's little to be said for "The Bride Who Died Twice." The Latin setting gives it a touch of novelty, and Ida Lupino's direction makes it seem better than it is. But the script is talky and the story far too straightforward. A little ambiguity would have helped; some uncertainty as to whether the lovers were alive or ghosts or merely figments of Sangriento's imagination might have lent a certain macabre atmosphere, which the episode sorely lacks. The story line bears a resemblance to *Romeo and Juliet*, but little is made of this.

The acting is variable. Mala Powers, a former child actress, is adequate as Consuelo; genre fans may recall her from *The Unknown Terror* (1957) and *Colos-*

sus of New York (1958). Joe de Santis, who bears a striking resemblance to Omar Sharif, is suitably villainous as Sangriento. On the other hand, Robert Colbert (who played Tony on *The Time Tunnel*) is thoroughly Anglo-Saxon, hence hardly believable as Fernandez (perhaps Alejandro Rey was unavailable).

The strongest performance is Eduardo Cianelli's as General De La Verra. A solid character actor who made an impression as the gangster Trock Estrella in Maxwell Anderson's *Winterset* (1936), Cianelli was also seen in *Gunga Din* (1939), *The Mummy's Hand* (1940), *The Mask of Dimitrios* (1944), and many other films (he also appeared in the *Thriller* episode "Man in the Cage"). As Leslie Halliwell wrote: "His finely etched features and incisive speech were usually employed in villainous roles, but he could also strike sympathetic chords." He does so here, making General De La Verra an anguished, believable, and finally tragic figure. It's too bad the story line does not provide a more worthy vehicle for his performance.

"Kill My Love" (airdate: March 26, 1962). Produced by William Frye. Directed by Herschel Daugherty. Teleplay by Donald S. Sanford, from the novel by Kyle Hunt. Director of Photography: Benjamin Kline. Music: Morton Stevens. Art Director: Howard E. Johnson. Editor: Danny Landres. Set Decorators: John McCarthy and Julia Heron. Assistant Director: Ben Bishop. Associate Producer: Doug Benton.

Cast: Richard Carlson (Guy Guthrie), K. T. Stevens (Olive Guthrie), David Kent (Julian Guthrie), Patricia Breslin (Dinah Duffay), Kasey Rogers (Anthea Jason), Raymond Greenleaf (Harold Carson), Amy Douglass (Mrs.

Carson), Larry Blake (Alex, the bartender).

"I'm a very peculiar fellow," Guy Guthrie (Richard Carlson) comments to a friend. "I'm full of surprises." This can hardly be denied: he's a multiple murderer, yet he cannot abide deceit. Likewise, he's devoted to his son, despite the fact that he blew his mother to smithereens.

Guy, a traveling salesman, is first seen having troubles with his mistress, Anthea Jason (Kasey Rogers): she wants him to leave his wife. Guy protests that the separation would be traumatic for his son, Julian. Anthea accuses him of making a "positive fetish" of his son, saying it is unnatural. She threatens to inform Guy's wife of their affair, so Guy strangles her with a pair of stockings while she is bathing.

Afterward, Guy goes to see attractive Dinah Duffay (Patricia Breslin) at a bar, then returns home to his wife, Olive (K. T. Stevens), and son, Julian (David Kent). He was supposedly away on business, but his son finds a picture of him with Anthea Jason, whose death has been widely reported. Guy tries to talk his way out of it, but Julian sees the dead woman's picture in the newspaper. Meanwhile, Olive wants Guy to give up his job on the road and work in her father's bank. Guy tells her he's not cut out for that kind of work; Olive shows him Anthea's picture and tells Guy she has had him followed by a private investigator. When Guy asks what she intends doing about it she ways she won't tell the police — as long as he never gives her provocation.

Guy waits until Olive has gone out, then sneaks down to the basement and overloads the light socket there, before filling the room with gas. He heads for the bar to establish an alibi. Olive returns home, smells the gas and turns on the light, which causes an electrical arc, blowing up the gas.

After the funeral, Guy calls Dinah and arranges to meet her. He sends Julian off to stay with his grandparents, but Julian runs away. He has figured out Guy's murder plot, and confronts him with it; Guy's glib reassurances do not convince the boy. "How do you tell someone your father's a murderer?" Julian asks. Guy gives him Seconal, then carries Julian out to his car and leaves him inside with the motor running. But after drinking to ease his conscience, he has a sudden change of heart and saves Julian's life.

The final eight *Thrillers* are mostly a lackluster group. Among this group, "Kill My Love" rises slightly above the average, mostly because of Richard Carlson's performance. He works hard to make Guy Guthrie believable, and it's fun to see him stretch his acting muscles a bit by playing such a totally villainous part (he played a similar character in Bert I. Gordon's *Tormented*). Guthrie is a salesman and, appropriately, he has a glib explanation for all his actions, yet as a multiple murderer he's surprisingly slipshod (he leaves a flyer in his car linking him to the murdered girl, and both his wife and his son are onto him). He's simply too self-destructive to be believable. His final decision to kill Julian makes no sense at all ("You know, he lives for that kid," one character remarks of him early on). Given Guy's inherent self-contradictions, Carlson does a creditable job, even though he seems a little old to be such a lothario. Nevertheless, it's a genuine star turn for a generally underrated actor.

Normally cast as the hero, Carlson was a busy man during the fifties in sci-fi and horror films such as *It Came from Outer Space* (1953), *The Creature from the Black Lagoon* (1954), *The Maze*

(1953), *The Magnetic Monster* (1953), and *Riders to the Stars* (1954), which he also directed. He had started out as a more conventional leading man during the late thirties, with roles in *The Ghost Breakers* (1940), and *The Little Foxes* (1941). Leslie Halliwell wrote that he "played the diffident juvenile so long that he had nothing to give to mature roles." Whether or not this is true, he always projected intelligence and determination. On television he played Communist-hunting Herbert Philbrick on *I Led Three Lives*. Apart from John Newland, he's the only actor to appear in one episode of *Thriller* and direct another ("Choose a Victim"). He died in 1977.

K. T. Stevens is adequate as his wife. It doesn't speak well of Olive Guthrie's common sense for her to trust her murderous mate, particularly after he's cheated on her *and* killed his mistress, yet that's exactly what she does, with the expected result. Stevens, an attractive brunette, was seen as Virginia Grant in the *Thriller* episode "The Merriweather File." Her films include the execrable *Missile to the Moon* (1958).

Patricia Breslin is attractive but wasted as Dinah Duffay. We keep expecting her to play a pivotal role, but she's just another of the women Guy keeps juggling. She was a regular on the popular fifties sitcom "The People's Choice," and co-starred with William Shatner in the memorable *Twilight Zone* episode, "Nick of Time." Her film credits include two for William Castle: *Homicidal* (1961) and *I Saw What You Did!* (1965).

David Kent is quite good as Julian. It's a relief to find a young actor who isn't cloyingly cute; Julian is an intelligent young man who sees through his father's schemes and even figures out how he killed his mother with the electrical arc, making it that much more

difficult to understand why he would take the Seconal which Guy gives him.

"Kill My Love" is hardly an exceptional episode. It maintains interest throughout, and constantly gives promise of being better than it actually is, but ultimately it disappoints. If it is slightly better than the rather dispirited *Thrillers* which preceded it, that's more a comment on their lack of suspense than anything else.

"Man of Mystery" (airdate: April 2, 1962). Produced by William Frye. Directed by John Newland. Teleplay by Robert Bloch, based on his story. Director of Photography: Benjamin H. Kline, A.S.C. Music: Morton Stevens. Edited by Danny Landres. Art Director: Howard E. Johnson. Editorial Department Head: David J. O'Connell. Musical Supervision: Stanley Wilson. Sound: John W. Rixey. Associate Producer: Doug Benton. Assistant Director: George Bisk. Set Decorators: John McCarthy and Julia Heron.

Cast: Mary Tyler Moore (Sherry Smith), John Van Dreelen (Joel Stone), William Windom (Lou Waters), Walter Burke (Lucas), Mercedes Shirley (Jill Naylor), Robert Sampson (Reporter), Willis Bouchey (Lieutenant Farnham), Ralph Clanton (Dr. John Grail), William Phipps (Harry Laxer), Ken Lynch (Rudolph), Yuki Shimoda (Koto).

The best of the last batch of *Thrillers*, "Man of Mystery" is an unexpectedly strong episode that points up, once again, the perils in judging by appearances.

Harry Laxer (William Phipps), an ex-public relations man for millionaire entrepreneur Joel Stone, finishes his manuscript, *Man of Mystery*, a biography of the reclusive tycoon. "He ain't a man of mystery, when I get through with him," Laxer tells his publisher. But before he can turn in his manuscript, he is brutally murdered and his book destroyed. A mysterious figure sets fire to his body.

Joel Stone (John Van Dreelen) expresses sadness over Laxer's death. He tells a reporter that Laxer's drinking caused the fire, and that at the time of Laxer's death, he was in Paris.

Stone, along with his deaf mute companion, Lucas (Walter Burke), go to see Sherry Smith (Mary Tyler Moore), a singer at a small nightclub. Lou Waters (William Windom), a small-time comic in love with Sherry, also works at the club, but he is unable to make much headway against Stone's advances. Stone buys the club and fires Lou, meanwhile building up Sherry's career.

Lou goes to see Jill Naylor (Mercedes Shirley), an old flame of Joel Stone's. She agrees to talk, telling Lou she knows Stone's secret. But before she can say anything, she is thrown to her death from a window. The death is made to look like suicide. And once again Stone has an alibi — he spent the evening with Sherry.

Sherry is disturbed by Lucas, who is always around, but Stone tells her "I would trust him with my life." "Don't you have any other friends?" Sherry asks. "Yes, I do," Stone says. He invites her to his home to meet them. They are all dummies, seated at the dinner table. "I have no real friends," Stone tells Sherry. "A man in my position has no one."

Stone is supposed to meet Lucas at the airport. Instead, he goes off with Sherry to a hunting lodge. He has more than $1 million in bonds and negotiable securities there. He asks Sherry to marry him. He tells her there have been many women in his life before, but this time he's serious. He also tells her there's a secret she must keep. He goes upstairs to get the bonds. There is the sound of

a struggle, and Stone falls back downstairs, dead.

Lucas emerges from the shadows, unaccountably able to speak. He accuses Stone of stealing. "But those bonds belonged to him," Sherry protests. "No, not to him," Lucas says. "They belonged to Joel Stone. *I* am Joel Stone." The other man was merely an actor. Lucas tells her they were penniless together in Europe; the other man had charm, good looks — everything but a brain. So Stone hired him to be his front man while he remained in the shadows, pulling the strings, pretending to be a deaf-mute. He killed the other women. "I hated them," he says. "I hated them all." But he felt that Sherry could see beyond the shadow. He wants to fly away with her. But she backs away from him, terrified.

Lou Waters breaks in. He knows the whole story. "Then we three are all who are left that know the secret," Stone says. "It's a pity that my empire must fall this way, that this must be the end of the man of mystery."

Shortly afterward, there is a new head of Joel Stone Enterprises — Harlan Croft, actually Lou Waters. Joel Stone's death was caused by Sherry Smith, who then jumped out of the window at Stone's hunting lodge. Croft is now in charge of everything, with the faithful Lucas at his side.

The grim one-two punch ending of "Man of Mystery," like much of Bloch's work, paints an unflattering portrait of mankind in general (even though Karloff, a la Hitchcock, makes a fleeting appearance in the epilogue to assure us that justice ultimately triumphed).

When asked about the episode, Bloch responded:

> "Man of Mystery" was written at a time when eccentric billionaire Howard Hughes was very much in

the news. I'd already written a short story predicting that actors might be chosen and groomed as political leaders (which, of course, came true!) but then I got to wondering why the same setup couldn't apply to financial tycoons. Maybe they too might be figureheads. So instead of writing another short story, I chose to present this one as a teleplay. And that's how "Man of Mystery" was born.

"Man of Mystery" is a crime episode that has the feel of a horror entry, particularly in the sequence at the dinner table with the dummies seated all around (a sequence reworked in Bloch's script for William Castle's *The Night Walker*). The use of shadows as metaphors is remarkably consistent throughout. Sherry Smith describes Lucas as Joel Stone's shadow, but in "Man of Mystery" everyone has a shadow. Sherry herself is the shadow of the other girls who have preceded her in Stone's life. And, of course, "Joel Stone" is actually Lucas's shadow. When Lucas, the real Joel Stone, finally emerges — literally and figuratively — from the shadows at the end, he casts off his shadow, and the imposter falls down the stairs. And Lou Waters becomes Stone's new shadow.

For an author as fascinated with wordplay as Bloch, names carry symbolic weight, and this shadow imagery is reflected (pun intended) in the characters' names. "Joel Stone" implies a personality with the solidity of a rock; it's doubly ironic that it belongs to the man Sherry describes as a shadow, rather than the actor (who is not even identified by name, emphasizing his essential anonymity) who assumes the part. Lou Waters' name serves a dual function: his first name links him to Lucas, whose shadow he will become, and his surname implies the reflecting waters that give back the image of the viewer, which, after all, is

another form of shadow. And Sherry Smith's name encapsulates both her sexual nature (sharing) with her commonality.

All these factors, along with John Newland's suspenseful and atmospheric direction, help to make "Man of Mystery" an above average episode. The casting is a bonus. John Van Dreelen is very good as the ersatz Joel Stone. His John Simon–like inflections give even his reassurances a sibilant note of sinister charm. With his smooth veneer and polished delivery, Van Dreelen naturally specialized in cultured villains, such as the waspish assassin in the memorable *Twilight Zone* episode "The Jeopardy Room." His genre films include *Beyond the Time Barrier*, *The Leech Woman*, and William Castle's *13 Ghosts* (all 1960).

Mary Tyler Moore is quite acceptable as the ill-fated Sherry Smith. She sings badly (on purpose, presumably) and is shallow and self-interested. (When the real Joel Stone approaches her, she cannot see beyond his unprepossessing appearance: she shrinks in fear and asks him not to touch her.) Moore had previously appeared in "The Fatal Impulse"; John Newland recalls that "Man of Mystery" was "one of the first things she'd done at that point." The *Dick Van Dyke Show* was already on the air, and she was well on her way to sitcom immortality as Laura Petrie.

William Windom was an all purpose actor: he could be heroic or villainous as the occasion demanded (and, of course, in "Man of Mystery," he's both). He played the lead in the sixties sitcom *The Farmer's Daughter* opposite Inger Stevens, and won an Emmy as the James Thurber inspired cartoonist in *My World and Welcome to It*.

Walter Burke was one of Hollywood's most distinctive character actors.

Standing just over five feet tall, he usually conveyed malevolence. One of his best roles came early: as Willie Stark's sinister henchman in the award-winning *All the King's Men* (1949). He also had memorable supporting roles in *Jack the Giant Killer* (1962) and *The President's Analyst* (1968), in which he played Henry Lux, head of the FBR (whose agents are all shorter than he is). He also appears in the *Thriller* episode "The Hollow Watcher." He died in 1984.

The other actors are competent. Mercedes Shirley has a good scene as the ill-fated Jill Naylor, and sci-fi fans with reliable memories may recognize William Phipps, the hero of Arch Oboler's film *Five* (1951), in a cameo as Harry Laxer.

The merits of "Man of Mystery" are somewhat relative; it's hardly one of the true *Thriller* classics, not is it the best of the Robert Bloch episodes, but it's a decided cut above the routine episodes that were being churned out as the series was nearing its close. It is also an episode that pulls no punches and features no contrived, last minute happy ending. It's true to its premise, and remarkably free of moralizing despite its very clear moral: always look beyond the surface.

"The Innocent Bystanders"

(airdate: April 9, 1962). Directed by John English. Written by Robert Hardy Andrews. Director of Photography: Benjamin H. Kline, A.S.C. Art Director: Howard E. Johnson. Edited by Danny Landres. Editorial Department Head: David J. O'Connell. Musical Supervision: Stanley Wilson. Set Decorators: John McCarthy and Julia Heron. Assistant Director: Carter DeHaven, III. Sound: Corson Jowett.

Cast: John Anderson (Jacob Grant), George Kennedy (John Paterson), Steven Terrell (Bruce Evans), Janet Lake (Elsie Evans), Gale Robbins (Mary Jerold), Jean Engstrom (Anne Grant), Carl Benton Reid (Dr. Marcus Graham), Than Wyenn (Vane), Clegg Hoyt (Kyle), Clancy Cooper (Chief Constable), Anthony Jochim (The Beggar), Dikki Lerner (Little Jamie).

One of the weakest *Thrillers* in this last batch, "The Innocent Bystanders" has an intriguing premise, but is let down by an uninteresting story line and bland characterizations.

In 19th-century England, Little Jamie (Dikki Lerner), a street entertainer, dances for pennies. Shortly afterward, one of his patrons is set upon by the team of Jacob Grant (John Anderson) and John Paterson (George Kennedy), two body snatchers who provide their own bodies when the supply is scarce. They pull him inside Grant's house; just then, there is the sound of someone at the door. Outside is Mary Jerold (Gale Robbins), the sister of Grant's wife, Anne (Jean Engstrom). With her are Bruce Evans (Steven Terrell) and his wife, Elsie (Janet Lake), who are in need of lodging.

Letting them stay in the house, Grant and Paterson carry the body off to the medical school where Dr. Marcus Graham (Carl Benton Reid) works. Grant and Paterson demand $50 for their business transaction. "Business — bodies for sale to the highest bidders," Graham sniffs. "You can't change the system," his servant, Vane (Than Wyenn), points out, "as long as the law says surgeons must graduate in anatomy, but forbids them to dissect, which is the proper way to learn — the only way." But Vane is taking a cut — $25, since he knows Grant and Paterson murdered the man. Vane tells them the next specimen should be female; accordingly, Mary Jerold is their next victim.

Later, Dr. Graham overhears Vane

arguing with Grant and Paterson over their fee. "It's too late in the day for murder to matter to you," Vane tells him. Meanwhile, Elsie overhears Anne accusing Grant of killing her sister and selling her body. "Your sister was never here," Grant warns her. Elsie tells Bruce what she has heard, and he follows Grant and Paterson on their nocturnal rounds. Their next victim is Little Jamie, the street entertainer, and Bruce hears Grant suggest that Elsie will be the next victim.

Bruce confronts Dr. Graham, who has already signed a confession and is about to take poison. "Dr. Marcus Graham — body buyer, murderer," Bruce says sneeringly. "I followed them up and down streets and byways since early morning, till I saw them kill. Now, what they've killed is in this house, bought and paid for, waiting for your knives." Bruce convinces Graham to go to the police. Vane goes to warn Grant — unwisely, since Paterson then murders him. When Grant enters a tavern he is set upon by his fellow body snatchers, who resent his habit of murder. Paterson returns home and attacks Elsie. Bruce arrives to defend her, but the sound of a police whistle rouses Paterson to flight, only to be stabbed by Anne Grant. The police take Paterson into custody; both he and Grant will be tried and hanged, and a new anatomy bill will be presented. "So, out of evil — good," Graham says, apparently having changed his mind about suicide. He offers a home to the three "innocent bystanders" — Bruce, Elsie and Anne.

As Karloff explains in his introduction to the episode, "Although the names and places have been changed, it is based upon documented facts." The characters of Grant and Paterson were, of course, based upon the notorious murderers Burke and Hare, who killed their victims and sold their corpses to an anatomist.

William Hare was the keeper of the Log's lodging house at Tanner's Close in Edinburgh. William Hare, Irish-born (as was Burke), arrived there in 1827. An old pensioner died in the house; instead of burying the corpse, Burke and Hare sold it to Dr. Robert Knox, a surgeon, for £7.10s. Thereafter they enticed at least 18 wayfarers into the lodging house, got them drunk, and then smothered them (so there would be no trace of violence) and sold the corpses to Knox's school of anatomy. They were finally found out when they murdered a local woman in 1828. Hare turned King's evidence and was eventually released; Burke was found guilty of murder and hanged on January 28, 1829.

Robert Louis Stevenson wrote a story, "The Body-Snatcher," using Burke and Hare as its source. This was fashioned into the best-remembered of all Val Lewton's films, featuring Karloff and Henry Daniell. Burke and Hare themselves were the subject of *The Flesh and The Fiends* (1960), featuring Peter Cushing as the surgeon, *The Anatomist* (1961), with Alastair Sim, *Burke and Hare* and *Dr. Jekyll and Sister Hyde* (both 1971), and *The Doctor and the Devils* (1985), based on a script originally written by Dylan Thomas.

This material would seem ideally suited to *Thriller*: unfortunately Robert Hardy Andrews' script is surprisingly unsuspenseful and even uninteresting. Part of the problem is its verbosity: Dr. Graham and his servant, Vane, stand around endlessly arguing the morality of Graham's actions. In addition, the good characters are simply too colorless and bland to be appealing (it might have been interesting for them to kill Grant and Paterson in self defense and then sell *their* bodies to the doctor out of financial necessity). There's some nice period flavor, and one or two semi-suspenseful moments, but for the most part, "The Innocent Bystanders" is a bust, one of the most disappointing second season *Thrillers*. (As with the final episode, "The Specialists," William Frye's name is missing from the credits.)

John Anderson is quite good as Jacob Grant: glib, well spoken and resourceful, he gives the episode what little life it has. A solid supporting actor, he's probably best remembered as the used car salesman in *Psycho*, though he was equally memorable in two *Twilight Zone* episodes, "The Odyssey of Flight 33" and "A Passage for Trumpet." His films include Sam Peckinpah's classic western *Ride the High Country* (1962), *The Satan Bug* (1965) and *A Man Called Gannon* (1969). He died in 1992.

George Kennedy is unfortunately cast as a one-dimensional heavy, and he plays him in the usual lumbering, menacing style he employed before finding great success in a sympathetic role in *Cool Hand Luke* (1967), for which he won an Academy Award. He was a memorable heavy in *Charade* (1963) and appeared in William Castle's *Strait-Jacket* (1964) before settling down to a career as a reliable supporting actor.

The other cast members are saddled with uninteresting roles. Steven Terrell is appropriately bland and forgettable as the hero, and the others fare little better. Even veteran Carl Benton Reid can do little to enliven things, since his role as Dr. Graham is so poorly developed. Only Dikki Lerner, seen as the dummy, Hans, in "The Weird Tailor," adds a soupcon of period flavor as Little Jamie (who was based on "Daft Jamie," an Edinburgh half-wit murdered by Burke and Hare); unfortunately, he's seen only briefly.

In all, "The Innocent Bystanders" is one of the more forgettable *Thrillers*: it had potential which is mostly frittered away by bland direction and writing. By any standard, it's a missed opportunity.

"The Lethal Ladies" (airdate: April 16, 1962). Produced by William Frye. Directed by Ida Lupino. Teleplay by Boris Sobelman, based on short stories by Joseph Payne Brennan. Director of Photography: Benjamin H. Kline, A.S.C. Art Director: Howard E. Johnson. Edited by Danny Landres. Editorial Department Head: David J. O'Connell. Musical Supervision: Stanley Wilson. Set Decorators: John McCarthy and Julia Heron. Associate Producer: Doug Benton. Assistant Director: Edward K. Dodds. Sound: John W. Rixey.

Cast: Howard Morris (Myron Sills/Dr. Wilfred Bliss), Rosemary Murphy (Lavinia Sills/Alice Quimby), Pamela Curran (Gloria), Marjorie Bennett (Mercedes), Robert Carson (Albert White), Jackie Russell (Martha Foster), Henry Brandt (Mr. Sutter), Chet Stratton (Mr. Delevant), Ralph Moody (Mr. Jacobson), William P. Remick (Mr. Grant), Jackie Joseph (Miss Martin).

Thriller's last multi-part episode, "The Lethal Ladies" is an entertaining mix of murder and mayhem, though it suffers from unevenness, the usual bane of short story compendiums.

"Murder on the Rocks": Rock-hunting Lavinia Sills (Rosemary Murphy) enjoys dominating her pipsqueak husband, Myron (Howard Morris). Myron is secretly carrying on with Gloria (Pamela Curran). Gloria suggests that Lavinia could fall during one of her climbs; Myron would then inherit her money.

Myron and Lavinia go climbing. Myron comments that a man could break his leg on a remote ledge and no one would ever find him. Lavinia tells him the stocks he put everything into dropped five points; he has been wiped out. Myron pushes Lavinia off the edge; she falls into the pool below. "I surprised you, didn't I, Lavinia?" Myron shouts.

But Lavinia has surprises of her own. She is not dead; she returns, and binds and gags Myron. "Poor Myron," she says. "Nothing ever works out right for you, does it?" She tells him she's altered her will, so he would never have inherited her money, then carries him back to the ledge above the pool. When she removes the gag, Myron appears to faint. Lavinia listens for a heartbeat, but in vain; Myron is dead. "You cheated me!" Lavinia shouts, but as she backs up, she loses her footing and falls to her death.

"Goodbye, Dr. Bliss": At Wharton Memorial Library, situated on a large campus, Miss Quimby (Rosemary Murphy) is passed over as chief librarian in favor of Dr. Wilfred Bliss (Howard Morris). Miss Quimby has five years to go before she will receive her pension. But she has no intention of retiring: "This place is my life," she tells Mr. Delevant (Chet Stratton). "There is nothing else. I could never leave."

Dr. Bliss takes over. He is an authoritarian type, and announces that the methods used by the library are old-fashioned and must be changed. He terminates Mr. Sutter (Henry Brandt) and says he intends to replace the entire staff.

At the end of the school term Dr. Bliss is planning his vacation — he is leaving no forwarding address, so there is no way he can be reached. He hands Miss Quimby her termination notice. When Miss Quimby makes a trip to the vault, to which she has the only key, she splashes water on the floor to make it appear the pipes are leaking, then summons Dr. Bliss. He goes down to investigate and tells her to get the custodian. She goes out, locking him in the vault.

As she leaves the college she turns to say, "Goodbye, Dr. Bliss."

"The Lethal Ladies" is based on two short stories by Joseph Payne Brennan (1918–90), one of the most underrated horror writers of the last 50 years. He was one of *Weird Tales'* last major discoveries; his ghost story "The Green Parrot" appeared in the magazine in 1952. His Arkham House collection, *Nine Horrors and a Dream* (1958), is a necessary item in any aficionado's library, and certain of his short stories — notably "Slime," "Levitation," and "Canavan's Back Yard" — have become minor classics. Brennan was also an accomplished poet, and Arkham House published a collection of his verse, *Nightmare Need* (1964). Given all that, it seems a shame *Thriller* never adapted one of his horror tales — "The Horror at Chilton Castle" might have made a splendid episode. The stories that comprise "The Lethal Ladies" are minor Brennan: they're both enjoyable, but hardly rank among his best work. They seem better suited to *Alfred Hitchcock Presents.*

As usual with multi-part episodes, one segment overshadows the other. "Murder on the Rocks" is an amusing trifle, but not much more. Director Ida Lupino supplies some clever camera angles to suggest the animal passions that motivate both characters: there are close-ups of stuffed tigers and a moose's head. But the story is slight and the final twist not particularly memorable.

"Goodbye, Dr. Bliss" is more gripping, perhaps because it reflects Brennan's own attitudes toward his profession. Writing was only a sideline for him; he worked as the senior assistant at Yale University Library, and the outrage Miss Quimby feels at being shunted aside reflects Brennan's own antiquarian views. Ida Lupino provides some notable high angle views of Dr. Bliss as he scurries about the vault like a trapped animal, and, in all, the segment comes across as more substantial than the first. (In a totally unnecessary coda, Karloff appears to assure us that Miss Quimby paid with her life for her crime.)

Both segments are really a showcase for the acting skills of the two leading players who enact dual roles. Howard Morris is best remembered for his appearances with Sid Caesar on the classic *Your Show of Shows* in the fifties. He plays the milksop Myron Sills and the authoritarian Dr. Bliss, and carries off the dual impersonation reasonably well. Morris was a familiar face on television throughout the fifties and sixties.

Rosemary Murphy, like Morris, plays antithetical parts: a domineering wife and a meek librarian, and seems to relish the challenge. She worked frequently on television and won an Emmy for her performance in *Franklin and Eleanor* (1976). Her films include *To Kill a Mockingbird* (1962), *Any Wednesday* (1966) and *Ben* (1972).

There's an amusing (if irrelevant) prologue in which a nurse throws acid into the face of a doctor; the camera then pulls back to reveal Karloff seated in a chair marked "*Thriller* Director." "Cut!" he says. "Delightful! That's a print."

Overall, "The Lethal Ladies" is one of the better entries in this last batch of *Thrillers*. As noted, it's uneven, but as a pleasant respite from the more harrowing episodes, it's a welcome surprise.

"The Specialists" (airdate: April 30, 1962). Directed by Ted Post. Teleplay by John Kneubuhl, based on a novel by Gordon Ash. Director of Photography: Benjamin Kline. Art Director: Russell Kimball. Associate Producer: Douglas Benton. Assistant Director: Carter DeHaven, III. Edited by Danny Landres.

Cast: Lin McCarthy (Peter Duncan), Suzanne Lloyd (Helen Coleman), Ronald Howard (Martin Gresham), David Frankham (Joe Carter), Sean McClory (Patrick Galt), Lauren Gilbert (Tracy), Robert Douglas (Swinburne), Doris Lloyd (Landlady), Anthony Scott (Montaigne), Lucy Prentis (Peggy Duncan), Alan Caillou (Police Superintendent).

It's sad to report that *Thriller*'s final episode is a thoroughly routine crime entry. It makes a singularly inappropriate finale for the series.

In Montreal, a well-dressed man (Ronald Howard) prowls the streets; inside one of the houses, a man agrees to take a group of men to see Ray Coleman. But when the man gets in his car, he turns the key in the ignition and it explodes.

At a house in the country, Martin Gresham, the well-dressed man seen earlier, drops in on Ray Coleman. He tells him he'll have to transport some stolen jewels for his employer, a man named Swinburne. But when Coleman's back is turned, Gresham shoots him, then leaves the gun behind along with a forged suicide note. Just then the "specialists" enter the house and find the dead man. They go to see his sister, Helen, but she has gone away. Gresham has faked her death without her knowledge and is taking her with him to London on a "business" trip for Swinburne. He is in love with Helen (Suzanne Lloyd) and has told her he is an art dealer, traveling from country to country.

The specialists, who were ready for Coleman to talk before his friends got to him, are working secretly for the federal government, and include Peter Duncan (Lin McCarthy) and Joe Carter (David Frankham). They find the body of "Helen," actually another woman, along with a faked suicide note, all arranged by Gresham.

In the meantime Carter has spotted the real Helen at the airport. They follow her to London, but lose her there. Another member of the team, Patrick Galt (Sean McClory), tells them that Gresham is known as a haberdasher named Morrison. They decide to buy his store. Swinburne (Robert Douglas) meets with Gresham, planning a robbery involving diamonds, but creates a diversion, making it impossible for the specialists to eavesdrop. They decide to pick up Gresham, but he kills Carter and escapes. Desperate, they put out the news that Helen Coleman's brother is dead. Swinburne orders Gresham to kill Helen, along with Peter Duncan. Swinburne is arrested immediately afterward. Gresham begins making a bomb.

Helen hears the news that her brother is dead. Gresham disarms her with a concocted story and arranges for her to call Duncan and agree to meet with him. Patrick Galt keeps watch from a rooftop. Duncan and Helen meet in an empty street; Gresham hurls his bomb, but Duncan shoves Helen to one side and it explodes harmlessly in the street. Gresham, trying to escape, gets into a fight with Duncan, who subdues him.

"The Specialists" resembles the pilot for an unproduced espionage series rather than an episode of *Thriller*, mainly because, according to Doug Benton, that's exactly what it was. "The guy who owned a part of the series — Hubbell Robinson — did it," Benton recalls. "I think it was a pilot that Universal sneaked in, to get the *Thriller* people to pay for it."

To its credit, there are several clever touches (when the smugglers are under electronic surveillance, Swinburne is tapping his fingers constantly, creating a cacophony of sound so their conversation cannot be overheard) and capable performances, but "The Specialists" is largely a washout. It resembles an episode of *Cain's Hundred*, an early sixties crime series, more than *Thriller*. And since the villains are far more personable and charming than the heroes, who seem a rather dull lot, it's hard to get involved. Lin McCarthy (also seen in the even duller "Rose's Last Summer") is, as usual, emotionless and even robotic, and his partner, played by David Frankham, is equally bland, so it's left up to Ronald Howard, a far more stylish actor, to provide what little interest there is. Admittedly, it's nice to see *Thriller* veterans McCarthy, Frankham, Howard, Sean McClory and Alan Caillou together, but this is meager compensation.

All in all, "The Specialists" is a sad farewell performance for a once great series. After its initial telecast, Doug Benton recalls, the only comment made on it was that "All the FBI men were wearing the wrong kind of hats."

Part III
Appendices

A. ANCESTORS OF *THRILLER*

Thriller's predecessors date back to the very dawn of network television. Not surprisingly, these pioneering efforts were modeled after the successful radio horror shows of the thirties and forties, most notably *Inner Sanctum* and *Lights Out* (both of which were reincarnated as early television series, though with little of the effectiveness of their radio counterparts).

One interesting early effort was the short-lived *Starring Boris Karloff* (also known as *Mystery Playhouse Starring Boris Karloff*), which lasted for 13 episodes on ABC in 1949. As with *Thriller*, Karloff served as host and occasional star. The comparison is heightened by consideration of one episode in particular, "Five Golden Guineas." It deals with an English hangman who is paid five guineas per execution. He enjoys his work with sadistic relish. When his pregnant wife learns of his profession, she leaves him. Twenty years later the hangman is called upon to execute a young man; despite having evidence that the boy is innocent, the hangman carries out the sentence, taking great pleasure in the act. His ex-wife then reappears to tell him he has hanged his own son. The hangman strangles his wife, and is sentenced to be executed by another hangman, who pockets five golden guineas for his services.

The episode is, as Stephen King points out in *Danse Macabre*, "kissing cousin" to the memorable *Thriller*, "Guillotine."

Other programs were direct spinoffs from radio: *Suspense* and *Lights Out* were two of the more successful. Although they emphasized mystery and suspense, they were not averse to the occasional horror yarn. *Lights Out* was the more horrific of the two, and featured Karloff in one episode, "The Leopard Lady," as well as such notable actors as Burgess Meredith, Basil Rathbone and Raymond Massey. It also featured a notable introduction; as Tim Brooks and Earle Marsh describe it: "At the beginning of each episode viewers would see only a close shot of a pair of eyes, then a bloody hand reaching to turn out the lights, followed by an eerie laugh and the words, 'Lights out, everybody....'"*

Hands of Destiny ran from 1949 to 1951 on the Dumont network, and presented notable supernatural and horror episodes. Brooks and Marsh note that "A

As described in The Complete Directory to Prime Time Network TV Shows *(Ballantine Books, 1979).*

novel aspect of the series ... was the almost complete absence of props and sets, with inventive camera angles and lighting used instead to suggest the locale." The series was also known as *Hands of Murder* and *Hands of Mystery*.

One early series, *Mr. Black* (September–November 1949), apparently featured the first "monster host," the sinister Mr. Black. Another early, little-seen series, *Tales of the Black Cat*, was hosted by James Monk, along with his cat, Thanatopsis.

Other series, while not specializing in the supernatural per se, offered occasional macabre or fantastic fare. *Favorite Story*, a syndicated anthology program broadcast in 1952, featured adaptations of Poe's "The Gold Bug" and "The Tell-Tale Heart," as well as H. G. Wells's "Strange Valley" and Oscar Wilde's "The Canterville Ghost." *The Conrad Nagel Theater* presented a notably frightening adaptation of "The Sandman," featuring Sebastian Cabot.

The Unexpected, hosted by urbane Herbert Marshall, ran on NBC in 1952, and featured mystery and supernatural tales. *Inner Sanctum*, another spinoff from radio, ran for 11 months in 1954. The episodes were occasionally horrific, and the same was true of *The Whistler*, which ran the same year, and featured such stars as Lon Chaney, Jr., Robert Hutton and Charles McGraw.

One exception to the usual run of anthology series was the short-lived *Tales of the Unknown*, which ran in 1954. Each episode featured a soliloquy performed by an actor or actress. *Panic* was a slightly more successful and certainly more traditional anthology series featuring an occasional supernatural or fantasy episode. It featured such performers as Alan Napier, Carolyn Jones and Darryl Hickman, and lasted for 31 episodes.

Suspicion, which aired on NBC for two seasons between 1957 and 1959, was, again, primarily a suspense-mystery anthology series, but occasionally featured a supernatural tale. It featured such notable guests as Burgess Meredith, Macdonald Carey, and Rod Taylor. One of its producers, interestingly enough, was William Frye.

The last of these precursors of *Thriller* was *Moment of Fear*, which ran from July to September 1960 on NBC, and gave up the ghost just as *Thriller* was debuting. To its credit, the program presented a faithful adaptation of Fritz Leiber's *Conjure Wife*, with Larry Blyden, but was otherwise undistinguished.

Most of these early shows remain sadly lost in time, seldom (if ever) rerun, and rarely available on videotape. Their chief weakness was their crudeness and poverty of production values, necessitated by the primitive technical facilities of early television; the best of them rose above this by imagination and ingenuity. As forerunners of *Thriller*, they deserve a nod of recognition, if only for their attempts to establish a beachhead in the domain of the macabre.

B. DESCENDANTS
OF *THRILLER*

When *Thriller* left the air in July 1962, the most immediate and obvious beneficiary was the venerable *Alfred Hitchcock Presents*. This show promptly moved from NBC to CBS, expanded to a full 60 minutes, and was retitled *The Alfred Hitchcock Hour*. Its stories became noticeably more macabre, and the show began to employ many *Thriller* directors, including John Brahm and John Newland. Ironically, the show that *Thriller* had once patterned itself after now seemed like an imitation.

Many episodes were notable ventures into the supernatural virtually indistinguishable from *Thriller*. "The Sign of Satan," scripted by Robert Bloch and based on his story "Return to the Sabbath," featured Christopher Lee as a European horror star reluctant to make his American debut because of a cult bent on killing him. It was an atmospheric episode with a memorably creepy denouement. Ray Bradbury's "The Life Work of Juan Diaz" was a macabre drama set in Mexico's catacombs where the dead are buried upright, and featured Alejandro Rey. "The Magic Shop" was a chilling adaptation of H. G. Wells' short story, scripted by John Collier, and featuring a notably downbeat ending. Perhaps the best episode of all, in terms of sheer mounting suspense, was "An Unlocked Window," featuring three nurses isolated in an old house with a strangler on the loose. Similar in several respects to the *Thriller* episode "The Storm," it built to an unforgettable ending. (Several of these episodes were remade for the updated *Alfred Hitchcock Presents* in the eighties, but with little of the old panache.)

By the time the Hitchcock series left the air in 1965, anthology shows were considered passé, despite sporadic (and ineffectual) attempts to bring them back. England's Hammer Films tried in 1968 with the short-lived *Journey to the Unknown*, but the stories were bland and ineffective. Robert Bloch, a sometime contributor, said of it:

> It seems that the network [ABC] decided early in the game it wanted none of the traditional supernatural elements. It was like doing a Western series without six-guns or horses. Therefore, there was no atmosphere, suspense, or any of the other qualities fans of that genre have come to expect from an offering of this sort.

"Journey" died an early and well-deserved death.

Rod Serling's "Night Gallery" promised a return to the glory days of *Twilight Zone*, but the show was a near-total disaster, featuring "hip" vampires and skits that were basically ghoulish one-liners. Serling himself, disgusted by the show's mediocrity, attempted, without success, to have his name removed from the title.

Later series fared little better. *Ghost Story*, also called *Circle of Fear*, was a vapid and uninvolving mix of supernatural elements. *Darkroom*, a brief series with James Coburn as host, presented stories in the *Thriller* mold (including an adaptation of "Guillotine") but the results were overpoweringly mediocre, and the series sank without a trace. Later attempts, ranging from *Tales from the Darkside* to *Friday the Thirteenth*, were also failures.

It's depressing but true that, with the exception of certain episodes of *The Alfred Hitchcock Hour*, *Thriller*'s successors were an undistinguished group, lacking both atmosphere and storytelling expertise, qualities that made the original series so memorable. Truly, *Thriller* left no heirs.

C. The Top 25
THRILLER Episodes

This listing is based on requests sent to the *Thriller* Fan Club. For more information (and to order specific episodes), write to: 537 Jones Street, Department 1850, San Francisco, CA 94102.

1. "Pigeons from Hell"
2. "The Hungry Glass"
3. "The Incredible Doktor Markesan"
4. "The Grim Reaper"
5. "The Cheaters"
6. "The Terror in Teakwood"
7. "Well of Doom"
8. "La Strega"
9. "The Devil's Ticket"
10. "The Prisoner in the Mirror"
11. "The Weird Tailor"
12. "Masquerade"
13. "Parasite Mansion"
14. "The Return of Andrew Bentley"
15. "A Wig for Miss Devore"
16. "Dialogues with Death"
17. "God Grante That She Lye Stille"
18. "The Remarkable Mrs. Hawk"
19. "The Premature Burial"
20. "Waxworks"
21. "The Hollow Watcher"
22. "The Purple Room"
23. "Dark Legacy"
24. "Trio for Terror"
25. "The Closed Cabinet"

BIBLIOGRAPHY

Ackerman, Forrest J. *The Frankenscience Monster.* New York: Ace Books, 1969.

Asherman, Allan. "John Newland Interviewed." *Filmfax*, No. 13, December 1988.

Beck, Calvin. *Heroes of the Horrors.* New York: Collier Books, 1975.

Bianculli, David. *Dictionary of Teleliteracy.* New York: Continuum Books, 1996.

Bloch, Robert. *Once Around the Bloch.* New York: Tor Books, 1993.

Brooks, Tim, and Earle Marsh. *The Complete Directory to Prime Time Network TV Shows.* New York: Ballantine Books, 1979.

Burlingame, Jon. *TV's Biggest Hits: The Story of Television Themes from "Dragnet" to "Friends."* New York: Schirmer Books, 1996.

Copner, Mike. "Fantastic Television." *Videosonic Arts* #2, 1990.

Corville, Gary, and Patrick Lucanio. "Jack the Ripper." *Filmfax*, No. 31, February-March 1992.

Daniels, Les. *Living in Fear.* New York: Scribner's, 1975.

DeCamp, L. Sprague, Catherine Crook deCamp and Jane Whittington Griffin. *Dark Valley Destiny: The Life of Robert E. Howard.* New York: Bluejay Books, 1983.

Delson, James. "Science Fiction on Television." *Fantastic Films*, April 1979.

Derleth, August, and Mark Schorer. *Colonel Markesan and Less Pleasant People.* Sauk City: Arkham House, 1966.

Donati, William. *Ida Lupino: A Biography.* Lexington: University Press of Kentucky, 1996.

Gerani, Gary, and Paul H. Schulman. *Fantastic Television.* New York: Harmony Books, 1977.

Gianakas, Larry James. *Television Drama Series Programming: A Comprehensive Chronicle, 1959–1975.* Metuchen, NJ: Scarecrow, 1978.

Goldstein, Fred, and Stanley Goldstein. *Prime-Time Television.* New York: Crown, 1983.

Hegenberger, John. "The Private Life of Boris Karloff." *Filmfax*, No. 13, December 1988.

Herndon, Ben. "TZ Interview: Douglas Heyes." *Twilight Zone*, August 1982.

Herron, Don, ed. *The Dark Barbarian: The Writings of Robert E. Howard.* Westport, CT: Greenwood, 1984.

Inman, David. *The TV Encyclopedia.* New York: Perigree Books, 1991.

Jensen, Paul. *Boris Karloff and His Films.* South Brunswick, N.J.: A. S. Barnes, 1974.

Kaffke, Ken, Matt Engle, and Rick Polizzi. "Prime Time Evil." *Spin Again* #3, 1993.

Kane, Charles F. "Charnel Chillers." *Castle of Frankenstein*, Vol. 1, No. 3, 1963.

King, Stephen. *Danse Macabre.* New York: Everest House, 1981.

Kuhn, Annette, ed. *Queen of the "B's": Ida Lupino Behind the Camera.* Westport, CT: Greenwood, 1995.

Larson, Randall. *Robert Bloch.* Mercer Island, WA: Starmont House, 1986.

_____. *Musique Fantastique: A Survey of Film Music in the Fantastic Cinema.* Metuchen, NJ: Scarecrow, 1985.

Lindsay, Cynthia. *Dear Boris.* New York: Knopf, 1975.

Lucas, Tim. "Laserdisc Thriller Colection." *Video Watchdog,* No. 25, September-October 1994.

Mank, Gregory William. *It's Alive!* San Diego, Calif.: A. S. Barnes, 1981.

_____. *Karloff and Lugosi.* Jefferson, N.C.: McFarland, 1990.

Neel, Mark D. "John Brahm." *Filmfax,* No. 31, February-March 1992.

Nevins, Francis M., Jr. *First You Dream, Then You Die.* New York: Mysterious Press, 1988.

"Newsmakers": "Scarecrower." *Newsweek,* September 5, 1960, p. 41.

Newton, Dwight. "Mort Sahl Stars in TV 'Thriller.'" San Francisco *Chronicle,* December 20, 1960, p. 9.

Nollen, Scott Allen. *Boris Karloff: A Critical Account of His Screen, Stage, Radio, Television and Recording Work.* Jefferson, N.C.: McFarland, 1991.

Sanford, Jay Allen. "Karloff Through the Looking Glass: Horror on *Thriller.*" *Midnight Marquee,* No. 39, fall 1989. (Reprinted in *Filmfax,* No. 29, October-November 1991, and No. 30, December-January 1992.)

Stanley, John. "An Interview with Robert Bloch." *Castle of Frankenstein,* No. 16, July 1971.

Stephens, Bob. "It's a Thrill to Be Terrorized." "Lasermania," San Francisco *Examiner,* September 3, 1994, p. c-1, c-11.

Sullivan, Jack, ed. *The Penguin Encyclopedia of Horror and the Supernatural.* New York: Viking, 1986.

Taves, Brian. *Robert Florey, the French Expressionist.* Metuchen, N.J.: Scarecrow Press, 1987.

Terrace, Vincent. *The Complete Encyclopedia of TV Programs.* San Diego: A.S. Barnes, 1985.

"Time Listings." *Time,* September 12, 1960, p. 120.

Underwood, Peter. *Karloff.* New York: Drake, 1972.

Waite, Ronald N. "The Golden Years of Terrorvision." *Famous Monsters of Filmland* #138, October 1977.

_____. "King Boris the Benign on TV Time." *Famous Monsters of Filmland* #147, September 1978.

Weaver, Tom. "His Life Was a Thriller," *Fangoria* No. 155, August 1996.

_____. "Licensed to Thrill." *Fangoria* No. 156, September 1996.

Wickstrom, Andy. "The Thriller Collection" (Video Recording Reviews), *Video,* December 1994, p. 73.

Wright, Gene. *Horrorshows.* New York: Facts on File, 1986.

INDEX

Abbott and Costello Meet Frankenstein 133
Abbott, John 80, 83, 85
Abdullah, Joe 65
Ackerman, Forrest J. vi, 14
Adams, Stanley 127
Adventures of Sherlock Holmes 87
Advise and Consent 29, 98
Aidman, Charles 51–52, 53, 100, 102
Airplane! 29
Airport 1975 24
Airport 1977 24, 25
Albertson, Frank 54
Albertson, Grace 54
Albright, Hardie 35
"The Alfred Hitchcock Hour" 5, 94, 160, 188
"Alfred Hitchcock Presents" 5, 10, 11, 15, 16, 18, 30, 41, 58, 61, 64, 67, 70, 88, 98, 128, 169, 162, 169, 182, 188
All the King's Men 86, 179
Allen, Elizabeth 59, 61, 116, 117, 118
The Alligator People 53, 129
Allyn, William 95
Alper, Murray 52
Alpert, David 52
Alvin, John 33
The Americanization of Emily 99
Ames, Rachel 33
The Anatomist 180
Anderson, John 179, 181
Anderson, Richard 37, 38, 40, 41
Andress, Ursula 156, 157
Andrews, Edward 95, 98, 137, 138, 165, 166
Andrews, Robert H. 73
Andrews, Robert Hardy 62, 64, 129, 173, 179, 180
Andy Hardy Comes Home 99

Anthony Adverse 91
Arlen, Michael 41
Armstrong, Charlotte 33, 43, 53
Arnold, Phil 172
Arrigo, Frank 145, 158
Arsenic and Old Lace 9, 51, 138
Arthur, Robert 103, 105, 140, 142, 151
Ash, Gordon 183
Asquith, Lady Cynthia 129
Assault on a Queen 64
Astor, Mary 20, 34, 35
Astro-Zombies 147
"An Attractive Family" 151–153
Aubry, Daniele 65

Baby Doll 58
"Back There" 61
Backes, Alice 48
The Bad Seed 128, 160
Baer, Donald 73, 153, 156, 171, 173
Baer, Parley 30
Bainter, Fay 43
Bal, Jeanne 84
Banner, John 146, 149, 150
Bannon, Jim 95, 165
"Banquo's Chair" 73
Baragrey, John 31, 160
Barron, Jack 15, 58, 162, 169
Barry, Patricia 37, 40, 41, 95, 98, 160, 162
Barselow, Paul 151
Bartell, Harry 48
Barton, Anne 36
Barty, Billy 67
"Batman" 46, 70
Bava, Mario 24, 140
Baxter, Alan 42, 153
Baylor, Hal 145

The Beast of Hollow Mountain 93
The Beast with Five Fingers 102, 168
Beaumont, Charles 14, 43, 44, 122, 123, 126
Beck, Billy 74, 167
Beckman, Evelyn 31
Beckner, Neal 42
Bedlam 9, 45
Beir, Frederick 54
Belding, Richard 48, 51, 62, 71, 74, 80, 87
Bell, Hurley 145, 172
Bellak, George 67
Ben 183
"Ben Casey" 20
Bender, Russ 65
Benedek, Laszlo 78
Bennett, Marjorie 181
Benton, Douglas (Doug) vi, 2, 10, 14–15, 19, 20, 21, 22, 23, 24, 41, 47, 76–77, 91, 94, 95, 98, 100, 103, 106, 109, 115, 116, 120, 122, 124, 127, 129, 131, 133, 136, 137, 138, 140, 143, 145, 146, 151, 153, 156, 158, 160, 163, 165, 167, 170, 171, 173, 174, 176, 181, 183, 184
Beregi, Oscar 143, 145
Berke, Les 160
Bernard, Barry 68, 161
Bevans, Clem 59, 165
Bewitched (movie) 135
"Bewitched" (TV series) 132, 132, 169
Beyond the Time Barrier 178
"The Big Blackout" 11, 13, 50–51, 147, 189
The Big Heat 96
The Big Steal 150
Binns, Edward 71, 72, 74
Bishop, Ben 80, 91, 106, 133, 174
Bishop, Bunny 52
Bisk, George 103, 176
Black Alibi 86
The Black Castle 87
The Black Cat 9
"The Black Madonna" 118
Black Magic 105
Black Sabbath 24
The Black Sleep 163
Blackmer, Sidney 124, 126
Blake, Larry 175
Blake, Whitney 48, 49
Bloch, Robert vi, 2, 5, 11, 13, 15–16, 19,

23, 24, 29, 56, 59, 61, 60, 83, 86, 88, 90, 91, 92, 93, 94, 95, 97–98, 114, 116, 118, 119, 126, 128, 129, 153, 155, 169, 189, 171, 172, 176–179, 188
Blondell, Gloria 88
Bluebeard 147
Blunk, John 67
Blyden, Larry 70, 67, 68, 187
Bochner, Lloyd 103, 104, 106
The Body Snatcher 9, 58, 180
Bogart, Humphrey 55
Bond, Nelson 80, 87
Booth, Nesdon 71
Boris Karloff's Tales of Mystery 17
Boris Karloff's Thriller 17
Bouchey, Willis 176
Bourbon, Diana 74
Bourneuf, Philip 143, 144
Bower, Antoinette 143, 144, 153, 154, 169
Bowman, John 37, 67
Bowman, John Clarke 87, 100, 124, 138, 165, 167
Bradbury, Ray 14, 188
Bradford, Lane 163
Brahm, John 15, 24, 41, 43, 45, 47, 56, 57, 64, 71, 72, 74, 76, 90, 95, 106, 108, 145, 147, 151, 152, 160, 162, 165, 166, 169, 171, 188
Brando, Jocelyn 31, 172
Brandt, Henry 181
Brennan, Joseph Payne 181, 182
Breslin, Patricia 174
Bricken, Jules 36, 73, 91
The Bride of Frankenstein 9
"The Bride Who Died Twice" 70, 173–174
The Brides of Dracula 135
Bristol, Iris 68, 80
"Broadside" 98
Brocco, Peter 80, 103, 122, 173
Brodie, Steve 48
Bronson, Lillian 98
Brown, Fredric 51
Brown, Helen 78
Brown, James H. 30, 136, 137
Brunetti, Argentina 36
Buchanan, Edgar 172
Bulifant, Joyce 151, 166
Bullitt 84
Bunny Lake Is Missing 135

Buono, Victor 43, 46, 129, 130, 131
Burke and Hare 180
Burke, Walter 20, 163, 165, 176, 177, 178
Burnham, Terry 33
"Bus Stop" 30, 45

The Cabinet of Caligari 16
Caillou, Alan 15, 45, 47, 68, 69, 70, 99, 101–102, 157, 183
Cain, Lyle 129
Camille 57
Camlin, Peter 122
Canfield, Grace 95
Canfield, Mary Grace 163
Caps, John 74
Captain Sinbad 129
Carbone, Antony 48
The Cardinal 138
Carey, Macdonald vi, 20, 91, 92–93
Carey, Philip 65–70
Carlson, Richard 20, 67, 174, 175
Carneol, Jess 138
Carney, Alan 56
Carr, John Dickson 137
Carradine, John 22, 131, 132, 132, 145, 146, 147
Carricart, Robert 50
Carroll, Leo G. 151, 153
Carson, Jack 50, 51
Carson, Robert 181
Carter, Myra 139
Caruso, Tony 36
Casablanca 55, 102
Casbah 163
Casino Royale 33, 157
Cassavetes, John 12, 29
Castiglione, Iphigenie 127
Castle, William 32, 45, 86, 91, 102, 106, 122, 169, 164, 176, 178, 181
The Catman of Paris 122
Cavaleri, Raymond 145
Cavallaro, Gaylord 122
Cavanagh, James P. 10, 28, 30, 31, 33, 34, 36, 43, 53
Cavanaugh, Jimmy 50
Chamberlain, Richard 12, 17, 42, 43
Chaney, Lon, Jr. 22, 32, 115, 187
Chaney, Lon, Sr. 15, 49, 76
"Channing" 128
Chauvin, Lilyan 65

"The Cheaters" 2, 9, 13, 56–59, 77, 103, 106, 108, 142, 147, 158, 163, 171, 190
"Checkmate" 18, 64
"Child's Play" 10, 30–31, 97
"Choose a Victim" 67–68, 166, 176
Christie, Agatha 90, 137
Christine, Virginia 28
Cianelli, Eduardo 65, 67, 173, 174
Citizen Kane 37
Clanton, Ralph 56, 176
Clark, Arlette 65
Clark, Gloria 42
Clarke, Gage 146, 149, 150
Clarke, Gary 127
Claxton, William F. 163
Clemons, John 74
Cleopatra 73
"The Closed Cabinet" 106, 138–140
The Cocoanuts 168
Cocteau, Jean 105, 106
Colbert, Robert 173, 174
Cold Wind in August 125, 126, *A*
Colean, Chuck 145, 163
Collier, John 97, 146, 188
Collins, Wilkie 80, 86
Colman, Booth 65, 153
Colman, Ronald 12
The Colossus of New York 153, 174
"The Colour Out of Space" 24
The Comedy of Terrors 24
Conjure Wife 71, 187
"The Conrad Nagel Theatre" 187
Conway, Russ 78, 82, 80
Cook, Elisha 48, 49
Cool Hand Luke 147, 181
Cooper, Clancy 52, 179
Cooper, Jeannie 50
Copage, Alibe 84
Corby, Ellen 43
Corden, Henry 67
Corman, Roger 24, 109, 126
Cornthwaite, Robert 91, 94, 116, 119
The Couch 16
Coulouris, George 94
Counselman, Mary Elizabeth 94, 95
The Court Jester 78
Court, Hazel 100, 102, 126
"Cousin Tundifer" 71, 98, 165–167
Cowan, Ashley 54
The Cowboys 148
Crain, Earl, Jr. 143, 145, 153, 156, 160

Crain, Lyle 109
Crane, Norma 140, 143
Craven, John 100
The Creature from the Black Lagoon 175
Cregar, Laird 46, 57, 79, 90
Cross, David P. 122
Crowder, Judy 87
Crowley, Kathleen 78, 82, 80
Cry of the Werewolf 87
Curran, Pamela 88, 103, 181
The Curse of Frankenstein 102
Curse of the Demon 108
Curse of the Faceless Man 122
Curse of the Mummy's Tomb 81
Curse of the Undead 84, 83
Curucu, Beast of the Amazon 53
Cushing, Peter 155

Dale, Esther 44
Dallimore, Maurice 62, 161
Dalton, Audrey 45, 48, 68, 69, 70, 163, 164
The Damned 93
Daniell, Henry 22, 56, 57, 58, 74, 75–77, 103, 106, 116, 129, 131, 180
Dark Intruder 29, 55
"Dark Legacy" 106–109
"Dark Night of the Scarecrow" 165
Daugherty, Herschel 15, 21, 24, 62, 64, 68, 87, 94, 103, 116, 126, 129, 131, 135, 137, 140, 153, 158, 160, 171, 174
Davion, Alex 45
Davis, Jim 172
"Days of Our Lives" 93
Dead Men Tell 109
Dead of Night 84
The Deadly Bees 16
Dearing, Edgar 165
Death of a Salesman 58
deCorsia, Ted 73
Deebank, Felix 136
DeHaven, Carter, III 28, 59, 62, 84, 116, 122, 146, 151, 170, 179, 183
Dekker, Albert 94
de Kova, Frank 156
DeLeon, Raoul 50
Delevanti, Cyril 165
Deluge 126
DeMarney, Terence 80, 86, 143
DeMetz, Danielle 122, 123, 124

Denton, Crahan 109, 110–111, 114–115
Derleth, August 5, 23, 80, 82, 98, 99, 113, 143, 144, 160, 162, 167, 168
Dern, Bruce 17, 145, 146, 148
Dern, Laura 148
de Santis, Joe 173
The Desperate Hours 78
De Vestel, Guy 122
"The Devil's Ticket" 16, 91–94, 119, 126, 153, 190
DeWilde, Brandon 20, 109, 110, 114, 116
di Cagliostro, Adessandro 104–106
Les Diaboliques 121
Dial M for Murder 91
"Dialogues with Death" 88, 105, 126, 140–142
"The Dick Van Dyke Show" 109, 178
Die, Monster, Die 24, 82
Dillon, Brendon 136
Dr. Blood's Coffin 102
"Dr. Kildare" 22, 24, 44
Dr. Terror's House of Horrors 86
Dodds, Edward K. 34, 45, 48, 56, 68, 74, 94, 158, 181
Dominique 122
Don, Carl 173
Doran, Jack 31, 43
Dorfman, William 42, 65
D'Orsay, Fifi 116, 119
Douglas, Donna 59
Douglas, Robert 183
Douglass, Amy 174
Dozier, Robert 30
Dracula's Daughter 153
Drayton, Noel 80
Dreyer, Carl Theodor 126
Duff, Howard 87
Duncan, Bob and Wanda 21
Dunnock, Mildred 56, 58
"Dust" 103

East of Eden 147
Edmiston, Walker 172
Edwards, Elaine 48
Edwards, Sam 62
Eegah! 81
"87th Precinct" 8, 49
Elephant Walk 129
Ellenstein, Robert 78
Eller, Barbara 56

Ellerbe, Harry 43
Elliott, Ross 71, 72, 74
Elmer Gantry 98
Elson, Donald 145
Ely, Ron 17, 153, 154, 169
Emery, John 91, 93–94
English, John 179
Engstrom, Jean 50, 179
Enright, Kevin 145
Epstein, Howard 65
Eric, Martin 145
Erwin, Stu 42
Evelyn, Judith 120, 122
"Execution" 61
"The Extra Passenger" *see* "Trio for Terror"
"Eye of the Beholder" 41, 62

Fahey, Myrna 43
Fair, Jody 87
Family Plot 148
Fantastic Television 9–10, 32
"The Farmer's Daughter" 178
Farrell, Tommy 137
"The Fatal Impulse" 11, 17, 18, 48–50, 142, 178
Fate Is the Hunter 78
"Favorite Story" 187
The Feasting Dead 165
Fein, Bernard 71, 100, 160
Fiedler, John 160, 162
Fields, Amy 153
The Film Actor 87
Fine, Sidney 163
"The Fingers of Fear" 13, 73–74, 124, 171
Finlayson, Alex 84
Five 179
"Five Characters in Search of an Exit" 64
"Five Fingers" 171
"Five Golden Guineas" 186
Flato, Richard 124
Fleet, Jo Van 145
The Flesh and the Fiends 180
The Flesh Eaters 169
Flin, Ray 145
Flippen, Jay C. 36, 38
Florey, Robert 167
"Flowers of Evil" 58, 74, 103, 115, 170–171

For Whom the Bell Tolls 103
Forbes, Brenda 62
Forbidden Planet 29
Ford, Constance 28, 31
Forey, Robert 168, 169
Forster, Peter 84, 139
The Fortune Cookie 138
Foster, Dianne 28
The Four Skulls of Jonathan Drake 58
"Four Star Playhouse" 12, 83
Frankenstein 9, 168
Frankham, David 62, 68, 103, 106, 139, 140, 183, 184
Freeman, Howard 98
Freeman, Mona 33, 35
Freulich, Henry 151
"Friday the 13th" 189
Frye, William vi, 1, 2, 11–14, 19, 21–22, 23, 24, 25, 37, 39, 41, 45, 48, 56, 59, 61, 60, 62, 68, 73, 74, 80, 83, 84, 87, 88, 91, 94, 95, 98, 99, 103, 106, 109, 114, 116, 120, 122, 124, 126, 129, 131, 133, 135, 137, 138, 140, 142, 145, 146, 151, 153156, 158, 160, 163, 165, 167, 169, 171, 173, 174, 176, 181, 187
Fuller, Lance 48

Gabbay, Naji 65
Gable, Martin 42, 43–44
Gaffikin, Brian 146
Garbo, Greta 57
Garcia, David 170
Garland, Beverly 51, 53
Gausman, Hal 68, 74
Gay, Gregory 170
"General Electric Theatre" 12, 14, 39
Geraghty, Maury 50
"Get Smart" 88
The Ghost Breakers 133
"The Ghost of A. Chantz" 109
Ghost Ship 102
Ghosts of Berkeley Square 135
Gibney, Sheridan 135
Gilbert, Lauren 183
Gillespie, Gina 98, 99
"Gilligan's Island" 61, 118
Gilman, Sam 73, 88
Giovannini, Oscar 99, 103
"The Girl from U.N.C.L.E." 18, 24, 153

"Girl with a Secret" 43–45
"The Glass Eye" 61
Glass, Ned 106
Glessing, Molly 56, 74, 139
"God Grante That She Lye Stille" 64, 76–77, 106, 129–131, 133
The Godfather 37
Goldberg, Mel 31
Goldsmith, Jerry 1, 13, 17, 18, 56, 62, 58, 68, 74, 87, 88, 70, 88, 90, 98, 99103, 106, 116, 118, 120, 122, 126, 129, 131, 133, 138, 173
"Good Imagination" 16, 97–99, 138, 162, A
Good Stuff 21
Gordon, Barry 65, 66
Gordon, Bert I. 169
Gordon, William D. 124, 158
The Gorgon 87
Gorss, Saul 50
Gould, Charles S. 54, 109, 120, 127
Graft 9
Grandel, Janine 122
The Grapes of Wrath 147
The Great Dictator 58
Great Expectations 135
The Great Gatsby 148
"Great Ghost Tales" 5, 18, 25
The Greek Tycoon 171
Green, Dorothy 34
Green, Seymour 45, 62
Greene, Danford B. 133, 135, 138, 160, 165, 167
Greene, Dorothy 36
Greening, Jack 136
Greenleaf, Raymond 174
Greer, Jane 20, 146, 149, 150
Gregg, Virginia 98, 99
Gregory, James 71, 72, 74
Grendon, Stephen *see* Derleth, August
Grey, Duane 59
Gridge, Lois E. 35
Griffith, James 100, 94, 96, 158, 160
"The Grim Reaper" 16, 17, 19, 25, 61, 68, 94, 109, 116–119, 147, 150, 190
Grizzard, George 28, 29–30
"The Guiding Light" 162
"Guillotine" 13, 20, 74, 84, 86, 122–124, 186, 189
"The Guilty Men" 36–37
Gunga Din 174

Hagen, Kevin 73, 76–77, 74, 170, 171
Haigh, Kenneth 69, 70
Haire, Edward 99, 106, 116
Hairston, Jester 84
Hale, Richard 106, 167
Halliwell, Leslie 94, 138, 174, 176
"Halls of Ivy" 12
Hammer, Ben 140
"Hands of Destiny" 186
Hangover Square 57, 79
Hanna, Mark 137
"Happy Days" 106
Hard Day's Night 73, A
Hard, Fast and Beautiful 87
Hare, Lumsden 68
Harper 150
Harper, Ron 50
Harris, Robert H. 84
Hartman, Paul 43
The Haunted Palace 46, 50, 109
"Have Gun, Will Travel" 88
Hawks, Howard 86
"Hay-Fork and Bill-Hook" 13, 47, 68–70, 109
"Hazel" 50
Helmore, Tom 120–122
Helton, Percy 35
Hennesy, Ton 143
Henreid, Monica 100
Henreid, Paul 33, 35, 99, 102
Herbert, Pitt 54, 59
Here Comes Mr. Jordan 94
Hern, Pepe 173
Herndon, Ben 41
Heron, Julia 30, 33, 34, 36, 37, 42, 43, 54, 62, 71, 95, 98, 100, 103, 109, 116, 120, 122, 124, 127, 129, 131, 133, 137, 138, 140, 143, 145, 151, 153, 156, 160, 163, 165, 167, 170, 171, 173, 174, 176, 179, 181
Herrmann, Bernard 160
Hervey, Irene 42, 44
Heyes, Douglas 12, 37, 39–41, 59, 61, 124, 126
Heyes, Joanna 37, 41, 59, 61
Hickman, Darryl 187
The Hidden Hand 109
High Sierra 87
Hill, Hallene 165
Hillaire, Marcel 122
Hiller, Arthur 28, 30, 31

Hills, Miss Beverly 88
Hitchcock, Alfred 8, 13, 16, 17, 23, 24,
  34, 43, 68, 70, 86, 88, 90, 91, 93, 102,
  105, 114, 122, 124, 145, 148, 153, 169,
  177
Hitchcock, Keith 62
Hitchens, Dolores 41
The Hitchhiker 87–88
Hoffman, Herman 51
"Hogan's Heroes" 55, 150
Hogan, James 33, 36, 50, 88, 129, 131
"The Hollow Watcher" 53, 163–165,
  173, 179
Holman, Rex 44
Holmes, Madeleine 129
Homicidal 176
Homolka, Oscar 20, 93, 153, 169
"Hong Kong" 88
House of Dracula 147
House of Fear 44
House of Frankenstein 147
House of Horrors 99, 169
House of the Damned 81
House of the Seven Gables 74
The House of Usher 45
House on Haunted Hill 50, 153
The House That Dripped Blood 155
How to Make a Monster 87, 129
Howard, Leslie 81
Howard, Robert E. 5, 19, 109, 112–113, 114
Howard, Ronald 74, 79, 76–77, 129,
  130, 131, 183, 184
Howard, Vance 122
Howes, Basil 68, 167
"The Howling Man" 45, 82
Hoyt, Clegg 179
Hughes, Robin 80, 82, 85
The Human Comedy 45
The Human Duplicators 129
"The Hungry Glass" 13, 17, 41, 59–62,
  109, 114–115, 118, 190
Hunt, Kyle 174
Hunt, Marita 133, 135
Hunter, Henry 67, 167
Hush ... Hush, Sweet Charlotte 148
Hutton, Robert 187
Huxham, Kendrick 68, 139, 161

"I Heard You Calling Me" 32
"I Kiss Your Shadow" 30

"I Led Three Lives" 176
I Saw What You Did! 176
I Spy 24
I Was a Teenage Werewolf 103
In Love and War 55
"Incident in a Small Jail" 162
"The Incredible Doktor Markesan" 23,
  25, 109, 144, 167–169, 171, 190
The Indestructible Man 76
Inescourt, Frieda 103
"Inner Sanctum" 187
"The Innocent Bystanders" 19, 129,
  179–181
"The Invaders" 41
Invisible Ghost 115
The Invisible Man Returns 74
Ireland, John 20, 84, 86
Isle of the Dead 9
It Came from Outer Space 175
"It's About Time" 106

Jack the Giant Killer 81, 179
Jack the Ripper 88–91
Jacobs, Arthur P. 30
Janssen, David 160
"The Jeopardy Room" 178
Jerome, Stuart 65
Jezebel 45
Jochim, Anthony 54, 179
"Johnny Dollar" 12
"Johnny Staccato" 12
Johnson, Chubby 50
Johnson, Howard E. 31, 33, 34, 36, 37,
  42, 45, 48, 50, 51, 54, 56, 59, 62, 67,
  68, 74, 78, 84, 91, 95, 100, 120, 122,
  126, 129, 131, 133, 135, 137, 138, 140,
  146, 151, 153, 156, 163, 165, 167, 170,
  171, 173, 174, 176, 179, 181
Johnson, Russell vi, 59, 61
Jones, Carolyn 187
Jones, Henry 127, 128, 172, 173
Jory, Victor 22
Joseph, Jackie 181
Journeaux, Donald P. 62
Journey to the Center of the Earth 74
"Journey to the Unknown" 16, 188–189
Jowett, Corson 167, 179
Joyce, Jimmy 140
Judgment at Nuremberg 55, 61
"The Jungle" 164

Jurassic Park 148
Just Imagine 55

Kaffke, Ken 25, 119
Kane, George 100, 140
Karloff, Boris ii, 1, 8–10, 13, 17, 20, 21, 22, 23, 24, 25, 29, 45–48, 50, 56, 60, 62, 70, 76, 80, 82, 109, 110, 122, 124, 125, 126, 133, 134, 135, 140, 151, 141, 142, 147, 167, 169, 177, 180, 183, 186
Karloff, Evelyn 21, 122
Kearney, Carolyn 167
Kelly, Carol 28
Kelly, Nancy 158, 160
Kennedy, George 179, 181
Kenney, June 153
Kent, David 174
Kenyon, Sandy 163
Kerr, Sondra 127
Kidd, Jonathan 65
Kiel, Richard 74, 79, 77
"Kill My Love" 174–176
Killer's Kiss 38
The Killing 38, 50, 71
Kimball, Russell 65, 71, 73, 80, 87, 94, 183
King Hearts and Coronets 64, 152
King Rat 140
King, Stephen 8, 15, 186
Kish, Joseph 88
Kiss Me Deadly 46
Kitten with a Whip 162
The Klansman 171
Klemperer, Werner 54, 55
Kline, Benjamin H. 48, 50, 51, 62, 68, 73, 78, 95, 103, 106, 122, 126, 129, 131, 135, 137, 138, 153, 156, 160, 163, 167, 170, 173, 174, 176, 179, 181, 183
Kneubuhl, John 15, 51, 71, 84, 86, 109, 114, 183
"Knock Three-One-Two" 51–53
Kosleck, Martin 153, 154, 169
Kramer, Vernon W. 84
Kroeger, Berry 33, 34
Kruger, Otto 151, 153
Kubrick, Stanley 38, 41, 71
Kuttner, Henry 131

The Lady from Shanghai 37, 61
Lake, Janet 179

Lambert, Jack 131
Landis, Jessie Royce 33
Landres, Danny B. 28, 30, 31, 33, 34, 37, 45, 50, 54, 56, 68, 73, 78, 84, 88, 91, 94, 98, 109, 120, 122, 124, 127, 129, 131, 137, 140, 143, 145, 151, 153, 156, 158, 163, 170, 171, 173, 174, 176, 179, 181, 183
Lang, Cora C. 84
Langdon, Sue Ane 165, 166
Lansing, Robert 48, 49, 49
Lapis, Joe 127
Larson, Randall 17, 18, 70, 90
"The Last of the Sommervilles" 133–135
The Last Picture Show 46
"Late Date" 86, 87–88
Lava, William 163
Law and the Lady 118
"The Law of the Plainsman" 99
The Lawless 93
Lawlor, Harold 15, 21, 99, 101, 116, 118, 120, 121
Leachman, Cloris 43
"Leave It to Beaver" 55
Leavitt, Norman 52, 163
Lee, Christopher 24, 94, 188
The Leech Woman 178
Leiber, Fritz 71, 187
Leisen, Mitchell 31, 32, 43
Lenard, Kay 138
The Leopard Man 86
Lerner, Dikki 127, 129, 179, 181
Leslie, Bethel 30, 31, 71, 72
Leslie, Nan 50
"The Lethal Ladies" 181–183
LeTorre, Charles 122
"Letter to a Lover" 64, 135–137
Lewton, Val 9, 58, 145, 180
"The Life and Legend of Wyatt Earp" 148
"The Life Work of Juan Diaz" 188
The Light in the Forest 64
"Lights Out" 186
Lindon, Lionel 28, 43, 59, 67, 74, 80, 84, 109, 115, 146, 151
The List of Adrian Messenger 90
The Little Foxes 176
Livesey, Jack 34
Livesey, Jill 88
Lloyd, Doris 68, 73, 106, 139, 183
Lloyd, John J. 116

Lloyd, Suzanne 183
"Lock-Up" 16, 93
The Lodger 57, 90
Lomond, Britt 95
London After Midnight 50, 76
The London Blackout Murders 87
Lonergan, Arthur 28
Long, Richard 151, 152
Long, Ronald 68
Look Back in Anger 73
Lormer, Jon 33
Lorre, Peter 22, 102, 169
Losee, Frank 51, 71, 95, 143
Lossee, Frank 78
Lovecraft, H.P. 15, 16, 24, 90, 96, 98, 99, 113
Lugosi, Bela 86, 142
Lummis, Dayton 56, 165
Lupino, Ida 1, 12, 15, 20, 22, 24, 64, 80, 82–84, 98, 99, 120, 122, 123, 124, 134, 138, 156, 157, 173, 174, 181
Lupino, R. M. H. 133
Lupino, Richard 80, 82, 84
Lynch, Ken 95, 137, 138, 176
Lynch, William 98
Lyndon, Barre 80, 88, 169

"M Squad" 33, 147
Macabre 32–33, 45
McAdam, Michael R. 59
McCarthy, John 30, 37, 42, 43, 50, 51, 54, 59, 62, 65, 68, 71, 74, 78, 84, 87, 88, 91, 94, 95, 98, 100, 103, 106, 109, 116, 120, 122, 124, 127, 129, 131, 133, 137, 138, 140, 143, 145, 151, 153, 156, 160, 163, 165, 167, 170, 171, 173, 174, 176, 179, 181
McCarthy, Lin 34, 35, 183, 184
McClory, Sean 163, 164–165, 183, 184, 184
McConnell, Keith 45
MacDonald, John D. 48
MacDonald, Philip 48
McGibbon, Harriet 31
McGraw, Charles 50, 51
McLean, David 158
McNear, Howard 165
Macready, George 20, 127–129
McVeagh, Eve 163, 172
The Mad Magician 94

"The Magic Shop" 187
The Magic Sword 124, 142
The Magnificent Seven 84
Malmar, McKnight 158, 159
The Maltese Falcon 36, 50
"The Man from U.N.C.L.E." 18, 80, 153
"Man in the Cage" 65–67, 174
"Man in the Middle" 13, 53–56
The Man of a Thousand Faces 150
"Man of Mystery" 13, 17, 23, 116, 171, 176–179
The Man Who Could Cheat Death 102
The Man Who Knew Too Much 103
Man with a Cloak 10
The Manchurian Candidate 76
Manning, Patricia 139, 140
Mara, Adele 120, 122
Marcuse, Theo 65, 70
Margulies, William 171
"The Mark of the Hand" 1, 33–34
Markle, Fletcher 10, 11, 28, 30, 31, 33, 34, 36, 43, 53
Marley, John 36, 38
Marlowe, Scott 124
Maross, Joe 51, 52, 53
Marshall, Herbert 131
Marshall, Sarah 62, 64, 129, 130, 130–131
"Martin Kane, Private Eye" 33
Martin Lowitz Galleries 88, 91, 146
Martin, Meade 52
Marvin, Lee 147
The Mask of Dimitrios 174
The Mask of Fu Manchu 9
"The Mask of Medusa" *see* "Trio for Terror"
The Masque of the Red Death 102
"Masquerade" 17, 22, 25, 131–133, 147, 190
Massey, Raymond 186
Master of the World 140
Matheson, Murray 58, 62, 64, 136, 137
Matheson, Richard 142–143
Matinee 94
"Maverick" 40
Mayer, Alex 103, 143
Mayer, Gerald 65
The Maze 87, 175
Medina, Patricia 91, 93, 124, 126
Meehan, John 160

Merande, Doro 137, 138
Mercier, Louis 103, 122
Meredith, Burgess 187
Merrill, Scott 116
"The Merriweather File" 71–73
Meyer, Gerald 48
Meyler, Fintan 74
Michon, Pat 103
Middleton, Robert 73, 76, 73, 74, 122, 123, 124
Midnight Lace 91
Midway 2, 3, 24
Milland, Ray 12, 88, 90, 91, 126
Millard, Oscar 50
Millay, Diana 65, 68, 66
Milo, George 50, 51, 59, 65
Mims, William 151
Mirage 87
Missile to the Moon 129, 176
"Mr. Adams and Eve" 87
"Mr. Black" 187
"Mr. George" 1, 98–99
Mr. Moses 45
"Mr. Novak" 86
Mr. Sardonicus 102, 103, 169, 164
Mitchell, George 50, 146
Mitchell, Guy 67
Mitchell, Steve 87
Mitchum, John 56
"Moment of Fear" 71, 187
The Monster and the Ape 129
Monster on the Campus 76
Monster That Challenged the World, The 109
Montgomery, Elizabeth 17, 131, 132, 132
Montgomery, Ray 28
Montoya, Alex 173
Moody, Ralph 181
Moonraker 81
Moore, Mary Tyler 17, 48, 50, 176, 178
Moriarty, David H. 124, 137
Morris, Frances 172
Morris, Howard 181, 183
Morris, Jonathan 161
Morton, Gregory 122
"Mortuis", De 97
Mosquito Squadron 33
Mullaney, Jack 103
The Mummy 9
The Mummy's Curse 169
The Mummy's Hand 11, 174

Murder by the Clock 126
Murders in the Rue Morgue 168
Murphy, Rosemary 181, 183
Mustin, Burt 137
"My World and Welcome to It" 178

Nagel, Conrad 48
Naked Gun 29
Nalder, Reggie 20, 100, 102, 143, 145
Napier, Alan 37, 68, 73–74, 106, 109
Neff, Ralph 36
Neise, George N. 35
Nelson, Alberta 146
Nelson, Ed 48, 50, 56, 95, 97, 140, 142
Nesmith, Mike 115
Nesmith, Ottola 59, 62, 109, 110, 115–115
Neumann, Dorothy 131
Never Fear 87
Nevins, Francis M., Jr. 86
Newlan, Paul 50, 51, 56, 116, 118, 145, 146, 147
Newland, John 19, 24, 109, 115–116, 142, 143, 144, 146, 148, 150, 176, 178, 188
"Next Step Beyond" 24
Nicholas and Alexandra 102
Nicholson, George 36, 146
Nicholson, Jack 44
Nielsen, Leslie 28, 29
"Night Gallery" 132, 189
Night Into Morning 10
Night Monster 44
"The Night of the Gruesome Games" 103
"The Night of the Returning Dead" 102
The Night Strangler 42
The Night Walker 16, 106, 178
Nightmare 11
Nine Horrors and a Dream 182
Nolan, Jeanette 100, 94, 96, 156, 157, 158
Nolan, Tommy 30, 31, 94, 97
North by Northwest 13, 88, 90
Not of This Earth 53
Novarro, Ramon 156, 158

Oates, Warren 52, 53, 163, 165
Ober, Philip 172
O'Connell, David J. 30, 36, 74, 84, 91,

98, 106, 109, 116, 122, 124, 126–127, 129, 137, 140, 143, 145, 151, 153, 156, 160, 163, 167, 170, 176, 179, 181
O'Connell, William 161
The Odd Couple 162
O'Donnell, David J. 165
"The Odyssey of Flight 33" 181
O'Farrell, William 28
The Old Dark House 9, 132
Oliver, Susan 67, 70
Olmsted, Nelson 42
O'Malley, J. Pat 88, 88, 124, 153
O'Malley, Lillian 52, 124
The Omen 18
On the Waterfront 78
Once Upon a Time 99
"One Step Beyond" 25, 47, 115
Operation Eichmann 55
Operation Mad Ball 169
"The Ordeal of Dr. Cordell" 17, 18–19, 78–80
Orpheus 106
Our Town 45
Out of the Past 150
"The Outer Limits" 25, 32, 144
Overton, Frank 30
Owen, Deirdre 151
Owen, Reginald 80, 86

Paluzzi, Luciana 170, 171
Panic 187
"Papa Benjamin" 84–87
Papez, Loyd S. 88, 98, 106
"Parasite Mansion" 31, 94–97, 158, 160, 190
Parnell, James 145
Parsons, Milton 106, 109
"Passage for Trumpet" 181, A
Pate, Michael 80, 85, 83
Paths of Glory 42
Patrick, George 30, 109, 124
Patton 18
Patton, Bart 165
Payday 42
Peach, Kenneth D. 88
Peel, Richard 45, 62, 68, 80, 136
Pennell, Larry 87, 88
Pepper, Cynthia 48
"Perchance to Dream" 46
Perfect Friday 157

Perkins, Gil 50, 71
Perrott, Ruth 98
Perry, Barbara 137
Perry Mason 32, 33
Persoff, Nehemiah 73, 76, 74
Peters, Eric 33
Peters, Erika 103
Peterson, Caleb 84
Petulia 43, 96
Phantom Lady 85
The Phantom of the Opera 15
The Phantom of the Rue Morgue 93
The Phantom Planet 81
The Phantom Ship 86
The Phenix City Story 98
Phipps, William 176
"Phyllis" 128
Piazza, Lida 52
"Pigeons from Hell" 17, 18, 19, 62, 109–116, 141, 144, 150, 158, 171, 190
"The Plainclothesman" 33
Planet of the Apes 30
Plato, Reginald 80
Platt, Edward 87, 88
"Playhouse 90" 8
Poe, Edgar Allan 20, 124, 125–126
"The Poisoner" 62–65, 106, 137
Poor Devil 18
"Portrait Without a Face" 23, 116, 148–151
Post, Ted 84, 183
Poston, Tom 131, 132
Poverty Row Horrors! 145
The Power 78
Powers, Mala 173, 174
Pratt, Judson 33
"The Prediction" 2, 13, 20, 25, 29, 45–48, 126, 129
The Premature Burial (film) 102, 126
"The Premature Burial" 9, 20, 25, 93, 124–126, 134
Prentis, Lucy 183
The President's Analyst 179
Price, Vincent 44
"Printer's Devil" 45
"The Prisoner in the Mirror" 18, 65, 103–106, 190
The Prisoner of Zenda 150
Psychic Killer 78
Psycho 16, 17, 55, 64, 68, 96, 131, 151, 160, 181

Puritan Passions 165
"The Purple Room" 12, 13, 33, 37–41,
    45, 61, 109, 114, 121, 134, 160 162
Pursuit to Algiers 87
Pyle, Denver 163

Qualen, John 98
Queen of Outer Space 45
The Queen of Spades 81

The Rabbit Trap 96
The Rack 46
The Raiders 65
Raine, Jennifer 62, 139
Randall, Stuart 87
Randall, Sue 54, 55
Rathbone, Basil 22, 186
The Raven 24, 43
Raw Edge 163
Rear Window 122
Reason, Rhodes 43
Rebel Without a Cause 88
Red River 86
"The Red Skelton Show" 10
Reed, Walter 103
Reeves, Richard 71, 87
Regas, Pedro 65
Reid, Carl Benton 179, 181
"The Remarkable Mrs. Hawk" 2, 17, 22,
    23, 145–148
Remick, William P. 181
Remsen, Bert 54
Renard, Ken 109, 112, 115, 143
Rennahan, Ray 87
"Rescue 911" 61
"The Return of Andrew Bentley" 22–23,
    82, 103, 116, 142–145, 150, 169, 190
Return of Count Yorga 129
Return of the Fly 124, 140
Return of the Vampire 115
Rey, Alejandro 122, 124, 156, 157, 174,
    188
Rhodes, Grandon 56
"The Richard Boone Show" 96
Richards, Lorrie 78
Rickard, Dennis 113
Ride the High Country 181
Riders to the Stars 176
"Ripcord" 88

Rixey, John W. 74, 176, 181
Robbins, Gale 179
Roberts, Thayer 73
Roberts, Tracy 67
Robinson, Bartlett 91
Robinson, Hubbell 8, 9, 10, 11, 19, 21,
    23, 184
Rocketship X-M 94
Rodman, Howard 53
Rogers, Kasey 174
Rolfe, Guy 100, 102
Rondell, Ronnie 140
Room Service 55
Rorke, Hayden 91
Rosemary's Baby 50, 126
"Rose's Last Summer" 11, 34–36, 171
Ross, Marion 103
Roter, Ted 122
Rudley, Herbert 160
Rugolo, Pete 13, 17, 18, 28, 30, 31, 33,
    34, 36, 37, 42, 43, 45, 48, 50, 51, 53,
    59, 65, 67, 71, 73, 84
Ruscio, Al 65
Russell, Jackie 181
Russell, John L. 33, 34, 36, 45, 53–54,
    56, 65, 71, 91, 94
Ryan, Edmond 88

S.O.B. 150
Sabrina 91
Sahl, Mort 20, 54–55
St. Clair, Margaret 15, 145, 146
"Salem's Lot" 103
Sampson, Robert 176
Sanford, Donald S. vi, 1–3, 8, 11, 13, 14,
    15, 18–21, 24, 32, 41–42, 45, 56, 58,
    74, 76, 78, 87, 94, 96, 98, 99, 120,
    121, 131, 133, 135, 145–147, 160, 162,
    167, 168, 174
Sanford, Jay Allen 11, 13, 14, 29, 43, 60,
    82, 100, 119, 133, 142, 144, 145
Sarracino, Ernest 156
Sarris, Andrew 57
The Satan Bug 181
The Scarf 16, 86
Schafer, Natalie 116, 117, 118
Schallert, William 140
Schorer, Mark 143, 144, 167, 168
Scott, Anthony 183
Scott, Avis 129, 136

Scott, Henry 84
Scott, Pippa 94, 96
Scotti, Vito 137, 138
Scream of Fear 137
The Sea Hawk 57
Searle, Pamela 161
Seay, James 43
Seitz, Chris 87
Sen Yung, Victor 30
Seven Days in May 18, 129
The Seventh Veil 137
The 7th Voyage of Sinbad 81
"77 Sunset Strip" 55, 83, 153
Sexton, Pat 65
Seymour, Anne 44
Shadow of a Doubt 93
Shane 50, 114
Shane, Maxwell 11, 18, 34, 48, 50, 51,
    65, 67, 71, 78, 79, 80, 84, 87
Shatner, William 17, 59, 61, 116, 117, 118,
    145, 176
Shaw, Reta 172
She 157
Sherman, Fred 54
Sherman, Ransom 88
Shimoda, Yuki 176
Ship of Fools 55
Shirley, Mercedes 176
Shoemaker, Ann 137, 138
"The Sign of Satan" 94, 188
Silva, Henry 106, 107, 108
Silvera, Frank 36
Simms, Jay 163, 164
Singer, Stuffy 87
Siodmak, Curt 102
Sloane, Everett 36, 37
Smith, Clark Ashton 96, 113
Snow White and the Three Stooges 102
Sobelman, Boris 137, 138, 165, 181
Sofaer, Abraham 45, 48, 127
Sokoloff, Vladimir 100, 103, 170, 171
Some Like It Hot 78
The Space Children 61
Spartacus 86
"The Specialists" 19, 21, 23, 24, 36, 77,
    106, 165, 181, 183–184
Spellbound 94, 153
Spicer, George 153
The Spy Who Loved Me 81
Squire, Jacqueline 80
Squire, Katharine 146

Stagecoach 147
"Stagecoach West" 10
Stanley and Livingston 160
Stanley, Wilson 120
"Star Trek" 61, 162
Starlog 138
"Starring Boris Karloff" 9, 186
"Stay Tuned for Terror" 16
Stevens, K.T. 71, 174, 176
Stevens, Morton 13, 17, 18, 78, 80, 84,
    87, 91, 94, 95, 103, 105, 109, 115, 124,
    135, 137, 140, 143, 145, 146, 151, 153,
    156, 158, 160, 165, 167, 170, 174, 176
Stevens, William L. 78, 84, 87, 91, 94
Stevenson, Robert 65
Stevenson, Robert J. 73
Stewart, James 25
Stockwell, Guy 65
"The Storm" 126, 158–160
Strait-Jacket 16, 181
The Strange Door 87
The Strangler 46, 160
The Stranglers of Bombay 102
Stratton, Chet 133, 165, 181
"Strega" 17, 47, 84, 96, 124, 156–158,
    190, La
Strudwick, Shepperd 33
Stuart, Gil 68, 80
"Studio One" 8, 9
Sturgess, Olive 42, 139
Submarine X-1 33
Sunrise at Campobello 138
Sunset Boulevard 115
Superman 135
"Suspicion" 187
Swanson, Audrey 56, 91
Sweet Bird of Youth 42

Tailspin 160
Tale of Two Cities 91, A
"Tales from the Crypt" 5
Tales of Terror 140
"Tales of the Black Cat" 187
"Tales of the Texas Rangers" 12
"Tales of the Unknown" 187
"Tales of Tomorrow" 115
Talman, William 87
"Tamara, the Georgian Queen" 21, 119
Tarantula 76
Targets 24

Taylor, Don 102
Taylor, Rod 187
Taylor, Vaughn 67, 71, 165, 166
Teal, Ray 37
The Tenant 147
The Tenth Victim 157
Terrell, Steven 179, 181
"Terribly Strange Bed" see "Trio for Terror", A
The Terror (1928) 50
"The Terror in Teakwood" 25, 47, 100–103, 145, 163, 190
Tetzel, Joan 91, 93, 151, 153
The Texas Chainsaw Massacre 133
Thackery, Bud 30, 37, 116, 124, 140, 165
That Night 115
Thatcher, Torin 74, 77, 79
Thaxter, Phyllis 133, 135
They Came to Cordura 169
They Drive by Night 87
The Thief 44
The Thing 94
The Thing That Couldn't Die 86, 169
"Third for Pinochle" 22, 98, 137–138, A
Thirteen Ghosts 91, 119, 178
This Angry Age 78
This Island Earth 61
Thomas, Marlo 17, 78, 80
The Thousand Plane Raid 3, 33
"Three O'Clock" 86
"Thriller" Fan Club 25, 119, 190
Thunderball 171
"'Til Death Do Us Part" 171–173
The Time Machine 122
The Tingler 122
To Catch a Thief 91
To Have and Have Not 55
To Kill a Mockingbird 183
"To Serve Man" 106
Tobin, Dan 31
Todd, Ann 136, 137
Tol'able David 147
"The Tom Ewell Show" 10
Tomerlin, John 106
Tompkins, Joan 56, 98
"Topper" 153
Tormented 175
Torn, Rip 37, 38, 41
Townes, Harry 56, 57, 58, 106, 108
Tracy, Don 50
Treasure Hunt 135

"Trio for Terror" 80–84, 142
Tropic of Cancer 42
The Trouble with Angels 24, 84
Trundy, Natalie 28, 30
Tuttle, Frank 106
Twelve Angry Men 151, 162
"Twelve O'Clock High" 31, 49
Twice Told Tales 129
"The Twilight Zone" 5, 15, 17, 18, 25, 29–30, 31, 32, 37, 39–41, 53, 55, 58, 61, 64, 68, 103, 106, 145, 145, 169, 164, 166, 167, 169, 176, 178
The Twilight Zone Companion 53
Twilight Zone Magazine 41
Twilight Zone — The Movie 64
"The Twisted Image" 10, 28–29
Two on a Guillotine 99

The Undying Monster 57
"The Unexpected" 187
The Unguarded Moment 98, 166
The Uninvited 74
Universal Horrors 81, 168
"An Unlocked Window" 160, 188
"The Untouchables" 32, 37, 83

Valentine, Nancy 88
Valley of the Dragons 124, 164–165
The Vampire 160
The Vampire's Ghost 87, 122
Vampyr 126
Vance, John Holbrook 65
Van Dreelen, John 176, 178
Van Fleet, Jo 20, 145, 146, 147
Vaughn, Robert 17, 78–80
"The Veil" 47
Vertigo 122, 128
"The Victim" 160
Victor, Ina 160
Villon, Jacques 122
The Violators 115
"The Virginian" 96, 129
Vlahos, John 36
Voodoo Island 50
Vye, Murvyn 45

Wainewright, Thomas Griffiths 64
Walk on the Wild Side 99

Walker, June 137
Walker, Peter 133
Walpole, Hugh 169
Warning Shot 29
Warren, Bill 35, 53, 102, 129, 162, 164
Warren, John F. 31, 98, 99, 106, 120, 133, 143, 158
Warren, Ruth 87
Washburn, Beverly 94
Wasserman, Lew 22
"The Watcher" 2, 12, 17, 41–43
Watkins, Linda 56, 100, 103, 160, 163
"Waxworks" 17, 23, 64, 144, 153, 153–156, 171
"Way Out" 5, 18, 25, 32, 58, 128
Weaver, Tom 145
Webber, Robert 20, 146, 150, 151
"The Weird Tailor" 16, 127–129, 181, 191
Weird Tales 14–15, 57, 82, 90, 92, 95, 99, 101, 105, 113, 113, 118, 121, 128, 132, 144, 146, 155, 162, 168, 182
Welch, Nelson 62, 80
"Well of Doom" 2, 74–77, 106, 131, 171, 190
Welles, Orson 37, 96, 105, 153
Wells, Delores 172
Wells, H.G. 187
Werier, George 30
Wessel, Dick 73
Westerfield, James 42
Weston, Jack 56, 58, 170, 171
Whale, James 9, 70, 168
"What Beckoning Ghost?" 19, 20, 120–122, 134
What Ever Happened to Baby Jane? 21–22, 45
"What Makes Sammy Run?" 71
What's New, Pussycat? 157
Where Angels Go, Trouble Follows 24
"The Whistler" 187
White, Christine 31, 32–33
White, Lionel 71
White, Will J. 52
Who's Minding the Mint? 46
Whorf, David 109, 115, 170, 171
Whorf, Richard 115
"Wig for Miss Devore" 23, 41, 98, 103, 160–163, 171, 190, A
Wilbanks, Don 50

Wilcox, Frank 120
Wild at Heart 148
Wild River 147
"The Wild, Wild West" 24, 53, 77, 102–103
Wilde, Oscar 64, 187
Wilkerson, Guy 109
Wilkinson, Frank H. 91, 122, 170
Will Success Spoil Rock Hunter? 128
Williams, Adam 88
Williams, John 88, 90–91
Williams, Norm 78
Wilson, Stanley 36, 74, 84, 91, 98, 106, 109, 116, 122, 124, 127, 129, 137, 140, 143, 145, 151, 153, 156, 160, 163, 165, 167, 170, 176, 179, 181
Windish, Ilka 106
Windom, William 176, 178
Wingreen, Jason 146
Winterset 174
Winwood, Estelle 140, 141, 142
Witness for the Prosecution 91
The Wizard of Oz 165
"Wolf in the Fold" 162
The Wolf Man 115
The Wonderful World of the Brothers Grimm 45, 153
Woods, Donald 88, 91
Woolrich, Cornell 15, 20, 84, 85–88, 122, 123, 124
The World of Henry Orient 135, 162
"Worse Than Murder" 1, 11, 31–33
Worsley, Wallace 98
Wright, Will 151
Wyenn, Than 65, 179
Wynant, H. M. 73

X-15 160

York, Dick 167, 169
The Young Philadelphians 84
"Your Show of Shows" 183
"Yours Truly, Jack the Ripper" 15, 18, 88–91
Yung, Victor Sen 28

Zicree, Marc Scott 53